North Korean Military Proliferation
in the Middle East and Africa

NORTH KOREAN MILITARY PROLIFERATION IN THE MIDDLE EAST AND AFRICA

ENABLING VIOLENCE AND INSTABILITY

BRUCE E. BECHTOL JR.

UNIVERSITY PRESS OF KENTUCKY

Paperback edition 2025
Copyright © 2018 by The University Press of Kentucky

Scholarly publisher for the Commonwealth,
serving Bellarmine University, Berea College, Centre College of Kentucky,
Eastern Kentucky University, The Filson Historical Society, Georgetown
College, Kentucky Historical Society, Kentucky State University, Morehead State
University, Murray State University, Northern Kentucky University, Transylvania
University, University of Kentucky, University of Louisville, and Western
Kentucky University.
All rights reserved.

Editorial and Sales Offices: The University Press of Kentucky
663 South Limestone Street, Lexington, Kentucky 40508-4008
www.kentuckypress.com

Cataloging-in-Publication data is available from the Library of Congress.

ISBN 978-0-8131-7588-1 (hardcover : alk. paper)
ISBN 978-1-9859-0216-9 (pbk. : alk. paper)
ISBN 978-0-8131-7591-1 (epub)
ISBN 978-0-8131-7590-4 (pdf)

ASSOCIATION
of UNIVERSITY
PRESSES

Member of the Association
of University Presses

For Sara Beth, a gifted writer, an amazing daughter,
and the inspiration for this book.
On Iowa!

Contents

Preface

North Korea has gained a great deal of attention on the world stage since Kim Jong-un became that nation's leader in late 2011. The small, isolated nation has detonated a nuclear device (probably a weapon) several times, has tested a wide variety of ballistic missiles, naval systems, and ground systems that could threaten the security of its neighbor to the south (the missiles now have ranges that can threaten most of Asia and probably the United States), and has routinely engaged in rhetoric espousing its intent to use these systems if the leadership in Pyongyang feels threatened by the United States or its allies. But behind all this weapons development is another threat—that of military proliferation.

North Korea is not just a threat to American interests in East Asia because of its advancing weapons systems. In fact, it is not only just a threat to the United States with its advancing ballistic missiles—missiles with ranges that now appear to be able to target the West Coast of America at a minimum. North Korea is in fact an equally menacing threat to American interests and the interests of the international community because of its military proliferation to other volatile and unstable regions worldwide. It conducts military proliferation to regions and countries where these weapons systems, which range from typical conventional small arms all the way up to ballistic missiles and nuclear weapons technology, are most needed—in other words, regions that are rife with violence and regions where nation-states and non-state actors are in need of a variety of weapons systems because of the conflict they are engaged in or have the potential to be engaged in. For better or worse, this has been (for many years) a perfect opportunity for North Korea. The nations it proliferates to are often rogue states themselves (such as Iran, Syria, or Sudan), but there are also other nations in need (or perceived need) of North Korea's systems that have excellent economic and political relations with America and the international community (such as Ethiopia or Egypt). The North Koreans sell to anyone who will pay.

The reason that we should always consider weapons development to be as much of a threat to American interests because of proliferation as what North Korea will do with them militarily in its own region or against the

United States (via ballistic missiles) is because of whom these systems go to and because of the regions in which they sit. Thus, I specifically address North Korean military proliferation to the Middle East and Africa. In the Middle East, it is a foregone conclusion that Iran wants to threaten Israel. But Iran also has shown a goal of being the hegemon in the Middle East. This threatens Washington's Arab allies in the region. We have seen this in Tehran's support for Syria in its civil war as well as the support that Iran has provided to nonstate actors such as Hezbollah, Hamas, and the Houthis. In Africa, there are many nations struggling to attain political and economic stability. But, especially since the end of the Cold War, this has been hampered by instability and violence that show no signs of ending. The United States has interests and allies in both these regions. It is because of the importance of American interests in the Middle East and Africa that I have chosen these two regions for an examination and analysis of their involvement with North Korean military proliferation.

I will address several key issues in this book regarding North Korea's military capabilities, how they are tied in to Pyongyang's proliferation goals, and how this proliferation serves to support the regime while promoting instability elsewhere. Since arriving on the scene as leader following his father's death, Kim Jong-un has promoted an uptick in military weapons development. Of that there can be no doubt. The data support such an assessment. But why is this important for military proliferation? What role has North Korea played in the Syrian civil war? How has North Korea supported Iran's nuclear program? Is the evidence strong enough to reasonably come up with an assessment that this support exists? And what of North Korea's support to the Iranian ballistic missile program? A final question that one would ask regarding the Middle East is, How does North Korea support nonstate actors (terrorists) in the Middle East such as Hezbollah and Hamas? And, of course, since this book will address military proliferation to Africa in detail, the question is, Just how extensive is this? I will answer all these questions in this book. In fact, once the reader has finished it, he or she will be able to make assessments and gain perspective regarding North Korea's military proliferation to key regions and, hopefully, gain insight into the kind of policy that Washington and the international community must embrace in order to contain it.

I wrote this book for what will hopefully be a diverse audience. Individuals who will find it useful will be those who specialize in international security issues, regional specialists (for East Asia, the Middle East, and Africa), scholars of Korea (North and South), military planners, counterproliferation specialists, and anyone who has an interest in the North Korean threat and how it affects American interests abroad. This work and the assessments that it leaves the reader will be of interest to specialists and broader-range analysts alike in the United States, the Middle East, Africa, and East Asia. My goal in writing this book was not only to offer an accurate picture of the current DPRK threat but also to present predictive analysis that will be useful for policy in the future. Thus, this book will hopefully be useful for not only those who have an operational or scholarly interest in these issues but also those who have a practical interest in seeing these challenges resolved.

There are a number of people whom I would like to acknowledge who were helpful in the building of this project, the compiling of research, and the writing of this manuscript. William Newcomb, a retired former member of the State Department and a former member of the UN Panel of Experts was extremely helpful and offered very useful advice. Dr. Chun Seong Whun, a former presidential adviser in the Blue House in South Korea, was an excellent source of information and collaboration. Mr. Greg Scarlatoiu, the current executive director of the Committee for Human Rights in North Korea, has been an excellent resource for addressing sources and methods and seeking out resources for my research. I would like to thank Dr. Hugo Kim, my friend and mentor and a founding member of the International Council on Korean Studies, Lieutenant General Ray Ayres, USMC (Ret.), General John Tilelli, USA (Ret.), Dr. Patrick Morgan of the University of California Irvine, Dr. Andrew Scobell of the Rand Corporation, Dr. Richard Bush of the Brookings Institution, the former Congressional Research Service analyst Larry Niksch (now retired), the author Gordon Chang, Dr. Nicholas Eberstadt of the American Enterprise Institute, and my longtime friend and mentor Dr. Lee Choong-mook, who at the time I conducted much of my research was associated with the Institute of Korean Studies.

Because this book is written about Korean security issues (and I thus use many Korean names in the book), I feel it is important to address how the Korean language is used in this work. The written form of Korean (Hangul) has never been transliterated in one specific form. Until about fifteen years ago (though there is no exact date), the form most commonly used by Westerners to transliterate Korean was the McCune-Reischauer system—though this was never universal. The South Korean government changed to a different system in 2002, although this system is also not universally used by all and other systems remain in use (including sometimes the McCune-

Reischauer system). Because of these various forms of transliteration, it is likely that most South Korean government sources used before 2002 will be under the old system, that sources after that time will be under the new system (both systems discussed earlier), and that nongovernment sources from South Korea (such as press sources or think tanks) are likely to have used a variety of different systems for transliteration. For this work I will use the new system whenever possible (the system initiated by the South Korean government in 2002). Thus, I will quote sources exactly as written, whether using the new system or a different one. So it may appear that I sometimes use a different spelling for some of the names in this work, but, in the interest of consistency, I believe the methodology described above will be the most practical for the reader. In this work, I used the Korean practice of placing family names first, not last, whenever possible, unless individuals requested otherwise or the sources used articulated the names in the Western style of placing family names last. The reader will also note that sometimes I refer to South Korea as *the Republic of Korea* or *the ROK*. Both are accepted in South Korea—in fact, many South Koreans refer to their country as simply *Korea*. While I most commonly refer to the Democratic People's Republic of Korea as *North Korea,* some sources refer to it as *the DPRK*. Both are considered acceptable, and, thus, the reader will at times see both in this work.

The responsibility for the writing and research of this work is solely my own. Thus, the views that I express in it do not necessarily reflect the policy or position of any US government agency or any university that I have been affiliated with. References to Internet sites were accurate at the time of publication. As this book went to press, all the information included in it was up to date. Because North Korea is a moving target, it is likely that events will continue to unfold rapidly. Nevertheless, the information contained in this work will remain relevant and provide value to scholars, students, the media, pundits, and the general public in understanding North Korea's strategy and activities. Neither I nor the University Press of Kentucky is responsible for Web sites that have expired or changed since this book was prepared.

1

Setting the Context

North Korea has been engaged in proliferation to both state and nonstate actors on a large scale for many years. This is an issue that has gone largely unnoticed in both policy and academic circles—unless a headline-grabbing incident occurs (such as when North Korea was caught proliferating Scud missiles to Yemen in 2002). In fact, some scholars have even published relatively minor studies claiming that North Korea's military proliferation has nearly shut down since the end of the Cold War. This is clearly untrue. Following the collapse of the Soviet Union, North Korea needed to find another way to finance its elite and its very large military. One of the key ways to do this has proved to be profits from proliferation. This proliferation has been both robust and widespread.

Nation-states that North Korea has proliferated to in recent years include Iran (ongoing), Syria (ongoing), Libya, Burma, Pakistan, Ethiopia (ongoing), and a plethora of countries in sub-Saharan Africa (ongoing). But it does not stop there. North Korea has proliferated weapons to nonstate actors (and continues to do so) such as the Tamil Tigers, Hezbollah, al-Shabab, and Hamas. This issue is important because it affects security in the Middle East, Africa, and East Asia. In addition, the WMD and related platforms (ballistic missiles) that North Korea continues to proliferate in the Middle East present a threat that could directly challenge the United States or nations in Europe. The key substantive aspects of this issue (which have never truly been addressed in a public forum) are how widespread the proliferation is, how much money North Korea is making from this proliferation, and how can it be contained or stopped. Clearly the impact of this proliferation has been quite compelling. Rogue nation-states armed with both chemical weapons and nuclear weapons, terrorists armed with weaponry that threatens the daily security of citizens in some of our closest allied countries (such as Israel), and conventional weapons that continue to disrupt security and stability in key regions where stability is already tenuous are all aspects of this issue that make it an important one for both American foreign policy and that of our allies (important allies such as Israel and the Republic of Korea).

North Korea has expanded and enhanced its proliferation efforts around the world since the end of the Cold War. Whether it is in the Middle East, Africa, or even someplace as far away as Cuba, North Korea continues to change its tactics, techniques, and procedures in order to bring in money for the regime and to support the elite as well as the military and its programs. North Korea's proliferation program really consists of four key parts: (1) WMD and the platforms to carry them (ballistic missiles), (2) conventional weapons sales, (3) refurbishment of Soviet-era weapons for countries that still use them, and (4) technical and military assistance and advising. These programs have continued in the Kim Jong-un era and have in some instances even expanded. North Korean proliferation presents an international security dilemma that policy makers in many nations should address—and take efforts to contain. The profits from North Korea's proliferation may be as high as in the billions of dollars, and they are contained in illicit networks and front companies so sophisticated and complex that the North Korean government has even had trouble tracking and controlling them.

The proliferation that North Korea engages in presents a number of foreign policy challenges to the United States. First of all, because Pyongyang proliferates to rogue nation-states such as Syria and Iran (among others), the threat to Washington's key allies in the Middle East is profound (from both conventional weapons and WMD). In addition, the funds that North Korea is able to generate from its widespread proliferation to state and nonstate actors serve to maintain the regime's ability to maintain its large military (which threatens the Republic of Korea) and to provide rewards to the small number of members in the elite who keep the government infrastructure running. Finally, the support to nonstate actors (terrorist groups) creates instability and violence in both the Middle East and Africa. It will be important for American policy—and a key focus for decision-making processes—to determine not only how widespread and dangerous North Korea's proliferation and illicit activities are but also how to effectively contain and/or shut down these activities, something that has not yet occurred despite concerns in the United States, South Korea, Israel, and other allied nations. Thus, an important focus for American foreign policy can and should be on North Korea's key centers of gravity (when it comes to proliferation) and Pyongyang's vulnerabilities to American interdiction from foreign policy initiatives.

The weakened position of Kim Jong-un as compared to his father and grandfather and the instability in North Korea that has occurred as a result mean that proliferation of WMD (nuclear and chemical weapons technology) and the platforms that will carry that technology (ballistic missiles and artillery) as well as the array of conventional weapons that Pyongyang sells to state and nonstate actors are used as a key source of finance for military R&D, the lavish lifestyles of the elite, and other elements of North Korean society meant to maintain the Kim family regime. This should be a basic core assessment of any American analysis of North Korean capabilities—and should also be a basis for strategy regarding the DPRK. The DPRK has shown no indications of slowing down its military proliferation. In fact, evidence from recent years suggests stepped-up cooperation with Iran. Syria is even more troubling. The civil war there has created a customer in need of weapons and advising much more than during most of Kim Jong-il's reign, a factor putting funds into North Korea's coffers. Because North Korean proliferation to both the Middle East and Africa (and elsewhere) is ongoing, if unchecked, these activities will enable exacerbated threats to American security interests in both regions and (because of the range of ballistic missiles that Iran now possesses) Europe as well.

Research Methodology

I have employed traditional research methods as I have conducted this research. Several visits to Seoul have provided me the opportunity to conduct interviews with key defectors from numerous entities dealing with proliferation and illicit activities in North Korea. They have also offered the opportunity to collaborate with fellow scholars in both policy circles and academic circles there. In 2014, and again in 2015, I briefed members of the national security staff at the Blue House in Seoul (the South Korean equivalent of the White House) on North Korean proliferation. We also engaged in information sharing. The overriding theme at the conclusion of the briefing was, We want more information. Thus, my research has taken me (and will continue to take me) to where the weapons are going—the Middle East and Africa—more than anywhere else. My collaboration has included (and will continue to include) fellow scholars, law-enforcement officials, military officials, and policy makers. I have built an extensive network in some of these key areas, and this has allowed me to conduct in-depth research that has benefited the writing of this book.

Because in my view this issue is so compelling—and unique—it has been important to address it in a logical, practical manner. Thus, a prism to look through in order to clearly lay out what the aspects of this issue are in order to make policy-relevant assessments has been key. An analysis of the diplomatic, informational, military, and economic (DIME) aspects of this issue have allowed me to understand and articulate the challenges for international security that North Korea's proliferation presents. The advanced paradigm that North Korea presents with its proliferation since the end of the Cold War is unique, difficult to analyze, and extremely dangerous to the national security of the United States (and its allies). Thus, research conducted on this issue has resulted in new, groundbreaking assessments relevant to policy makers on both sides of the Pacific and in the Middle East. This book will use the case studies methodology. In other words, once the tactics, techniques, and procedures (TTP) that North Korea uses are described—in relation to their proliferation, financial networks, and the way the money is used for regime policy and survival—I will conduct analysis entity by entity. Thus, there are individual chapters in my book that cover Iran, Syria, and African nations and also include nonstate actors (e.g., Hezbollah and Hamas are included in the chapters on Iran and Syria because they are so closely connected in their business dealings with North Korea). It is important to understand that this book must—by the very nature of the project that has been conducted to write it—be descriptive in nature. Thus, it analyzes what the North Koreans have that they proliferate, key players they proliferate to, how they proliferate and get around sanctions, and how their proliferation can better be contained.

I have used very diverse sources to conduct the research necessary for this book. These sources include but are not limited to interviews, scholarship and books by experts in East Asia, Africa, the Middle East, and the United States regarding North Korean military proliferation and the infrastructure that supports it, papers and presentations from conferences and symposia, analysis of speeches, press releases, press reports, and press conferences, interviews with defectors as well as current and former government officials in the United States, Israel, Ethiopia, and South Korea, US, Middle Eastern, African, and South Korean government reports, white papers, and legislative testimony, declassified defector reports, speeches and statements by policy makers in the United States, Africa, the Middle East, and East Asia, and papers, reports, and special releases by important think tanks, government agencies, public policy institutes, and universities. To provide further enlightenment on the sources used in this work, a selected bibliography is included.

This is the first book to address the weapons, systems, capabilities, training, and military infrastructure support that North Korea proliferates to the Middle East and Africa, how all this is proliferated (and the financial system that supports this proliferation and uses it to gain profit for the regime), whom these systems are going to, the types of proliferation that have occurred to specific state and nonstate actors, and methodologies for better containing this illicit activity. Everything I describe will be tied together in an analysis that will generate assessments previously unreported in whole prior to the publication of this book.

Importance of Study and Existing Literature

North Korea's proliferation to state and nonstate actors has been an active part of its foreign policy since the Cold War. It continues today, yet many still do not understand the extent of these activities or the damage caused to stability in key regions important to the national security interests of the United States. There are some important reasons why Pyongyang's proliferation and illicit activities have not gained a lot of attention in the West (though this seems to be changing since 2017) or been placed as a top foreign policy priority in either Seoul or Washington.

During the Cold War, North Korea essentially served as a proxy for the Soviet Union, contributing to, supporting, and often participating in proxy wars that Moscow found too distasteful for direct involvement. Thus, during the Cold War, North Korea frequently helped guerrilla and/or terrorist groups that believed in Communist ideology—often helping them attempt the overthrow of the governments in power. Most of these activities occurred in the Middle East and Africa. In return for these widespread activities, the Soviet Union completely subsidized the North Korean economy—and its military. Cuba played a very similar role during the Cold War. Because of the nature of North Korea's support to these groups, it was largely seen as a small part of a larger picture; in other words, it was seen as simply another Soviet-supported and -funded operation for proxy violence, and a routine part of the Cold War. Because North Korea was seen as a satellite state, its participation in these activities was never a high priority—and thus the focus was more on their sponsor.

By the end of the Cold War, North Korea had contacts all over the world. It was these contacts that had been built up during the Cold War that helped Pyongyang create illicit activities following the fall of the Soviet Union.

North Korea was already proliferating ballistic missiles to Iran beginning in the early 1980s, and the contacts with Iran's Republican Guard Corps would later prove to be quite useful as Pyongyang would eventually use them to set up business (largely the sale of conventional weapons and training) with groups such as Hezbollah and Hamas (groups with close ties to Iran). In fact, largely because subsidies from the Soviet Union ended in 1990, North Korea increased it proliferation activities, building them up to the high levels we continue to see today. Customers have included (but are not limited to) nation-states and nonstate actors in the Middle East, Africa, and South Asia. Yet, as in the Cold War time period, these activities—which threaten the stability of regions where key American allies are—received very little attention (a phenomenon that continues today). The reasons for their being a low priority (and the fact that North Korea's proliferation receives very little attention) are different now than they were during the Cold War time period, but perhaps more profound. Since 1993, the United States and North Korea have been in on-again, off-again negotiations regarding Pyongyang's nuclear weaponization program. These talks have been considered very sensitive, and, thus, aspects of North Korea's rogue state activities have been overlooked in the interest of going after more important issues. Unfortunately, because of evidence showing that Pyongyang is now proliferating WMD and the platforms that support it as well as conventional weapons to some of the most rogue regimes on earth (as I will describe later), I believe it is important to explore the details of North Korea's proliferation and illicit activities. I also believe it is important to analyze policy options that will work to contain and (eventually) shut down key aspects of these activities that threaten the security of the United States and key allies.

While there have been contributions to the scholarship regarding international security and North Korea's illicit activities (to include proliferation), they have been far and few between. In addition, while much of this scholarship has been well researched and accurate, it typically focuses on other (nonmilitary) aspects of North Korea's illicit activities, which can lead to confusion and misconceptions among readers, particularly policy makers. It is my intention for this book to cover all aspects of North Korean military proliferation, to include key nations and nonstate actors, the weapons being proliferated, methods of laundering the money, financial networks, and the role that these operations play in the DPRK infrastructure. Military proliferation—what is being proliferated, how it is proliferated, whom it goes to and the effects it causes in these regions, and case studies that provide in-depth details—has never before been the focus of a book. In fact, this book will be the first to focus on this unique yet important aspect of how North Korea generates funds for the regime, an important aspect of North Korea's national security and economic survival.[1]

Outline of Chapters

The following chapters will focus on key issues. While chapter 2 will focus on the capabilities the North Koreans have (vital if one is to understand the impact these weapons will have in volatile regions like the Middle East and Africa), chapter 3 will focus on the many methods and procedures they use in their proliferation. Chapters 4–6 will focus on case studies, and chapter 7 wraps up this work with conclusions and policy recommendations.

Chapter 2 will be important because policy makers, academics, and specialists cannot truly understand North Korea's military proliferation unless they understand the capabilities and numbers of the systems North Korea is selling in unstable regions. North Korea's nuclear weaponization program and its ballistic missile programs have developed compelling capabilities that can potentially threaten all the Middle East, Africa, and Europe when proliferated (and many of these systems have already been proliferated). North Korea's advances in maritime capabilities are important as well, including a new submarine with long-range capabilities and a developing capability to fire a ballistic missile. The North's ground forces have not been idle as high training levels and important initiatives in training have added to potential capabilities, including artillery and rocket systems that could create havoc in ongoing conventional conflicts in both the Middle East and Africa. Pyongyang continues to show no hesitancy in using its military capabilities to test and upgrade systems that, when proliferated, can raise important profits that support the elite and the military.

In chapter 3, I will address how North Korea has always been able to get around sanctions using some very clever TTP for getting its arms distributed. This has been an ongoing situation no matter what sanctions are imposed or the methods used to impose them. According to a North Korea defector who was an individual in charge of illicit arms deals, North Korean arms dealers often have studied at Pyongyang University of Foreign Studies. There, they would often undergo training making them fluent in English and Chinese. These are the people who deal with traders in other countries. There are several methods that North Korea uses to get around sanctions (and they are often changing). One method is to send containers across the Yalu River into China one-third or half filled with weapons. "The forwarder who received this cargo enters a port in a third country, where the containers are filled with freight unrelated to weapons and the paperwork is completed," according to the North Korean defector. The containers are then laundered someplace like Hong Kong, Singapore, or some other large port in East Asia that has heavy traffic. The defector further states: "The containers are mixed with other cargo in those transit points. They are searched, but not thoroughly." He further comments: "Even if customs or other officials roll their sleeves up and search for weapons, how can they possibly find the arms among the mountains of other containers headed to other countries?"[2] It is important to note that this method is one of many the North Koreans have used—as they are constantly adjusting their TTP to avoid detection and sanctions.

Another method the DPRK often uses is that of reflagging its ships. North Koreans have been documented in the past often changing the flagging on their merchant ships (using foreign-flagged ships with North Korean crews to carry cargo and often changing flags). This makes it more difficult for those ships to be detected or boarded by international law enforcement or military personnel.[3] The North Koreans are constantly changing their TTP in order to adjust to the complex international law enforcement environment, and the two examples cited above (combining illicit arms with legitimate cargo in containers placed on ships and the reflagging of ships) point to the fact that they are adjusting their TTP in order to adapt to sanctions, avoid detection by the maritime forces of other nations, and stay below the radar of law enforcement around the world, which is often very wary of shipments tagged as North Korean. There are several other methods that North Korea uses to get around sanctions and to conceal its illicit financial networks as well (all described in chapter 3). Thus far, it appears that these methods have been largely successful, and I will examine in detail how the DPRK uses its government powers to get around sanctions and proliferate its arms for profit.

In chapter 4, I will address North Korean proliferation to Iran from soup to nuts. This begins with the evidence that North Korea has been proliferating conventional and unconventional weapons to Iran since the early 1980s. Since that time, it has shipped nearly every kind of ballistic missile it builds as well as related military advisers, engineers, technicians, and trainers to Iran. It has proliferated nuclear technology, missile technology, conventional weapons, and numerous spare parts to Iran. But it has also shipped conventional weapons and spare parts to Iran's proxy, Hezbollah. This has been going on for years. I will also reflect—in detail—on what North Korea has proliferated to Iran in the Kim Jong-un era, beginning in December 2013.

In chapter 5, I will discuss how North Korea has been proliferating chemical weapons, ballistic missiles, conventional arms, advisers, trainers, engineers, and technicians for a variety of projects to Syria for many years. But in the 1990s the rate of proliferation really picked up steam. In fact, one of the principal front men coordinating proliferation and support operations in Syria was the all-powerful Kim Kyok-sik (one of the key elite figures in North Korea). Kim was the deputy military attaché to Syria back in the early 1970s.[4] But North Korean proliferation has been stepped up significantly during the Kim Jong-un era in light of a needy Syrian customer fighting a civil war (North Korea has also supported Syria through proliferation and advisers in past conflicts).[5] In this chapter, I will address this issue and the fact that it is perhaps the most compelling proliferation dilemma regarding North Korea since the death of Kim Jong-il.

In chapter 6, I will address the interesting and complex case of North Korean military proliferation to Africa. There are so many countries in Africa that North Korea provides goods and services to that I cannot list all the activities here in the interest of space. In this chapter, I will key in on the proliferation activities that have occurred since the beginning of the Kim Jong-un era (with context on how many of these activities began long before Kim Jong-un became the North Korean leader). African countries that North Korea continues to sell military weapons, refurbishment, and training to in Africa during the Kim Jong-un era have included (but are not limited to) Ethiopia, Eritrea, Congo (Brazzaville), Congo (DRC), Zimbabwe, Uganda, and even Egypt.[6] I will go through all the key examples of this proliferation throughout the chapter on DPRK proliferation to Africa.

In chapter 7, I will provide policy recommendations and will also summarize and assess the results of this research, results that have the potential to be quite useful for policy makers, the general public, and academics and specialists who have an interest in the region. By providing details on what types of weapons systems are proliferated and how much money is generated from illicit deals with other rogue nations such as Iran and Syria (as well as terrorist groups such as Hezbollah and Hamas), this work will contribute to more than just the scholarship; it will contribute to the evidence chain. This evidence of North Korea's proliferation and other illicit activities will be entirely unclassified and thus also releasable to an often uniformed or underinformed audience. By providing clear, actionable data on how North Korea's financial networks operate, this chapter offers policy makers choices as to how to deter and defeat these networks. By providing evidence-based assessments of how North Korea actually disseminates its weapons systems (both conventional weapons and WMD), it offers policy makers the opportunity to enhance current initiatives such as the Proliferation Security Initiative or open up new multinational initiatives that can more effectively interdict these often large-scale yet difficult-to-detect activities. By providing recommendations on key methods that will enable Washington and its allies to target regime funding, it offers policy makers options (and evidence supporting these options) that will be important for both planning and operations. Like everything else that I have written, these policy recommendations will be clear, concise, and unambiguous. The intention of my policy recommendations will be an end state that equals new action that can be taken against North Korea—action that will actually give the United States and its allies leverage in changing the rogue state behavior of the DPRK.

2

Understanding the Product

North Korea's Military Capabilities

Before one can understand how North Korea proliferates to state and non-state actors or who these actors are (and why these particular systems and training are going to them) and how this proliferation will enhance their capabilities and, perhaps just as important, create instability in the regions and nations where it occurs, it is first important to have knowledge of exactly what North Korea is proliferating. Understanding the capabilities that North Korea is able to provide other rogue states and nonstate actors (as well as states that may be friendly to the United States) will enhance knowledge of how this changes the balance of power in regions where—as often as not—power is often tenuous or contested. Thus, in this chapter, I will address the weapons, systems, and training that are part of the North Korean military. Many of these capabilities are proliferated to various regions around the world, but here I will focus on the Middle East and Africa. Analyzing these systems, how they are used, and how they improve the capabilities of what many consider to be a primitive military (North Korea) will be important because it will also give us insight into how Pyongyang can enhance the capabilities of other nations (and nonstate actors) or pariah states that may not have the resources to buy arms and training elsewhere.

If one is to look at North Korea's military capabilities, certainly the capability that gets the most headlines and is arguably the biggest threat is Pyongyang's two-headed (plutonium and highly enriched uranium [HEU]) nuclear weapons program. This program has been the focus of discussion, diplomacy, and military planning since the early 1990s. Thus, in this chapter, I will address the very latest developments and analyze some key assessments that have come out in recent times. Closely tied into North Korea's nuclear weaponization program—but often not directly—is its growing missile program. A nuclear weapon must have an efficient platform to carry it, and there have been several very significant new advances assessed by US officials in announcements and congressional testimony. But that is not all there is to North Korea's advancing missile programs. There have also been advances in Pyongyang's naval surface-to-surface missiles and to short-range missiles, which form one of the key threats to bases and population centers in and around Seoul. The sections on WMD (nuclear weapons and missiles) will address all these issues.

There have been other advances in North Korea's capabilities. Maritime forces have fielded systems showing that the North Korean navy is finally moving forward in its efforts to go toe-to-toe with South Korean and American naval forces. These maritime advances include new (or improved) types of ships and submarines and even a developing SLBM. In concert with the maritime developments, North Korea's conventional air and ground forces continue to make moves that show an active intention to advance readiness and capabilities. These moves include not only new or improved weapons systems but also exercises and training that reflect an adjustment to the capabilities of the ROK-US military alliance. This training is of course (no doubt) passed on to countries where North Korea provides assistance on the same or similar systems—both in the Middle East and in Africa. And, finally, one of North Korea's capabilities that has received a significant amount of press coverage is the growing cyber-warfare entity. Much of this is due to the issues surrounding the release of the American movie *The Interview,* but, that having been said, the cyber-warfare capability North Korea possesses is both real and growing. All the capabilities I have addressed in this section are important. In the sections that follow, I will look at details and sources that will give the reader a broad view of not only the new systems, capabilities, and doctrine that have evolved in North Korea's military but also what the likely intentions are for these often-compelling moves.

North Korea's Nuclear Weapons Programs: Advances and Questions

There can be no doubt that the nuclear weapons programs in North Korea receive more attention and debate than any other part of the military threat. The reasons for this are, in my opinion, twofold. First of all, any rogue nation-state with a nuclear capability will be near the top of the concerns list for policy makers in the United States and in the region in which the country resides. Second, the North Korean conventional threat (and perhaps even the ballistic missile threat as well) is a subject that the overwhelming majority of academic personnel know almost nothing about. Thus, when addressing the North Korean threat, it is simply easier to focus on the nukes since the conventional and missile threat is far more diverse and complicated than most analysts are able to address in their research. And, even then, most of those in the academic and policy communities tend to focus far more on the politics of the nuclear program than on North Korea's intent or the actual capabilities of the nuclear weapons Pyongyang possesses. This is an unfortunate situation, but the fact of the matter is that North Korea's nuclear program is not just a threat but a growing threat. Thus, in this section, I will address some key recent issues and advances in North Korea's nuclear program and the effects these issues will have on geopolitics in the region.

North Korea's nuclear program success goes back to the 1990s and is now assessed by many to be capable of weaponizing both plutonium and HEU.[1] North Korea has likely had nuclear weapons for more than a decade (and, thus, the newness of the threat now tends to be more about the platforms that will carry the nukes more than the nukes themselves).[2] In fact, despite the denials of some in the Clinton administration, by the late 1990s it had become obvious that North Korea was already working toward this two-headed threat. To quote Robert Gallucci, a State Department official during the Clinton administration: "In addition, our intelligence community detected significant numbers of components for a gas centrifuge uranium enrichment program being transferred from Pakistan to the DPRK during the late nineteen nineties through the early part of this decade."[3]

North Korea's first series of three underground nuclear tests each produced higher yields. The first underground test in 2006 produced what many analysts assessed to be a yield of 0.5–1.0 kilotons, while in 2009 an underground nuclear test produced a yield of up to 4 kilotons.[4] The third North Korean underground nuclear test is assessed to have produced a yield of 6–7 kilotons.[5] The third test was not only larger and thus "more successful" than the first two tests; it was also largely more concealed, meaning that, unlike with the first two tests, American and allied intelligence collection was unable to determine whether the test was of a plutonium or an HEU weapon.[6] Reportedly, high-ranking Iranian officials were present at North Korea's third underground nuclear test.[7] North Korea is assessed—and has been for several years—to have the designs and probably the capability to build a five-hundred-kilogram HEU warhead that can fit on a missile. The missile is the No Dong, and the designs for the warhead came from a nuclear deal with Pakistan, which purchased several No Dong systems from North Korea beginning in the 1990s and ending around 2002.[8] The No Dong missile has a range of up to fifteen hundred kilometers and can hit key nodes in Japan, including American military bases and Tokyo.[9]

In 2016, the North Koreans did something that to date had been unprecedented in their nuclear weaponization history—they conducted two nuclear tests in one year. In the fall of 2015, new activity was imaged at the Yongbyon nuclear facility. By late October, imagery revealed that the North Koreans were digging a new tunnel at their test facility near Punggye-ri in the far northeastern section of the country. In January 2016, they conducted their fourth nuclear test. Pyongyang claimed it was a hydrogen bomb, but there is no proof of this to date (at least not in unclassified channels). In fact, the test appeared to be similar in size to North Korea's third underground nuclear test. Nevertheless, if nothing else, it showed that North Korea continued to march forward with its nuclear weapons program—and the quest to put that weapons capability on a missile.[10]

In September 2016, North Korea conducted its fifth nuclear weapons test. This test was (by far) the largest ever conducted by Pyongyang. It was conducted only eight months after the test conducted in January of the same year. While there were (as usual) many estimates, most analysts estimated the yield from the nuclear device to be 10–12 kilotons. The North Koreans also made a point to announce publicly that this was a "smaller, lighter" device that could be mounted on a ballistic missile. One thing is clear. North Korea has slowly but surely advanced the capabilities and yield of it nuclear weapons.[11]

In September 2017, almost exactly a year following its fifth nuclear weapons test, the DPRK conducted a test that was at least five times larger than any other test conducted previously. At a minimum, the blast from the test was around 50 kilotons, while many analysts assessed it to be over 100 kilotons, and others assessed it to be even higher. In fact, a think tank in Norway showed scientific estimates assessing that the yield of the blast was approximately 250 kilotons. The day before the test of 2017 (North Korea's sixth nuclear test), Kim Jong-un was shown in published North Korea propaganda photos being briefed on a two-stage thermonuclear device. The photos indicated that the missile that would carry this warhead would likely be what the North Koreans call the Hwasong-14, which has proved its ICBM range. (I will address this missile later in this chapter.) Immediately after the test, the North Koreans announced that this was a thermonuclear device, which would be a distinct improvement in yield over previous nuclear devices tested. They claimed that they had tested a hydrogen bomb that could be mounted on an ICBM. If this weapon could be launched on an ICBM with the thermonuclear device displayed in their propaganda, it would easily be the most deadly weapon the North Koreans have.[12] Earthquakes and tremors detected near the Punggye-ri nuclear test site during the late fall of 2017 indicate that the North Koreans may have conducted so many nuclear tests there that further tests may no longer be safe.[13]

While the developments addressed above are quite troubling (and highly debated) and certainly high on the priorities list for the United States and key players in Northeast Asia, recently other developments and assessments have created yet more debate and challenges for policy makers and military planners. In 2015, the most compelling disclosure regarding North Korea's nuclear program has been the assessment by high-ranking American officials that North Korea has now developed the technology to build a nuclear warhead that could be placed on a ballistic missile with the range to hit the United States.[14] This is a significant upgrade from previous assessments (including mine) that North Korea has the capability to put a nuclear warhead on one of its key MRBM systems, the No Dong (which, as earlier discussed, can hit Japan), but not on an ICBM.[15]

In early 2015, in congressional testimony, the head of US Northern Command addressed North Korea's ability to place a nuclear warhead on its developing (and, as of the writing of this book, untested) mobile ICBM, known as the KN-08. Later, when addressing reporters at the Pentagon, Admiral William Gortney stated: "Our assessment is that they have the ability to put a nuclear weapon on a KN-08 and shoot it at the homeland." The admiral also responded, "Yes sir," when asked whether North Korea had succeeded in the process of miniaturizing a nuclear warhead for an ICBM.[16] Other high-ranking officials also made similar statements in 2015. The commander of USFK/CFC/UNC, General Curtis Scaparrotti, made very similar statements in his own congressional testimony in April 2015. The general also made important statements regarding the ICBM, which I will cover in the next section.[17]

Adding credibility to the now open assessment of North Korea's new, potentially deadly long-range strike capability with a nuclear weapon by the American government is the fact that the Pentagon has not rushed to correct or deny the statements made by these high-ranking military officers. In addition, none of the agencies in the intelligence community have corrected these statements or stated disagreement. During April 2015, South Korean officials stated that their government was less confident in making an assessment about North Korea's ability to put a nuclear warhead on an ICBM with the range to hit the United States.[18] Thus, as with many weapons systems that North Korea has, there is likely to be continued debate about this new capability assessed by US Department of Defense officials. One thing is certain—American officials appear very confident of this assessment. Thus, there is likely some very important information in classified channels that was behind this assessment, information not yet made available in open sources.

To further complicate matters when it comes to North Korean nuclear weaponization and long-range strike capabilities, Pyongyang decided to go public with the development of its ability to place a nuclear warhead on an ICBM capable of hitting the United States. In fact, the National Defense Commission, the top military body in the country at the time and a powerful political entity within the ruling infrastructure, made an announcement in May 2015 confirming that the DPRK military has now manufactured a warhead small enough to be placed on a long-range missile. To quote the announcement: "It is long since the DPRK's nuclear striking means have entered the stage of producing smaller nukes and diversifying them." The announcement further stated: "The DPRK has reached the stage of ensuring the highest precision and intelligence and best accuracy of not only medium and short-range missiles but long range ones."[19] North Korea has (at times) exaggerated its military capabilities. But, at the same time, it has often surprised the world with its development of weapons systems.[20] Thus, the North Korean announcement, combined with the public assessments of high-ranking American officials, means that the debate over North Korea's ability to develop a warhead small enough to be placed on a long-range missile is likely to continue. In my opinion, the confidence with which US DOD officials have made their statements means that a test may be in the offing in the future and that there is more evidence than what has been made available in public channels to date.

To exacerbate the debate, during early March 2016, North Korea publicly exhibited what it claimed was the actual nuclear warhead for a ballistic missile—presumably the KN-08 or some similar system. Kim Jong-un was photographed posing next to the warhead. To add credibility to the North Korean claim, highly regarded *Jane's* published a study (quoted in the international press) reporting that Pyongyang's missile reentry vehicles appear to be stable enough to launch successfully and that the warheads publicly exhibited "appear to be small and light enough to fit into the vehicles."[21]

DPRK Ballistic Missile Programs: Compelling Advances in the Threat

North Korea's ballistic missile program has been considered a threat to regional and international security ever since the 1980s, when the DPRK successfully manufactured Scud Bs and soon thereafter (*a*) deployed them, pointing them at the South, and (*b*) proliferated them to Iran (which almost immediately began firing them at Iraq as the Iran-Iraq War was in high octane at the time).[22] Since that time, the array of missiles that North Korea has produced, deployed, and proliferated can be considered nothing less than stunning, particularly when one considers the tragic shape Pyongyang's economy is in. The list includes Scud B/C/D/ER, No Dong, Musudan, and the Taepo Dong series. Another key missile is the KN-02, the North Korean version of the Soviet SS-21 (now with a longer range). These are only those ballistic missiles that have actually been deployed and test-launched. There are also other missiles that are in development (which I will discuss) and that have caused great concern for American and South Korean policy makers. In this section, I will address developments in North Korea's missile programs that have occurred recently and how these development pose a threat to the ROK-US alliance and security in the region (as well as to the United States).

North Korea has recently—particularly since 2013—made several advances in its missile programs. It has also enhanced training for its missile units (as I will address below). But the focus of much of the debate and controversy for many years has been the Taepo Dong program. Many pundits and experts said that North Korea would never be able to put an ICBM through all three of its stages, meaning that it would not be able to hit the United States (which has now been proved to be false). In fact, some have said that North Korea's ballistic missile program is fake, an assessment that can only be considered silly by any serious analyst. To quote the Rand analyst Markus Schiller (in a report that fails to address many of the facts regarding North Korean missile development): "The security community generally believes that North Korea has obtained its missiles by producing large numbers of reverse-engineered Soviet ballistic missiles. But the data on North Korean missile tests and missile performance raise questions about this explanation: North Korea tests too few missiles to achieve the level of reliability that its missiles appear to possess. North Korea may have achieved this level of reliability by using missiles supplied directly by Russia or produced as part of a licensed production arrangement."[23] Schiller obviously failed to address the tests that other countries conducted of missiles purchased from Pyongyang. He also showed no evidence to prove his allegation that somehow Russia was supplying any missiles to North Korea (in other words, his assessment was based on a guess with no supporting data).

What recent data show us is that the Chinese may be assisting North Korea with its ballistic missile program. There is no evidence to suggest that this has been going on for many years, but there is certainly evidence that small yet important initiatives have occurred in recent years. One key example of this is the training that the Chinese have provided to North Korean technicians on the Beidou satellite navigation system. North Koreans, along with specialists from seven other nations, received intensive and useful training on the GPS-associated technology from the system—in China—and are most likely to use this technology in systems such as the Taepo Dong.[24] Speaking of the Taepo Dong, the North Koreans used many components from foreign sources (including the United States) for their successful launch of the three-stage system in 2012.[25] In other news regarding the ongoing development and testing of the Taepo Dong series of ballistic missiles, in 2014, construction at the Sohae launching site near Tongchang-ri in February 2014 showed near completion of a larger rocket launch pad. Imagery from July 2014 showed other improvements to the launch site that would enhance the capability to launch a larger rocket than seen in past launches. New buildings have also been constructed at the site that will add to the efficiency of future launches. Assessments by many analysts indicated that the improved facility was being designed to launch a more powerful ballistic missile with a heavier payload.[26]

Development and testing of the Taepo Dong missile continued into 2016. In October 2015, a freight train (apparently moving missile components) was spotted moving in the direction of North Korea's long-range missile launching site located near Tongchang-ri. In late January 2016, suspicious activity was imaged at the site. In early February, an American radar ship capable of tracking what appeared to be an imminent launch was reported at Sasebo, Japan, which would be the perfect area for the ship to depart from as it monitored a North Korean launch. Imagery from February 5 showed renewed activity at North Korea's launch site, including the presence of tanker trucks. On February 6, North Korea informed the International Maritime Organization that the launch window would be February 7–14. Also on February 6, press reports indicated that the North Koreans had a backup missile ready in case the first launch was unsuccessful. The American secretary of defense, Ashton Carter, publicly announced that the United States was going to use its missile defense system to monitor the launch. Perhaps in response to all of this, both Japanese and South Korean airlines altered their planned flight routes during the launch period. During this same time period, North Korea built a viewing booth for the launch, apparently for Kim Jong-un (who did in fact observe the launch). On February 7, North Korea conducted a successful launch of the Taepo Dong, putting a satellite into space. South Korea was able to retrieve parts of the first stage soon after the launch. Results of analysis following the test revealed that the missile had a range of up to twelve thousand kilometers, meaning it could hit many key nodes in the United States if launched as a ballistic missile vice a satellite launch vehicle. Following the launch, it was also revealed that North Korea had built a secret underground railway at the launch site, allowing technicians to ready the missile for launch in a way that significantly shortened the warning time for the United States and others. Warning time for launch has now been changed (apparently) from several weeks to several days, an ominous prospect for American and allied intelligence. According to some reports, the newer version of the long-range missile system can now also carry a larger payload.[27]

While the continuing development of the Taepo Dong series of missiles is certainly troubling, also troubling is the significant increase in the testing of a variety of missile systems since early 2014. One example of this was the several dozen launches conducted of the free rocket over ground systems during March 2014. The 1950s-era system has been in North Korea's inventory for a long time and can be aimed at Seoul, but this large number of launches has not been noted since before even the Kim Jong-il era.[28] Continuing with the trend of conducting a high number of missile launches, during both 2014 and 2015 North Korea conducted several launches of its Scud systems.[29] Another interesting set of missile launches occurred when it conducted No Dong firings during March 2014. Launches were simulated during 2015. The 2014 test launches were reportedly conducted with a modified version of the missile, a version that could carry a nuclear warhead. The firing angle for the launches indicates attempts to modify the missile in order to evade ballistic missile defense systems such as the PAC-3.[30] Another important—and deadly—missile that was tested several times during the 2014–2015 time frame was the KN-02. This missile is the North Korean variant of the

Soviet SS-21, a missile deployed against NATO forces by Soviet and Warsaw Pact forces during the Cold War. The KN-02 has a range of up to 170 kilometers, uses solid fuel (making it easier to transport and fire), and has an advanced GPS system for nearly pinpoint guidance. North Korea reportedly has at least 100 KN-02 systems, and at least 30 mobile launches have been deployed with the system.[31] The KN-02 will be a key weapon in an attack against the South.

In 2016, North Korea continued active testing of it ballistic missile systems. In early March of that year, it fired two Scuds off its east coast, each traveling around three hundred miles.[32] About a week later, it fired off what appeared to be a Nodong, which flew about the same distance.[33] In April 2016, the North Koreans launched what appeared to be two Nodong missiles off their east coast, and the missiles landed in Japan's Air Defense Identification Zone (ADIZ).[34] In fact, by late July, analysts assessed that North Korea had fired off thirty-one ballistic missiles up to that date in the Kim Jong-un era, twice the number of missiles launched during Kim Jong-il's entire term.[35] But the North Koreans were not done with the many launches of their land-based missiles for that year. During late July, they launched three Scuds that flew between five and six hundred kilometers. Pyongyang claimed that the launches were simulated attacks on South Korean airfields and ports.[36] In early August, the North Koreans launched what appeared to be two more Nodong missiles off their east coast. The missiles landed in Japan's Economic Exclusion Zone.[37] In September 2016, North Korea launched what appeared to be three more Nodong missiles, all of which landed in Japan's ADIZ. Of interest, once an analysis of video footage released by Pyongyang occurred, it showed a tunnel immediately behind the launchers.[38] This means that the North Koreans have the capability to hide the missiles in tunnels until right before launch preparations, making them harder to detect in wartime. The North Koreans have not been idle in advancing their antiair systems. The KN-06 is a system apparently based on the Chinese HQ-9 system, and testing of it has been going on in one way or another since at least 2011. With a range of sixty to ninety miles, it is North Korea's best antiair system. After a test in 2017 at which Kim Jong-un was present, Pyongyang announced that it was going into what was called mass production.[39]

While the number of short- and midrange North Korean missile systems tested has been quite compelling in recent times, there are other systems that have been tested that also created quite a stir. The North Korean Musudan missile was not tested on the Korean Peninsula until 2016 but reportedly had been tested in Iran in 2006.[40] Despite the fact that many American analysts have tended to ignore the fact that the Musudan was tested in Iran and has now been field deployed in North Korea,[41] there continued to be quite a bit of debate about whether the missile was operational. But, if one is to wonder how seriously the US government takes the Musudan threat, one can simply look back to the last time Musudan missiles were deployed on launchers for a possible launch. During April 2013, Pyongyang deployed a Musudan missile in firing mode on its east coast. The United States reacted by deploying a THAAD ballistic missile defense system to Guam, US sovereign territory within range of the missile.[42] Obviously, Washington takes the Musudan threat seriously, and there are now many systems deployed, both in North Korea and Iran.

The North Koreans finally decided to test-launch the Musudan from the Korean Peninsula during March 2016. Though, as we have seen, the Musudan was reportedly tested by the Iranians during 2006 (the North Koreans proliferated eighteen Musudan systems to Iran during the fall of 2005), the North Koreans had waited until 2016 for home testing, in order to leave its status on the peninsula ambiguous.[43] There were several launches during 2016, with several failures, before success was achieved. During one of the first launches, the missile reportedly exploded on the launch pad, resulting in several North Korean casualties. Later tests (three) were not as catastrophic; however, there were no successful launches during April 2016.[44]

North Korea again conducted Musudan test launches in June 2016. There were two launches, with the first missile apparently failing in launch (unless it was a decoy), followed by a second launch that was deemed successful and showed analysts valuable and previously unknown technical details about North Korean capabilities. The successful missile launched in June 2016 reached an altitude of more than fourteen hundred kilometers, perhaps to avoid flying over Japan. The missile launch proved that, if the flight trajectory was leveled out, the Musudan has the range to hit Guam (which is within a range of thirty-five hundred to four thousand kilometers). But those who analyzed the launch were able to detect other new capabilities in the Musudan, one of them being North Korean–designed grid fins and what appeared to be new engines. The Musudan flew at a speed and an altitude showing that it can possibly evade South Korea's Patriot PAC-2 or even upgraded PAC-3 systems.[45] Because of the new analysis, THAAD will be an important addition to the on-peninsula arsenal for the ROK-US alliance. While there are many naysayers when it comes to Pyongyang's missile capabilities, it is important to note that, in two short months, North Korea went from the missile blowing up on the launch pad during its attempted test launch to a successful launch that proved menacing capabilities.[46]

A missile system that has not yet been tested has become the focus of military analysts and policy makers in recent years. This is tied in to the miniaturization debate. As addressed earlier, this debate began with public assessments by high-ranking policy makers and intelligence specialists that North Korea had the ability to make a nuclear warhead small enough to be put on a road-mobile ICBM. The ICBM that these officials have been addressing in this now widely publicized US government assessment is the KN-08. The KN-08 is road mobile—deployed on a wheeled transporter-erector-launcher—an ICBM that has been publicly displayed in military parades in Pyongyang. During November 2013, the first high-ranking official to speak of KN-08 capabilities (Admiral Samuel Locklear, commander of US Forces Pacific) stated that the KN-08 was potentially a serious threat to the United States.[47] This was followed up by congressional testimony by James Clapper, the director of national intelligence, who in January 2014 stated in part: "North Korea has publicly displayed its KN08 road-mobile ICBM twice. We assess that North Korea has already taken initial steps towards fielding this system, although it remains untested. North Korea is committed to developing long-range missile technology that is capable of posing a direct threat to the United States."[48]

While there is scant evidence in open sources regarding the capabilities, development, and deployment of the KN-08, military and intelligence officials have been increasingly open and progressively alarming about the missile system. Of course, this missile would be the most compelling North Korean threat to the United States—ever—if it was to become completely operational. This is because, if that was the case, (a) it would be a road-mobile system and thus harder to target, (b) it would have the range to target US mainland territory, and (c) it would have the capability to carry a nuclear warhead.

Admiral C. D. Haney, the commander of the US Strategic Command, testified to Congress on March 19, 2015, that North Korea continues to advance its ballistic missile programs, including the development of a new road-mobile missile (presumably he was referring to the KN-08).[49] During the same month, the vice director of the Missile Defense Agency, Navy vice admiral James Syring, stated that both Iran and North Korea could have the ability to launch an ICBM by "this year," that is, by 2015. He also remarked in February 2015 that the United States was striving to "stay ahead" of the KN-08 missile threat. Syring made his remarks at press briefings.[50] And, of course, there were the remarks (during April 2015) of NORAD commander Admiral William Gortney regarding the KN-08 that left no doubt the assessment was now that the missile system was ready to hit the United States. Gortney stated: "We assess that it's operational today, and so we practice to go against that."[51] And perhaps the most compelling testimony regarding the KN-08 came from the commander of USFK during April 2015, when in open testimony he told the Senate Armed Services Committee that he believed that North Korea had the ability to miniaturize a nuclear warhead to place on the missile. He also stated that "we must assume" that the North Koreans had the capability to hit the United States with a KN-08.[52]

The KN-08 is an interesting and unique ICBM. On the basis of analysis by those who have examined the few pictures that exist of it, it appears to be about seventeen meters long. It is a three-stage missile, with the first stage likely to be a cluster of four Scud engines, the second stage being a Musudan engine (SS-N-6), and the third stage being a cluster of Musudan engines (also called the R-27).[53] It appears to be a simple yet very practical design and one that is highly mobile. It should be stressed, however, that, as of the writing of this chapter, the KN-08 remains untested in flight. Thus, the logical analysis would point to the assessment that there is unreleased evidence in classified channels that has led to the flurry of high-ranking military and intelligence officials making statements that clearly show that the United States believes this missile to be operational and thus ready to strike at any time. While this evidence has not yet been released, one thing is for sure; North Korea has made much faster progress on this missile that many called a mock-up in 2012 than anyone would have predicted. If, as several senior officials have stated, it truly is operational—and the North Koreans have successfully manufactured a nuclear warhead that can fit on it—it now presents the most compelling DPRK threat to American national security that has ever existed.

Development of technology—publicly—that continues to advance the readiness of the KN-08 was ongoing in 2016. It was in March of that year that North Korea tested a ballistic missile nose cone that appeared to be for the KN-08. According to the North Koreans and also many analysts, the test of the nose cone was successful. Thus, if true, this confirms that the nose cone of the KN-08 is probably capable of atmospheric reentry, showing that, if launched, a nuclear-armed KN-08 can get to its target (presumably the United States) without burning up or falling apart.[54] In the development of the KN-08, North Korea successfully conducted an engine test for what appeared to the KN-08 in April 2016. The engine tested consisted of two clustered SS-N-6 (R-27) engines (also known as the engine for the Musudan missile) with "double plumes" seen coming from the clustered engines.[55] Perhaps in response to the advances in KN-08 development, in February 2016, the North Koreans reportedly formed a KN-08 brigade, presumably also deploying actual systems to the field. The brigade is subordinate to the Strategic Forces, a corps-level unit within the North Korean People's Army.[56]

During October 2015, the North Koreans revealed what is possibly an advanced version of what has been designated as the KN-08. The modified version may be able to more effectively target the United States and is perhaps a more sophisticated missile than the KN-08. This missile, designated by some as the KN-14, can likely also carry a nuclear warhead. Little information was available in open sources at the time, but the new version was publicly displayed in a North Korean parade, which typically signals a system already deployed or in later stages of development.[57] In 2017, the North Koreans revealed what appeared to be yet another new version of a road-mobile ICBM that can be launched from a TEL (this one looks nothing like the KN-08 or the KN-14). If one is to look at the pictures or the film released by the North Koreans of the weaponry that was displayed in a military parade, the missile looks quite similar to the Chinese DF-31, though there is little known of the new missile (including where the North Koreans may have acquired it). If the development of the missile comes to fruition (and there is no evidence to date of how close to being deployed it is), this means that, in the future, the North Koreans will have the capability to field and launch a variety of ICBMs. This would make BMD more challenging and would be a particularly difficult challenge if these systems (any of them) were deployed to a North Korean customer such as Iran.[58]

As if North Korea had not tested enough missiles by the spring of 2017, it decided to test yet another ballistic missile system in May. The North Koreans called this system the Hwasong 12, and it was identified by the US government as the KN-17. The missile appears to be very similar to the Musudan, just longer (or at least it appears to be). While the engine appears to be similar to the Musudan engine—or exactly the same—the missile also comes with Vernier engines that appear to have given it extended range. On the basis of data analyzed following the successful test launch, it appears that, if the very high trajectory the missile was launched at was leveled out to realistic ballistic missile launch patterns (in other words, a maximum flight pattern), it would have a range of forty-five hundred kilometers, thus leaving no doubt that North Korea has, not one, but two ballistic missile systems capable of targeting Guam, its military bases (including those that house aircraft that would be used to fly missions against North Korea in wartime), and its American population of nearly 170,000 people.

Analysts have assessed that the Hwasong-12 missile may be able to hit outer islands that are part of Alaska. Conclusions regarding the specifications of the missile varied after the launch. Ralph Savelsberg (who was writing for the Johns Hopkins University Web site 38 North), the Center for Strategic and International Studies, and the South Korean government all assessed it to be a one-stage missile, while Jonathan Pollack of Brookings and John Schilling (also of 38 North) initially assessed it to be a two-stage missile (my judgment is that it was a one-stage missile). The trajectory the missile was launched on once again proved that North Korea has atmospheric reentry capability for its intermediate-range missiles. This liquid-fueled ballistic missile presents a new threat to the United States and its allies in Asia.[59] Since the spring of 2017, the North Koreans have successfully test-launched the Hwasong-12 several times, including once on a trajectory that took it over Japan.[60]

On July 4, 2017, the North Koreans changed all the paradigms when it comes to being able to threaten the United States. It was then that they launched a mobile missile with ICBM range and probably with successful atmospheric reentry capability. The missile, which the North Koreans called the Hwasong-14, appeared (at least initially) to be a variant of the KN-14 missile described earlier that was displayed in parades—but with several different characteristics (which may have been updates). The US designated this missile the KN-20.[61] A two-stage missile, it was launched at a very steep angle that, if leveled out, would give it a range of at least sixty-seven hundred kilometers, meaning it could hit most of Alaska, including Anchorage, where 40 percent of the state's population lives (nearly 300,000 people). The missile was transported to the launch site using a Chinese-manufactured vehicle. It was then dismounted from the vehicle, set up, and launched in the same location. Kim Jong-un attended the launch. According to several reports, the United States observed the North Koreans fueling the missile. Pyongyang probably wanted this because it conducted the launch near an aircraft facility and set up an observation site and launch pad in advance, activities that were likely imaged by American intelligence collection (which the North Koreans would have rightly estimated). The mobility of the missile, combined with a range that could directly threaten American population centers, meant that, on that day, Pyongyang's ability to threaten the United States experienced a profound paradigm shift and made North Korea the sixth nation in the world to have a proven ICBM capability.[62]

On July 28, 2017, North Korea once again proved to the world that it had the capability to launch a mobile ICBM that could hit the United States. This time the missile flew higher and longer than the system launched on July 4. The missile launched on July 28 flew about forty-five minutes (at least eight minutes longer than the missile launched on July 4) and went on a longer range than the missile launched on July 4. If it had been launched on a more conventional, flatter trajectory, it could, many analysts have assessed, hit cities on the West Coast of the United States or perhaps even in the Midwest. This missile fired on July 28 appeared to be of the same basic design as the one launched earlier in the month, but it appeared to have a longer second stage that featured engines with improved thrust (among other improvements). Kim Jong-un and several senior military officials also attended this launch, which occurred at night (and, once again, the preparations for their attendance were likely intentionally left for American intelligence to observe).[63] There were some questions about reentry capabilities for this particular launch, but these appeared to have been minor and unconfirmed.[64] By late July 2017, the North Koreans had proved that they now had a missile probably capable of carrying a nuclear weapon that at a minimum could hit cities perhaps as far away as the West Coast of the United States.

Following the tests of North Korea's first proven ICBM platforms, further assessments from other analysts articulated that, with the size and weight of the warhead (on the basis of what the North Koreans reportedly acquired from Pakistan, many believed that this would be a five-hundred-kilogram HEU warhead), the missile would likely be able to hit Alaska and Hawaii, though being able to target cities farther west could entail having a lighter nuclear warhead (something the North Koreans may or may not have). Some analysts assessed at the time that North Korea likely acquired engines from a former Soviet missile company now located in Ukraine (and owned by the Ukraine government). The government of Ukraine vehemently denied this, and US government officials also stated that the press reports were not accurate. Other analysts looking at the missiles launched and their capabilities also disagreed with the assessment that North Korea acquired engines for its Hwasong-12 and Hwasong-14 missiles from Ukraine. Nevertheless, the possibility exists that it may have acquired designs and/or blue-prints from rogue individuals at the company in Ukraine or elsewhere. The possibility also exists that it simply improved on Musudan technology in order to field and successfully test-launch these platforms.[65] To date, no definitive unclassified evidence exists to prove either theory about how the North Koreans were able to successfully improve on and bring success to their IRBM and ICBM ballistic missile platforms. Reportedly, soon after its second successful ICBM test launch, American intelligence officials formally assessed that the DPRK is capable of building nuclear warheads that can be launched using the country's long-range missiles.[66] This assessment was probably based on the smaller and less powerful devices tested before North Korea successfully tested what appears to be a thermonuclear device in early September 2017.

On November 29, 2017, the North Koreans test-launched yet another new two-stage ICBM (apparently successfully). They called this missile the Hwasong-15, and the US military has referred to it as the KN-22. The KN-22 appeared to be both longer and more capable than its immediate predecessor, the KN-20 (Hwasong-14). It was bigger and more powerful than any mobile missile tested previously by the North Koreans. The first stage appeared to be powered by two clustered engines—giving the missile greater range and more thrust than previous models. The transporter-erector-launcher (TEL) vehicle is bigger than the KN-20 (Hwasong-14) and has an extra axle. The missile has a blunt reentry vehicle (instead of a pointed one like the KN-20) and appears to have a bigger, more powerful engine for its second stage. Many analysts believe that this missile can fly farther than the Hwasong-14 (KN-20). In fact, in November 2017, the KN-22 flew at a higher altitude and for a longer time than either of the KN-20 test-flights. This may mean that the newer missile can hit more targets and targets farther inside the United States than its predecessor. But, of course, it once again depends on the size and weight of the warhead—which makes most estimates guesswork until more data are available. The missile also appears to be capable of carrying more fuel than other previous test-launched platforms—an important capability for any ICBM. The fact that it is mobile also makes it a warning nightmare for allied ballistic missile defense systems. This two-stage, liquid-fueled missile appears to be able to operate with eighty tons of liftoff thrust, which is what the North Koreans seem to have been pushing for.[67] It is my assessment that North Korea is likely to proliferate this missile (or related technology) to Iran.

North Korea's Maritime Threat:
Systems for the DPRK and for Proliferation

While its nuclear capabilities and its ground-based ballistic missile capabilities have certainly rated watching in recent times, the more traditional military capabilities that the DPRK possesses cannot be overlooked, and the North Korean navy has certainly not been idle. Thus, in this section, I will address the maritime capabilities that have grown with almost unprecedented speed in the Kim Jong-un era. Among these many advances are improvements in ships, submarines, missiles, and even base improvements. The rise in capabilities is matched only by the speed with which they have occurred.

One of the most surprising updates in naval capabilities is to North Korea's Najin-class frigate ships. Several long-overdue upgrades to weapons systems are apparently being installed on these ships.[68] Among the weapons systems now being installed on at least one of North Korea's Najin-class ships and others in the North Korean fleet as well is an advanced (for the North Koreans) antiship missile. This system appears to be a North Korean version of the Russian KH-35, which flies at a speed of three hundred kilometers and can also fly at very low altitudes. While South Korea's more advanced ships, such as its Aegis-equipped vessels, are well prepared to defend against this type of missile, its older ships are much more vulnerable.[69] There is also an air force version of the missile that the North Koreans could potentially use on their IL-28 bomber aircraft. During one of the tests for the missile, the ship launching it was a recently developed catamaran-hulled missile patrol craft (PTGF) that incorporates stealth technology in its hull—reducing detection from enemy radar. The missile patrol craft is around 38.5 meters long and 13 meters wide. It carries other sophisticated weaponry in addition to the KH-35. The North Koreans have reportedly produced at least six of these ships thus far.[70] Proliferation of this ship (with sophisticated capabilities) is a concern, especially to Iran. North Korea also continues to make improvements in its KN-01 antiship missile.[71]

Speaking of radar-evading naval craft, North Korea has also built another (very new) highly capable craft that was detected in open sources—and probably deployed—since 2014. The craft is reportedly cylindrical and about thirty meters long. It is armed with thirty-millimeter guns and torpedoes. It can travel at speeds of sixty miles per hour or more, which makes it even faster than the air-cushion craft North Korea has stationed on both coasts. The biggest threat from this craft appears to be the fact that such a high-speed vessel is designed to infiltrate special operations forces (SOF).[72] The high speed of the vessel, combined with its formidable weapons systems, means that Pyongyang has now increased the odds of successfully infiltrating SOF into the South during wartime using maritime means.

Ironically, what many analysts consider the most important development in maritime capabilities that North Korea has made involves an aspect of their navy that not many have paid attention to until recently—submarines. North Korea has about seventy submarines, but the majority are the very small Yugo-class or Sango-class infiltration subs or the now-infamous Yeono-class sub (also primarily an infiltration sub and a craft that has been proliferated to Iran)[73] that sank the Cheonan-class South Korean corvette in 2010.[74] North Korea also has about twenty Romeo-class submarines, which until recently could be considered the largest of its submarine fleet. The Romeo-class sub is very noisy and, with modern means, relatively easy to detect.[75] But, in 2014, the world began to pay more attention to North Korean submarines as a regional and international threat.

During the summer of 2014, it was disclosed that the North Koreans were working on a submarine capable of launching ballistic missiles. According to press sources, US intelligence agencies confirmed a missile launch tube on a North Korean submarine in imagery. The submarine—which would easily be the most sophisticated in Pyongyang's inventory—appears to be either a modified version, a copy, or a derivative of the Soviet-era Golf-class submarine. The North Koreans purchased several decommissioned Golf-class submarines from Russia in 1994. They also have SS-N-6 missiles—their own version—that they purchased from rogue Russian technocrats during the early 1990s. Those who follow the North and its military know that these missiles are now known as the Musudan. The technology for the missile tubes spotted in imagery was likely derived from the decommissioned subs the North acquired.[76] The submarine could potentially be a threat to targets such as Hawaii (with a nuclear-tipped missile if the North Koreans have the technology to do so) as it (or a later, advanced version) potentially has a range that takes it out of littoral waters, and, with the right missile, it would be able to range areas outside Northeast Asia.[77] The submarine (which most assess to be a DPRK version or a variant of the Golf class) appears to be well on the way to being operational. It is 67 meters long with a beam of 6.6 meters and a diving displacement of approximately three thousand tons. It is capable of carrying a North Korean variant of a nuclear-tipped ballistic missile (which I will address next), and, in fact, the North Koreans are driving toward that goal. The analyst Joseph Bermudez confirms that the sub houses vertical launch tubes and has designated it the Sinpo class.[78]

Speaking of the new, longer-range ballistic missile–carrying submarine that the North Koreans are developing, the missile that it will fire has been the focus of a great deal of analysis since the summer of 2014. The possibility of a North Korean submarine equipped with a submarine-launched ballistic missile (SLBM) was confirmed by South Korean officials during September 2014. During November 2014, it was confirmed that North Korea had conducted tests of an ejection launcher for an SLBM. In March 2015, senior US officials confirmed that, in February, the North Koreans had conducted a flight test of the same SLBM that would go on the new submarine the DPRK had developed (or copied). Perhaps in the most shocking aspect of what looks to be lightning-fast development of both the submarine and the missile that it will fire, in May 2015, the North Korean government claimed it had successfully test-launched an SLBM from a submarine while it was submerged. Pyongyang also showed film and images of what it said was a successful test launch. South Korean defense officials assessed that the North Koreans are still about four to five years away from an operational, SLBM-launching submarine. American officials also reportedly think North Korea is several years away from an operational submarine/SLBM. American intelligence agencies reportedly watched the May test very closely, and, in photos taken at the time, the missile appeared to be a variant of the SS-N-6 or the Musudan (which now seems to be incorrect). Admiral James Winnefeld of the US Joint Chiefs of Staff suggested the test was a fake and that the photos were manipulated. Others disagreed, however, stating that, at the very least, the missile was launched from a submerged barge, which means development and testing were advancing.[79]

According to the arms expert Hong Seong-min of the South Korea–based think tank Security Policy Networks, the North Koreans developed the launching device for the new SLBM by modeling it after a Soviet-era device that they imported (obviously illegally) through a Japanese trade partner back in 2003. Hong also said that it was his assessment that the SLBM had actually been successfully mounted on the Sinpo-class submarine. According to press reports, there are some in the South Korean Defense Ministry who assessed (in 2015) that the Sinpo-class submarines could operationally deploy equipped with the new SLBM in two to three years.[80]

While the test of the new launching device for the SLBM (and what appears to be an initial testing of the missile itself) has been downplayed by some analysts, others disagreed. According to one report, the test in May 2015 reveals a preliminary capability to conduct missile launches beneath the surface of the water (the missile flew about 150 meters). If one is to judge the test by assessing that it was to determine whether the ejection system and rocket motors are proficient in getting the missile through the water and above the surface successfully, then it can be seen as a solid first step for the DPRK in moving forward with its SLBM program.[81]

Later steps followed. During November 2015, North Korea conducted another underwater ejection test of its SLBM—this time from an actual submarine. The test proved to be a failure and apparently actually caused serious damage to the submarine. During December 2015, the North Koreans again attempted a test launch of their SLBM from a submarine, only this time the missile successfully ejected from under water. It is not clear how far it flew, but it is clear that it did not fly very far. So, while it could be considered a successful ejection test, the actual flight of the missile remained in question. In April 2016, the North Koreans again conducted a test launch of their SLBM from the Sinpo-class submarine. This time the missile flew for approximately twenty kilometers. Analysts determined that the missile launched was a solid-fuel one, a significant advancement. In July of the same year, North Korea conducted another SLBM test launch. This time, the missile exploded in the air after flying about ten kilometers. During August 2016, the North Koreans conducted what appeared to be a completely successful test of their SLBM and accompanying submarine. This time, after being launched from under water, the missile traveled five hundred kilometers. Experts in the South Korean military estimated that the missile has a range of up to two thousand kilometers. This means that, if the Sinpo-class submarine or an upgraded larger submarine were able to travel within two thousand kilometers of someplace like Hawaii or Guam (a distinct possibility), North Korea could threaten American sovereign territory with an SLBM.[82]

As if North Korea's submarine and accompanying SLBM technology are not moving forward fast enough, in August 2016 yet another advancement was uncovered that appears to be quite compelling. According to experts, it appears a larger and more advanced submarine than the Sinpo class (perhaps with a longer deployment capability and underwater dwell time) is currently under construction.[83] In addition, on further analysis of the launches in 2016 of the North Korean SLBM from the Sinpo-class submarine, it appears that the missile being launched is very similar in appearance and capabilities to the Chinese-made JL-1 solid-fuel SLBM. This is particularly interesting because the North Korean Sinpo-class submarine appears to be either a derivative or based on the design of the Golf-class submarine. The Chinese have tested the JL-1 from their own Golf-class submarine.[84] As launches continue, it will be interesting to see exactly what the origins of North Korea's SLBM are and what country may have provided the technology.

During February 2017, the North Koreans launched what can only be assessed to be the land variant of the solid-fueled SLBM launched successfully by a submarine during the fall of 2016. The missile, which the North Koreans called the Pukguksong-2, looks very much like the sea-based version (the North Koreans call the sea-based version Pukguksong-1). In fact, it even uses the cold-launch system employed by the SLBM. The missile is assessed by some military analysts to have a range of two to three thousand kilometers. It appears that what the North Koreans did was take their SLBM and simply convert it to a slightly longer, land-launched missile. They even used the exact same technology utilized by a submarine (cold launch), only the missile is launched from a TEL on land instead of underwater, as the sea-based version is. Because it is solid fuel and mounted on a TEL, this missile can present a threat to all South Korea and Japan and has the potential of being very difficult to track down.[85] The second successful test of this missile (designated the KN-15 by the United States) occurred during May 2017. Because it is a solid-fueled system, this missile may end up being the most reliable of North Korea's land-based midrange ballistic missiles (MRBMs).[86]

North Korea's Air and Ground Forces: New Systems and Training Trends

I believe the evidence shows that North Korea has made important strides in its WMD systems and platforms and also in its development of maritime systems. But, especially when it comes to conventional forces, in North Korea the focus has always been on ground forces. Air forces play an ancillary yet important role as well. In the North Korean military, the systems are important—and often outdated—but the readiness and capabilities of this million-man military are also important. Thus, when it comes to air and ground forces, I will address not only systems but planning and recent exercises and training as well. In recent times, the North Korean military has reportedly been rife with corruption. Activities such as the trading of classified information for money across the Chinese border (likely to reporters), illegally allowing North Korean citizens to slip across the border into China, and bribing

senior officers in order to obtain furloughs and long leave passes are reportedly rampant now within the North Korean army.[87] Indeed, there continue
to be anecdotal reports of malnourishment among some units.[88] And this is
despite the fact that, according to the US State Department, North Korea
spends more than 23 percent of its GDP on defense.[89] One thus must ask,
What is the status of the readiness and capabilities of DPRK air and ground
forces?

When it comes to air platforms, North Korea has made advances that
have an impact on the way the ROK-US alliance must defend the South
against attacks and North Korea–based intelligence gathering. Among these
airborne platforms that have the potential to make a significant impact on
the battle space are the drones the North Koreans have utilized against the
South, particularly since early 2014. Among the drones that targeted South
Korea—two of which were downed during March 2014—were unmanned
aircraft that appeared to be of Chinese design. The downed drones caused
a stir among the ROK populace about ROK defenses against these small,
newly utilized (at least that has been seen in open sources) unmanned aircraft.[90] According to reports from the spring of 2014, North Korea has developed a drone (now indigenously produced) capable of attacking US and
ROK ground targets, one based on the American MQM-107 Streaker target
drone.[91] How North Korea got the exact technology to make copies of American unmanned aerial vehicles (UAVs) is unclear but clearly quite compelling. North Korea is also reportedly developing a long-endurance drone with
capabilities advanced over previous models, and, perhaps in related activity,
according to *Popular Mechanics,* it is developing a drone called the Banghyun
5 that can fly up to ten hours and carry a dirty bomb as its payload. If this is
true, it will be something that will certainly bear watching, including to see
whether Pyongyang plans to proliferate the system.[92] The UAVs now pose a
threat to South Korean and American forces on the Korean Peninsula using
US technology.

While UAVs are a new aspect of the threat that North Korea poses to the
South and to the ROK-US alliance, they are not the only airborne platform
that rates interest. While North Korea's jets get a lot of attention, Pyongyang
continues to struggle to find spare parts and to gain training time for its best
pilots.[93] But the aircraft that keeps military planners awake at night is a plane
that most would rarely give much respect to. The AN-2 is a biplane that
can fly at extremely low altitudes, avoiding radar, and is able to carry eight
or more fully equipped SOF troops. The North Korean air force has about

three hundred (or more) of these old yet very reliable and highly capable aircraft. The AN-2 would be the initial platform for airlifting thousands of SOF troops into the South during a war, giving Pyongyang the ability to develop a second front, and forcing troops off the front lines.[94] In early 2015, it was confirmed that North Korea had made changes to the camouflage patterns on most or all of its AN-2s. The belly of each plane is now painted sky blue. The AN-2, which can fly through gorges and small valleys carrying SOF troops on hard-to-detect parachute drops, reportedly was involved in a large number of training events during 2014, with ten to fifteen thousand SOF troops participating.[95]

North Korea has also continued to improve the numbers and capabilities of its ground forces. It has around twenty-five hundred armored personnel carriers (APCs) as of 2014—up around three hundred units from 2012. This of course also means that the North Korean APCs continue to outnumber those of the ROK.[96] The APCs that the North Korean army has recently fielded are of at least two types—a six-wheeled vehicle and an eight-wheeled vehicle. Both come with two 14.5-millimeter machine guns and one coaxial 7.62-millimeter machine gun. Both vehicles are amphibious and when waterborne are powered by a single water jet. The 6×6 APC can carry up to six fully equipped troops, while the 8×8 APC can carry up to eight fully equipped troops.[97] Meanwhile, North Korea has recently upgraded its main battle tank, known as the Songun-ho, with several important features. The tank is reportedly now equipped with ninety-three-millimeter-round thermobaric rocket launchers and SA-16 portable missiles.[98] Other ground-based systems are being brought into the North Korean army as well.

Throughout 2014, the North Koreans tested—successfully—a three-hundred-millimeter multiple rocket launcher (MRL) system that can now target all of Seoul and American military bases south of the city. The system has a range of up to 180 kilometers or more and can carry a payload of 150 kilograms. The MRL system may be based on the Russian BM-30 SMERCH or a similar weapon. North Korea already has thirteen thousand MRLs and artillery systems, many of them deployed along the DMZ. But the deployment of this new MRL will enhance the quick strike threat the North already poses to the South with its missiles and long-range artillery.[99] Other revealed details show that the vehicle carrying the launching system appears to be of Chinese design, matching as it does the specifications for a vehicle manufactured by the China National Heavy-Duty Truck Group. There are eight launch tubes in two pods. The North Koreans have reportedly tested the new long-range system with fragmentation shells and underground penetration shells. The system, which can fire far beyond Seoul, has been tested numerous times in recent years (including several times during 2016) and will likely be deployed along the DMZ.[100]

Another North Korean asymmetrical weapons issue has gained some traction in recent years. In congressional testimony during 2014, former CIA director James Woolsey warned that North Korea is developing and expected to be soon capable of fielding electromagnetic-pulse weapons (EMP). Reportedly, the South Korean Defense Ministry agrees that the weapons are being developed in North Korea, but it does not assess that the EMP weaponry has been fielded. If and when such weapons are fielded, they could neutralize airborne defense systems, radar, ships at sea, and aircraft.[101] Reportedly, the EMP actions of North Korea (or anyone with EMP capability) could come from "an enemy initiating what's called a 'high-altitude EMP' by attaching a nuclear weapon onto a satellite, then detonating it as the satellite passes over the center of the U.S., inflicting the most possible damage."[102]

According to a report from a Johns Hopkins University–affiliated think tank in 2017, two Russian generals who were experts on EMP warned a congressional commission in 2004 that a Russian design for an EMP warhead had unintentionally been transferred to the North Koreans. If this is true, there is no telling how far the North Koreans are from fielding such a system, one that, if successfully launched in space, could cause a great deal of damage.[103] If the EMP weapon was launched from a missile and detonated at a relatively low altitude—perhaps the same type of altitude at which North Korea has already successfully placed satellites—it could cause massive damage to unhardened sites in an area encompassing hundreds of miles.[104] How far along North Korea is in advancing to this kind of capability is to date unknown, at least in unclassified channels.

In another piece of evidence that could be relevant to its ongoing development of an EMP weapon, Pyongyang conducted a test of a nuclear weapon during early September 2017. The test was at least five times larger than previous tests it had conducted. But, of the utmost importance, the North Koreans claimed that the test was also of an EMP weapon. To quote the state news agency statement, the weapon "is a multifunctional thermonuclear nuke with great destructive power which can be detonated even at high altitudes for super-powerful EMP attack." A thermonuclear EMP weapon detonated in the atmosphere over the United States would have profound and long-lasting effects on the infrastructure for a huge swath of territory.[105]

According to Peter Vincent Pry, an EMP weapon "would need not re-enter the earth's atmosphere before exploding and generating a high-frequency electromagnetic pulse that would damage a broad range of electronics."[106] Thus, the North Korean claim of EMP weaponization capability is troubling and must be taken seriously. Nevertheless, to date, there is no evidence in unclassified channels that proves Pyongyang actually has the capability to field an EMP weapon.

While North Korea has been active in developing and upgrading its military capabilities, it has not been idle in the exercises and training that are used to maintain the readiness of its military units. This is not strictly limited to conventional units. In fact, North Korea carried out at least a dozen biological and chemical exercises between February 2014 and February 2015. The drills were assessed to be offensive in nature, being used to plan for a biochemical attack. There is also assessed to be a significant increase in biochemical training as in the past these exercises have typically been limited to small drills during the summertime.[107] North Korea is suspected of building a biological weapons program, though the evidence is not as strong as that regarding the country's chemical warfare programs. The North Koreans are suspected of having several different types of biological weapons programs.[108]

North Korea is assessed to have at least forty-five hundred tons of chemical agents, including hydrogen cyanide, mustard gas, sarin, phosgene, tabun, and chlorine. In fact, if one has any doubts about not only North Korea's chemical weapons capabilities but also its willingness to use these capabilities, one can simply turn to the assassination in Malaysia of Kim Jong-un's older brother, Kim Jong-nam, which was accomplished using VX. According to press sources, the attack was coordinated by the North Korean military under the guidance of the Reconnaissance General Bureau.[109] Again according to press sources, North Korea has been a key provider of chemical weapons to Syria during its ongoing civil war and has also provided most of the training that the Syrian chemical units receive, so these drills have helped not only North Korea (because of the real-world expertise that it gives their operators) but also the Syrian military.[110] In 2017, Japan's prime minister publicly admitted that North Korea may be capable of mounting a missile with a sarin gas warhead aimed at his country.[111] Sarin gas is likely to be used in any war against the South as well and would cause a high number of casualties as well as mass panic.[112]

North Korea's drills since 2014 (or ever) have not been limited to chemical weapons exercises. There has reportedly been an increase in offensive exercises, including coastal landings and river crossings. During January 2015, the scope and focus of North Korean military exercises was quite compelling. In early January, several units from the frontline corps conducted recoilless gun-firing drills (recoilless rifles are deployed along the DMZ opposite South Korean guard posts). Later in the month, fighter and attack squadrons conducted drills that involved MiG-23, MiG-29, and Su-25 aircraft. On January 27, the KPA conducted a large-scale river-crossing drill, and, on January 31, an antinaval drill was conducted on the east coast.[113] Also during January 2015, and perhaps the most compelling event seen that month, the DPRK reportedly conducted an exercise simulating a raid on Incheon airport. The exercise involved SOF troops and infiltration aircraft (likely the AN-2). The North Korean military is also said to have a plan—and to have conducted drills to support it—to invade and occupy the five islands along the Northern Limit Line (NLL) on the western border of the two nations.[114] But there is more on what has been happening along the NLL that is directly related to North Korea's ambitions for military action there.

Exercises in 2016 also proved to be compelling and a source of information that will be useful for analysts. These exercises show that North Korea continues to place a high priority on both artillery and SOF readiness. Major artillery exercises in 2016 involved more weapons than ever observed in the past (a significant issue since North Korea has engaged in many large-scale exercises in the past). Large-scale exercises in both March and December 2016 included dozens of systems (pictures were released to the public), including the largest and most capable in Pyongyang's arsenal.[115] Another compelling exercise that occurred in 2016 was also attended by Kim Jong-un. This exercise, conducted by North Korean SOF, appeared to be a simulated attack on South Korea's presidential Blue House, the seat of power in the nation. According to South Korea's top military and defense issues think tank, the Korea Institute for Defense Analysis, North Korea's special operations warfare capabilities have improved in recent years. Improvements have included upgraded equipment, beefed-up and modernized training, and an increase in the number of units.[116] Relating to proliferation, these units are often the types of units that train both state and nonstate actors in special warfare.[117]

As an important follow-up to the apparent increase in scope and focus of North Korean military exercises, it has recently been revealed that, at a meeting in August 2012, Kim Jong-un and his senior military officials hastened in a new war plan for the invasion of the South. The plan, called the Seven-Day War, proposes that the invasion can be ended in fifteen days (much longer than that would be disastrous for the North Korean army). It calls for the use of asymmetrical weapons to kick off the attack—long-range artillery, missiles, chemical and biological weapons, and, perhaps, nuclear weapons. SOF troops would open up a second front, and then conventional forces would move into the gaps created by the confusion and destruction. Kim Jong-un is said to have ordered his corps commanders to come up with operational-level plans to support the Seven-Day War.[118]

In direct correlation to the war plan, and tied in to violence in the NLL that has occurred off and on continuously since 1999, there have been more incidents in the disputed area since the winter of 2014. During March 2014, the North and South Koreans exchanged artillery fire (hundreds of shells) along the NLL, causing residents of the five islands along the violent border to be evacuated to shelters. North Korea continues to beef up its forces facing the islands and the waters in the NLL area. The DPRK has up to a thousand coastal artillery guns and MRLs facing the islands. It also has antiship cruise missiles along the shoreline and naval bases to launch hovercraft carrying invading troops nearby. As recently as May 2015, it was confirmed that North Korea had built new bunkers to support 122-millimeter MRL units on the island of Gal, which is only 4.5 kilometers from Yeonpyeong Island, an island targeted for artillery attack in 2010 with the very same weaponry. Tied into all the military construction and brinkmanship in the disputed area, during May 2014, North Korea fired artillery rounds at a South Korean ship conducting routine patrols near the NLL. Continued tension and rhetoric remain a norm for this area, and violent North Korean actions there are likely to continue.[119] During February 2016, North Korea units conducted coastal artillery drills, likely with 122-millimeter systems. These systems fired shells so close to South Korean offshore islands that the citizens could hear the boom of the gunfire. Ironically, these are the same systems sold to Syria, systems that Damascus has used to target its own people with chemical weapons—weapons sold to them (both the MRLs and the chemical shells) by the North Koreans, who also trained them.[120]

North Korea and Cyber Warfare: A Growing Threat

The focus that the international press and policy makers have had on North Korea's cyber-warfare capabilities has drastically increased since the highly publicized hacking of Sony Corporation because of the projected release of *The Interview* in late 2014.[121] But the North Koreans have been building up their cyber-warfare capability for a number of years. And, in recent years, North Korea has hacked South Korean business, government, and nonprofit entities several times, to an extent that has caused Seoul to increase its own counter cyber-warfare capabilities.[122] Thus, in this section, it will be my goal to introduce the reader to the growing threat that North Korea's cyber-warfare force presents to the security and stability of networks in both South Korea and the United States.

Experts in South Korea now assess that cyber warfare is among North Korea's highest priorities.[123] Experts also say that South Korea is highly vulnerable to cyber warfare conducted by North Korea.[124] In addition, reports indicate that North Korea has doubled the number of cyber warriors in its arsenal since 2012.[125] It has bolstered its cyber-warfare capabilities by deploying agents outside its borders. Recent estimates from 2014 placed the number of personnel working in this field to be around six thousand, many of them in the Reconnaissance General Bureau (RGB).[126] During December 2014, the United States sought the help of the Chinese government in blocking hacking attempts against ROK and US targets, though Beijing did not respond with action that would stop these activities.[127]

Because the RGB has been in reality subordinate to the National Defense Commission (NDC)—and not the Ministry of Peoples Armed Forces (MPAF) like the rest of the military—it is able to operate in a less bureaucratic environment than most military units. (As of January 2016, the NDC is no longer the supreme body in the country; thus, the RGB may now report directly to the State Affairs Commission [SAC]).[128] The RGB is where the largest portion of North Korea's cyber warriors are housed. According to a high-ranking defector, most of the highly trained specialists who go to cyber units are educated and trained at Mirim University. They are treated better and live better than most military personnel, and many are children of the elite families in North Korea. North Korea has been able to achieve the technological capabilities necessary to conduct sophisticated operations using cyber warfare thanks to a variety of sources and resources, including help from China. Reportedly, those gifted students who show outstanding math skills are targeted by the DPRK regime for service within units that conduct cyber warfare.[129]

The skilled cyber experts who are now housed in North Korea's RGB and other units have proved their technical skills, both in attacks on the South and in other instances. In late 2014, a nuclear power plant in South Korea was targeted. Of course, the most infamous episode of successful cyber warfare targeted not South Korea but the United States. FBI officials have formally and publicly confirmed that North Korean operatives working for the RGB hacked into Sony's networks. The operatives were reportedly working out of Shenyang in China and were part of Office 121, a unit subordinate to the RGB and manned by highly trusted personnel. Why China allows North Korea to operate such a unit within its sovereign territory is an open question, but claiming ignorance is an excuse not likely to be taken seriously by officials in the United States.[130] According to defectors, there is also another unit, one actively involved in stealing cash and other activities. This is Unit 180, and it too is directly subordinate to the RGB.[131]

During November 2015, an inspection conducted by the Intelligence Committee of the South Korean National Assembly reported that North Korea had hacked into foreign affairs and intelligence ministries and apparently some members of the National Assembly. The attacks appear to have occurred from locations in China (and to have been launched by North Koreans). In early 2016, it was revealed that senior officials in South Korea had their smart phones hacked into.[132] On March 16, 2016, the commander of Cyber Command in the United States, Admiral Mike Rogers, stated: "Iran and North Korea represent lesser but still serious challenges to U.S. interests. Although both states have been more restrained in this last year in terms of cyber activity directed against us, they remain quite active and are steadily improving their capabilities, which often hide in the overall worldwide noise of cybercrime. Both of these nations have encouraged malicious cyber activity against the United States and their neighbors, but they currently devote the bulk of their resources and effort to working against their neighbors."[133] This statement is particularly compelling, because it means that, if North Korea is collaborating with Iran on cyber warfare as it has been for years in both WMD and conventional weapons programs, these two states can present a threat that will be challenging to deal with.

During June 2016, it was revealed that North Koreans had hacked into defense-related companies in South Korea, the SK Group and the Hanjin Group. More than forty-two thousand documents were stolen, including some containing sensitive military information.[134] In July 2016, the malicious behavior using cyber means continued when North Korea reportedly stole the personal data from millions of online customers at a shopping mall in South Korea. The event appears to have been purely an attempt to steal money from South Korean citizens.[135] The cyber events and attacks show no sign of easing up, and this capability will no doubt be shared with North Korea's fellow rogue states (as long as they are willing to pay for the capability).

During March 2017, South Korea's Ministry of National Defense reported an increase in hacking attacks believed to be emanating from North Korea. In addition, according to the Korea Institute for National Unification, by 2017 North Korea had increased the number of its cyber hackers to an estimated seventy-seven hundred personnel. The hacking operations are said to be spread out over seven organizations contained in both the Korea Workers' Party and the North Korea People's Army.[136] As if this was not enough to show the increased threat, in what can be described only as a bizarre story of international intrigue, in 2017 it was disclosed that the primary suspect (North Korea) in an electronic robbery of the Bangladesh Central Bank got away with $81 million (thanks to its great hackers). It appears (at least for now) that the hackers were Chinese citizen intermediaries under the control of North Korea. According to allegations, the money was transferred to banks in the Philippines and then laundered through casinos there. The theft of the money from Bangladesh shows the sophistication and skill of North Korean cyber operators—if proved.[137] According to reports that came out during July 2017, the North Koreans continue to keep attacks on banks as one of their key areas of focus.[138]

In addition to the accusations of their attacks against banks from Bangladesh, the North Koreans have again in 2017 been accused of attacking multiple accounts in countries located around the world. North Korea may in fact be involved in ransomware and other cyber-attack-related software that is stealing cash from banks and other financial entities. According to press sources, it is involved in the Wannacry software and ransomware scandal, which involved numerous countries worldwide. Technical analysis of who was targeting these legitimate financial entities points to the North Koreans. There have been naysayers, who more often than not have pointed to China, not North Korea. But perhaps the most important development is that, during June 2017, the NSA reportedly made an assessment that the RGB was involved in the Wannacry scandal, an event that involved numerous large corporations being attacked in a way that led to yet another compelling demand that funds be paid to the mysterious entity who had attacked them.[139] During December 2017, the US government announced that North Korea would be held accountable for the Wannacry debacle, which caused serious damage worldwide but may have been meant as much to get money into Pyongyang's coffers as anything else.[140] During the fall of 2017, it was also disclosed that North Korean hackers were able to steal US and South Korean military plans for going after North Korean leadership during wartime. Pyongyang's cyber warriors were also able to steal blueprints for South Korean warships and submarines.[141]

Using Its Military Capabilities:
North Korea and Violent Provocations in 2015

North Korea has made interesting advances in its military capabilities, but it is not hesitant to use its capabilities in violent actions against the South. Its violent provocations almost always have four key things in common (as I have written previously): (1) they are intentionally initiated at moments when they have the likelihood of garnering the greatest attention on the regional and perhaps even the world stage; (2) they initially appear to be incidents that are relatively small, easily contained, and quickly resolved; (3) they involve continuously changing tactics and techniques; and (4) North Korea denies responsibility for them.[142]

On August 4, 2015, two South Korean soldiers on patrol 1,440 feet south of the military demarcation line stepped on what were clearly North Korean wooden box mines. Both were severely wounded, with one needing to have one of his feet amputated and the other needing to have parts of both his legs amputated.[143] The mines were planted well south of the North-South demarcation line, which means North Korean troops (likely SOF personnel) successfully snuck into the DMZ, planted the mines, and then snuck back out, without taking any casualties. This was the first successful DPRK violent provocation since the artillery attack on Yeonpyeong Island during November 2010. Many in South Korea placed this provocation on par with incidents such as the Cheonan sinking and other provocations, thus proving that the North Koreans have no intention of ceasing violent military provocations meant to inflict casualties on the South.[144]

Following the North Korean provocation, the South Koreans began broadcasting loudspeaker propaganda into the North. North Korea, in response, made threats that they would attack the loudspeakers. The result was that, on August 20, 2015, North Korea ended up firing weapons systems at targets across the border into the South. The South Korean army responded with artillery fire back into the North. In other words, Seoul's response was quick and authoritative. After the exchange of fire across the

DMZ, the North Korean Central Military Commission reportedly convened a meeting to organize yet another counterattack. The meeting included eight of the highest-ranking military and security personnel in the country. Of course, after the exchange of fire and the subsequent talks, there was no North Korean counterattack.[145] In addition to responding with appropriate and compelling force following provocation, South Korea took measures to look out for the safety of its troops in the future. Under the improved guidelines, South Korean troops patrolling the advanced scouting missions along the DMZ will wear mine-proof boots and carry special mine detectors.[146] The weapons and tactics that the North Koreans have used in provocations present an interesting template that can be used when they proliferate military training and arms to other states. These tactics can prove useful if applied to a variety of low-intensity conflicts ongoing in both the Middle East and Africa.

The evidence shows—clearly—that North Korea in the Kim Jong-un era has continued to pursue the weapons programs and the brinkmanship that Kim Jong-il was well-known for. The only difference is that this appears to be happening at a stepped-up rate under Kim Jong-un. One is thus forced to wonder, What are the reasons for this? To date, there have been no real moves to engage in realistic talks with South Korea. There have also been no moves to ramp down tensions that exist on the Korean Peninsula. In fact, missile firings, incidents in disputed areas, and bombastic rhetoric from North Korean government authorized sources have been the order of the day. This leads one to believe that there has to be specific motivations for the spate of military developments, testing of advanced systems, and stepped-up exercises occurring in North Korea since late 2013.

Given the available evidence, one would tend to believe that there are three key reasons why there has been the flurry of diverse military activity in North Korea since late 2013. The first reason is that it may be a reaction to the increase in unification planning and focus that has been coming from Seoul during this time period. This increased focus on unification may be a motivator for Pyongyang to show that it remains a strong military power, having no intention of compromising with the South. In fact, this is what has actually occurred during the Kim Jong-un regime. There has been no real engagement, and the focus has been on showing off and developing new and advanced weapons systems that would be used for offensive purposes against South Korea and/or the United States. These advanced systems can also be (and often have been) proliferated to other states or nonstate actors.

There is another reason that North Korea may be conducting this flurry of activity relating to its military. Kim Jong-un still has not fully consolidated his power in the three key institutions of the DPRK—the Party, the security services, and the military. But the military has been the institution with the most instability. The constant rotating of senior-level uniformed officials, the purges and executions, the anecdotal reports of corruption and morale issues in a number of units, and the high number of defense chiefs is evidence that Kim still is attempting to build a power base in the military but has not even come close to building the loyalty and security that his father commanded. Thus, one way to gain credibility with the military would be to support the building of new systems, to provide resources for advanced and sophisticated exercises, and to take a strong military approach in policy making.

The third likely reason—and perhaps the most compelling—that there has been a flurry of military activity is because North Korea is developing most of these systems not only for deployment on its own but also for proliferation in order to gain valuable funds to support the regime. It should be noted that all the systems and capabilities described in this chapter either have been proliferated to the Middle East or Africa (or both) or have the likelihood of being proliferated once operational. It is a fact that North Korea looks to proliferation and other illicit activity as one of its key means of generating billions of dollars for the regime, a regime that is clearly not as stable as Kim Jong-un wants it to be and that could use the valuable funds generated by this proliferation. This shadow economy has become vital for support of the regime and the elite who run the country.[147] Thus, in following chapters, I will address how North Korea is able to get around sanctions to proliferate arms and services in key (often unstable) areas around the globe, how it is able to use illicit finance and banking activities to support and profit from its proliferation, who it is proliferating military goods and services to, and how this can be contained more effectively than it has been in the past.

3

How Do They Do It?

North Korea's Illicit Financial Networks and Proliferation Modus Operandi

North Korea is a nation-state that for many years (including the years following the Cold War) has been off the main radar of American foreign policy. Whether it was because the United States was worried about other issues, such as problems in the Balkans in the 1990s, or fighting wars in Iraq and Afghanistan in the new millennium, challenges from the DPRK never seemed to be at the top of the priorities list with American foreign policy makers. This has changed. It has now become obvious to the world that North Korea has an active nuclear weapons program and that Pyongyang has not been shy about threatening to use it. It is also obvious that North Korea has long- and short-range ballistic missiles that can threaten not only the region but also, potentially, the United States and, through proliferation, areas as far away as the Middle East. So, since North Korea is now acknowledged as a threat not only to the international order but also, in a very potentially violent way, to the American homeland, one wonders how this regime, highly threatening and more sanctioned than almost any nation on earth, continues to survive. The answer is largely through its illicit activities that support and enable the Kim family regime.

Because its rogue state activities have put it on several sanctions lists, one would think that the DPRK would be economically squeezed. This is true, yet, because of an incredibly sophisticated financial network that operates worldwide (much like a crime family network), it is able to get its tentacles into numerous banks, supported by dozens and perhaps hundreds of front companies. But it does not stop there. I will also consider, in detail, the highly nuanced measures that North Korea takes to get around sanctions and other initiatives that the United States and the international community have taken to contain its proliferation, other illicit activities, and illegal banking actions.

Because military proliferation of both conventional weapons and WMD is the main focus of this book, I will refer to North Korea's military proliferation from time to time in this chapter, largely because it will become obvious how much this proliferation contributes to Pyongyang's economy. Thus, it will also be necessary to conduct a brief analysis of the nonmilitary illicit activities that the DPRK continues to conduct, highlighting key aspects of it. While descriptions of the activities I have described above are important, it is also important to know what the United States has done to contain those illicit activities. Of course, it will also be necessary to look at how the international community has attempted to do the same and how successful both the United States and the international community have been at attempting to curb both the activities and the financial network that supports them. Finally, I will address China's role (often highly debated) in containing North Korea's illicit activities and in enforcing sanctions. I believe the conclusions will be quite compelling.

North Korea's Illicit Financial Networks

In September 2016, the South Korean press reported that two key entities within the Korea Workers' Party (KWP) that handled funds for the Kim family regime (and reportedly Kim Jong-un's private slush fund) had merged into one. Office 38 and Office 39 merged, becoming simply Office 39.[1] In reality, it has always been Office 39 that has been the entity managing North Korea's illicit money. In fact, Office 39 (originally formed by Kim Jong-il during his father's reign) has for many years managed everything from military proliferation, to counterfeit currency, to a variety of other illicit and illegal activities.[2] It will be the purpose of this section not only to analyze and evaluate the activities of Office 39 but also to show the reader the sophisticated financial networks that run these illicit activities. These financial networks are interconnected and highly nuanced. But they all end up in one place—in the coffers of the Kim family regime.

Office 39 was formed in the 1970s when Kim Il-sung was still in power, but it was under Kim Jong-il. Since that time, its activities have been significant, reportedly raising billions of dollars annually. Those activities are incredibly diverse and show that North Korea is now the only government on earth actively promoting and engaging in large-scale criminal activities, activities run by operatives sanctioned by the party. These activities include (but are not limited to) counterfeit US currency, counterfeit cigarettes, sales of illegal drugs, illegal export of minerals (including gold), and of course the most concerning moneymaker when it comes to national security concerns, arms sales (I do not include the large, government-organized operations of North Korean overseas workers in these activities as the greatest number of workers have served or are serving in places such as China, Russia, and the Middle East and, for the most part, their activities have not been hidden). I will discuss in detail later how North Korea's Office 39 operatives—diplomats, businessmen, and others—use a variety of illegal methods to conduct their criminal and sanctions-busting operations, but the methods are many.[3] According to Dr. Andrei Lankov of Kookmin University in South Korea, the use of foreign currency has risen greatly in North Korea, largely as a result of all the illicit foreign trade Pyongyang has conducted. In the areas of the country along the Chinese border, much of the illicit trade is conducted using yuan.[4]

According to the North Korean defector and former overseas trade official Choi Kin-chol, North Korea's diverse banking and trading activities have greatly diversified since 2005 when the US Treasury Department sanctioned Banco Delta Asia in Macao, setting off a snowball effect that left North Korean finances out in the cold in banks all over Asia and elsewhere. According to the defector, individuals (using individual accounts) and front companies work together to mask their North Korean identity, and then deposits are made in small banks in China, Italy, Russia, and Africa (my research shows it is even more diverse than this).[5] According to the international economic expert Bradley Babson: "The North Korean system evolved over decades in a fragmented way." He goes on to articulate: "As a result, North Korea has no financial statistics, no significant banking supervision, and no capacity for macroeconomic management of an increasingly mixed economy." Babson also goes on to point out that that the army's ownership "of significant foreign exchange earning enterprises and affiliated banks was one way that Kim Jong-il maintained the support of the military during his tenure."[6] Thus, the military has been involved in literally owning and running overseas endeavors that make money for the regime (and for itself), as was, previously, Office 38. Nevertheless, the dominating force in North Korea's shadow economy (or the "royal court economy," as a high-ranking defector will, we will see, refer to it later) has always been Office 39, and this entity has overseen this secretive aspect of North Korea's economy and enhanced its growth since the 1970s.

Kim Kwang-jin, a high-ranking North Korean defector who was a key member of North Korea's illicit activities network operating out of Singapore, gives us some interesting insight into this shadow economy that then and now continues to support Pyongyang's military and keep the elite living in high style. He states: "The same economy that cannot produce a usable toothbrush is now armed to the teeth with nuclear weapons. I say this as someone who knows, having been involved, however obliquely, in providing the funds that made the atom splitting possible." Kim goes on to state in part: "This hidden financial system I'm referring to has no written records; most of the documents that tell the story—receipts, bank transactions, and the rest—are destroyed annually by Kim's direct order (less to prevent outside audit than for fear that North Korean citizens might learn what was done with all the money secretly generated while they starved). Yet this same private financial network, which belongs exclusively to Kim and the elite ruling class, produces, by my estimates, fully two hundred times the foreign cash revenue of the Cabinet-run People's Economy." He further states: "The Royal Court Economy, which supports this development, emerged from necessity. Kim's dilemma in the early 1990s was straightforward enough: The collapse of the North Korean economic regime was total, laid waste by his father Kim Il-sung's decision to move to a derivative economy dozens of years earlier, exposing North Korea to the financial bust of the Soviet bloc."[7] We thus see an illegal and illicit economy that is based on the sale of largely illegal goods and sanctioned weapons sales, that began as a result of a failed legitimate economy during the Cold War, and that continued, and even grew, in the post–Cold War era as the Kim family regime struggled to find ways to survive despite its isolation from the global financial system. Of course, all this illegal activity has led to North Korea becoming one of the most corrupt countries on earth.[8]

According to sources in the South Korean press, the current North Korean leader, Kim Jong-un, has slush funds of between $4 and $5 billion hidden in bank accounts (not in his name) in such diverse countries as Austria, China, Lichtenstein, Luxembourg, Russia, Singapore, and Switzerland. The North Koreans typically use smaller banks that are under less scrutiny and often are not as strict in enforcing regulations. They reportedly even have deals with the Russian Mafia to help them launder their funds, which are being managed by officials at the Russian embassy.[9] A North Korean diplomat who was posted in Russia as a trade representative reportedly defected in Vladivostok in 2016. He is only one of several I will address in this essay, and he is reported to have been working for Office 39.[10]

Speaking of the Russian Mafia, it is not an exaggeration to say that this spiderweb of individuals, front companies, and banks, all working under Office 39, is very much a Mafia-like organization. The difference is that this organization was planned, was founded, and is now manned by members of North Korea's government infrastructure, including military members, trade representatives, and diplomats.[11] As the UN Panel of Experts has noted, this vast network of North Korean shady entities has created such a complex network that it is often quite challenging to trace either the true ownership of front companies or how the money is moved around.[12] In 2014, a group of North Korean defectors implored the Swiss government to crack down on and freeze all the assets of the North Korean leadership, to no avail.[13] Thus, the money continues to flow into these essentially untouchable accounts with no accountability to the international community.

Kim Jong-un reportedly requires diplomats and others who are posted overseas to raise millions for celebrations and other activities that promote the regime. Those individuals include even military members of the RGB, a key SOF entity that is often involved in military proliferation to rogue states on Pyongyang's behalf.[14] All the recent activities show that there may be trouble brewing in Office 39's network. During August 2016, it was reported that Thae Yong-ho, the DPRK deputy ambassador to the United Kingdom, defected with $58 million. He is said to have been one of the managers of Kim Jong-un's secret money. In June of that year, another official from Office 39 defected in Europe. He allegedly made off with $400 million. In 2015, an official from Office 39 defected and escaped from China, while another escaped with millions from Singapore. In 2014, Yoon Tae-hyung, who was then in charge of the Russian branch of Daesung Bank (a front bank answering to Office 39) escaped and defected—taking $5 million with him.[15] All these defections by money people show, in my assessment, three things: (1) there is a great deal of corruption now within North Korea's illicit financial networks, (2) this corruption likely has led to top officials stealing money from the regime in what will ultimately in many cases lead to defection, and (3) a great deal of fear continues to exist everywhere in North Korea for anyone who crosses the regime, and even the members of the elite who work within the shadow economy of Office 39 are vulnerable.

When one examines North Korea's spiderweb of global financial networks, the result is fascinating. One sees the only true government-run, highly sophisticated set of criminal financial networks in existence since Nazi Germany.[16] This is not an exaggeration. The evidence shows that Office 39 was founded specifically for the purpose of raising funds for the regime. It is this series of networks, run like a modern-day crime family, which enables the DPRK to operate around the global financial system, using phony front companies, empty banks, and conspiring individuals (including criminals) in nations all over the world. Office 39 continues to operate around the world, constantly generating funds that go into Kim Jong-un's slush funds, support the North Korean military, and keep the elite living in a high fashion. But an examination of North Korea's financial networks is not enough. In the next section, I will show how North Korea gets around sanctions and counterproliferation initiatives.

How North Korea Gets around Sanctions

North Korea has an efficient yet corrupt illicit financial system. But, in order for the system to work, it must be able to get around the sanctions and counterproliferation regimes that the international community has imposed on the DPRK. This is no easy matter. But, for many years, the North Koreans have been able to get around banking regulations, unilateral sanctions from several states, counterproliferation initiatives imposed by the international community, and UN sanctions that have become ever tougher and broader with time. The answer to the question how they have been able to do this—successfully—is complex and often confusing. But asking the question is a necessary undertaking if one is to truly understand North Korea's illicit activities, their proliferation, and the vast set of tactics, techniques, and procedures (TTP) that Pyongyang uses in order to protect its business assets overseas that are so important to the survival of the regime. And we must keep this in mind—these activities are *truly* essential for the survival of the regime.

According to press sources in South Korea, sanctioned banks are very clever about getting their funds into legitimate banks (these sanctioned banks often have very little cash—it is getting the money into a nonsanctioned bank that is important). As often as not, these legitimate banks have proved to be smaller ones in China and elsewhere. Reportedly, this is because many individuals in China can be bribed to transfer the funds (those who are used as go-betweens are said to get a 15–30 percent cut depending on how strict sanctions or local law enforcement may be). The North Koreans transfer the cash to a Chinese intermediary, who then deposits the funds into a small Chinese bank. Many of North Korea's funds are said to be going through Guangzhou, Shenzhen, and Zhuhai. In addition to individuals, front companies are often used, and often these companies are used only one time.[17] According to a former North Korean diplomat who spoke to the South Korean press, North Korean diplomats change counterfeit money into real money and then send it back to the DPRK. North Korea is infamous for its "super notes," counterfeit $100 bills that are so close to the real thing it is almost impossible to tell the difference. The defector described the modus operandi for the counterfeit exchange thusly: "An agent working at the embassy goes to a safe house and brings a box full of them." He further stated: "When the bills arrive, embassy staff bundle them up into $10,000 units. They then travel to major cities in their host country to exchange it."[18] By 2013, China was said to have closed down the accounts of North Korean entities in major banks (including the Bank of China).[19] Of course, using the method outlined above, North Korea could easily get around such actions, and the North Koreans typically use smaller banks anyway.

An excellent example of North Korea's use of various resources and its amazingly adept use of shell front companies, easily bribed individuals, and phony banks can be seen if one is to look at one of the few times the North Koreans were actually caught—a shipment of arms to the Middle East intercepted in Thailand in 2009. The shell companies for the operation were in sixteen countries, including New Zealand, Hong Kong, and Ukraine. The officers listed on the registration papers did not know the identities of the real owners, or their nationalities, or even where the companies were located. They simply got their money and moved on. The Russian-made cargo plane carrying the thirty-five-ton shipment was owned by an international arms trafficker whose company was registered in the United Arab Emirates. A Georgian company had the operating license for the aircraft. The aircraft was then chartered by a Hong Kong–registered company. After being chartered, the aircraft departed Azerbaijan, eventually landing in Pyongyang. From there, it departed for Tehran, where thirty-five tons of weapons such as rocket-propelled grenades, surface-to-air missiles, and many other light arms were to be delivered to Hezbollah by the Iranians. The non–North Korean individuals who were involved in the operation knew almost nothing about what was going on outside their compartmentalized information sphere. The front company in New Zealand listed as the director a twenty-five-year-old

Chinese immigrant who held a day job at a Burger King in Auckland.[20] It was only through luck and good intelligence work that the aircraft—which had landed in Thailand for refueling—was found and the arms shipment stopped. Otherwise, thirty-five tons of military gear destined for Hezbollah would have arrived in the Middle East to be used in the violent conflicts that have caused many casualties.

In 2014, Japanese police officials disclosed that they had discovered an illegal North Korean account belonging to a client of a firm in Shizuoka Prefecture. The North Korean Reconnaissance Bureau reportedly controlled the account through a Chinese individual. The funds from the account were then used for the illegal arms trade.[21] This is another great example of North Koreans using easily bribed individuals to cover their illicit activities and proliferation actions. During 2014, the government of Singapore filed charges against the Chinpo Shipping Company, and the company was ordered to pay a fine. Singapore has proved to be a key hub for North Korea's proliferation and illicit activities—largely because of the lax banking laws and regulations that make Singapore the Switzerland of Asia. Owing to a technicality, in 2017 Chinpo was able to appeal the charges successfully.[22] The North Koreans are said to use several different banks in Singapore.[23]

Money from transactions made with Iran is also reportedly laundered through banks in Singapore. Citizens of African countries (including at least Zimbabwe)—perhaps hundreds of them—are often used as intermediaries to launder the money for the North Koreans in banks located in Singapore.[24] According to the UN Panel of Experts report released in early 2014 (as reported in Reuters), North Korea is using "the complicated financial countermeasures and techniques 'pioneered by drug trafficking organizations.'" According to further reporting from Reuters quoting the Panel of Experts: "The panel said it found a relatively complex 'corporate ecosystem' of foreign based firms and individuals that helped North Korea evade scrutiny of its assets as well as its financial and trade dealings."[25]

Speaking of Singapore, in 2017 it was revealed that North Korea's Glocom and Pan Systems were in fact front companies and were being used to conduct military proliferation through a network of agents and illicit bank accounts. Pan Systems also reportedly operates in Malaysia and China. Pan Systems and Glocom are said to be operating under the direction of North Korea's RGB.[26] Malaysia, a place that until recently required no visa for travel from North Korea, has also been a key area that North Korea's financial networks have used as an operating base. To quote the North Korean analyst

Scott Snyder: "The visa-free access to Malaysia that North Korean citizens have enjoyed until it was rescinded earlier this month following the murder of Kim—the half-brother of the isolated regime's leader, Kim Jong Un—had provided Pyongyang with a base for both illegal procurement and financing activities that have enabled it to import sensitive materials and finance its WMD development."[27]

According to Hugh Griffiths and Lawrence Dermody, who conducted a study for the Stockholm International Peace Research Institute (SIPRI), foreign companies and individuals traveling on foreign passports are the majority of those who have violated sanctions, both the unilateral sanctions of individual nation-states and UN sanctions. In other words, the majority of operations overseas that violate sanctions, international law, and counterproliferation initiatives are conducted by foreign individuals and foreign front companies operating on behalf of the DPRK. This brings up an interesting point regarding sanctions and how they are targeted. The SIPRI study found that most of the activities on behalf of the North Koreans in the illicit underworld were actually conducted by compensated third parties operating on Pyongyang's behalf. Yet almost all the sanctions to the date of the SIPRI study had been focused on entities within the DPRK.[28] Thus, targeting entities within foreign countries appears to be the best way to pursue operations countering illicit activities. Unfortunately, given the nature of front companies and shell companies as well as the compensated (bribed) individuals, this appears to be what will often be a game of whack-a-mole.

According to the two SIPRI analysts just referenced, North Korea is fully capable of operating outside the international system quite successfully, and as those analysts state: "One reason is that the sanctions have targeted North Korean companies and state institutions that are impervious to sanctions because they are not embedded in the global economy." They also state: "North Korea–linked proliferation activity is now firmly established beyond North Korea's borders and sometimes beyond the borders of any regulated state, in what can be described as the offshore economy: companies operating in deregulated business or free-trade zones, ports and financial centres that have proved so conducive to legitimate forms of international trade. Shipments involve the outriders of globalization: offshore bank accounts, flag-of-convenience ships and passports, honorary consuls, free-trade zones and containerization."[29] As the former high-ranking government official Juan Zarate stated in congressional testimony: "The North Korean schemes outside their borders rely heavily on front companies, layered transactions, opaque ownership structures, and trusted or corrupt relationships, making it difficult for legitimate banks and compliance systems to detect and stop its nefarious activities."[30] These various, often-untraceable means are now better known to analysts, but what is even more troubling is that North Korea is now known to be using civilian airliners to transport illicitly gained hard currency.[31] In 2015, the US Treasury Department sanctioned individuals from North Korea operating in Russia, Syria, and Vietnam. Clearly, North Korea's spiderweb of operations had proved to be diverse, prosperous, and capable of evading authorities, at least for an extended period of time.[32]

In 2016, another study released by the UN Security Council Panel of Experts was quite compelling. It showed that North Korea continues to evade sanctions successfully. It also shows that North Korea continues to use the international system and its many loopholes to get around international counterproliferation initiatives. It further points out that North Korea continues to proliferate military gear in the Middle East and Africa, among other places. According to the Voice of America, the report also said that North Korean companies used methods now known to those analysts who closely follow their proliferation and illicit activities: "They adopted concealment techniques such as the use of foreign intermediaries, front company networks and incomplete documentation." Other highlights of the report showed that North Korea was even sending spare parts for ballistic missiles (Scuds) to one of Washington's allies—Egypt![33] This appears to be on the cusp of changing. In March 2017, the US State Department sanctioned companies, entities (sometimes government entities), and individuals in North Korea—but also China, Burma, Iran, Sudan, Saudi Arabia, Egypt, Eritrea, and even the United Arab Emirates—for activities in violation of Section 3 of the Iran, North Korea, and Syria Nonproliferation Act. Though it is a small first step, going after front companies and individuals who are not North Korean (often referred to as *secondary sanctions*) can be an effective way of containing North Korea's illicit and illegal proliferation networks.[34]

Evidence that had been compiled over a period of several years and released in 2016 showed banks in both Singapore and China cooperated with members of the North Korean illicit financial network. The money trail then goes back to Panama, where shipping agents provided cover for North Korean activities, including proliferation. (The firm of Mossack Fonseca helped serve as a shipping agent in Panama but reportedly did not realize that it was fronting for North Koreans until 2010, at which point it stopped working for them.) As often as not, the transactions appear to have gone through Chinese banks, in this instance the Bank of China (which of course also denied knowing the funds were North Korean). Sophisticated networks that run through North Korea to China, Singapore, and then Panama are only one example of how complicated and difficult it is to track these activities, which more often than not are run through intermediaries who are not North Korean and thus often escape scrutiny initially.[35] In March 2017, the US Treasury Department levied sanctions against several North Korean individuals involved in illicit financial activities supporting proliferation in diverse places such as China, Russia, and Vietnam.[36]

In 2016, when North Korean entities were listed by the US Treasury Department as a "primary money laundering concern," many thought that it might actually slow down the North's proliferation and illicit activities. But not everyone concurred. In referring to BDA (the Chinese bank sanctioned by the United States in 2005, an action that set off a snowball effect on North Korean illicit bank accounts all over Asia), John Park remarked: "If you look at the BDA period . . . North Korea was caught off guard. It was a big shock to them. But what comes out of that shock is that they moved a lot of their banking activities inside of China and then they started using private Chinese companies to do their activities in between them and smaller banks." The interview conducted with Park evolved into even more compelling assessments. As the interviewers stated: "Park said that there are always Chinese middlemen and private firms who are willing to do financial transactions on behalf of North Korea for money, and commission fees go up as sanctions on the regime in Pyongyang become tighter."[37] Park also made an interesting—and important—statement in another article (of which he was the author) when discussing the role of Chinese middlemen, intermediaries who (for a fee) help the North Koreans launder and mask the money used to carry out illicit activities and proliferation: "As sanctions have become tougher, these local Chinese middlemen have charged higher fees to reflect the elevated risk of doing business with North Korean clients. Instead of hindering procurement activities, we found that sanctions have actually helped to attract more capable middlemen, who are drawn by the larger payday."[38]

Thus far I have not (at least in detail) discussed the methods by which North Korea ships its weapons, weapons that bring in billions to Kim Jong-un's coffers. But, when it comes to proliferation of arms to other nations, North Korea has turned this into an art form. In the early 2000s, the United States helped create the Proliferation Security Initiative (PSI). The PSI has to date been endorsed by more than one hundred nations, and it more often than not focuses on maritime interdiction.[39] This is a noble effort, yet the results have been, at best, mixed.[40] North Korea has proved quite adept at getting around a variety of PSI methodologies, and one of the key ways it has done this is by using a legal loophole in maritime law, the reflagging of ships. In 2014, despite many sanctions—including the sanctioning of North Korean merchant ships—the trade and proliferation did not slow down. The reason? North Korea (like many other nations) chose to use flags of convenience to carry its goods and services to other nations despite the fact that this was banned by sanctions. In fact, Pyongyang has even made use of South Korean ports. The North Koreans collude in this practice with front companies to maintain their network of merchant ships that proliferate and operate illegally in violation of international sanctions.[41] In 2015, disclosures indicated that North Korea was using (to say the least) the flags of Mongolia, Kiribati, Tuvalu, and Niue on its merchant ships in defiance of sanctions. In 2016, it was exposed as flying the flags of Sierra Leone on some of its merchant ships. In the same year, nearly fifty North Korean ships were reported to be flying under the flag of Tanzania. This is, no doubt, only the tip of the iceberg. North Korea has for many years moved its merchant ships from flag to flag in order to avoid detection.[42] In 2017, it was caught proliferating weapons on a Cambodia-flagged ship.[43] The DPRK is also known to have used the flags of both Comoros and Fiji.[44]

As I discussed in *The Last Days of Kim Jong-il,* a North Korean defector who formerly worked within networks that conducted illicit arms deals has disclosed to the press in South Korea that the DPRK's arms dealers frequently have been students at Pyongyang University of Foreign Studies. There, their training was designed to make them fluent in English and Chinese because Pyongyang's plan was to use these people to deal with traders in other countries. A key method that the DPRK defector described as a tactic Pyongyang has used to get past sanctions enforcement is to transport containers across the Yalu River to China (presumably under the cover of legal trade) one-third or half filled with weapons: "The forwarder who received this cargo enters a port in a third country, where the containers are filled with freight unrelated to weapons and the paperwork is completed." But this is not the end of the story. The containers are then moved to a third major port (one with heavy traffic). What typically happens next? "The containers are mixed with other cargo in those transit points. They are searched, but not thoroughly. . . . Even if customs or other officials roll their sleeves up and search for weapons, how can they possibly find the arms among the mountains of other containers headed to other countries?"[45] Methods like this are among several diverse ways that North Korea gets around sanctions.

So we see a North Korean financial network that is so complex and nuanced that it has baffled even the most sophisticated law enforcement networks and international organizations. North Korea has used—and continues to use—a variety of TTP to get around sanctions and counter-proliferation initiatives. These techniques at times seem to be so clever that one wonders whether the international community will ever be able to truly contain them. Not the least of the reasons for this is because the DPRK uses so many nearly untraceable foreign entities (under the control of its financial network managers) to conduct its transactions and launder its money. As Anthony Ruggiero of the Foundation for Defense of Democracies stated in 2017 when speaking about the UN Panel of Experts report released early that year: "The report highlights Pyongyang's habitual use of front companies with no visible ties to the regime, a practice that the Treasury Department has called 'a threat to the integrity of the U.S. financial system.'"[46]

The lack of enforcement of sanctions on North Korea by governments all over the world—from China, to the Middle East, to Africa—can be highlighted by the words of Richard Nephew when referring to the UN Panel of Experts Report from early 2017: "The UNSC Sanctions Committee and UNSC more generally should consider imposing sanctions, even if just targeted designations, on officials and entities involved in the willful refusal to implement UNSC sanctions. Pertinent examples could include the African nations who have continued to purchase arms from North Korea as well as some of the traffickers described in the report. It is too much to expect that China or Russia would agree to impose sanctions on entities or individuals operating in their own territory (and there is more than a touch of hypocrisy involved in supporting designations of citizens of other countries engaged in evasion), but they may be willing to support certain other non-DPRK designations at this stage."[47] As we move on to the next section, it is important to point out that these constantly changing and evolving networks continue to make billions annually for the Kim family regime.

North Korean Nonmilitary Illicit Activities: Focus on Illegal Drugs and Counterfeiting

North Korea has been able to successfully work around being largely banned from working within the international, globalized system. This shows the cleverness of its Party members and leaders within the government. It also shows the long-range vision of Kim Il-sung, who, even in the 1970s, foresaw the weakness of the Soviet system (and his own) and tasked his son, Kim Jong-il, to set up an illicit economic infrastructure that has survived and even thrived for nearly fifty years. This system has been able to bring in billions annually for Kim Jong-un's coffers.[48] It is my assessment that North Korea makes the largest chunk of its illicit money from proliferation and that the largest chunk of that comes from the Middle East, especially Iran.[49] (A lot comes from largely conventional arms sales to several nations in Africa as well, but not as much as from the Middle East.)[50] But, for the purposes of this chapter, I will examine two key aspects of North Korea's illicit activities that are not related to military proliferation—illegal drugs and counterfeit currency. By examining these two key marketing items in North Korea's annual inventory of bad deeds, I will show how truly unethical the government-blessed and -financed activities of these illicit financial networks can be.

According to a defector who wrote his testimony in 2012, North Korea's government has an interesting methodology for sponsoring those who run its opium industry (largely used for heroin, according to most analysts): "The DPRK regime conducts its drugs trade clandestinely, through what seems at first glance a legitimate company. Situated between Pyongyang's Botong-gang Hotel and Chungru-gwan is a gigantic building called 'Ryugyong.' It is the home of Ryugyong Corporation, which trades under the auspices of the Party's Foreign Relations Department." The defector goes on to state: "With the absolute support and full protection of the regime, Ryugyong Corporation oversees the DPRK drug industry and its production chain: from cultivation of opium plants to point-of-sale."[51] Reportedly, opium dealers on the North Korea–China border are overseen by Office 39, and the DPRK government is also involved in production and distribution.[52] According to a variety of sources (including defectors), one of the key resources that North Korea uses to distribute its illegal drugs is its diplomatic corps. As diplomats work within North Korea's illicit system, they come under the control (of course) of Office 39. South Korean government sources estimate that North Korean illegal drug sales overseas amount to up to $200 million annually.[53] While North Korea has, over the years, sold traditional opium-based drugs (largely heroin), the biggest moneymaker and the largest sales item for several years is now methamphetamine, sometimes known as *ice*. North Korean operatives are now known to be working with drug-distribution organizations in Southeast Asia, including Thailand. They also operate on a large scale in China. Methamphetamine has reportedly become more popular and profitable because the growing of opium has become more difficult over the years, with often tenuous crop conditions and frequent droughts and/or floods.[54]

The quality of the meth coming out of North Korea is reportedly very high. One would expect nothing less from a government-sanctioned and -sponsored business endeavor. The finished product is reportedly often smuggled into China and then moved on to Shandong and then other provinces. From there, it likely moves on to places like Southeast Asia and Japan. In North Korea, the security services are compliant with individual manufacturers who distribute the drugs in China and North Korea. According to a North Korean defector named Kim Young-min, some security services individuals were actual users of the drug.[55] For those who are worried that North Korea's drug-smuggling networks might reach all over Asia and perhaps even to the United States, I can tell you that that train has already left the station. According to studies by Chinese scholars conducted in 2014, North Korean–manufactured illegal drugs are getting into not only China but also Japan (and routinely). According to Zhang Li, a professor at the People's Public Security University, North Korean drugs bound for foreign nations first enter China (by sea), are transferred to other ships, and are then smuggled into countries such as Taiwan, South Korea, Indonesia, and Japan.[56] Reportedly, the manufacture and sale of the drugs sold internationally are under surveillance by Kim Jong-un's henchmen. Their purview includes the overseas market, where the handling of the drugs and the sales that follow are under the close surveillance of Kim Jong-un's security people.[57]

Obviously, the North Koreans use a variety of means to generate hard currency for the regime (military proliferation being the primary means, but other ancillary means are important as well). While illegal and illicit drug activity is a fascinating case study (largely because this is the only illegal drug network in the world actually sponsored by a sovereign government), there are other means that are not related to military proliferation that North Korea uses. One of the key means among these other methods of raising money is counterfeiting. North Korean counterfeiting was considered a key threat in the international community during the 1990s and the early years of the twenty-first century. North Korean $100 bills were of such fine quality that the Treasury Department called them super notes. But, in 2005, with the crackdown on Banco Delta Asia (by the Treasury Department), many analysts assessed that North Korea had drastically pulled back on its counterfeiting operations.[58] Indeed, it did seem—at least given the number of incidents being reported—that North Korea had toned down its counterfeiting operations after 2005. But, in 2016, it appeared that, perhaps out of a motivation to raise more cash for the regime, it was resuming its large-scale counterfeiting operations.[59] In June 2016, press sources reported that North Korea appeared to be working with both terrorist groups and international criminal organizations in order to distribute counterfeit $100 bills. Some analysts believe that—much like illegal drug sales—this is under the auspices of Office 39. To quote the North Korean defector Park Sang-hak: "Japanese yakuza and terrorist groups in the Middle East, such as the Islamic State may be among those who are circulating North Korea's fake money."[60] Sales and attempted sales of counterfeit American currency may have been a reflection of North Korean efforts to raise more money for the regime at a time when international pressure may have been as high as it has ever been.[61]

Illicit drugs and counterfeit currency are only two types of illicit and illegal trade that North Korean engages in. They are particularly interesting ways of raising money for the regime because it is so unambiguously clear that they are—without a doubt—criminal activities carried out with the consent and support of the very top leaders in the North Korean ruling government. There are other types of illicit activities that the regime engages in. These activities (including what I described earlier in this section) are designed by entities who answer largely to Office 39, exclusively for the purposes for raising money for the regime.[62] These activities are important and raise significant cash for the regime. But it should be pointed out that probably by far the most important illicit moneymaker for the regime is the military proliferation it conducts, especially in the Middle East and Africa. As I have noted previously about North Korean military proliferation: "It essentially involves four efforts: 1) WMD and the platforms to carry it (ballistic missiles), 2) Conventional Weapons sales, 3) Refurbishment of Soviet era weapons for countries that still use them, and 4) Technical and Military assistance and advising. Some have suggested that because North Korea has partially adjusted its tactics, techniques and procedures by actually building facilities (usually actual factories) where countries can assemble WMD, related platforms, and conventional weapons systems, that this somehow means the proliferation has 'declined.' In fact, the opposite is true. North Korea builds these facilities for countries like Syria, Iran, and non-state actors such as Hezbollah, and then remains on board to maintain and supervise assembly of weapons systems—with parts (less detectable than entire systems) that continue to roll in from North Korea."[63]

How Has the United States Taken Action to Stop North Korea's Illicit Activities and Proliferation?

The United States has instituted a variety of initiatives and sanctions that have been designed to counter North Korea's illicit and illegal activities and the financial networks that support these activities. While some of these initiatives and sanctions have been less than successful, I would assess that the reasons—for many years now—have been largely because of difficulties in enforcement, not because the sanctions and initiatives did not have the potential to legitimately contain North Korea's criminal and sanctions-busting actions. The way America's actions have evolved during recent years, and how they can continue to improve, is what I will address in this section.

During 2013, it became obvious that Washington was going to go after individuals and front companies that supported North Korea's illicit actions, or who gained profit from them, when the Obama administration sanctioned Burmese general Thein Htay for buying North Korean military equipment, apparently missile related (the general was at the time the head of a missile research-and-development facility).[64] In 2013, after the Obama administration had initiated a number of sanctions against various North Korean entities, the US House of Representatives passed a bill that probably (certainly at the time) had more teeth than other sanctions. The bill brought about new banking restrictions. It denied North Koreans or any of their third-party cohorts all access to American property or banking institutions and, perhaps as important, allowed Washington to sanction any third parties—or banks—that facilitate North Korean illicit activities and/or human rights abuses.[65] Almost as if on cue, in August 2014, the US Treasury Department issued an advisory on financial transactions with the DPRK. This came in the wake of an earlier initiative that came out of the Financial Action Task Force, an international body with thirty-four member jurisdictions that put North Korea on a list of nations needing to improve countermeasures against terrorist financial transactions and money laundering. The Treasury Department advisory urged financial institutions to consult existing guidance on any transactions that had the possibility of involving North Korea.[66]

In early January 2015, in what many analysts thought was an American reaction to what has now been proved to have been a North Korean cyberattack launched against Sony, the Treasury Department took financial measures against North Korean government agencies and ten individuals who were at the time reported to be operating out of such diverse places as China, Syria, Iran, and Russia. The sanctions were also noteworthy because they included the Korea Mining Development Corporation, the Tangun Trading Corporation, and even the elite (SOF) RGB, showing once again the dynamic between government trading organizations and the military when it comes to proliferation and even illicit activities and banking.[67] This was followed up on in March 2015 when the US Treasury Department issued another advisory naming North Korea as a country at high risk for money laundering and terrorist financing.[68]

After all of the actions initiated above—all with good reason and ample evidence—in June 2015 the US State Department once again left North Korea off the list of nations sponsoring terrorism. To quote: "[It] is not known to have sponsored any terrorist acts since the bombing of a Korean Airlines flight in 1987."[69] This is, in my assessment, an interesting statement, given the evidence showing that North Korea has supported—and continues to actively support—terrorist-designated groups such as Hezbollah and Hamas. Secretary of Defense Gates, who in 2010 was in a better position to know that than just about anyone else, stated: "The fact is that North Korea continues to smuggle missiles and weapons to other countries around the world—Burma, Iran, Hezbollah, Hamas— and they continue with their development of their nuclear program."[70] It is also interesting given the wording that the Treasury Department used in its advisories during 2014 and 2015. Despite the State Department's rather confusing nondesignation of North Korea, the sanctions continued in 2015, largely because of proliferation. In November of that year, the Treasury Department's Office of Foreign Asset Control, which publishes a list of individuals and entities that act on behalf of targeted countries (e.g., North Korea), released a list of four new individuals who were designated as supporting activities already sanctioned. Two of these individuals were working for KOMID (the Korea Mining Development Trading Corporation, a widely known proliferation front company already sanctioned), and one is known to have worked for Office 39. As 2015 ended (in December 2015), the United States initiated new sanctions against North Korea. This time, another major military entity was targeted (probably for proliferation)—the Strategic Rocket Forces. Banks and front companies also again came under scrutiny and were the targets of action, as were North Korean citizens who were based in places like Syria and Vietnam.[71] (Vietnam has a very lax banking system).[72]

The year 2016 brought many interesting developments. US actions continued as they did in 2015. Clearly, North Korea's proliferation and other illicit activities had caught the attention of both the White House and Congress. On March 16, 2016, the president issued an executive order regarding blocking the property of the North Korean government and the Party and prohibiting several types of transactions that North Korea had used to get around sanctions in the past. Some of the highlights of the new executive order included: "All property and interests in property that are in the United States, that hereafter come within the United States, or that are or hereafter come within the possession or control of any United States person of the Government of North Korea or the Workers' Party of Korea are blocked and may not be transferred, paid, exported, withdrawn, or otherwise dealt in." In addition, the following things were prohibited:

(i) the exportation or reexportation, direct or indirect, from the United States, or by a United States person, wherever located, of any goods, services, or technology to North Korea;

(ii) new investment in North Korea by a United States person, wherever located; and

(iii) any approval, financing, facilitation, or guarantee by a United States person, wherever located, of a transaction by a foreign person where the transaction by that foreign person would be prohibited by this section if performed by a United States person or within the United States.

Finally, in a very important measure, the executive order states in part: "The Secretary of the Treasury, in consultation with the Secretary of State, is hereby authorized to take such actions, including the promulgation of rules and regulations, and to employ all powers granted to the President by IEEPA and the UNPA as may be necessary to carry out the purposes of this order. The Secretary of the Treasury may redelegate any of these functions to other officers and agencies of the United States Government consistent with applicable law. All agencies of the United States Government are hereby directed to take all appropriate measures within their authority to carry out the provisions of this order."[73]

Despite the many sanctions and other actions taken by Washington during the years 2009–2016, reports that assessed the impact of these actions on North Korea showed that Pyongyang appeared to be accomplishing its goals. For example, according to reports coming out of Northeast Asia, prices of commodities in North Korea did not seem to be affected by the sanctions in 2016, years after many sanctions had been imposed by the United States (as well as financial initiatives imposed by the US Treasury Department).[74] Whether or not these reports were true, Washington continued to take action. In June 2016 (in an action related to the initiative taken in November of the same year), the US Treasury Department declared that North Korea is a jurisdiction of primary money laundering concern under the Patriot Act, section 311. The designation was particularly important because it forbade third-country banks to use US bank accounts to process financial transactions for the DPRK. This could have made foreign banks vulnerable to US sanctions if they did business with North Korea (though it is unclear how much it did).[75] In September 2016, legislation was introduced in the US House of Representatives that would ban North Korea from the worldwide bank transfer of electronic funds system, the Society for Worldwide Interbank Financial Telecommunications, otherwise known as SWIFT. SWIFT system regulations are controlled out of Belgium. Thus, it would take European cooperation to shut down the North Korean accounts that utilized this system.[76] For anyone who has transferred electronic funds to a bank overseas, this system is quite familiar.

The Korean specialist Scott Snyder stated in September 2016 that one way to strengthen sanctions against North Korea (out of four that he mentioned) would be as follows: "Target Chinese small and medium enterprises that continue to do business as usual with North Korea. There are companies similar to the Hongxiang group that play a gateway role for both legitimate trade and embedded North Korean procurement of dual use items." He also stated in part: "Push Chinese authorities to crack down [on] Chinese banks that deal with North Korean citizens since they use multiple personal accounts containing millions of dollars for state purposes. Since opening an account requires identification, Chinese authorities should be able to identify and cut off all North Korean account holders. If necessary, impose secondary sanctions on these banks."[77] In November 2016, the US Treasury Department finalized actions taken that would (and did) restrict North Korea's access to the US financial system. To quote the press release from the Treasury Department: "'North Korea continues to use front companies and agents to conduct illicit financial transactions—some of which support the proliferation of WMD and the development of ballistic missiles—and evade international sanctions,' said Adam J. Szubin, Acting Under Secretary for Terrorism and Financial Intelligence. 'Such funds have no place in any reputable financial system.'"[78] In December 2016, in reaction to North Korea's nuclear test, Washington sanctioned sixteen North Korean companies and seven individuals, largely for North Korea's involvement in proliferation.[79]

The year 2017 brought in a new administration and a new philosophy regarding dealing with North Korea's proliferation and illicit financial networks. On August 22, 2017, the US Treasury Department designated (sanctioned) several entities and individuals "in response to North Korea's ongoing development of weapons of mass destruction (WMD), violations of United Nations (UN) Security Council resolutions, and attempted evasion of U.S. sanctions." The report went on to say in part: "Today's sanctions target third-country companies and individuals that assist already-designated persons who support North Korea's nuclear and ballistic missile programs." It designated entities and individuals in Russia, China, and even Namibia.[80] In September 2017, it was announced that the Treasury Department was taking further actions against North Korean entities and banks, including those doing business with third-party banks and front companies, at least one of which was located in Singapore.[81]

In late September 2017, it was publicly announced that, months earlier, President Trump had signed an executive order expanding the authority of both the State and the Treasury Departments to target both entities and individuals trading with North Korea and those banks that are running the dirty money. A press report quoted the president as saying that "'the new executive order will cut off sources of revenue that fund North Korea's efforts to develop' weapons of mass destruction." It continued: "'For much too long,' he said, 'North Korea has been allowed to abuse the international financial system to facilitate funding for its nuclear weapons and missile programs.'"[82] Later that year, in October 2017, the UN Panel of Experts identified fifty-seven Chinese, Malaysian, and North Korean companies that have helped North Korea evade sanctions and financed its WMD programs. Of those companies, forty-three had yet to be sanctioned, opening up new opportunities to be exploited by the United States. The networks of banks, front companies, and phony financial entities reportedly was (and likely is) operating in China, Malaysia, Singapore, and countries in Africa.[83] The renewed proactive engagement with the international community to pressure the DPRK began paying dividends on a small scale almost immediately. There was initial pressure from the United States to get North Koreans off reflagged ships (those from Fiji being a key example). In addition, the pressure on nations with North Korean embassies was intensified, with Mexico, Peru, Spain, and Kuwait, among others, expelling the DPRK's ambassadors. The US requests were reportedly targeted and quite specific.[84]

As reported on November 2, 2017, the United States officially cut off the Bank of Dandong from the American financial system that same month. According to the *Wall Street Journal,* Dandong is the 148th largest of 196 banks in the Chinese sector. This is an excellent first step, but there is no doubt that there are several other banks against whom action needs to be taken. Going after banks that launder North Korea's dirty money is important, though a report by the think tank the Center for Advanced Defense Studies (C4ADS) in Washington, DC, suggests that—at least in China— North Korea's financial holdings and laundered money are far more vulnerable to targeting by US and international agencies than many would think. As the report states in its executive summary: "Today the regime is dependent on the flow of hard currency to function. Maintaining this access and evading international sanctions have required the regime's foreign exchange banks to offshore critical financial infrastructure overseas. The resulting illicit overseas networks play a vital role as proxies for the North Korean banking and foreign exchange systems. However, being integrated into the international systems of banking, commerce, and logistics, leaves these networks exposed to international law enforcement actions."[85]

During November 2017, in a long-overdue move, the United States redesignated North Korea a state sponsor of terrorism. This is an important political move not only because of all the legitimate moves that it allows nation-states to make against North Korea's rogue state illicit arms deals but also because it completely discredits the move made by the George W. Bush administration in 2008 simply because it was thought that the initiative would bring Pyongyang back to the bargaining table (which it did, accomplishing nothing). North Korea should be and always should have been on the list of nations that are state sponsors of terrorism because it is now and has been since before the Cold War a state sponsor of terrorism.[86]

As this section has hopefully shown, North Korea has not slowed down its proliferation activities, its illicit activities, or its involvement in the international banking system despite a variety of sanctions and other actions targeting Pyongyang's activities. This is not because of a lack of sanctions or other actions taken by the United States. But the actions taken by the

United States, right up until January 2017, all have one major issue that takes away from their effectiveness—enforcement. While the actions taken have all looked good on paper, they are no more useful than the paper they are printed on unless the initiatives are actually acted on. For the most part, during the Obama administration this did not happen. It is unfortunate because some of these sanctions could have truly put North Korea in a place that would have made the government vulnerable to actions on the part of the international community. As the noted Korean specialist Bruce Klingner has stated: "Even the most reclusive regime, criminal organization or terrorist group is tied to the global financial order. Dirty money eventually flows across borders and—given that the U.S. dollar serves as the global reserve currency—95 percent of all international financial transactions are denominated in dollars. As such, virtually all international transactions must pass through a U.S. Treasury Department–controlled bank account in the United States."[87]

The initiatives and actions taken by the Trump administration during 2017 are important and relevant. Yet they need to be stepped up and initiated in a comprehensive manner. This is not a criticism but simply a lesson learned from past lessons of North Korea's issues. Unless or until these actions are taken in a way that puts pressure on all North Korean proliferation, illicit trade, and illegal bank accounts and front companies, Pyongyang will simply morph its modus operandi once again and continue to function as it has been. As we move through 2018 and 2019, we may very well see stepped-up pressure on North Korea, including the United States working with its allies to achieve diplomatic isolation and with the international community to contain and suppress Pyongyang's sophisticated illicit financial networks. It is important to keep in mind that the threat from North Korea's conventional and WMD-associated programs is every bit as (if not more) compelling because of proliferation as it is because of potential conflict in the region in which the DPRK sits.[88]

How Has the International Community Taken Action Regarding DPRK Illicit Activities?

The international community has attempted to take action against North Korea in ways that would truly affect the regime since the very first nuclear crisis culminated in the Agreed Framework freezing Pyongyang's plutonium nuclear program in 1994.[89] In fact, North Korea's successful dance with the international community has often been compared with Iran's recent talks that resulted in the Joint Comprehensive Plan of Action (JCPOA) in 2015.[90] I have already addressed several initiatives (such as the PSI) that have attempted either to coerce North Korea into changing its rogue state behavior or to contain that behavior via nonkinetic means. In this section, I will look at the highlights in recent years. This international activity has (as often as not) been conducted through the United Nations, and, thus, this has dominated much of the international and multinational action taken against the DPRK.

In early March 2013, in what came as a surprise to many analysts, China was able to reach an agreement with American officials to draft a resolution targeting North Korea's illicit trade, specifically "the illicit activities of North Korea's diplomats, banking relationships, and illicit transfers of bulk cash."[91] Later in the month, Japan and Australia sanctioned North Korea's Foreign Trade Bank (FTB). In April, the US Treasury Department publicly encouraged other nations to join it in sanctioning the FTB. In May 2013, the Bank of China announced that it would sever ties with the FTB (though, as I have stated earlier, North Korea is known to typically use smaller banks in China).[92]

In February and March 2015, the international anti-money-laundering body known as the Financial Action Task Force (FATF) called on North Korea to combat money laundering. This call was supported by the US Treasury Department and passed on in one of its financial advisories. Later in that year, in late June, the FATF warned all thirty-four member states that they "should pay 'special attention' to financial transactions with North Korea."[93] As 2015 turned into 2016, the FATF issued another important report. This time, the international body highlighted (among others) Iran and North Korea. To quote a published report: "FATF . . . expressed concern about 'significant deficiencies' in North Korea's systems. It specifically warned member agencies to 'protect against correspondent relationships being used to bypass or evade counter-measures' and to be wary when considering requests to allow North Korean financial institutions to open branches or subsidiaries in their countries."[94] The United Nations imposed new sanctions on North Korea in 2016 following that nation's nuclear test. In fact, the United Nations has imposed several separate sanctions measures since North Korea began its rogue state behavior—particularly nuclear weapons tests.[95] The sanctions imposed on North Korea in March 2016 involved harsh new regulations regarding cargo inspections and targeted North Korean agents of trade in places such as Syria, Iran, and Vietnam. The sanctions truly went after DPRK trade with any nations belonging to the United Nations. Unfortunately, the sanctions had several loopholes that countries such as China could exploit.[96] In addition, many nations trading with North Korea (such as Iran) simply ignore UN sanctions at will.

During October 2016, the FATF again took action against North Korea and alerted nations all over the world (specifically FATF member states) to terminate any relationships with North Korean financial institutions. To quote the South Korean press piece, which quoted the official announcement: "FATF has serious concerns about the threat posed by DPRK's illicit activities related to the proliferation of weapons of mass destruction (WMDs) and its financing." The report proceeded: "Jurisdictions should take the necessary measures to close existing branches, subsidiaries and representative offices of DPRK banks within their territories and terminate correspondent relationships with DPRK banks."[97] In November 2016, following North Korea's second test of a nuclear device in that year, the United Nations again issued what many saw as harsh new sanctions. The sanctions appeared to be largely designed to take further action against North Korea's illicit activities, which as we have seen are a key aspect of maintaining the regime's power. Some, however, have said that North Korea continues to be skillful at working around UN sanctions, a disturbing assessment.[98]

In 2017, SWIFT banned several North Korean banks from participating in its system. As noted earlier, SWIFT is well-known to anyone sending money or exchanging money overseas; it must be used if one is to be able to easily access banks using intercountry telecommunications. This action was (at least in my view) finally taken because of recent information confirmed and released by the United Nations in 2017 documenting North Korean use of the system.[99] While North Korea will likely still be able to access the system using foreign intermediaries (as it has done for numerous other worldwide financial activities), the action taken by SWIFT will still make it more difficult for it to abuse the international financial system.

It appears that there has been no shortage of international action taken against North Korea, particularly since it detonated its first nuclear device in 2006 (more UN sanctions followed in the summer of 2017).[100] The issue is not whether the international community has issued initiatives and, in the case of the United Nations, resolutions. There have been many. In fact, the seriousness of these resolutions has increased over time. How effective have banks and financial institutions around the world been at containing North Korean illicit and illegal activities and banking practices? The answer appears to be that, thus far, there are many issues with containing the billions of dollars annually that North Korea continues to successfully raise, put into international banking institutions, and funnel back to slush funds. The key is enforcement. There continue to be many issues with the enforcement of what can legitimately be considered far-reaching measures taken by the international community in an effort to contain North Korea's rogue state actions. Unless or until enforcement becomes the focus of these measures, North Korea will continue to maintain and perhaps even enhance its ability to maintain its worldwide network of proliferation, illicit activities, and underground financial transactions supporting the Kim family regime.[101] As a report released in September 2017 by the UN Panel of Experts says: "Lax enforcement of the sanctions regime coupled with the DPRK's evolving evasion techniques are [sic] undermining the goals of the resolutions that the DPRK abandon all WMD and cease all related programs and activities."[102]

There has also been a plethora of UN sanctions against the North Koreans, typically immediately after Pyongyang's nuclear tests or test launches of long-range ballistic missiles. The last two resolutions in 2017 were 2375, issued in September 2017, and 2397, issued in December 2017. Both focused on limiting North Korea's access to refined petroleum products and sets standards for repatriating DPRK workers overseas (among other measures). The North Korean overseas workers are not illicit, at least for now. But they represent a big moneymaker for the regime, and much of this money earned is probably used for weapons development and the sponsorship of the elite. Supposedly, workers will be gone from countries where they are employed twenty-four months from December 2017.[103] For a variety of reasons, all these sanctions have been largely ineffective. But the most important reason is because China and Russia are permanent members of the UN Security Council and have insisted on watering down those sanctions.[104] This is something that is unlikely to change. Another reason that these UN sanctions have thus far been largely ineffective at putting any real pressure on North Korea is because enforcement is weak—from countries like Russia and China but also from other nations, such as several nation-states on the African continent.[105]

China's Role in Containing North Korea's Illicit Activities

China has been an interesting part of the puzzle both for the role many of the entities within its borders play in being complicit with North Korea's illicit activities and for accusations (which appear legitimate) of not being transparent in going along with UN resolutions to which Beijing is a signatory. It is this unusual role that China plays in the North Korean illicit activities and underground financial networks that I will address in this section. For many years, American policy makers have been calling on China to play a bigger role in putting pressure on North Korea for its many rogue state activities.[106] But there are some analysts (like myself) who, on the basis of available evidence, assess that the government in China has no intention (at least not yet) of putting any strong pressure on North Korea economically or politically. In fact, as the evidence in this section will show, if one is to pick one statement on what China does about entities within its borders that deal with North Koreans or the illegal activities of its own banks, that one statement would be, It looks the other way.

While there have been many muted hints by academics and others that China may have been somewhat supporting North Korea militarily over the years, in 2013 a disturbing analysis of North Korean transporter erector launchers carrying ICBM's in a parade in Pyongyang revealed that these vehicles came from China. Beijing of course claimed that they were selling Pyongyang lumber transporters, and of course everyone then moved on.[107] In 2014, a variety of reports stated that the Chinese had put in place a number of plans regarding what to do in the case of North Korean collapse. The plans reportedly included such things as reconnaissance units along the border to monitor any crossings and setting up camps in China near the border. They also reportedly take into account what to do if other powers (presumably the United States) cross into North Korea during a crisis. Many analysts assess that China considers North Korea a buffer against South Korea and of course the American troops stationed there.[108] China is said to supply 90 percent of North Korea's oil. Russia supplies some, but on a much smaller scale.[109] Thus, it was no doubt disturbing to Pyongyang when China suspended the provision of North Korea with aviation fuel in 2014. But the supply lines were restored in late 2014.[110] This was no doubt a relief for the North Korean air force, which relies on the fuel for its exercises and operations and also has stockpiled it (though its reserves are not unlimited).[111]

Perhaps because of what I would consider largely token actions taken by China in 2014, North Korean exports to Russia reportedly rose 32 percent in that year.[112] Despite this reporting, it is important to note that in May 2015, according to imagery analysis, North Korea was constructing a new transport corridor in order to conduct trade with China.[113] During 2015, despite some increases in trade with Russia, China remained by far the DPRK's most significant trade partner.[114] Then—and now—China continues to be a valuable trade partner and also allows things to happen that enable North Korea's illicit activities and underground finance. As 2015 turned into 2016, there were many revealing things that came out about the unique China–North Korea relationship. In March 2016, as China supposedly implemented sanctions imposed following a North Korean nuclear test by suspending certain financial transactions with the DPRK, money continued to flow across the border on trains, often hidden in luggage, according to a source reporting from China. Again, this appears to be a case of the Chinese government simply looking the other way.[115] During April 2016, military supplies continued to be smuggled across the China–North Korea border despite sanctions. In fact, front companies working for North Korea's military were reported to be continuing operations in China. Thus, while China had signed off on sanctions against North Korea, by April 2016 it was clear that the sanctions were not being seriously enforced.[116]

China's official list of things that would be sanctioned was released in April 2016 following the UN resolution issued in response to North Korea's nuclear test of that year (the first one). The list was quite extensive, but, perhaps as important, the key was what was excluded. Many items were allowed to be traded for "public welfare purposes." In addition, there were loopholes for the trading of aircraft fuel. The government of China also allowed for trade dealing with several key items as long as the trade benefited "livelihood purposes" and did not support nuclear or missile programs.[117] One wonders how a nation could determine such a thing. Of interest, first-quarter trade between China and North Korea was up 20 percent over 2015 in 2016—before sanctions were enforced.[118] Of course, transparency is key here because there is likely a great deal of trade that occurred after the sanctions were incurred that was never made official. Despite the rigorous official sanctions China had placed on North Korea—including the export of oil—a reporter from a South Korean newspaper visiting the Chinese city of Dandong during May 2016 witnessed oil being staged to be shipped across the border into the DPRK.[119] During June 2016, the North Korean envoy Ri Su-yong visited with China's leader, Xi Jinping. At Ri's request, China reportedly agreed to provide 500,000 tons of food supplies to its neighbor to the south (about half of what the North Koreans reportedly requested).[120] In addition to the oil flowing across the border, goods and commodities banned under the UN resolution were also reportedly crossing into North Korea as of June 2016.[121]

In the fall 2016, the South Korean press reported that trade between North Korea and China in August of that year had actually gone up nearly 30 percent over the previous year. The reported trade figures indicated that China had found many loopholes to get around the UN sanctions that they had supported and still claimed to be enforcing.[122] In fact, reportedly, North Korea made $1.1 billion just in sales of coal to China during 2016.[123] During late September 2016, at a Senate hearing, both senators and those testifying from the Obama administration State Department acknowledged essentially that China was not enforcing sanctions. One of the senators (Rubio) even remarked that no Chinese entities had been sanctioned as of that date (likely a reference to the fact that it is now an accepted norm that there are many Chinese front companies, individuals, and banks who continued then as they do now to cooperate with the North Koreans).[124] In October 2016, North Korea and China were reportedly engaged in maritime clandestine trade near the coastal North Korean city of Cholsan (with dozens of Chinese ships supposedly involved), perhaps to avoid be seen along the land border. Other reports (citing Korea International Trade Association data) showed that Chinese exports of jet fuel to the DPRK jumped 391 percent during September 2016 when compared to a year earlier.[125]

At the same September Senate hearing just mentioned, the US State Department's coordinator for sanctions policy, Daniel Fried, admitted that several Chinese firms were under investigation. It was in September that the United States sanctioned the China-based Hongxiang Industrial Development Company. The Treasury Department froze all its US-based assets, and the Justice Department pressed charges against four individuals.[126] The Hongxiang Company is an interesting case study in how Chinese companies get around sanctions while making big profits working with North Korean entities to make and process cash for the Kim regime, and this is likely only the tip of the iceberg (many other companies, banks, and individuals are likely involved in these types of illegal and illicit activities).

According to an official report released by the US Department of Justice: "Four Chinese nationals and a trading company based in Dandong, China, were charged by criminal complaint unsealed today with conspiring to evade U.S. economic sanctions and violating the Weapons of Mass Destruction Proliferators Sanctions Regulations (WMDPSR) through front companies by facilitating prohibited U.S. dollar transactions through the United States on behalf of a sanctioned entity in the Democratic People's

Republic of Korea (North Korea) and to launder the proceeds of that criminal conduct through U.S. financial institutions." In referring to other action taken, the report stated in part: "In addition, the department filed a civil forfeiture action for all funds contained in 25 Chinese bank accounts that allegedly belong to DHID and its front companies. The department has also requested that the federal court in the District of New Jersey issue a restraining order for all of the funds named in the civil forfeiture action, based upon the allegation that the funds represent property involved in money laundering, which makes them forfeitable to the United States. There are no allegations of wrongdoing by the U.S. correspondent banks or foreign banks that maintain these accounts." It is also important to note that the report states: "'The charges and forfeiture action announced today allege that defendants in China established and used shell companies around the world, surreptitiously moved money through the United States and violated the sanctions imposed on North Korea in response to, among other things, its nuclear weapons program,' said Assistant Attorney General Caldwell." Assistant Attorney General Carlin remarked in part: "Denying the use of the U.S. financial system can greatly curtail illegal activities and disrupt efforts to provide weapons of mass destruction to terrorists and rogue nations."[127] I completely agree with the last part of this statement. By using the US financial system to curtail the support that Chinese entities provide North Korea, real pressure can be put on the Kim regime. With only minor exceptions (like the prosecuting of the Hongxiang Company), this did not happen in the Obama administration. In early 2017, it was revealed that China was still importing from North Korea minerals banned under UN sanctions.[128] In early 2017, it was also reported that China had continued to export items valued at several million dollars to North Korea the previous year, items banned under UN sanctions.[129]

China reportedly banned North Korean citizens residing in China from opening new accounts in several banks and ordered the closing of existing accounts in these banks as well. The government order occurred during September 2017. It is not clear how this affected smaller banks (which is where North Korean operatives or their intermediaries often launder their money). In addition, given the modus operandi that North Korean operatives follow of using paid intermediaries and other loopholes, the success of this move can easily be called into doubt.[130] In 2017, China agreed to sanctions that would severely limit North Korea's imports of petroleum products, but anecdotal evidence (including imagery) suggests that it continues to allow its traders to export these products to the DPRK. On what scale this is occurring is unknown.[131]

If one is to look back at the actions of the North Korean regime in recent years, it is clear that this is a regime that engages in rogue state behavior in so many ways that one almost loses count. But it is important to consider that the illicit activities that North Korea engages in (and the illegal financial networks that support them) are not just a small aspect of the Kim regime. Rather, these activities are a key part of what the North Korean leadership infrastructure needs to do in order to simply survive. North Korea is more heavily sanctioned than most nations on earth. Thus, in order to survive, the government must literally work as a criminal entity in order to raise money for the regime. This explains both North Korea's many clever TTPs as well as its ties to international crime networks.[132]

In the past, the United States has tried several initiatives, from PSI to unilateral sanctions, to Treasury Department actions, to joining with the international community to bring about UN sanctions. But many of these actions have not produced results for two key reasons: (1) the United States has frequently failed to sufficiently enforce initiatives that could contain North Korea's proliferation, illicit sales of illegal goods, and illegal banking activities, and (2) North Korea does not play by the rules in the international system and is, thus, often able to escape enforcement. American sanctions have been important. There was an initiative that was successful back in 2005. American pressure (largely from the Treasury Department) forced Banco Delta Asia (BDA) to freeze its North Korea assets; then American officials were able to contain North Korean efforts to move funds to places like Europe, Vietnam, Singapore, and Mongolia. The threat of banks being blacklisted by the United States was enough to get many banks to turn down North Korean deposits. The snowball effect was quite compelling. Even banks in China were known to freeze North Korean accounts.[133] The actions (and the freezing) ended when the United States unfroze the BDA accounts. Since that time (and the failed nuclear agreement that followed the unfreezing), North Korea has diversified its banking practices and has spread its spiderweb financial network to places like Russia, China, Southeast Asia, and Singapore.[134] Thus, to take actions that will once again truly contain or at least slow down North Korea's proliferation and illegal financial activities, the United States would need to target several banks (usually smaller ones) in places all over Asia, Europe, Africa, and even the Middle

East. To date, this has not happened on a large scale, but things may be changing.

On May 16, 2017, UN ambassador Nikki Haley announced that the United States would be tightening sanctions against North Korea. She also announced that the United States would go after entities in third countries that were helping with North Korea's proliferation and the illicit financial activities that support it.[135] In June 2017, the Treasury and State Departments imposed new sanctions on North Korean entities and individuals, including the Tangun Trading Corporation and one of its partners in Moscow that had been operating in violation of sanctions. To quote the Treasury Department release: "Treasury is working with our allies to counter networks that enable North Korea's destabilizing activities, and we urge our partners to take parallel steps to cut off their funding sources."[136] Thus, one is led to believe that—finally—a new presidential administration may take the necessary steps to make enforcement of sanctions a high priority. If focus on enforcement becomes a reality, secondary sanctions on countries outside North Korea will become key, and this needs to include entities within countries like China, Singapore, Vietnam, Russia, and Iran (to name several of the many countries housing entities supporting North Korea's proliferation through illicit financial activities). Exactly what are we referring to when we say *secondary sanctions?* To quote Aaron Arnold of Curry College: "Secondary sanctions, sometimes referred to as extraterritorial sanctions, are an often discussed but rarely understood policy instrument. Whereas primary sanctions apply restrictions directly to U.S. persons and companies, secondary sanctions leverage the strength and role of the U.S. financial system to target businesses and persons outside the typical jurisdiction of the United States. Generally, these types of sanctions focus on blocking or restricting foreign banks' access to the U.S. financial system."[137] These sanctions can be used particularly well by the United States because of the power of the dollar in financial markets.

The first year of the Trump presidency reflected more action—real action—against North Korea proliferation than was seen in the entire eight years of the Obama administration. This is not a political statement. It is simply a statement of facts. There are two reasons that this is so compellingly true: enforcement and the imposition of secondary sanctions with teeth. Moves made that began during 2017 were important. But it must be pointed out that, while this is a good start, it is only a start for much broader initiatives that must occur if we are to truly pressure North Korea. In June 2017, for the first time since the Treasury Department took action against BDA in 2005, it again took action against a Chinese bank—the Bank of Dandong. It designated it a primary laundering concern and stated that it was an entity that facilitated funds used by front companies operating in support of North Korea's WMD programs. This will also mean that the Bank of Dandong will not have access to the US financial system. The government of China of course protested the move, but the US government made it clear at the time that it was going after illicit entities, not governments.[138]

According to press reports in mid-July 2017, Washington was preparing still more initiatives and sanctions against other banks in China and other entities there as well. In addition, State Department officials visited Singapore and elsewhere in Southeast Asia during mid-July 2017, reportedly to gain help in going after entities (banks and front companies) working with North Korea.[139] The expected actions came in late August 2017 when the US Treasury Department specifically targeted entities in Russia, China, Singapore, and even Namibia that were either directly dealing in trade with North Korea's WMD program, ballistic missile programs, or other arms programs, raising funds that could be used to provide financial support for arms programs, or helping launder the money.[140]

In June and August 2017, the US Attorney's Office in Washington, DC, filed three civil forfeiture actions worth millions of dollars against shell companies that were accused of laundering funds used to finance North Korea's WMD programs.[141] In a Department of Justice public report, one of the front companies based in China was addressed: "The United States has filed a complaint to civilly forfeit $1,902,976 from Mingzheng International Trading Limited (Mingzheng), a company based in Shenyang, China." The report continued: "'This complaint alleges that parties in China established and used a front company to surreptitiously move North Korean money through the United States and violated the sanctions imposed by our government on North Korea,' said U.S. Attorney Phillips." Finally, it stated: "Specifically, despite strengthened financial sanctions, North Korean networks are adapting by using greater ingenuity in accessing formal banking channels. This includes maintaining correspondent bank accounts and representative offices abroad, which are staffed by foreign nationals making use of front companies. These broad interwoven networks allow the North Korean banks to conduct illicit procurement and banking activity."[142]

On September 21, 2017, the United States took action that was, in my view, the most important and potentially damaging to North Korea's rogue state behavior since the BDA initiative in 2005. This is not an exaggeration. On that day, President Trump issued an executive order that essentially gave the Treasury Department full authorization to completely cut off North Korea's access to the US dollar and thus to go after any front company, bank, or individual attempting to do business with North Korea. In other words, any institution caught doing business with North Korea will not be allowed to do business with the United States. This action mirrors the type of initiatives taken by Treasury against North Korea in 2005 that had North Korea on the ropes by late 2006.[143] The difference is that this action is expected to be more comprehensive and much more widespread because North Korea's illicit financial networks are much more diversified and widespread than they were in 2005–2006. The United States can—and likely will—go after banks and front companies all over China, but it will also go after such entities in places such as Singapore, Malaysia, and several countries in Africa. Now that the executive order has been issued, the specific targeting of those entities that are laundering North Korea's dirty money need to be designated, an action that is likely to be ongoing and large scale.

All these are important moves and a good start. But widespread and comprehensive action must be taken against a wide variety of banks, front companies, and individuals, and it is important to remember that these elements exist all over Asia, Africa, and the Middle East, not just in China. It is also important to remember that token action (as was often taken in past years leading to 2017) is nothing more than exactly that—token action. This action must cover all known entities and individuals who are supporting North Korea's illicit programs, and it must be a series of routine and continuous acts that constantly apply the pressure and readjust as the North Koreans readjust.

The international community is another matter. The United States remains the economic leader of the world, but many other international organizations and nation-states continue to be very critical of North Korea's financial activity. Key among the international community in recent years has been the United Nations. UN sanctions are now as tough as they have ever been, and many have expressed a hope that these sanctions may actually bring about a change in the DPRK's behavior.[144] Despite the fact that the international community is now (in my opinion) more serious than it has ever been about containing and/or slowing North Korea's illicit trade, illegal banking, and military proliferation, the country that could make the biggest dent in these practices continues to be at best reluctant to take full measures against Pyongyang. China remains at a crossroads: it can choose to join the international community in putting real pressure on North Korea, or it can simply maintain the status quo.[145] At least for now, the latter appears to be the most likely option. Thus, North Korea's rogue state activities are likely to continue until sanctions and other initiatives implemented by nations other than China put real pressure on Pyongyang.

4

North Korea and Military Proliferation to Iran

Pyongyang's Most Important Customer

During the second week of September 2015, the US Congress came through with enough of a vote (a distinct minority in both houses) on President Obama's Iran nuclear deal (a deal brokered by Secretary of State John Kerry) for it to go through. One cannot help but note that many questions remained.[1] The Obama deal, known as the Joint Comprehensive Plan of Action (JCPOA),[2] has eased many sanctions and allows the means for Tehran's economy (and, many would argue, its nuclear program) to make great gains. Thus, one tends to question why Iran's nuclear program was addressed in isolation, as if human rights, terrorism, the ballistic missiles that carry the nuclear weapons, and violations of UN sanctions, along with many other matters, are totally unrelated. A key element of foreign support to this nuclear weaponization program has been North Korea, which has contributed to this program by providing technical expertise, raw materials, and advisers as well as engineers, technicians, and scientists.

Despite a wide variety of evidence in open source channels, the Obama administration did not comment on this long-standing and compelling relationship (at least when it comes to the nukes), and, even more troubling, it was not even addressed in the talks between US and Iranian negotiators. In fact, there is a very long history of North Korean assistance to the Iranian nuclear programs and the platforms that would carry these nuclear weapons. Though the Iran–North Korea relationship regarding nuclear weaponization has been long and prosperous for both Pyongyang and Tehran, there are several other elements of North Korean proliferation to Iran that are important to consider (such as ballistic missile and conventional weapons sales as well as support to terrorist groups) as the relationship between Washington and Tehran during the Obama administration changed in a way that many no doubt considered to represent a major paradigm shift.

Iran has had profound and compelling military-to-military and weapons program exchanges with North Korea since at least the very early 1980s. In fact, I will describe this relationship in detail. But, while the nuclear weaponization relationship with North Korea may have existed as early as the late 1990s, it truly picked up steam around 2003, when (under American pressure) Pakistan cut off the nuclear bazaar proliferation network, run by A. Q. Khan but supported and enabled by the Pakistani government.[3] I will address this relationship and how it has evolved from the genesis of cooperation that began because of a lack of Pakistani support right up to events occurring today.

Iran's nuclear program is quite fascinating, as is the support it has received from outsiders (and in this chapter I will address a key outsider, North Korea). But nuclear weapons are only as good as the platforms that carry them—typically ballistic missiles. I will address the missiles that North Korea has proliferated to Iran and the programs it has set up there so that the Iranians could assemble these missiles on their own soil (though vital components continue to come from North Korea). While Iran has several ballistic missiles with the potential to carry nuclear warheads, it also has a plethora of missiles that are used in conventional operations. It received many of these missiles from North Korea as well, and I will address them in great detail.

While nuclear weaponization programs and ballistic missiles are certainly the sexiest programs that North Korea proliferates to Iran, conventional weapons are also very important. North Korea proliferates a variety of ground, naval, and other systems that are important for Tehran's military capabilities.[4] Tied in with this is the fact that North Korea and Iran have collaborated to support terrorist groups—specifically, Hezbollah and Hamas. I will address this support, the methods used, and the weapons systems proliferated in this chapter.

The North Korea–Iran Nuclear Connection

Iran probably began to develop its nuclear weaponization program during the late 1990s, largely with the help of the A. Q. Khan network, supported and enabled by the government and the military of Pakistan.[5] Unfortunately for Iran, the cookie jar had slammed shut by 2003. It was then that, at least partially due to pressure from the United States, Pakistan shut down the pro-liferation network being run by A. Q. Khan.[6] The network reportedly trans-ferred nuclear technology, parts, and scientific know-how to at least three countries—Iran, Libya, and North Korea.[7] By 2003, North Korea was tak-ing advantage of the void left by Pakistan, having stepped in to provide assis-tance (for a price of course) for what at the time was Iran's fledgling nuclear weaponization program. North Korea was then—and is now—ahead of Iran in its path for nuclear weaponization.[8]

It was in 2003 that, in an article for the *Los Angeles Times,* the veteran reporter Douglas Frantz wrote: "A three-month investigation by The Times—drawing on previously secret reports, international officials, independent experts, Iranian exiles and intelligence sources in Europe and the Middle East—uncovered strong evidence that Iran's commercial program masks a plan to become the world's next nuclear power." He continued: "Technol-ogy and scientists from Russia, China, North Korea and Pakistan have pro-pelled Iran's nuclear program much closer to producing a bomb than Iraq ever was." He concluded: "North Korean military scientists recently were monitored entering Iranian nuclear facilities. They are assisting in the design of a nuclear warhead, according to people inside Iran and foreign intelligence officials. So many North Koreans are working on nuclear and missile projects in Iran that a resort on the Caspian coast is set aside for their exclusive use."[9] In an interesting bit of irony, following his long and distinguished career as a reporter, Frantz worked for then senator John Kerry as deputy staff direc-tor and chief investigator of the Senate Foreign Relations Committee. When Kerry moved to the State Department as the secretary, Frantz moved as well and became the assistant secretary of state for public affairs (beginning in 2013).[10] Thus, one wonders why Frantz—and Kerry—have been so close-mouthed about North Korea's support to Iran's nuclear program.

It is important to note that the year 2003 is key, it being the first year that North Korea's assistance to Iran's nuclear weaponization program clearly occurred, though there may be evidence of earlier cooperation in classified channels that has not been released to the public. The nuclear warhead design that North Korea was (and likely still is) assisting Iran's scientists and engi-neers with most likely was one that Pakistani proliferators reportedly sold to North Korea, Libya, and Iran. But the North Koreans would have the great-est knowledge about the warhead because it goes on a No Dong ballistic missile. North Korea sold the No Dong to Pakistan, assisted the Pakistanis with launches, and worked closely with Pakistan in all phases of deploying the missile on Pakistani soil.[11] The warhead designs, based on original Chinese designs, were discovered when Libya gave up its nuclear program (and according to unnamed officials the designs were also sold to North Korea and Iran). It is a design for a 500 kilogram highly enriched uranium (HEU) warhead.[12] Iran also has the No Dong, which they call the Shahab-3. In fact, Iran and Pakistan began acquiring No Dongs and No Dong technology to build their own versions (assisted by the North Koreans) at almost the exact same time period.[13]

The assessment that North Korea has already perfected the technology to fit a small nuclear warhead on the No Dong has been shown to be credible by a statement issued by the former senior US intelligence official Arthur Brown, who said: "The fact that [the North Koreans] have a warhead that's fitable to the Nodong (ballistic missile) is pretty much given." Brown was speaking to the Foreign Correspondents Club in Japan in 2008.[14] At a minimum, it is a given that North Korea and Iran have been cooperating on perfecting this design and putting it on a No Dong, but I would assess that it is likely that they are working on nuclear warhead designs for other, longer-range missiles as well.[15]

North Korean assistance to Iran's nuclear weaponization program did not end in 2003, nor was this support limited to simply assisting with nuclear warhead technology. North Korea reportedly constructed more than ten thousand meters of nuclear infrastructure underground facilities for Iran. The facilities were reported to have reinforced concrete ceilings as well as doors and walls constructed to withstand bunker buster attacks. During 2005, Myong Lyu-do (a leading underground facilities expert in North Korea at the time) arrived in Tehran to lead the construction efforts.[16] During 2007, Syrian plutonium facilities that were well on their way to having the capability to produce weaponized nuclear material were destroyed by Israeli aircraft. The facilities were constructed with assistance (and guidance) from North Korea. In fact, according to Michael Hayden, the former director of the CIA: "The depth of that relationship was revealed in the spring of last year." Hayden was referring to the plutonium nuclear reactor built with a great deal of North Korean assistance. He further stated that the plutonium reactor was "similar to Yongbyon in North Korea, but with its outer structure heavily disguised." He made it very clear that the evidence was overwhelming and that there was a lot of it to show North Korean involvement when he said: "Virtually every form of intelligence—imagery, signals, human source, you name it—informed their assessments, so that they were never completely dependent on any single channel."[17] Why is this relevant to the North Korea–Iran nuclear weaponization relationship? Because evidence that Iran financed Syria's plutonium nuclear weapons program was uncovered later. Specifically, former deputy minister of defense Ali Reza Asghari made the allegations to the press following his defection from Iran in February 2007.[18] Iran reportedly paid the North Koreans up to $2 billion to lead the construction of Syria's plutonium facility.[19] As a result of the North Korea–Syria deal (and perhaps as a result of the destruction of the Syrian reactor), forty-five tons of yellow cake originally delivered by North Korea was reportedly transferred from Syria, through Turkey, and then into Iran.[20]

North Korea's support to the Iranian nuclear weapons program continued as the years advanced. In 2011, it was disclosed in the European press that North Korea had just supplied Iran with a computer program that would aid in the development of nuclear weapons. The software, originally developed in the United States, simulates neutron flows. Reportedly, a delegation traveled from Pyongyang to Tehran that year to train Iranian defense specialists in maintaining proficiency with the software.[21] Also in 2011, North Korea continued large-scale support to Iran's nuclear and missile programs (I will discuss support to missile programs in the next section). According to a diplomat quoted in the South Korean press: "Hundreds of North Korean scientists and engineers are working at about 10 nuclear and missile facilities in Iran, including Natanz." This source also stated: "The North Koreans enter Iran clandestinely via third countries like Russia and China."[22] During November 2011, in a report that quoted intelligence provided to UN nuclear officials, the *Washington Post* reporter Joby Warrick stated: "Crucial technology linked to experts in Pakistan and North Korea also helped propel Iran to the threshold of nuclear capability." He added later in his report: "Iran relied on foreign experts to supply mathematical formulas and codes for theoretical design work—some of which appear to have originated in North Korea, diplomats and weapons experts say."[23]

While there are many aspects of North Korean assistance to Iran's nuclear weaponization program that are quite compelling, perhaps one of the most compelling regarding cooperation is the report that Iranians observed North Korea's underground nuclear test during February 2013. Iran is not assessed by most analysts to have a plutonium weaponization program to date (it is building a plutonium nuclear reactor as of the writing of this chapter, reportedly with North Korean assistance, but some analysts allege that, though Tehran is not capable of producing plutonium-based weapons currently, it may be able to do so in the near future).[24] But, reportedly, the Iranian government requested the government in North Korea to permit key experts from Iran to come to the DPRK to observe the underground nuclear test of 2013. Tehran paid Pyongyang tens of millions of dollars for its people to observe the test. Iran's Atomic Energy Organization is said to have made the request. Mahmoud Ahmadinejad (the Iranian president at the time) made the final approval for the request. Among those in attendance at the nuclear test was Mohsen Fakhrizadeh-Mahabadi. A high-ranking official within the government of Iran, he is widely reported to be in charge of Iran's collaboration effort with Pyongyang to develop a highly enriched uranium (HEU) nuclear warhead for a missile. Some analysts have suggested that the test in 2013 was of a miniaturized nuclear warhead. In fact, the North Koreans actually claimed that they tested a "miniaturized and lighter nuclear device with greater explosive force than previously."[25]

The ties between Iran and the DPRK have not receded in recent years. Trips of officials going back and forth and scientists, engineers, and technicians routinely conducting missions in both counties continue as of the writing of this chapter. In 2014, Iranian foreign minister Mohammad Javad Zarif and North Korean deputy foreign minister Ri Gil Song met in Tehran, where they both stressed further expansion of bilateral ties.[26] In 2015, allegations were made by several analysts that Iran is actually housing nuclear materials in North Korea. While these allegations are to date unproved, it is my assessment that further investigation and analysis should be conducted in order to validate (or invalidate) their credibility. The US State Department remains mum thus far on these allegations. In fact, it has said nothing about the overwhelming evidence regarding North Korea–Iran nuclear weaponization cooperation.[27]

During May 2015, the National Council of Resistance of Iran (NCRI), a dissident group, made some very important allegations regarding North Korea's assistance to the Iranian nuclear weapons program. The NCRI has had a controversial history, yet the group has deep sources within Iran's nuclear community, and it has also made compelling, verified disclosures in the past, including breaking news about Iran's Natanz uranium enrichment facility and the Arak plutonium reactor. According to the NCRI, a delegation of North Korean nuclear and missile experts visited a military site near Tehran during April 2015. The seven-man team was making its third trip, with more trips to follow later in the year. The team included nuclear experts and experts on nuclear warheads. It was said to have been taken to the Khomeini complex. According to the reports provided, the North Koreans stayed in a secret guesthouse near key facilities. Arrangements for the visit were made by Brigadier General Nassorllah Ezati and Iranian Republican Guard Corps (IRGC) brigadier general Alireza Tamizi. Much of the information showing extensive exchanges of information regarding nuclear weapons and nuclear warhead design was provided to the NCRI by Iran's main opposition movement, the Mujahedin-e-Khalq.[28] During September 2017, a meeting between high-ranking Iranian and North Korean officials occurred in Tehran very soon after North Korea's largest nuclear test ever. The meeting was reportedly a matter of great concern to American government officials, who had fears that the North Koreans were providing the latest nuclear technology and know-how to their biggest proliferation customer.[29]

The evidence over a period that now spans well over a decade is clear. Whether it is assisting in the design and building of a nuclear warhead, providing computer software that will aid in building a nuclear weapon, building nuclear facilities that are capable of resisting bunker buster bombing attacks, or even providing yellow cake materials for Tehran's nuclear program, North Korea has been knee-deep in assisting Iran's nuclear program. Iranian specialists and VIPs even reportedly attended North Korea's underground nuclear test in 2013. And who can forget that the Iranian government paid up to $2 billion in order to finance North Korean construction of and assistance on a plutonium reactor in Syria? The North Korea–Iran nuclear connection is one that is compelling, widespread, and of long duration. And the fact that sanctions on Iran were lifted by the Obama administration in 2016 can only help this very lucrative relationship. As the respected former Congressional Research Service scholar Larry Niksch has stated: "There also are the significant financial earnings of these programs, especially through North Korea's nuclear and missile collaboration with Iran. Iran's willingness to increase financial support for North Korea's nuclear and missile programs may grow with the lifting of international sanctions against Iran and the resultant flow of billions of dollars to the Iranian Government."[30] But there is another issue that is equally of concern to policy makers and the international community—North Korea's sales of a wide variety of ballistic missiles to Iran.

The North Korea–Iran Ballistic Missile Connection

North Korea had been seeking to develop ballistic missiles like its allies the Soviet Union and China since the 1960s. But these efforts did not come to fruition. By the late 1970s, North Korea had acquired several Scud B missiles from Egypt.[31] These missiles served as the feeders—the genesis if you will—for a whole series of ballistic missile systems, systems that would be proliferated to nations in both the Middle East and South Asia. By 1984, North Korea had completed the process for indigenously building (and had successfully test-launched) its own ballistic missile systems, the Scud B.[32] What is important about the whole pattern of North Korea ballistic missile development and proliferation to rogue states (or states that cannot get such weaponry anywhere else) is relating this to the state that has been—from the very beginning—the largest buyer of North Korea's ballistic missile programs, Iran. In fact, as this section will show, Iran seemingly has bottomless pockets when it comes to purchasing missiles, missile programs, or missile assistance for its own ballistic program from North Korea.

Probably around 1985, North Korea and Iran entered into a contract where Pyongyang would proliferate Scud Bs to Tehran. The Iranians very quickly put the systems they had acquired to use in combat, in tit-for-tat ballistic missile battles conducted during what was at the time a long war with Iraq and in battles that historians now call the War of the Cities.[33] Even as it was proliferating Scud Bs to Iran, North Korea was working on a more capable Scud, the Scud C. Thus, in 1986, it successfully produced and tested its own version of the SCUD C. Of course, the Iranians bought it soon thereafter. The Scud C sale to Iran represents a key milestone in the Pyongyang-Tehran proliferation relationship. It was beginning with the Scud C that North Korea began the modus operandi of first selling Tehran actual missile systems and later converting this sale into setting up assembly and manufacturing facilities.[34] These facilities create confusion among analysts in the international security arena because Iran then claims that it is indigenously producing the weapons systems. Yet these systems cannot be produced without North Korean assistance and parts that are manufactured in North Korea. That said, it is far easier to import weapons parts than entire missile systems, and this also makes it (as a practical matter) far easier to get past sanctions regimes.[35] North Korea has also reportedly proliferated the Scud D to Iran as well as the Scud ER, which appears to be a variant of the Scud D. The Scud D is assembled in Syria (with North Korean assistance and components of course), and, thus, the Scud Ds that Iran has in its inventory may be coming directly from Syria.[36]

Pyongyang conducted its first (known) successful test launch of the No Dong in 1993, and, of course, Iranians were at the launch, observing the missile that many have acknowledged has a range of up to fifteen hundred kilometers.[37] Soon after the test, Iran began to acquire the No Dong, paying hard currency and, according to some reports, oil to the North Koreans.[38] But that is not where the story ends. As I have earlier stated, the North Koreans reportedly began assisting the Iranians as early as 2003 with the technology and expertise to construct five-hundred-kilogram HEU warheads for the No Dong missile (known as the Shahab-3 in Iran). By 2008, the Iranians had successfully test-launched the No Dong several times.[39] More recently, in 2015 the Iranians test-launched yet another upgraded version of the No Dong. Known as the Emad, the new missile is essentially nothing more than a No Dong with its range increased (by about two hundred kilometers) and an improved guidance system.[40] This missile was probably built with both assistance and parts from the North Koreans, who likely have the same missile.

During the early 1990s, the North Koreans were able to obtain a complete SS-N-6 system (also called the R-27) from what were apparently rogue Russians, who were not acting under the guise of the Russian government, at least according to the Russian government. The North Koreans then turned this missile into a road-mobile, land-based missile system. They also began to produce the missile on their own and to deploy it in the DPRK.[41] The missile has gone by many names since the West first discovered it but is now commonly known as the Musudan. In 2005, soon after Pyongyang had begun to manufacture and deploy the Musudan, the North Koreans proliferated (according to several sources) eighteen of the missiles to Iran.[42] Tehran reportedly conducted its initial test launch of the Musudan (deemed the Shahab-4 in Iran) on January 17, 2006. The Musudan (read Shahab-4) traveled approximately three thousand kilometers and was intentionally destroyed in midflight by technicians.[43] Analysis of the launch showed data leading to an assessment of a range of four thousand kilometers for the missile.[44] It is likely that North Koreans were on the ground in Iran to advise and assist in the launch. The Iranians may have tested an improved variant of the Musudan as recently as January 2017.[45] That missile, designated the Khorramshahr, was also displayed in a parade during the same year.[46] To see a compelling example of the ranges of several of the missile systems that Iran has acquired from North Korea that are tested, deployed, and operational, please see the map that is displayed on the next page (note that the Shahab-3 is essentially the No Dong and that the Shahab-4 is the Musudan).[47]

Iranian engineers reportedly observed North Korea's first Taepo Dong test launch in 1998.[48] Iranians also observed the Taepo Dong test launch of 2006. The engineers were said to be from the Iranian Republican Guard Corps and were at the launch to set up possible Iranian procurement of Taepo Dong technology.[49] North Korea conducted yet another failed Taepo Dong test launch on April 5, 2009, but this time the missile went through two of its three stages (i.e., it was more successful than the previous launch). Iranians were reportedly on hand for this launch as well, and, soon after the test was conducted, at least fifty North Korean engineers went to Iran (likely to assess the results of the 2009 test and assist the Iranian ballistic missile program).[50] Iranians were reportedly also present at the North Korean Taepo Dong 2 ballistic missile test launch on December 12, 2012.[51] The test was successful as the Taepo Dong missile (North Koreans called it the Unha-3) went through all three stages of its launch successfully, propelling a satellite into orbit (had the payload been a warhead instead of a satellite, the missile had the range to hit the United States).[52] So one must ask, If the Iranians were present at all these North Korean ICBM test launches, has anything come of this? The evidence points to an affirmative answer.

In January 2015, the Israeli press uncovered an Iranian (apparently multistage missile) system that has a range far beyond Europe. This missile is, according to the imagery that was exposed in the news report, twenty-seven meters long, almost the same size as a Taepo Dong 1.[53] Thus, one is compelled to ask, Is this missile the result of Taepo Dong technology passed to the Iranians after four missile test launches observed by its specialists (in addition to the numerous trips made by North Korean scientists, engineers, and technicians to Iran)? The answer appears to be that this latest missile, a possible threat to the United States and Europe, likely came from technology and assistance obtained from the North Koreans.

In recent years, there have been a variety of missile systems that have come to light in Iran, systems that would not exist without North Korean parts and assistance. For example, according to State Department cables revealed on WikiLeaks, one stage of Iran's Safir system (a two-stage missile that has successfully launched a satellite into space) is actually a No Dong. Furthermore, the Safir features steering engines in its second stage that are derived from Musudan technology.[54] In 2013, Thomas Countryman, the assistant secretary of state for international security and nonproliferation, gave a news briefing in Geneva at which he stated in part: "Both Iran and North Korea have developed channels that enable them to continue to export and continue to procure the items they need for their weapons industry."[55]

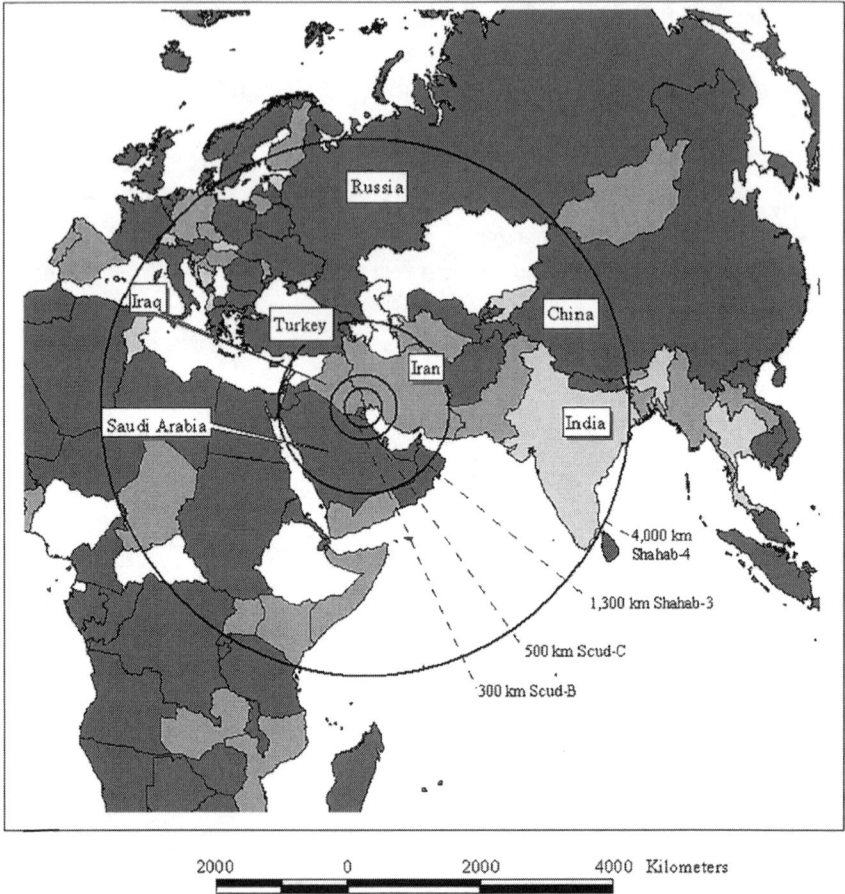

Ranges of Iran's Missiles. *Source:* "Recognizing Iran as a Strategic Threat: An Intelligence Challenge for the United States," Staff Report of the US House of Representatives Permanent Select Committee on Intelligence, Subcommittee on Intelligence Policy, August 23, 2006, http://permanent.access.gpo.gov/lps73446/IranReport082206v2.pdf.

In addition to a variety of activities dealing with rockets and missiles, in 2013 it was revealed that Iran and North Korea were collaborating on a new, eighty-ton long-range rocket booster for an ICBM. A variety of experts and specialists from Iran made several trips to North Korea to collaborate on the development of the rocket during 2013. In addition, at the same time, according to publicly released imagery, North Korea expanded its long-range missile launch facilities in the northwest area of the country, even building what appeared to be the largest launch tower that had ever been confirmed in the isolated state (obviously, the expanded facilities appear to be meant to accommodate a larger rocket booster).[56] Later in 2013, in a shocking disclosure, according to unidentified US intelligence community officials as reported in the *World Tribune,* it was disclosed that Iran is at least partially financing North Korea's ballistic missile program. In exchange, the DPRK is proliferating its technology, missile components, and expertise to Iran.[57] More evidence regarding North Korea's missile proliferation to Iran came out in 2015 when it was revealed that Pyongyang had supplied several shipments of missile components to Iran even as nuclear talks were ongoing between Iran and the United States.[58] Also in 2015, Tal Inbar, the head of the Space Research Center at the Fisher Institute for Air and Space Strategic Studies, stated in an interview regarding North Korean proliferation to Iran: "All the infrastructure we see in Iran, very large launch pads and all the test stands for rocket engines, are [sic] made after North Korean design."[59]

In 2016, following North Korea's fourth nuclear test, the US Treasury Department imposed sanctions on Iranian officials who were acting on behalf of the Shahid Hemmat Industrial Group and Iran's Ministry of Defense for Armed Forces Logistics. These individuals violated sanctions imposed by the United States and also both unilateral US and UN sanctions in dealing with one of North Korea's key proliferating front companies, the Korea Mining Development Trading Corporation (KOMID). Specifically, North Korean officials had visited Iran, and Iranian officials and technicians had visited North Korea, in order to procure an eighty-ton rocket booster for a missile (which could have been either for the Taepo Dong or for another system). There was thus now a smoking gun—officially designated by the US government—that the Iranians collaborated with North Korea to build (i.e., the North Koreans would build the missile and the Iranians would get it) a new eighty-ton rocket booster for one of the largest missiles ever test-launched in the DPRK.[60]

Unfortunately, even after sanctions and the Treasury Department actions, according to press sources high-ranking North Korean KOMID officials once again were reported active in Iran during March 2016.[61] To put the cherry on top, if you will, this whole cycle was completed when the North Koreans for the second time successfully put an ICBM-capable missile through all three of its stages in February 2016 (calling the test of course a *satellite launch*). The missile was the largest ever launched with the longest range and from the most improved facilities.[62] It is unclear whether the missile launched (under the cover of a space launch vehicle) was the missile equipped with the eighty-ton rocket booster (or a variant leading to the next generation that would house the rocket booster) that the Iranians had been collaborating with the North Koreans on since at least 2014. During March 2017, the North Koreans conducted an engine test of a powerful rocket booster with the most thrust seen to that date. This too is likely related to the capability the North Koreans are building for Iran (and probably for themselves as well).[63] Thus, the latest development of ballistic missile proliferation from North Korea to Iran is likely an upgrade or a variant of a long-range missile that is now likely to be spotted in Iran in the near future (since the Iranians have paid for it).[64]

According to a report that came out in June 2017: "Underground facilities and tunnels to produce, store, and maintain missiles have also been modeled after North Korean sites and were created with the collaboration of the North Korea's experts." In fact, the North Korean experts assisting Iran have such a constant and routine presence that they have permanent facilities there. As the report goes on to say: "These ties have been strengthened to a degree where the IRGC has built a special residence for North Korean experts beside the command center of the Hemmat Missile Industry Group in Tehran—Damavand Street, Azmayesh three-way junction, 2nd kilometer of Telo road. These experts have had a continuous presence in the IRGC's key missile industries, including building a warhead and the guidance systems." The report provides even greater detail: "According to specific information, since nuclear negotiations in 2013, this trend has not stopped and North Korea's experts constantly travel to Iran while the IRGC's missile experts visit North Korea."[65]

The implications of North Korea's proliferation of ballistic missiles to Iran and assistance to many (if not most) of Tehran's missile programs are quite clear. If one is to look at the development of Iran's ballistic missile program—from its genesis until today—in many ways it looks as if one is also following the development of North Korea's missile program. From the very beginning, when North Korea provided Scuds that were used in the Iran-Iraq War, to the No Dong missile that Pyongyang proliferated to Iran that has the range to hit Israel, to the later sale of the Musudan IRBM that can range NATO targets in Europe, it has been clear that the very next step Pyongyang takes after development and deployment of most of its ballistic missiles is to sell these systems to Iran. Even systems that Iran has deployed that are not in North Korea's arsenal are a concern. The best example of this is the Safir rocket, a two-stage space-launched vehicle featuring one stage that is derived from a No Dong and a second stage that shows elements of Musudan technology. Thus, through its missile sales and missile assistance programs, North Korea has proliferated to Iran capabilities that are a threat not only to the region but also to key areas outside the Middle East. This leads to the inevitable question, What is the next missile system that North Korea will proliferate to Iran, and will it be capable of targeting the United States?

In what some might consider a surprising move, in 2017 the Iranian government formally acknowledged that it was abandoning its human space-flight program (citing costs).[66] This means of course that any future long-range or multistage missile launches will have less of a cover when it comes to identifying the real purpose of the missile test launch, or so one would think. (Though in a confusing state of affairs, Iran continues to claim that many of its rockets are for its space program.) In late July 2017, the Iranians launched what they called a two-stage satellite launch vehicle that was probably simply a test of their two-stage ballistic missile technology (initial reports showed no indications of an actual satellite being deployed). In yet another example of how Iran is dependent on North Korea for technology and assistance in its missile program, the missile (satellite launch vehicle), named the Simorgh, consisted of two stages, with the first stage reportedly consisting of a cluster of No Dong engines.[67]

During September 2017, the Iranians released footage showing the test launch of a missile called the Khorramshahr that, when viewed on film (and the film appears to have been of a launch conducted earlier in 2017), looked remarkably like the Musudan missile system that the North Koreans have proliferated to Tehran.[68] In addition, during 2017 the Iranians for the first time known used what they called the Shahab-3 (No Dong) in combat, firing it at rebel forces in Syria, thus proving the effectiveness of yet another system supplied by North Korea.[69] The overwhelming majority of Iranian ballistic missiles tested to date or used in combat have had their genesis in North Korea, were built with North Korean assistance and parts, and remain the key component of Tehran's missile program. It is my assessment that Iran will continue to develop its missile program, pushing for missiles with long ranges and potential nuclear capability. It is also my assessment that North Korea will continue—as it always has—to assist Iran down this path (for a price of course). It bears repeating to say that, if you see it in North Korea

today, you will see it in Iran tomorrow. Thus, tests and new weapons development described in chapter 2 should be considered directly relevant to Iran's
ongoing missile development.

The North Korea–Iran Conventional Weapons Connection

One might express surprise at the fact that North Korea also engages in
large-scale proliferation of small arms and conventional weapons to Iran.
This essentially began during the Iran-Iraq War, when few nations would
provide arms to what the world largely saw as a religiously radical government in Tehran. During that war, North Korea sold long-range artillery systems to Iran. In fact, the North sold its most advanced (and longest-range)
systems to Iran—the 170-millimeter Koksan gun and the 240-millimeter
multiple rocket launcher system. Hundreds of these systems are currently
deployed along the DMZ in Korea, and both systems are capable of firing
chemical munitions. In fact, by the end of the Iran-Iraq War, Pyongyang
had sold the Iranians antitank weapons, antiaircraft systems, and a variety
of small arms and provided both advisers and trainers as needed. As the war
ended, there were more than three hundred North Korean military advisers
on the ground in Iran. During the war, North Koreans also provided such
practical expertise as building tactical and floating bridges and instruction in
small arms. By the time the war had ended, North Korea reportedly had sold
more than $1 billion in conventional arms to Iran.[70] The acquisition of North
Korean conventional weapons systems of all types continues today.[71] In fact,
an excellent example of how Iran acquires conventional weapons from North
Korea not only for its own needs but also for those of its proxies and allies, in
2017 Syria took delivery of a large conventional weapons shipment consisting
of a variety of weapons, including rocket-propelled grenades, heavy machine
guns, and mortars. Payment for the shipment went directly from Iran to
North Korea through several front companies based in Malaysia.[72]

One excellent example of North Korean proliferation that continues
to affect security in the Middle East today is the Yeono-class submarine.
The North Koreans built this submarine to survive the muddy waters off its
west coast, waters with rapidly changing tides. Where else do such waters
exist? Off the coast of Iran.[73] The effectiveness of the Yeono-class submarine
was seen in 2010 when one of these subs sank the South Korean corvette
Cheonan, killing forty-six sailors. North Korea has proliferated this submarine to Tehran, and reportedly fourteen of these submarines are now in

Iran's arsenal.[74] During April 2017, the Iranian navy conducted a test of what appeared to be a cruise missile from a Yeono-class submarine—or what it is called in Iran a Ghadir-class submarine (which appears to be an exact duplicate). The submarine, originally proliferated from North Korea to Iran, is now being produced indigenously by the Iranians. If the North Korea–Iran relationship with this submarine is to follow the same pattern that other proliferation has in the past, the North Koreans proliferated the original systems to Iran, then helped the Iranians set up a facility that could manufacture the systems there. But the systems will still of course need spare parts and manufacturing assistance from the DPRK. The test that the Iranians conducted of what appeared to be a cruise missile from the Yeono/Ghadir-class submarine proved (at least initially) to be unsuccessful. But tests are likely to continue. Again, if past precedent is to be followed here, the North Koreans will continue to assist the Iranians, not only with the operational capabilities of the Yeono-class submarine, but also with the test-launching of the cruise missile that the Iranians want to equip the submarine with. According to press sources, experts assess that the cruise missile is a copy of a missile previously tested in North Korea. Of note, the North Koreans have (as discussed earlier in this work) also been developing a submarine that launches a missile, though their submarine (named the Sinpo) and the missile both have far greater capabilities than do what the Iranians are testing thus far. It is likely that the North Koreans will continue to proliferate to Iran and assist with naval programs that Iran can use to create instability and disrupt the military status quo in maritime areas of the Middle East.[75]

Another excellent example of conventional weapons acquisition by Iran from North Korea that continues today came to light during March 2016. A fishing vessel believed to be of Iranian origin was intercepted by the Australian navy ship the HMAS *Darwin* off the coast of Oman. Once the ship was boarded, thousands of small arms, including rifles, mortars, and RPGs, were found hidden under fishing nets. But of particular interest were the North Korean Type-73 light machine guns confiscated. These guns are of a design that is uniquely North Korean. The weapons confiscated matched the weapon types used by the Houthi rebels in Yemen. This was one of several probable shipments from Iran to rebels in Yemen that were interdicted during a months-long time period in the area. Thus, we see a pattern here. North Korea sold weapons (light machine guns) to Iran, which turned around and proliferated them to nonstate actors (the Houthi rebels) in Yemen.[76] Iran probably uses the same weapons for its own conventional forces.

But North Korean weapons in the hands of the Houthi rebels do not end with small arms. The Houthis have now fired several Scud ballistic missiles at Saudi targets. The North Koreans proliferated Scud missiles to Yemen during the 1990s and in 2002 (and reportedly assisted them with the operation of the missiles). When the Houthis were able to capture many important military nodes and arms caches during the civil war in that nation, they were probably also able to capture some of the Scud missiles purchased from North Korea by the previous government in power. Thus, it is likely that the Scuds launched at Saudi Arabia (which had conducted air strikes against Houthi targets) had their genesis in North Korea and, thus, have now been used in Yemen's violent civil war—and against American allies such as Saudi Arabia. It is also likely that Iran, which is widely known to be providing large-scale assistance to the Houthis, is now assisting them with the operation of their missiles, missiles of the type that Iran also acquired from Pyongyang and that are now also manufactured in Iran (with North Korean assistance and probably spare parts as well).[77] We have seen additional evidence of this from the US State Department, which in a public statement issued on March 24, 2017, indicated: "We have seen indications Iran is providing missile support to the Houthis in Yemen."[78]

During the fall of 2017, the Houthis fired missiles with longer ranges than previously seen. Many analysts at the time assessed the missiles to be variants or advanced-capability Scud Cs (though the ranges some, including press sources, have determined the ballistic missiles to have match those of the No Dong system). The Houthis called the system the Burqan-2. The Houthi missile attack on Saudi Arabia in 2017 hit close to Riyadh. Lieutenant General Jeffrey L. Harrington of Central Command in Qatar stated that there were Iranian markings on the missiles. The United States afterward opened the way for the Saudis to buy more BMD systems capable of shooting down Houthi ballistic missiles. Thus, the fall 2017 spate of attacks during used missiles originally proliferated from North Korea to Iran, improved in Iran (likely with North Korean assistance), and then proliferated to the Houthis.[79]

While land systems constitute much of North Korea's conventional weapons proliferation to Iran, there have also been significant sales of naval craft and naval weapons systems. One compelling example actually came front and center in 2014. The North Koreans successfully test-launched a North Korean version of the Russian KH-35, an antiship missile capable of threatening many of South Korea's ships.[80] What makes this successful test launch so interesting when it comes to Iran is the naval craft from which the missile was launched. If one is to analyze publicly released pictures of the ship that launched the missile, it becomes obvious that this craft is a catamaran-hulled missile patrol craft (PTGF). What makes this ship a threat is that its hull contains stealth technology that gives it a reduced signature to enemy radar.[81] This craft, which is estimated to be 38.5 meters long and 13 meters wide, is similar to ships that North Korea has sold to Iran initially known as the Peykaap design and some variants with the same (or improved) capabilities.[82]

North Korean Proliferation to Terrorist Groups: Using Iran as a Conduit

North Korea proliferates military systems, advisers, trainers, and assistance to several states in the Middle East. But perhaps the most disturbing proliferation that North Korea conducts using Iran as a conduit deals with two very unpleasant entities in the region—Hezbollah and Hamas. In fact, former secretary of defense Robert M. Gates stated in 2010: "The fact is that North Korea continues to smuggle missiles and weapons to other countries around the world—Burma, Iran, Hezbollah, Hamas—and they continue with their development of their nuclear program."[83] Both these nonstate actors have proved numerous times that they practice acts of terror as a matter of policy. It will be the purpose of this section to address how North Korea deals with these two nonstate actors through Pyongyang's main customer, Iran.

North Korea has been dealing with Hezbollah since at least the 1980s. It was then that several key members of Hezbollah's combat leadership traveled to North Korea to receive several months' special training—at Iran's request.[84] But there is far more to North Korean support to Hezbollah through the Iranians (Iranian support comes largely from the IRGC). Moon Chung-in, a well-known and respected professor at Yonsei University in Korea, remarked publicly on Mossad's evidence that Hezbollah had the capability to target Tel Aviv with what he called short-range missiles (in reality probably rockets). The rockets were equipped with components that originated in North Korea. Moon asserted that the North Korean missile components were first shipped to Iran. Iranian personnel actually assembled the weapons, which were then moved to Syria and then on to Hezbollah.[85]

One of the more compelling developments of North Korean assistance to Hezbollah through Iran is the now well-documented construction of sophisticated Hezbollah underground facilities in Lebanon. Several reports provide evidence that these underground facilities were constructed under North Korean supervision and advising in 2003–2004. These facilities included sophisticated entities such as dispensaries, arms dumps, and food stocks.[86] They were far more extensive and well built than Israeli forces anticipated as they fought their war with Hezbollah in 2006. According to an article in the Israeli press: "Hizbullah's military bases, armories, bunkers and communications networks were much more extensive than Israel's intelligence services estimated on the eve of the 2006 war."[87] North Korean underground construction experts reportedly were able to get into Lebanon "disguised as servants for the Iranian embassy and its officers."[88] Following the 2006 war with Israel, North Korea continued to assist Hezbollah working through the IRGC. In 2007, reportedly under cover a trip arranged by officials in Iran, Hezbollah sent approximately one hundred so-called field commanders to attend special forces courses in North Korea whose curricula included such things as intelligence and counterespionage operations and commando tactics, curricula taught by Pyongyang's elite special operations forces.[89] North Korea continues to supply arms to Hezbollah—through Iran—as of the writing of this chapter.[90]

Hamas has been an entity that received arms from North Korea (going first through Iran originally but now reportedly directly) for a number of years. It is important to note that most shipments get through (much like drug shipments), so any that are uncovered and foiled are almost certainly nothing more than the tip of the iceberg.[91] Perhaps the most remarkable (known) deal between North Korea and Hamas (perhaps brokered through Iran) was uncovered in 2014. The deal gave Hamas communications gear and rockets and is said to have earned the North Koreans several hundred thousand dollars.[92]

North Korea is infamous for its expertise in building underground facilities for a variety of entities, but in the Middle East the most well-known recipients of this expertise have been Hezbollah and Iran (for Tehran's nuclear facilities).[93] Thus, it should come as no surprise that numerous reports have now surfaced alleging that North Korea provided either assistance or training—or both—for what has now proved to be a sophisticated Hamas tunnel network. The soil in the Gaza is much softer than the often-rock-hard soil in southern Lebanon. Nevertheless, the IDF displayed one underground network that was 1.5 miles in length, 66 feet below the surface, and featured 350 tons of concrete in its construction. This level of sophistication in underground facilities is puzzling unless one is to examine and analyze North Korea's underground construction abilities, already shared with the ally Hamas shares with Iran, Hezbollah. North Korea has—according to several reports—proliferated an underground construction capability to Hamas that it would be unable to use without assistance and training from Pyongyang.[94] In fact, the scholars Victor Cha and Gabriel Scheinmann stated in 2014: "Hamas' vast tunnel network almost certainly benefited from outside assistance, whether directly from North Korea or via Iran. Any true solution to the terrorist threat in Gaza must not only involve the full disarmament of terrorist groups, but also sever their links to foreign sponsorship."[95] To quote the IDF: "Hamas uses these tunnels as weapons caches, bunkers, command centers and a concealed transportation artery for terrorists and weapons."[96]

In 2016 and 2017, several reports revealed more North Korean proliferation to Hamas and Hamas military splinter elements. The Izz ad-Din al-Qassam Brigades are reportedly now equipped with North Korean shoulder-launched antiaircraft missiles and North Korean antitank missiles. Reportedly, the antiaircraft missiles were purchased through black market channels, then moved from ports in Somalia and Sudan and brought into Gaza after being transported over land through Egypt. The antitank weapons are said to be old Soviet 1960s technology, laser guided and capable of attacking NATO quality tanks. According to several reports, the antitank weapons have already been successful in taking out at least one Israeli tank. Hamas allegedly has acquired fifteen hundred of these antitank systems from North Korea.[97]

An understanding of the Iranian threat to security and stability in the Middle East must first be tied to North Korea. Pyongyang's weapons sales to Iran began in earnest well before the Cold War ended (the early to mid-1980s) and if anything, only picked up steam after. Those in both the policy and the defense communities should take note. Because proliferation from North Korea to the Middle East is certainly no pinprick, it is certainly much more than merely an irritant.

North Korea's proliferation to the Middle East (not just Iran) can be described as a legitimate threat to the security of the Middle East and the stability of the governments that exist in the region and a destabilizing factor because of the influence of the nonstate actors that play a role in violent conflicts in both Israel and Syria. As the distinguished retired Congressional Research Service scholar Larry Niksch said in congressional testimony in

July 2015: "The reports of the different facets of Iranian–North Korean collaboration sometimes contain estimates from the non-U.S. intelligence and government sources that Iran has paid North Korea huge sums of money for cooperative projects related to missiles, nuclear warheads, and Pyongyang's assistance to Hezbollah and Hamas." Niksch further clarifies: "It seems to me that North Korea may receive from Iran upwards of $2 to $3 billion annually from Iran [*sic*] for the various forms of collaboration between them."[98] Thus, since using violent measures to stop the proliferation flow between North Korea and the Middle East does not seem to be a policy option, a key alternative would be for the international community to clamp down on North Korean and Iranian illicit and illegal arms-related bank transactions, front companies, and individuals. Doing so may eventually stop (or contain) these two rogue states' regionally disruptive behavior.

5

North Korea and Syria

A Long and Ongoing History
of Military Trade

The Middle East has been a hotbed of violence and instability since the Arab Spring burst onto the scene. Some countries (such as Libya and Yemen) have now essentially become failed states, while others (such as Egypt) continue to be unstable. There are other nations mired in civil war. The nation-state that often comes to mind first is Syria. While Syria continues to be bogged down in a civil war as of the writing of this chapter, the international community has often posed the question of who is supplying the Assad regime with the weapons and support that are needed in order to fight the various groups who would seek to change the government in Damascus. While many have pointed to Russia and Iran (among others), there has been little reporting about the support and proliferation to the Assad regime in Syria that is generated by North Korea.[1] In fact, North Korea has been a constant source of both training and weapons for the Syrian military for many years, and this has increased in focus and tempo since the Syrian civil war began.

It will be the purpose of this chapter to address the long-standing relationship between the Assad regime (beginning with the older Assad) and the Kim family regime. This will be important because this relationship has been dependent on Syria's needs combined with North Korea's need to generate cash and resources. Throughout this relationship, there have been outside nations that have helped enable it and provide support for an authoritarian government in Damascus that has long been noted for human rights abuses. The relationship began during the Cold War and has continued, following the demise of the Soviet Union, with enabling actions from Iran (including cash), among others. Thus, I will examine the history of the North Korea–

Syria military proliferation relationship and the impact it has had on current events.

Certainly, one of the key concerns for policy makers and anyone interested in international geopolitics has been Syria's weapons of mass destruction (WMD). There has been a long-standing relationship between Pyongyang and Syria (North Korea being mostly the seller and Syria being mostly the buyer) for a variety of WMD programs. Whether it is the aid in construction of a nuclear reactor that North Korea provided to Syria, the chemical weapons programs that the North Koreans have proliferated to Syria, or the Scud missiles that the Syrians now have in their large arsenal thanks to Pyongyang, these issues should be of key concern to policy makers. An analysis of the WMD programs that Syria has thanks to North Korean assistance will be a key section of this chapter.

While WMD are of key concern to anyone with an interest in the Middle East or Northeast Asia, conventional weapons are also of key concern, particularly when Syria is mired down in a civil war. This will be an issue that I will cover. What weapons are going in, and how are they being used? Few have asked these questions, which I will answer in this chapter.

North Korea is (as we shall see) not the only state or nonstate actor providing weapons and/or support to the Syrian armed forces. A key player in this has been Hezbollah. Hezbollah fighters have played a key role in supporting Assad's military.[2] North Korea has been proliferating to Hezbollah for years, but, in this chapter, I will address how this has been stepped up owing to the Syrian civil war and what types of weapons and training North Korea has provided to this well-known terrorist group as it relates to Syria. Tied into this is the exact role that North Korea is playing in supporting the Syrian government and military in its quest to hold on to power and quash the various rebel groups attempting to overthrow it (including ISIS). This will be another key factor that I will address, and it will bring us up to the present regarding the ongoing concerns for stability and security in both the Middle East and Northeast Asia.

A Historical Look Back at the
North Korea–Syria Military Relationship

The military relationship between Pyongyang and Damascus goes back many years. Originally subsidized by the Soviet Union, it was a relationship that involved military personnel filling vital combat roles, training key units for war and operations other than direct war (such as reconnaissance), and the proliferation of both conventional weapons systems and WMD. Now that the Cold War is over, the Soviet Union no longer subsidizes this relationship (even though Russia continues to play a key role). But Syria now has a need for military assistance and support, perhaps more than it ever has in its history. Thus, the proliferation and military assistance provided by North Korea to Syria continues, with external assistance from others.

Pyongyang officially established diplomatic relations with Syria in 1966.[3] North Korea's military assistance to Syria goes back at least as far as 1967, when North Korean pilots assisted the Syrian air force during the Arab-Israeli War.[4] It continued for many years after that (and continues today). According to the Korean specialist Alexandre Mansourov: "In 1970, the DPRK dispatched 200 tank crewmen, 53 pilots, and 140 missile technicians to Syria. During the October 1973 Arab-Israeli War, the DPRK dispatched 30 pilots to Egypt and Syria, who provided training for Syrian pilots to fight against Israel. Moreover, the North Korean Air Force pilots themselves flew the Soviet-made Egyptian and Syrian airplanes during some key air battles. In 1975 and 1976, Pyongyang sent 75 Air Force instructors and 40 MIG pilots to Damascus, respectively. In 1982, during the Lebanese civil war, the DPRK government dispatched SOF (special operations forces) servicemen to Syria to provide training for guerrilla operations, some killed by the Israeli military. In 1984–1986 and 1990, 50 and 30 North Korean military instructors were sent to Syria, respectively."[5] In addition, starting in the early 1970s and continuing into the Syrian civil war, North Korea supplied Syria with conventional weapons such as tanks, rifles, artillery, multiple rocket launchers (MRL), antitank weapons, etc. During the 1982 Lebanon War, the Syrian army successfully and efficiently used 122-millimeter BM-11 systems sold to it by the North Koreans to target civilians. Reportedly, around twenty-five North Korean soldiers were killed during this conflict when the Israelis destroyed one of the MRL systems.[6] In later years, 122-millimeter MRLs would become very important for Syria and North Korea, as I will describe later.

There are other key historical factors that have (for many years) been important in the North Korea–Syria arms trade. In 2004, several Syrian technicians were killed on a train (in an apparent attempt to kill Kim Jong-il, who was not on the train). The explosion was created by a cell phone–enacted explosive device and killed dozens of people. The Syrians were employed by the Syrian Scientific Studies and Research Center (SSRC), the agency in charge of many of Syria's covert WMD-related programs. The Syrians killed were accompanying updated missile components and other materials (perhaps chemical weapons related) that were headed to the North Korean port of Nampo for trans-shipment to Syria.[7] North Korea is well known for having a large supply of such chemical materials as sarin gas, chlorine, and VX.[8] This was at a time when North Korea was developing both chemical and ballistic missile programs for Syria, programs that would largely be assembled in Syria but with parts and assistance from North Korea (and programs that are now fully developed). North Korea has long had an association with the SSRC, one going back probably to the early 1970s.[9]

Personal relationships have also been very important throughout the North Korea–Syria military relationship. Perhaps one of the most, if not the most, important personal relationships between a high-ranking North Korean military officer and counterparts in Syria is that of Kim Kyok-sik. Kim was a close personal confidant of Kim Jong-il's—and a family friend. In addition, he was widely believed to be one of the most trusted advisers of Kim Jong-un. The key here is that Kim Kyok-sik was a key player in the North Korea–Syria military arms/training relationship from 1971 until 2015. It was in 1971 that he began serving as the deputy military attaché in the North Korean embassy in Damascus. An artillery officer and an Arabic speaker, Kim was very useful when it came to setting up programs in Syria. He reportedly managed several key aspects of North Korea's military relationship with Syria. The projects he managed included helping rehabilitate the Syrian armed forces in the 1970s, coordinating shipments of MRL systems, including the now infamous 122-millimeter MRL systems (122 MRLs were used to attack Syrian citizens with chemical munitions during the Syrian civil war), and (in an important development that I will address in detail later) providing training and military support to nonstate actors (Hezbollah among them). Kim Kyok-sik last visited Syria in 2013, when he remained a key player in North Korea's dealings with Damascus.[10] He passed away, reportedly of respiratory failure, in May 2015.[11]

Of note, while the Soviet Union financed much of Syria's budget (not to mention North Korea's) during the Cold War, it appears that, since the end of the Cold War, much (if not most) of the cash that Syria uses to purchase weapons and advising comes from Iran.[12] Iran was not the only nation to fill the void left by the demise of the Soviet Union. Saudi Arabia rewarded Syria for its participation in the Gulf War against Iraq with several billion dollars, a mighty stipend that the Syrians used largely to purchase Scud-Cs and production equipment from the North Koreans.[13]

Syria and North Korea have also had a very important diplomatic relationship. Kim Il-sung and Hafez al-Assad had an important relationship that was mutually beneficial to both during the height of the Cold War.[14] The relationship continued as Kim Jong-il and Bashar al-Assad maintained good personal relations—and a robust proliferation and arms trade relationship.[15] The strong relationship has continued in the Kim Jong-un era. As mentioned earlier, Kim Kyok-sik continued to play a role in maintaining good relations between North Korea and Syria, particularly when it came to military affairs. During 2013, a Syrian diplomatic delegation officially visited North Korea (Syrians frequently visit North Korea because of arms deals, but these are events that get little to no publicity).[16] The delegation once again affirmed the strong relationship between the two countries—officially.[17] Meanwhile, in 2014, North Korea's foreign minister, Ri Su-yong (also known as Ri Chol), met with Syrian president Assad. They also reaffirmed that the relationship would remain strong and that the two countries would continue to stand against the West and make strong efforts to rebuild the Syrian landmass, war torn by the ravages of civil war.[18] Of one thing we can be sure: the long, mutually beneficial relationship between North Korea and Syria shows no signs of ending—or slowing down—anytime soon.

Nukes, Chemical Weapons, and Missiles: DPRK WMD Proliferation to Syria

There has been much made of Syria's chemical weapons capabilities that have been used during the ongoing civil war. The capabilities that Syria has are important, but they could not have come without a great deal of external support. Whether it is the nuclear weaponization capability that Israeli forces destroyed in 2007, the chemical weapons capabilities that may or may not have been largely destroyed by UN forces,[19] or the variety of ballistic missiles that Syria continues to use against rebel forces (many of these missiles can and have been equipped with chemical warheads, according to numerous reports), Syria has shown the world that its government will not hesitate to add whatever form of WMD to its military inventory that it can. High on the list of those nation-states who are supplying Syria with these capabilities is North Korea.

North Korea has—as the definitive evidence now shows—been cooperating on nuclear weaponization with Syria since the 1990s. In fact, the former director of the CIA, Michael Hayden, made some very important remarks about nuclear cooperation between North Korea and Syria to the World Affairs Council of Los Angeles in 2008. In referring to a plutonium reactor built by the North Koreans for the Syrians and destroyed by the Israeli air force in 2007, he said: "The depth of that relationship was revealed in the spring of last year." He went on to give more detailed evidence when he described the Syrian nuclear reactor as "similar to Yongbyon in North Korea, but with its outer structure heavily disguised." Finally (as noted earlier), he confirmed that the evidence regarding Syria's nuclear weaponization program and North Korean involvement was both diverse and clear cut: "Virtually every form of intelligence—imagery, signals, human source, you name it—informed their assessments, so that they were never completely dependent on any single channel."[20]

But there is far more compelling evidence that tells us the story of the proliferation of the North Korean plutonium nuclear weaponization program to Syria. According to a briefing given to the press by the Office of the Director of National Intelligence, sources began to reveal a nuclear weaponization relationship between North Korea and Syria going all the way back to 1997. But, during 2006, a facility in Syria that was under construction was identified. The next year, 2007, intelligence was collected showing key aspects of the interior and exterior of the facility, revealing that it was a plutonium nuclear reactor. Of note, the facility actually closely resembled that at Yongbyon in North Korea! Photographs inside the facility showed a gas-cooled, graphite-moderated reactor with a configuration very similar to the Yongbyon reactor.[21]

Some of the evidence revealed to the press during 2008 was almost comical. For example, a tin roof and thin curtain walls were added to the Syrian facility after construction was complete in an attempt to change the building's outline, which closely resembled that of the DPRK plutonium nuclear facility at Yongbyon. North Korean high-ranking officials made numerous visits to the facility once work on it began in 2001. Among these high-ranking officials was Chon Chi-bu, one of the key scientists in North Korea's nuclear weaponization program. In summary, as one of the intelligence officials stated at the press briefing: "Our information shows that Syria was building a gas-cooled, graphite-moderated reactor that was nearing operational capability in August 2007. The reactor would have been capable of producing plutonium for nuclear weapons. It was not configured to produce electricity and was ill-suited for research." The official finalized this statement by saying: "Only North Korea has built this type of reactor in the past 35 years."[22]

What likely spawned the attack on the Syrian plutonium facility was the port call of a North Korean ship at Tartus. Tartus has reportedly been the port of entry for missile components and other WMD-associated materials that are then transferred overground to Iran. Later reports revealed that the cargo of the ship was forty-five tons of yellow cake. The ship had originally departed Nampo, North Korea, and stopped at two different ports in China on its way to Syria. It arrived in Syria in September 2007. The yellow cake (as noted earlier) appears to have eventually ended up in Iran (instead of the Syrian facility).[23]

As discussed earlier in this chapter, Iran has financed many of the weapons programs used by the Syrian military and certainly a huge part of the WMD under development or fielded in Syria. Apparently, that was also the case with the plutonium nuclear reactor destroyed by the Israeli air force in 2007. It bears repeating that, according to the Iranian defector Ali Reza Asghari, the Iranians financed much (if not all) of the building of the Syrian nuclear reactor. Ali Reza Asghari is a former general in the Iranian RGC. He is also the former Iranian deputy defense minister. Iran reportedly spent $1–$2 billion to finance the Syrian nuclear project, perhaps hoping to keep a plutonium program for Tehran offshore.[24]

While the destruction of the plutonium nuclear reactor in Syria by the Israeli air force was quite a disturbing development, something much more disturbing that has been ongoing for many years is the support that the DPRK provides to Syria's chemical weapons program. The North Koreans have proliferated chemical weapons programs to Syria and have also brought Syrians to North Korea for training and weapons transfers.[25] On July 27, 2007, several Iranian advisers, Syrian technicians, and probably North Korean advisers were reportedly killed when they were loading a chemical warhead containing VX and sarin onto a SCUD missile for a test launch. The missile and the warhead were manufactured either in North Korea or in Syria with North Korean assistance.[26] In 2009, a Syrian Scud D veered off course during a test launch. It landed in the middle of a village and ended up killing at least twenty people and wounding sixty more. The missile may or may not have had a chemical warhead. Reportedly participating in the test launch gone wrong were both North Korean engineers and members of the Iranian Revolutionary Guard.[27]

The North Koreans have reportedly been providing support and training for the Syrian chemical weapons program since at least the 1990s. Pyongyang is currently helping Syria produce the precursors and is also providing chemical weapons parts to Syria. In addition, as mentioned earlier, North Korea has sold 122-millimeter MRL systems to Syria and is well known for assisting Damascus with its ballistic missile programs (as I will describe below). The chemical weapons used by the Syrians have reportedly been launched using ballistic missiles or 122-millimeter MRL systems (these appear to be the two key platforms). Thus, North Korea has been assisting—and continues to assist—Syria with both the chemical weapons and the platforms that are used to launch them.[28]

If one is to examine just how close the North Korea–Syria chemical weapons relationship is, there are many disturbing details that can be discussed. During 2013, an Israeli attack on a Syrian convoy of antiaircraft weapons also damaged Syria's key development center for WMD—the SSRC. This is a center that the North Koreans have been present at and served an active role in for many years, including during the Syrian civil war.[29] In fact, in an important report issued by a UN panel, an assessment was made that North Korea had in fact stepped up chemical weapons shipments and assistance to Syria, in no small part through the SSRC.[30]

North Korea is now, and has throughout its chemical weapons assistance program to Syria been, routinely providing after sales services. In other words, chemical weapons assistance from cradle to grave.[31] Indeed, as noted, the North Korean military capabilities analyst Joseph Bermudez has stated: "With regards to DPRK-Syria chemical weapons–related activity, reports originating in the Middle East indicate that there was an acceleration of such efforts beginning in early 2007. These reports identify the city of Aleppo as the center of this activity."[32] At the SSRC, North Koreans have, as previously mentioned, lived a life of luxury in an exclusive compound that has manicured lawns and a swimming pool. Compensation for North Korea's assistance to Syria's chemical weapons program reportedly comes from both Syria and Iran, and Syria also barters agricultural goods and computers (barter is common in North Korea's compensation for proliferation). According to reports from 2013, North Korea, Syria, and Iran have collaborated in the "planning, establishment, and management" of at least five Syrian chemical weapons facilities that are manufacturing precursors of chemical weapons.[33]

The chemical weapons program has been a subject of debate and horror worldwide as the world watched Assad gas his own people. But very important to not only the chemical weapons program but also Syria's battlefield readiness and capabilities overall is the robust ballistic missile program in this troubled nation's arsenal. One of the key supporters when it comes missiles and missile components, training of personnel, refurbishment and resupply of missiles, and matching missiles with chemical warheads is North Korea. The North Koreans working on ballistic missiles at the SSRC are working under the cover of the Tangun General Corporation (and other front companies) and are also often working with those who are chemical weapons specialists. North Koreans have provided support and supply beginning with Scud B missiles in the late 1980s.[34] But there is more to the WMD picture—the platforms that carry them (ballistic missiles being key).[35]

As the Cold War was winding down, the tight relationship Damascus had with Moscow began to wane. Thus, Syria began looking to other nations as options for acquiring its ballistic missiles. The North Korean official Yi Chong-ok traveled to Syria during 1990 in an effort to set up a new missile deal between Pyongyang and Damascus. By late 1990, thanks to money that Saudi Arabia donated to Syria for its efforts in the alliance against Iraq in the Gulf War ($2 billion), Syria had the financing to make a big deal with North Korea. The first big deal the two countries made for missiles was the sale of 150 Scud C missiles to Syria for $500 million. North Korea also agreed to build two missile assembly facilities in Syria (thus reducing the amount of maritime shipping and/or aircraft deliveries that would have to be made). The two facilities were completed by at least 1994—and continue to produce Scuds as of the writing of this chapter. During 1992, Syria conducted its initial Scud C test launch. Many more test launches have followed over the years.[36]

The Scud C was apparently not enough to satisfy the Syrian appetite for ballistic missiles. Thus, during May 2000, North Korea shipped its first set of Scud D systems to Syria. This was immediately followed up by a test launch of the Scud D during September 2000.[37] In 2005, a test-launched Scud D missile went off course and landed inside the Turkish border. After American intelligence specialists and missile experts examined the remaining fragments, it was determined that the missile contained components not seen in earlier models. In other words, it was an improved Scud D. This improved model was assessed by the experts who examined it to have a range of seven hundred kilometers and a separating warhead that was proved to have chemical warfare capability.[38]

If one is to fast-forward closer to the present time, in 2013 North Korea began a large-scale project to refurbish and resupply Syria with ballistic missiles, the obvious reason being that the many ballistic missiles used during the civil war meant that Syria needed more missiles. North Korea is also working with Syria to (once again) improve the capabilities of the Scud D missile.[39] Syria has reportedly stepped up missile production for two important reasons: (1) the ballistic missiles are an important component of the fight against rebel forces, and (2) Hezbollah has indicated a need to acquire missiles and rockets.[40] Indeed, continued North Korean support to Syria's ballistic missile program is quite compelling. According to *Jane's Defence Weekly*, Syria is most dependent on Iran and North Korea for the success of its ballistic missile program (and Iran acquires many of its missiles from North Korea). According to that respected British publication: "The SSRC is also returning to a deferred co-operative missile development programme with North Korea to upgrade Syrian 'Scud D' variant SSMs with a manoeuvring re-entry vehicle (MaRV) capability (essentially bringing them closer in capability to the original Russian 'Scud D' standard)." This is "in disregard of UN sanctions—Resolutions 1718 (2006) and 1874 (2009)." The *Jane's* report goes on to state in part: "This variant is designated 'Scud MD' (Manoeuvring D). The upgrade, which incorporates a bespoke canard system, will enable the MaRV of the 'Scud' to alter its original planned trajectory when it re-enters the atmosphere, significantly improving its accuracy and increasing warhead survivability by making its flight path problematical to assess for missile-defence interceptors."[41]

Conventional Weapons Proliferation to Syria: A Vital Aspect of Assad's Survival

North Korea's assistance to Syria when it comes to chemical weapons and ballistic missiles is quite troubling to say the least. But the Syrian army is also fighting its civil war using a variety of conventional weapons. In addition, the conventional weapons tie in to WMD when it comes to combat situations. For example, the 122-millimeter system is that has been supplied by North Korea to the Syrians for many years. But it is also the system that the UN inspectors have now proved to be one of the key platforms that the Syrian army uses for launching chemical weapons attacks on the rebels.[42] The North Koreans have been there all the way—before the civil war and no doubt after it is over (if Assad survives). Thus, it will be important to consider the various weapons systems that North Korea has provided to Syria over the years and especially leading up to (and during) the ongoing civil war.

When it comes to conventional weapons that North Korea has supplied to Syria, the list is actually quite staggering. Since the beginning of their relationship in the late 1960s, North Korea has supplied the Syrian military with rifles, artillery, mortars, machine guns, ammunition, bombs, armored vehicles, antitank weapons, and multiple rocket launchers, to name just a few.[43] But these are not the only weapons systems that the North Koreans have provided to Syria. North Korea upgraded several hundred T54/55 tanks for the Syrians during the 1980s. While these tanks are not considered top-of-the-line armor, they are relatively simple to operate and effective in combat. As Syria began to lose much of its armor in the war with the rebels, these older tanks have been recalled to duty. Confirmation that the North Korean variant of the T54/55 has been used on a large scale in combat occurred during 2014. The North Koreans are likely also assisting the Syrians in the maintenance and operations of these older tanks.[44] In addition, photos taken during 2014 revealed that Syrian rebels had captured—and were using—a North Korean variant of the Igla-1E man-portable air-defense system (MANPAD). The features of the system show that it can be nothing except a North Korean weapon, which means it was proliferated to the Syrians and then captured by rebels.[45] Even as the civil war in Syria was raging into massive casualties on both sides, North Korea continued to supply "vehicle parts, munitions component parts, and ordnance" to Syria in shipments rushed to the troubled nation.[46] It continues to ship as many conventional weapons to Syria as it can as fast as it can get them there.[47]

North Korea's Role in the Syrian Civil War

While, as described earlier, it is a well-documented fact that the North Koreans and the Syrians have established a mutually beneficial relationship that goes all the way back to Hafez al-Assad and Kim Il-sung, North Korea's role in providing arms, training, support, and even WMD to Syria has, in terms of international geopolitics, been played down by most governments. The reasons for this remain unclear. In fact, North Korea's support for the current Assad regime gets almost no notice, even in congressional testimony. While this remains an unfortunate aspect of American priorities, it is also something that needs to be fixed. North Korea has become a key aspect of the support that the current Assad regime needs in order to survive and fight on against the rebels. The DPRK is also benefiting a great deal from the civil war in Syria. If a nation is fighting a war, it must use artillery, tanks, ballistic missiles, small arms of all kinds, ammunition, and yes (in the case of the Assad regime), WMD. As (and if) the war continues, these expensive and vital items must be replaced and/or refurbished. Thus, Syria has gone from being one of North Korea's most important customers for many years to being almost on par with Iran as an important customer.[48] In this section, I will address how all the North Korean support and proliferation to Syria over the years has now reached an apex as the Syrian civil war rages on.

On July 24, 2013, Kim Jong-un met with a Syrian government delegation. At the meeting, he reportedly addressed how North Korea could increase support to Syria in its ongoing civil war (of course for a price). In fact, during 2013, the North Koreans did in fact step up the number of advisers assisting Syria's national defense. At facilities near Aleppo, North Koreans have played an important role in aiding the Syrians with engineering and construction, providing badly needed aid in repairing destroyed military infrastructure. North Korea has also assisted with operational planning and played a role (even on the front lines) in advising Syrian combat artillery warfare.[49] The nongovernment dissident group Syrian Observatory for Human Rights asserts that, in 2013, there were eleven to fifteen North Korean advisers serving in a several places but largely in and around Aleppo. At least some of these advisers were reported to actually be serving with combat units on or near the front lines.[50] Lebanese press sources claim that there are "confirmed reports that officers from North Korea are present with regular forces, and aiding them with logistics and operational plans in Aleppo."[51] The interesting facts regarding the wide variety of support functions that the North Koreans are serving in Syria continue with the reporting that North Korean military personnel are working with Iranian personnel (probably members of the IRGC), running an operations room for the Syrian military. The North Koreans and the Iranians were reportedly collaborating on plans to increase the effectiveness of Syria's air-defense systems and to upgrade Syria's missile effectiveness.[52] At the time—and now—Syria was using a large number of ballistic missiles in its attacks on rebels, particularly Scuds.

In another move reminiscent of the Cold War, North Korean pilots are, according to several reports, flying combat sorties for the Syrian air force. According to several reports, there are up to fifteen North Korean pilots flying in combat with the Syrians. It is unclear what type of rotary aircraft the North Korean pilots have been flying, but it appears that the helicopters are either Mi-2s or Mi-8s. This highlights the wide variety of missions and tasks that the North Koreans have taken on in support of the Syrian military since there is already evidence that North Koreans are playing key roles in supporting both artillery and Scud missile units during the ongoing Syrian civil war.[53] It appears that the reasons behind the augmentation of helicopter units by North Korean pilots is a shortage of trustworthy pilots (or pilots who are loyal to the Assad regime) in the Syrian air force.[54] Whether it is that or simply a shortage of trained pilots, North Korea's augmentation of air units with its own pilots is yet another disturbing aspect of its support to Syria in the ongoing civil war.

The North Koreans continue to benefit from both their missile and their chemical weapons assistance to Syria. They are reportedly assisting the Syrian military and its scientists and engineers with integrating chemical weapons and precursors into actual warheads for Scud missiles. They have also played a major role in helping repair damaged missiles, a key capability in any war. The same familiar players appear to be coordinating the whole effort—the SSRC on the Syrian side and the Tangun General Corporation on the North Korean side. These sanctions-busting activities are important for North Korea, as is its continued assistance to the Syrians with upgrading their Scud D missiles.[55] As of 2016, there are still reports that North Korean troops are on the ground in Syria in support of President Assad and serving in combat units.[56] In addition, the variety of weapons that the North Koreans have proliferated to Syria continues to be compelling. For example, in 2016, a Syrian soldier was actually photographed with a North Korean Type-73 machine gun, a unique weapon manufactured only in North Korea (or in facilities built and run by North Korean advisers).[57]

The plethora of weapons that North Korea is moving into Syria is quite interesting. During 2017, a large North Korean shipment of weapons that included rocket-propelled grenades, heavy machine guns, and mortars went there. The shipment was paid for by Iran, the funds going directly to North Korean front companies operating in Malaysia. According to the source for this information (a reliable human source used in the past with connections in the Middle East and Southeast Asia), the money from this shipment and others went from Iran (in other words, Iran sponsored this shipment from North Korea to Syria), to the DPRK front companies in Malaysia, to investment in casinos in Macao, where the profits were then placed in several bank accounts operated by Kim Jong-un's proxies.[58]

In a UN report released on September 5, 2017, quoted by Reuters during August 2017 from an early copy it was able to obtain written by what the British news service referred to as "a panel of independent UN experts," one key articulation that was highly important stated: "The panel is investigating reported prohibited chemical, ballistic missile and conventional arms cooperation between Syria and the DPRK (North Korea)." Regarding the interception of two Syria-bound North Korean shipments in 2017, the UN report indicated: "The consignees were Syrian entities designated by the European Union and the United States as front companies for Syria's Scientific Studies and Research Centre (SSRC), a Syrian entity identified by the Panel as cooperating with KOMID in previous prohibited item transfers." UN experts are said to be investigating the North Korea–Syria cooperation on Scud missile repairs as well as air defense systems.[59] These two North Korean shipments bound for the SSRC were reported to have been intercepted in the six months prior to late August 2017. As of August 2017, the UNSC was investigating DPRK chemical weapons sales to Syria as well as ballistic missile and conventional weapons proliferation.[60]

The same UN Panel of Experts report was released publicly in September 2017 and confirmed that North Korean front companies, Syrian front companies, and the same entities we have seen operating in Syria for many years continue to be highly active as Syria's civil war rages on.[61] In 2017, we have thus now seen at least one shipment of conventional weapons going to Syria from North Korea and two interdicted shipments of what may be WMD-related materials to the SSRC (and this is likely just the tip of the iceberg). The evidence suggests that the cooperation between North Korea and Syria in support of the Assad regime's prosecution of combat operations during the brutal Syrian civil war continues in high gear.

In a report issued in early 2018, the UN Panel of Experts confirmed even more evidence that adds to the compelling conclusions one must reach regarding these two pariah states and the military proliferation relationship they have maintained throughout Syria's violent civil war. A member state reported that a DPRK technical delegation visited Syria in August 2016 and was involved in the transfer of thermometers and special resistance valves for use in Syria's chemical weapons. DPRK ballistic missile technicians also traveled to Syria in April and November 2016. North Korean missile and chemical technicians continue to operate at facilities in Barzeh, Adra, and Hama. North Korea has used a variety of front companies to enable these efforts. Using sealed diplomatic shipments, which are normally not inspected, and phony foreign front companies, the North Koreans have been able to largely get past the interdiction of prohibited shipments to Syria. In fact, using these methods and front companies, the UN Panel of Experts has identified thirty-nine shipments from North Korea to Syria between 2012 and 2017. Another member state informed the panel that a likely shipment from yet another front company included grenade launchers, 7.62-mm machine-guns, and six-barrel 30-mm autocannons. These shipments are—again—just the tip of the iceberg. While it appears that most or none of the aforementioned arms shipments were not interdicted, during the same time period at least two other member states reportedly interdicted one arms shipment each. One interdicted shipment included tiles that can be used in the construction of chemical facilities. Thus, in 2018, North Korea continued the seemingly endless supply of weapons, dual-use materials, advisors, technicians, and engineers to help Syria fight its civil war.[62]

North Korean Proliferation to Terrorists through Syria

North Korea has for many years been providing assistance to Hezbollah, and this has occurred in a variety of ways. Pyongyang has been known to use Iran as a conduit (Iran pays for much of Hezbollah's weapons and training), through Syria (it appears nearly as often as through Iran, but it also appears that Iran is footing much of the bill for shipment through Syria as well) and sometimes directly. The purpose of this section will be to touch on some of the key weapons systems and forms of assistance that North Korea provides to Hezbollah through Syrian operatives.

North Korean assistance to Hezbollah reportedly began during the 1980s (as discussed earlier) when several key Hezbollah operatives had an extended visit in North Korea for training. The operatives—now well known to those who follow Hezbollah and security issues in the Middle East—were Hassan Nasrallah, the secretary-general, the security and intelligence chief Ibrahim Akil, and Mustapha Badreddine, the head of counterespionage operations. As one can imagine, this relationship likely began because of North Korea's long-standing ties to Iran.[63] While Hezbollah is now known for a variety of weapons systems that it has used both in the Syrian civil war and against Israel, rockets have always been its major weapon of choice. And the North Koreans (often through Syria) have been a longtime provider of components and/or actual complete systems of Katyusha and Grad rockets.[64]

In another example of the North Korea–Iran–Syria nexus and how it applies to Hezbollah, the M600 series rockets, a weapons system jointly produced by North Korea and Iran, come equipped with up to a three-hundred-kilometer range. They are supplied to both Hezbollah and Syria and have likely been used in the civil war.[65] In a joint deal between North Korea and Syria, Damascus provides Hezbollah with the Kornet antitank missile. North

Korea mass-produces the weapons, which are now used by both the Syrian army and Hezbollah.[66] Ballistic missiles may be the most disturbing example of North Korea's weapons ending up in the hands of Hezbollah thanks to the Syrian government. As with many of the deals taking place in the region, this one appears to be financed by Iran.[67] As discussed earlier, North Korea built a missile assembly facility for the Syrians where the Scuds are fabricated with the help of DPRK advisers. The North Koreans reportedly continue to advise on and help with the building of these missiles, including Scud Ds.[68] Hezbollah has now taken delivery of two Scud D platforms with a range of seven hundred kilometers. According to press sources, the deliveries occurred during 2010.[69] There may have been more deliveries since then; North Korea—largely through Syria (and Iran)—has also supplied Hezbollah with small arms that are now likely being used by Hezbollah fighters in the Syrian civil war.[70] Finally, a portion of the chemical weapons configured in Syria and assembled in the form of ordnance for 122-millimeter MRLs and warheads for Scud missiles (with North Korean assistance) has now been removed from storage and transferred to Hezbollah units in the southern Beqaa valley, according to a Syrian army defector.[71]

North Korea's military capabilities—conventional, unconventional, and WMD—present a real threat to security and stability in Northeast Asia. But, as this chapter has shown, through proliferation the DPRK has also contributed to the instability of another very important global region—the Middle East. North Korea's proliferation may have an ideological element, but we are kidding ourselves if we think this is the main reason Pyongyang proliferates to rogue states like Syria and terrorist groups like Hezbollah.

In this chapter, I have addressed North Korean proliferation to only one state actor—Syria. The fact that there is so much military proliferation to Syria that it rates an entire chapter is compelling if one thinks about it, Syria being only one of several customers that North Korea has in the Middle East. The fact that this military proliferation rarely appears in the headlines—even though it has an important impact on conflicts and potential conflict in the Middle East—is troubling. As the noted Israeli scholar (specializing in Korean studies) Alon Levkowitz has stated: "Israel might be able to intercept some North Korean military shipments to Syria or Hezbollah, but it will not be able to halt the majority of Pyongyang's conventional and nuclear exports to the Middle East without the assistance of the US and its allies. That is why Israel should continue to work on convincing the US, Europe, and its

Asian allies that North Korea is a rogue state that threatens the stability not only of Northeast Asia, but of the Middle East through its conventional and nuclear power."[72] Two things are clear from the evidence regarding large-scale North Korean arms sales to Syria, as Jay Solomon stated in 2017: "The longstanding cooperation between the two regimes seems to have intensified during Syria's war, with troubling implications for future missile, chemical, and even nuclear proliferation in the Middle East." That is important, but perhaps even more compelling is what Solomon says about what North Korea is learning from Syria's civil war battlefields: "Meanwhile, many North Korea analysts believe Kim is gleaning lessons from Assad's battlefield tactics, including the use of chemical weapons."[73] Thus, unless and until actions are taken that effectively stop or even slow North Korea's proliferation to the Middle East (and other global regions), we are likely to continue to see this rogue state behavior continue—or, as we have seen in Syria during its civil war, increase. North Korea has used Syria as its testing ground for platforms that launch chemical weapons, using 122-millimeter MRLs and Scud missiles. Military planners should pay close attention because what we are seeing is an effective training and testing ground for future North Korean planning in a conflict with the South.

6

North Korean Proliferation on the African Continent

North Korea has been well known for proliferation and the sanctions that follow for a number of years now. It is a good thing that North Korea's proliferation is coming out of the shadows. But many of the countries that it proliferates to remain relatively unknown. This is true nowhere more so than the continent of Africa. Though North Korea has been proliferating to the continent since the 1970s, most Americans do not even realize that it is active there.[1] It will be the purpose of this chapter to analyze and explain the very unusual military proliferation relationship that Pyongyang has with several countries in Africa. In fact, North Korea's relationship with some of these nations has actually enabled instability and violence.[2]

One is inclined to wonder why North Korea would deal with so many nations in Africa and why they (some of them American allies) would want to deal with North Korea. The answer is actually quite easy. North Korea trades mostly to poor, often-isolated nations in Africa that may not be able to get weapons or training anywhere else or simply cannot afford to purchase them anywhere else.[3] African enforcement of UN trade sanctions is lax, and, thus, it is difficult for UN inspectors or anyone else to enforce these sanctions that so many nations in Africa are clearly violating.[4] Much of what North Korea is currently trading or had recently traded when it comes to military proliferation was originally a legacy of the Cold War (when North Korea was often acting as a proxy for the Soviet Union). At least some of the current relationships were built on this legacy after the Cold War ended.[5] This is lucky for North Korea since many of these African nations still use old, Soviet-era arms and equipment in their militaries.[6] Indeed, these many relationships in Africa—often almost completely unnoticed in the West—are also quite useful to North Korea. As we shall see, there are many countries in Africa that North Korea proliferates weapons, training, and the upgrading/maintenance of military equipment to. The remainder of this chapter will go country by country and describe exactly what North Korea has proliferated to each country in recent years. In many cases, this proliferation appears to be ongoing. To date, the majority of African nations that North Korea has military proliferation relationships with continue to lack transparency when it comes to UN sanctions compliance.[7]

North Korea and Proliferation to Egypt: Missiles Remain Important

Egypt is a country that has been a longtime ally of the United States—since the peace talks between Israel and Egypt ended successfully during the Carter administration. This is despite the fact that Egypt has been guilty of numerous human rights violations and, even as this manuscript is being written, is not ruled by a transparent, credibly elected democracy.[8] Despite these facts, the United States continues, as of 2017, to contribute roughly $1.3 billion a year (or more) in assistance (foreign aid) annually to the Arab state.[9] Thus, it comes as something of a surprise to many that Egypt has had a long and very useful relationship with North Korea, one that has lasted nearly forty years.

The proliferation relationship between Egypt and North Korea began in the late 1970s. It was then that at least two Scud B missiles were shipped to North Korea for reverse engineering from Egypt, which received, in return, assistance for its fledgling ballistic missile program. (The initial Scuds Egypt had were of course supplied by the Soviet Union.) This led to North Korea then making several shipments of Scuds to Egypt (for a price of course) during the late 1990s. It also led to North Korean proliferation of Scud C technology and missile parts to Egypt, with the goal being Egyptian production of the missile (with North Korean assistance). Moving forward from what proved to be an apparently profitable relationship for both Egypt and North Korea in the 1990s, during 2001 and 2002 Egypt reportedly was involved in testing components of the No Dong missile in a program designed to field the missile from Egyptian soil. In 2013, amid rumors that continued ballistic missile trade was ongoing between North Korea and Egypt, Pyongyang and Cairo signed a cultural cooperation agreement even as the Egyptian company Orascom continued to build and expand North Korea's cell phone network. If one is to fast-forward to 2016, rumors of continued North Korea–Egypt cooperation circulated throughout the counterproliferation world. There were numerous press reports alleging continued North Korean sales of Scud missile components to Egypt. In fact, many of these reports were confirmed when the UN National Security Council (UNSC) Panel of Experts stated in a February 2017 report: "The Panel continued its investigation into the shipment of Scud spare parts to Egypt by focusing on the shipper, Ryongsong Trading Co. Ltd (Ryongsong); the seller, Rungrado General Trading Corporation (Rungrado); and the consignee, MODA Authority International Optronic." The report continued: "The Panel identified the intermediary companies and individuals involved in the shipment and determined that the Democratic People's Republic of Korea was operating out of its Beijing embassy, using cash to remit payment for shipping."[10] Thus, it appears that North Korea continues to proliferate technology and missile parts to Egypt to support its ballistic missile program.

During August 2017, the United States delayed $96 million of aid scheduled to go to Egypt while denying $195 million in military funding. The State Department confirmed that this was at least partially due to human rights concerns. But, when members of the press inquired whether North Korea's proliferation relationship with Egypt had played a role in the action, a State Department official "would say only that issues of concern have been raised with Cairo" and "refused to provide details about the talks."[11] Of note, Egyptian officials appeared to be genuinely surprised that Washington, which had apparently been overlooking this proliferation for years, was finally taking an interest. According to press sources, General Hamdi Bakhit, a member of Egypt's Parliament, stated: "The North Korean–American issue is a conflict between the US and its allies against North Korea—not the whole world against North Korea." He continued: "China, for example, has a balanced relationship with both the US and North Korea. . . . America is just fishing for a mistake to pressure Egypt." Emad Gad, another member of the Egyptian Parliament, reportedly stated: "The question is, if this North Korean issue is so important for the US, why didn't they ever mention it with us before?"[12]

Perhaps even more compelling when it comes to North Korean proliferation to Egypt, it was confirmed in the American press that, during August 2017, a Cambodia-flagged ship with a North Korean crew was caught and boarded as it entered Egyptian waters with thirty thousand rocket-propelled grenades onboard. Notification of Egypt by the United States of the ship's arrival apparently forced the Egyptians to take action to interdict receipt of their own shipment! A UN investigation later revealed that the weapons shipment was from North Korea and bound for the Egyptian army. American officials speaking on condition of anonymity said that it was because of this shipment and others that foreign aid from the United States to Egypt had been delayed.[13] Thus, it appears that Washington is finally taking action against an ally who has long been using North Korea as its supplier for weapons that the United States would not provide. If this is true, it is the beginning of a good trend, one that must be maintained in order to put as much pressure as possible on North Korea's rogue proliferation program.

Egypt is just the first country in Africa that I will discuss and one of the few confirmed to be engaged in military weapons trade with North Korea that is not in sub-Saharan Africa. It has a formal and long-standing relationship with the United States, one that includes a great deal of foreign aid from Washington. As we shall see, It is not the only US ally in Africa that conducts trade in military weaponry with North Korea. In the case of Egypt, the reasons for the ongoing trade are likely because the United States will not sell it ballistic missiles and other arms its army still uses left over from the Pro-Soviet era in and North Korea will. There are of course varying reasons why other American allies engage in military proliferation activities with North Korea, and these will be considered as we move through this chapter.

North Korea and Proliferation to Namibia

Until recent years (and probably even now), Namibia has been off the radar of those who were looking at North Korean proliferation. But a light was shone on the African nation in 2016 when it was revealed that it was knee-deep in military activities with the DPRK. Namibia has been—and, the evidence suggests, still is—involved with two well-known (and sanctioned) North Korean companies that are already known to be involved in proliferation and military assistance activities all over the globe but particularly in the Middle East and Africa.

The UNSC Panel of Experts confirmed in 2017 that Namibia has been getting military support from two key North Korean companies, the Korea Mining Development Corporation (KOMID) and Mansudae Overseas Projects. To quote in part what the UNSC report from 2017 said: "In its continued investigation of the involvement of KOMID in Mansudae's construction of a munitions factory in Namibia, the Panel confirmed that KOMID had provided key components to the Oamites munitions factory and that Mansudae had used labourers from the Democratic People's Republic of Korea." The report also stated: "Satellite imagery also shows that construction at the military base at Oamites continued until at least 2014."[14] According to *Defense News:* "The Namibian government has confirmed that North Korea built an arms and ammunition factory in the African country and is in the process of executing other contracts for the construction of the country's first military academy, military barracks and a new headquarters for the Ministry of Defense."[15]

The revelation of these North Korean activities in Namibia is shocking. The North Koreans built a munitions and small arms factory for Namibia. They also constructed (and may still be constructing) facilities at two key military bases as well as military headquarters, a military school, and museums. Some analysts have assessed that a chemical plant was moved to the area of Oamites during the fall of 2012. Dozens of computer-operated lathes spotted by an eyewitness at the factory location indicate a munitions plant. The contracts—most of which appear to have begun around 2000—were significant and enabled the firepower and efficiency of the Namibian military. The scope of the projects the North Koreans built for the Namibian government has been assessed by some analysts to be worth hundreds of millions of dollars.[16]

During 2016, there was a great deal of flurry and publicity involving Namibia's military relationship with the two North Korean companies discussed above. KOMID is a company well known for engaging in projects that create instability and violence in key regions globally, including the Middle East and sub-Saharan Africa.[17] The sight of North Koreans actively involved in construction projects in the Namibian capital had become commonplace by 2016. But, under pressure from the international community, the Namibian government formally declared that it had severed its military ties with North Korea. During 2016, leaders from the African nation actually traveled to the United Nations and explained that the relationship was over. In an odd development, no sanctions violations were ever formally admitted.[18] One would thus assume that this meant an end to North Korean illicit support for military projects in Namibia. Perhaps not. During early January 2017, there were once again reports that the Mansudae Overseas Project Group was still active in military construction projects in or near the Namibian capital of Windhoek.[19] Thus, as in several African countries, in Namibia compliance with UN sanctions appears to be lip service only—perhaps simply more subtle in an effort to avoid issues with the United Nations yet still gaining the vital support for military activities that North Korea has provided so well for so many years. Clearly, this is a niche that North Korea developed quite well in Namibia. During late October 2017, the Namibian government denied that it was not complying with UN sanctions against North Korea. Of course, Hugh Griffiths of the UN Panel of Experts said in an interview at the time that the UN panel had "not received responses from Namibia to specific queries for more than a year."[20]

North Korea and the Sudan: Two Rogue Regimes in Arms Deals

Another country in Africa that North Korea has had an arms relationship with in recent years is the Sudan. The Sudan is well known for violating the human rights of its own people.[21] It is also well known for using horrific weapons attacks against those in what is now the South Sudan in a war that raged on for many years.[22] But, thanks to North Korea, the Sudan was able to increase the sophistication and capabilities of its offensive weapons, weapons that were used to attack rebel forces and civilians and could be used again for these types of purposes in the future.

According to the UN Panel of Experts, in a report issued during February 2017: "According to a Member State, the Democratic People's Republic of Korea supplied 100 122-mm precision guided rocket control sections and 80 air attack satellite guided missiles (AGP-250, for ground attack) to Sudan Master Technology Engineering Company in two contracts of 29 August 2013, worth €5,144,075 and signed by reported KOMID president Mr. Kang Myong Chol (alias Pak Han Se), using a reported KOMID front company, Chosun Keuncheon Technology Trade Company."[23] This deal is fascinating as we begin to see the pattern that has been noted in several instances in Africa. KOMID once again was knee-deep in the military deal and used yet another front company in what eventually proved to be a failed attempt to hide the identity of the originating North Korean source.

The UN Panel of Experts report becomes even more fascinating if one considers the words of one of the experts. In speaking to the international media, Hugh Griffiths, a member of the panel that compiled the report, stated: "The Sudanese military have been criticized in the past for using barrel bombs that have targeted civilian populations in various parts of Sudan. That's just bombs kicked out of the back of Antonov aircraft." He continued:

"But what our report shows is that the North Koreans have been supplying far more sophisticated air-to-ground guided missiles that use GPS, satellite guidance systems and that those are being constructed and sent to Sudan together with longer-range ground-to-ground missiles as well." He further said something quite compelling when he remarked: "Sudan had never been documented before as a North Korean customer, but now they have and that's a very serious matter."[24]

The Sudan is a nation that has been under heavy UN sanctions (with good reason) and has often been less than responsive or transparent in its reporting of or compliance with sanctions placed on other nations (such as North Korea).[25] Thus, any analysis of where the military proliferation relationship between North Korea and the Sudan currently stands should be considered in that light. In November 2016, when the foreign minister of the Sudan announced that, while there had been a previous military relationship between his country and North Korea, it was now over, one must take this statement with a grain of salt.[26] Nevertheless, at least officially, the Sudan has now severed all ties with the DPRK.

It is important to keep in mind that both the Sudan and North Korea are widely viewed as pariah states. Thus, if—at least officially—the Sudan has severed ties with Pyongyang, one must remember that the Sudanese military still needs arms and maintenance/ammunition to support the fielding of those arms and as a pariah state can turn to few places other than North Korea. In fact, during July 2017, President Trump extended by three months the review period for Executive Order 13761, which would have lifted sanctions on the Sudan. One of the reasons for extending the sanctions? To ensure that the Sudan is committed to UNSC resolutions targeting North Korea.[27] By October 2017, the government of the Sudan had claimed that it had ended ties with Pyongyang.[28] Also in October 2017, the United States ended sanctions against the Sudan.[29] Despite the Sudan's announced moves and Washington's lifting of sanctions, ongoing North Korean proliferation to the troubled nation in Africa bears continued watching as more arms are likely to follow (if the Sudanese government thinks it can get away with it).

North Korea's Relationship with Uganda

One would not think that Uganda and North Korea would be typical partners in arms sales, military support, military/internal security forces training, or any of the other types of paid services that North Korea typically provides to countries in Africa. But the fact of the matter is that North Korea and Uganda have been involved in a mutually beneficial relationship for many years.[30] It is this unusual relationship that is quite fascinating given the fact that Uganda and the United States have typically had a very good relationship (except, of course, during the Amin era). This US-Uganda relationship has included foreign aid and even an important security partnership.[31] One must assume that the US government and those of other nations such as South Korea are not be pleased with Uganda's use of North Korea's services.

During June 2013, North Korean vice minister Ri Song Chol conducted an official visit to Uganda. Ri was even seen in a famous picture holding a tear gas gun (sold to Uganda, along with training on use). North Korea and Uganda had a contract for DPRK personnel to train Ugandan police forces. According to an official communiqué read by the Ugandan police chief Kale Kayihura, North Korea was assisting the African nation's police training (a frightening thought given the modus operandi of North Korea's internal forces) and also assisting marine forces and providing Uganda with medical training (likely for the military). At the time, it was not well known to most people that Uganda had a long-standing and diverse military relationship with North Korea. But the very public visit that year made it obvious that this was yet one more African nation that North Korea was profiting from.[32]

During October 2014, Kim Yong-nam, the chairman of the North Korean Supreme People's Assembly, visited several countries in Africa, including Uganda. All the countries Kim visited were nations that had a long-standing relationship with the DPRK. In fact, according to reporting in 2014, up until 2004 (and perhaps later, as we will see) North Korea was training Uganda's military, selling weapons to Uganda, and also involved in the refurbishment of that country's weapons systems. There are also allegations that it assisted the Ugandans with building and operating a factory for small arms. During this time period and afterward (2004–2007), the United States requested access to Uganda's budget (which at the time was not open to the public) but was denied.[33]

During May 2016, President Park Geun-hye made a friendship visit to several countries in Africa, including Uganda. During the visit, the South Korean president offered, many analysts believed, economic incentives to move Uganda away from its military and security relationship with North Korea. Perhaps as a result, the South Korean press announced that Uganda had agreed to sever its security and military cooperation relationship with North Korea. Unfortunately for Seoul, Ugandan officials almost immediately announced that this was not the case—at least not yet. In July 2016, Uganda acknowledged that it had active military contracts with North Korea. One key contract was for training pilots and technicians in the military. The contract was set to run through 2018. This was new and showed that, despite some statements to the contrary, Uganda continued to have a military relationship with the DPRK. Uganda did not at the time remark about its other contracts (discussed above) with North Korea. Toward the end of 2016, reports surfaced that it had decided to stop purchasing arms (and likely other services as well) from North Korea. The reasons for this were likely because it had now become strikingly obvious that its military and security relationship with North Korea was—without any ambiguity—a violation of UN sanctions. The February 2017 UN Panel of Experts report revealed that the investigations into Ugandan military collaboration with North Korea continued. Those investigations involved not only the (apparently ongoing) training program for Ugandan military pilots but also the reported involvement of the notorious (and sanctioned) KOMID in Uganda, both of which violated UN sanctions.[34]

North Korea and Angola: A Long and Profitable Relationship

Angola is a very interesting case study of North Korea's involvement on the African continent. In fact, North Korea's military relationship with Angola probably began in the early 1970s when the North Koreans supported Soviet-backed forces in the Angolan civil war. Other activities in Angola included training camps in the country for the African National Congress and the South West African People's Organization.[35] By 1987, North Korea reportedly had three thousand military troops in Angola as the civil war raged on.[36] North Korea's involvement in Angola started as part of an overall strategy of proxy warfare carried out on behalf of the Soviet Union in Africa and other unstable regions. North Korea assisted several African states during the Cold War in largely military activities (including guerrilla groups).[37] As the Cold War ended, it was able to turn its former Soviet proxy status into one of a more independent nation-state actor, still useful for African states that needed arms and training, but no longer tied to the Soviet Union (which no longer existed). Angola was part of this picture as well—beginning in the 1990s. The relationship continued until very recent times and is being investigated even as the writing of this chapter continues, as I will address in this section.

As the Cold War faded in the 1990s, a new world paradigm came into being. We no longer lived in a bipolar world. Rather, with the collapse of the Soviet Union, we lived in a world with only one super power, a world where there would no longer be proxy wars and where every nation-state was free to join the globalized world system.[38] Thus, it was no longer a world where we lived under a Cold War paradigm that was a battle of systems. Rather, beginning roughly in the very early 1990s, we lived (though most did not realize it then) in a world where, with the disappearance of the Soviet Union, Cold War threats were replaced by threats from rogue states and nonstate actors, a paradigm that continues today. In this new paradigm, North Korea was able to jump in with African nations, many of whom were anxious to keep the arms flowing as much as possible and as cheaply as possible to maintain their militaries—often militaries equipped with Soviet vintage systems. In the early 1990s, it was reported that North Korea was proliferating large-scale military arms shipments to Angola. According to a Human Rights Watch publication of the time, in 1993 North Korea made a deal worth $95 million that included SA-2 missiles, BMP-1 and BMP-2 armored personnel carriers, and training for Angolan military aviators. Human Rights Watch also asserted that its personnel had observed arms being offloaded at the airport in Luanda (likely from North Korea).[39]

Fast-forwarding to 2015, evidence was unearthed that North Korea was proliferating naval craft and the associated parts to Angola. In addition, it was reportedly providing training to Angolan presidential guards. All this was occurring under the auspices of a subsidiary of Green Pine Associated Corporation, a front company sanctioned by the United Nations. The proliferation operations were operating out of the North Korean embassy in Luanda and led by an individual named Kim Hyok-chan. The deal for naval craft (patrol boats), including spare parts and training, was potentially a long-term one. As for the military training (which includes instructors), this had reportedly been going on for at least twenty years. The instructors were coming to Angola in March and leaving in December. They were said to be housed either in Luanda or nearby.[40]

In April 2016, Angola's secretary of the interior discussed cooperation with the North Koreans on matters of security and public order. Secretary Hermenegildo José Félix met with the North Korean ambassador that month, according to an Angolan press release. No further details were given.[41] In March 2016, at least ten North Korean citizens were reported to have died from yellow fever in Angola. It is unknown what type of activity these individuals were involved in, but more than a thousand North Koreans were reportedly in Angola at the time. They were involved in construction projects in Angola in 2016 and were also serving in medical capacities (plus of course those involved in military proliferation and military training).[42] By August 2016, Angola had announced that it would fully comply with UN sanctions against North Korea and reportedly was no longer engaged in trade with the DPRK.[43] It seemed—at least at the time—that it was cutting off its long-term relationship with a sponsor that its government had dealt with in one form or another since the Cold War. But perhaps all was not as it seemed.

While Angola claimed that it had severed economic and military proliferation ties to North Korea during the summer of 2016, the UN Panel of Experts actually traveled to the African nation in September of that year. Regarding the continuing deal with Angola regarding naval craft (patrol boats), the UN Panel of Experts report stated in part: "The Panel continued its investigation into the refurbishment by the Democratic People's Republic of Korea of Angolan naval patrol boats through Green Pine. The Panel requested information from Angola and China about shipment of conventional arms dual-use exports to Angola by a front company linked to Green Pine." In addition, apparently reporting on the same visit, the UN Panel of Experts noted: "The Panel travelled to Angola in September 2016 to continue its investigation into the training by the Democratic People's Republic of Korea of the Presidential Guard. Angola informed the Panel that the training had been initiated around 1990 and that, at the time of the Panel's visit, 12 nationals of the Democratic People's Republic of Korea were providing martial arts and parade ground training. The Panel informed Angolan agencies that continuation of the training would constitute a violation of paragraph 9 of resolution 2270 (2016), which clarified the prohibition on the hosting of personnel from the Democratic People's Republic of Korea for security force training, established under resolution 1874 (2009). On 24 October 2016, the Panel enquired with the Government of Angola as to whether they had departed the country. The Panel has yet to receive a reply."[44] In other words, like several nations in Africa, Angola has made claims that it has cut ties with North Korea but, as of the writing of this chapter, has refused to support those claims. This lack of transparency is a common thread running through the stories of many of the nations in Africa when it comes to the reporting of compliance with UN sanctions.

North Korea and Proliferation to Eritrea

Eritrea is a country that has been rocked by war for much of its modern history. Even today, tensions exits with its neighbor, Ethiopia.[45] Thus, Eritrea remains a heavily armed country. Because of this, and because of the fact that it has been heavily sanctioned by the United Nations in one way or another since 2009, the East African nation is often badly in need of arms.[46] And that is where North Korea has stepped in.

The most recent incident involving North Korean military proliferation to Eritrea (as of the writing of this chapter) occurred in 2017 when the Eritrean navy was sanctioned by the United Nations for violating sanctions imposed on North Korea. The Eritreans bought forty-five boxes of encrypted radios for their military, but the equipment was caught and confiscated before it could be delivered. The equipment was of course sold to the Eritreans by North Korea. The North Koreans used a front company named Glocom operating out of Malaysia. The front company is associated with (and probably run by) the Reconnaissance General Bureau in North Korea, which in turn likely reports to Office 39 or directly to Kim Jong-un. While the latest North Korean actions are disturbing, they are not the first disturbing actions in recent times.[47] In 2009, the United Nations accused Eritrea of supporting al-Shabab, a terrorist group in Somalia. Speaking of al-Shabab, it was confirmed in November 2017 that an arms shipment seized by a French Navy frigate during March 2016 in the course of an interdiction of a cargo vessel discovered North Korean–made Type-73 machine guns (unique to the DPRK) among the various weapons onboard. The vessel was bound for Somalia, and the weapons were probably destined to end up in the hands of al-Shabab forces. The vessel originated in Iran and was thus probably an Iranian shipment to the forces in Somalia.[48]

The case of North Korean shipments of apparently high-tech military communications equipment to Eritrea is not the first time Pyongyang proliferators have been caught red-handed, nor is it the only type of activity that North Korea is involved in when it comes to supporting terrorism in Africa. During 2011, it was reported that NATO forces captured a cargo ship in the Indian Ocean bound for Eritrea and carrying fifteen tons of surface-to-air missiles, rockets, and explosives estimated to be worth $15 million. A UN monitoring group revealed during May 2011 that the cargo originated in North Korea.[49] It is unknown whether the arms were headed to the Eritrean army or to the Somali nonstate actors that they were assessed to be support-

ing at the time. (Eritrea was at the time under UN sanctions for providing arms to al-Shabab.)[50] Nevertheless, we once again see a sanctioned state
(North Korea) proliferating to another sanctioned state (Eritrea). This is a
pattern that we have seen not just in Africa but also in the Middle East and
elsewhere. Speaking of North Korean support of terrorism on the African
continent, as of 2015 North Koreans were, according to a South Korean
source, working with illicit Italian arms dealers to sell military equipment to
al-Shabab in Somalia and operating out of Ethiopia, where the arms deals
were occurring.[51] These allegations are unsubstantiated, but, given North
Korea's ties to Eritrea and Eritrea's past ties to al-Shabab (plus the kinds
of small arms that North Korea is so adept at proliferating), it is certainly
feasible. Despite the fact that Eritrea's government has spoken out against
both US- and UN-imposed sanctions, it appears obvious that the small African nation appears intent on maintaining its military readiness and perhaps
even its rogue state behavior. A 2017 meeting of the UN Security Council
revealed mixed assessments by member states about whether Somalia continued support to al-Shabab. Several member states alleged that it remained a
concern and called for a UN monitoring group visit.[52] Its continued lack of
transparency, rogue state activities, and thirst for military weaponry continues to make Eritrea a strong candidate for North Korean military proliferation in the future.

Ethiopia: One of North Korea's Best Customers in Africa

Ethiopia is a country that in recent years has served as an ally of the United
States. The East African nation has had a long-standing relationship with
Washington, a relationship temporarily put on hold when it became a satellite of the Soviet Union during the Cold War.[53] Ethiopia continues its long-
standing relationship with the United States today and remains a key African
recipient of American foreign aid.[54] Despite this, and perhaps surprisingly
because of this, it also has remained one of North Korea's key partners in arms
proliferation on the African continent, even when it was receiving American
foreign aid. There are important reasons for this, but the evidence suggests
that Ethiopia is, has been, and will likely continue to be involved with North
Korean support to its military, a military largely built with Soviet-era weapons and doctrine.

North Korean military involvement with Ethiopia began during the
Cold War. When Ethiopia overthrew its longtime monarch and became a

Communist state, what later ensued was a civil war against the province of Eritrea, which eventually became a sovereign nation. This long-lasting war remains one of the reasons why both Ethiopia and Eritrea continue to strive to maintain their militaries today.[55] During the 1980s, Ethiopia was a client state of the Soviet Union and, thus, also received support from other client states of Moscow. One of these was North Korea. According to Library of Congress researchers: "Beginning in 1985 P'yongyang deployed hundreds of military advisers to Ethiopia and provided an array of small arms, ammunition, and other materiel to the Mengistu regime."[56] During 1989 and 1990, the North Koreans are said to have trained fifteen Ethiopian special commando brigades. In addition, North Korea provided the Ethiopians with seventy-two thousand mortar shells. But, perhaps more important, beginning in 1989 it began assisting them with the establishment and operations of armaments factories. One of these, called the Gafat Engineering Plant, was designed to produce small arms, primarily Kalashnikov rifles. Another facility was part of the Hamat Project, which was a factory to produce ammunition for both mortars and larger field artillery. Both these projects are said to have gone into production but suspended after 1991 as the Communist government collapsed.[57]

By this time—the end of the Soviet Union—Ethiopia was, despite once again being an ally of the United States, completely dependent on old Soviet systems for its military, and North Korea was able to successfully step in and fulfill this need. One very important instance of this occurred in 2007, when Ethiopia was playing a key role in the global war against terror by taking the fight to Islamic militias in Somalia and was being supported by the United States.[58] Of course, in order to do this successfully, it needed supplies of important equipment and arms in order to conduct a large-scale military campaign. Unfortunately for Ethiopia, the United States had just convinced the United Nations to put strict sanctions on North Korea, which had become an important supplier of Soviet-era military weapons since the end of the Cold War. The Ethiopians thus requested that the United States allow them to complete an arms deal that would enable them supply themselves as they fought a campaign against extremists in Somalia, a campaign largely supplied by North Korean weapons. According to press sources, the decision was made in Washington to allow Ethiopia to make the arms deal, but it was strongly suggested that the Ethiopians move away from their North Korean suppliers in the future.[59] The North Koreans reportedly provided (at least) spare parts for tanks and other military equipment as part of the deal. Washington gave the green light to a transaction that was important for security in the Horn of Africa and a key aspect of the global war on terror.[60] Ethiopia continued to acquire systems that were based on Soviet-era technology as its military had not then (and still has not now) transitioned away from the infrastructure provided by the Soviet Union during the Cold War.

According to reports in 2014, North Korea was apparently still supporting the Ethiopian arms industry. As discussed earlier, in the late 1980s, during the Communist regime, North Korea assisted the Ethiopians in setting up two armament facilities. It appears that at least these two facilities (and perhaps more) were reactivated after the fall of the Communists and that once again North Korea stepped into the picture to support them. Specific systems required included such things as heavy ammunition, grenades, and 120-millimeter rockets. The interesting thing about the assembly lines set up by the North Koreans and the rest of the operations at the facilities is that these projects were originally intended to give the Ethiopian government more independent arms production, but it appears that the factories remained dependent on North Korea for spare parts and assistance. Evidence uncovered in 2014 by the UN Panel of Experts led to an assessment that at that time there continued to be an Ethiopia–North Korea link when it came to arms production.[61] Nevertheless, the Ethiopians have probably gone out of their way to discard evidence that may show their continued military involvement with the DPRK. The Ethiopian military continues to rely on vintage Soviet systems from the Cold War to support its military and seems unable to retool (Ethiopia simply cannot afford it). Thus, it likely that the relationship with North Korea continues as this is the cheapest way for Ethiopia to continue to maintain military readiness in its ongoing conflicts. Despite not being listed in the UN Panel of Experts report in 2017, Ethiopia continues to rate watching.[62]

North Korea and Zimbabwe:
Old Cold War Allies and Post–Cold War Proliferation

Zimbabwe is a country long ruled by the strongman Robert Mugabe. Mugabe was an individual noted for his corruption, lack of ethics, and horrifying human rights violations. He was the leader of a state that for the many years of its strongman rule has been considered a rogue state.[63] Mugabe has now apparently fallen from power, yet at least for now the government shows no signs of reform and is likely to continue as a dictatorship.[64] This makes Zimbabwe the perfect candidate for North Korean military proliferation. Not only does Zimbabwe fit the mold for North Korean proliferation; this status has borne real fruit since the Cold War and leading up to very recent times.

The North Korea military relationship with Zimbabwe began soon after the country was able to break itself from minority white rule. During the 1980s, North Korea sent special advisers there to train a specially equipped brigade, the now infamous Fifth Brigade. The elite unit was formed specifically to provide absolute loyalty to Mugabe. By 1988, it had become infamous for its brutality and ruthlessness. In fact, it was accused of slaughtering more than twenty thousand civilians.[65] The 1980s and 1990s marked a time when North Korea was involved in a number of ways in Zimbabwe. In fact, in 1991, it was reported that it had sold more than $16.5 million worth of arms to Zimbabwe.[66] By 2006, press reports suggested that its proliferation arrangements with Zimbabwe remained active.[67]

Zimbabwe's longtime association with North Korea did not end during the time of the Obama administration. According to several press reports, North Korea entered into an agreement with Zimbabwe in 2013 to ship yellow cake from the uranium mines there to the DPRK. In exchange, it provided arms to the African state.[68] This is not the first time Pyongyang has agreed to at least a partial barter trade in its proliferation to other rogue states. This is understandable given the fact that many of the states Pyongyang proliferates to are very poor (which is at least partially why they turn to North Korea, their deals with Pyongyang often being the cheapest to be found). One example of this is the arms for oil deals that North Korea has engaged in with Iran in the past.[69] The several types of deals that North Korea and Zimbabwe have engaged in over a time period of more than thirty years do not show signs of ending. While Mugabe denied that the relationship continued, once again the lack of transparency in Zimbabwe tells us that this could very easily be untrue.[70] As long as North Korea can provide arms and training for a price, why would Zimbabwe end this relationship if it thinks it can get away with it?

North Korean Proliferation to Mozambique

North Korea provided support to Mozambique during the Cold War following that country's independence from Portugal. Postindependence, Mozambique's government made a conscious effort to move away from Western powers and, instead, in 1977, signed a friendship treaty with the

Soviet Union. As a result of this, several countries in the Soviet Communist bloc also provided weapons and training to the new nation, including North Korea.[71] This has not ended in recent times. The February 2017 UN Panel of Experts report was quite specific in its allegations regarding North Korea and Mozambique. According to the allegations, in a contract signed in November 2013, North Korea agreed to provide components for MANPADS as well as the associated training equipment (which means that North Korean trainers are likely involved). The North Koreans also agreed to provide components for the P-18 early warning radar system and to refurbish Mozambique's aging T-55 tanks. Finally, they agreed to upgrade Mozambique's Pechora surface-to-air missile system. The panel was even provided photographs of North Korean army technicians posing in front of refurbished tanks. According to the UN report, the contract between the two countries is worth $6 million. As of the time of the publishing of the report, the government of Mozambique had not responded to any UN inquiries.[72]

North Korea and Military Support to Tanzania

North Korea has had a military relationship with Tanzania since at least the 1970s. It was then that it began to provide both military systems and training. During the 1980s, the North Koreans provided police forces to form a security team that guarded the Tanzanian leadership.[73] In 2013 at least, the relationship appeared to be ongoing. The East African nation stood accused of receiving North Korean advisers and technicians who came to the nation to refurbish its F-7 (MiG-21-equivalent) Cold War–era jets.[74] President Obama made a state visit to Tanzania in July 2013.[75] Thus, it is likely that this disclosure, revealed at a sensitive time, was embarrassing to the Tanzanian government, which had (and has) been working for many years to move closer to the West and to the United States in particular (Washington provides foreign aid to Tanzania). It is my assessment that Obama's visit in 2013 was evidence that this effort was moving in the right direction.[76] Nevertheless, reports coming out following the summer of 2013 alleged that Tanzania had in fact taken in North Korean advisers (and probably technicians) to refurbish its jets (apparently) and to build the facilities that would house them.[77] There were even allegations made in the African press that MiG-21 jets the North Koreans were transporting from Cuba (caught in the Panama Canal) were actually bound for Tanzania and not North Korea.[78]

The UN Panel of Experts Report for 2014 confirmed that, at an air base in Tanzania (Mwanza Air Force Base), facilities to support F-7 jets had been recently constructed (a probable indicator that work with the jets was ongoing or recently completed). It also reported that the panel had sent a request for information to the Tanzanian government but had not received a reply.[79] Tanzania later claimed that the North Korean technicians had been expelled.[80] According to a report from the UN Panel of Experts dated September 5, 2017, military ties to North Korea remain active, and a report by a member state that North Korea is upgrading Tanzania's Pechora surface-to-air missile systems as well as its P-12 air defense radar is being investigated. According to the panel's report: "The total value of the prohibited military-related contracts between Tanzania and the DPRK was reported as 10.49 million euros."[81] Ties to North Korean proliferation could jeopardize important American aid for an impoverished country like Tanzania.

North Korean Proliferation to the Democratic Republic of Congo

Since its independence, the Democratic Republic of Congo (DRC) has been a nation existing in a state of flux, often with anarchy in much of the country, instability in the government, bad relations with its neighbors, and a long history of violence.[82] It is into this quagmire of corruption and violence that North Korea has stepped. The North Korean government operatives—people who rarely miss an opportunity when it comes to proliferation—have taken advantage of a weak nation with a nontransparent government in order to make money for the Kim Jong-un regime.

During April 2000, it was publicly disclosed that North Korean military advisers were training and setting up a new special forces unit in the DRC army, the Tenth Special Infantry Brigade, which was, reportedly, equipped with artillery, infantry, and reconnaissance entities and several thousand troops strong. The unit apparently was used to fight rebels as well as nations backing the rebels such as Rwanda and Uganda.[83] North Korea was reportedly actively engaged in selling weapons in the DRC. According to a report issued in 2009, a member of the UN committee investigating the DRC at the time stated that during January of that year a North Korean ship carrying several tons of military weapons arrived at the port of Boma, where it offloaded its valuable cargo. According to the same report, during the same year, North Korea sent military instructors to train DRC troops.[84] In fact, according to a report by the Institute for Defense Analysis, North Korea has also constructed military facilities for the DRC in the past.[85]

During May 2016, UN experts informed the press that North Korea had provided DRC military personnel and police with pistols. It also provided around thirty military trainers to support the DRC presidential guard and special forces. Ironically, there are also reports from 2017 that Congolese army personnel deployed on a UN mission have been spotted armed with North Korean pistols. Evidently, the pistols were part of a series of shipments that also included small arms such as antitank mines and assault rifles.[86] The DRC government of course publicly denied that its personnel had been equipped with pistols from North Korea (which is a direct violation of international sanctions).[87] In February 2017, the UN Panel of Experts confirmed the allegations, even noting where the North Koreans were billeted: "The instructors were housed at the former Gulf Oil Company premises in the Binza district of Kinshasa. The Democratic Republic of the Congo has yet to respond to the Panel's enquiries."[88] The DRC shows no signs of breaking off ties to North Korea, its support being important for the military. Transparency with the international community appears not to be a priority of the DRC government.

It should be obvious from the contents of this chapter that North Korea's proliferation to nations on the African continent has a long history. It should also be obvious, given the evidence, that Pyongyang has continued its profitable relationship with a number of nations in Africa in recent years. I have covered many countries that have had deals with North Korea in recent years. But there are likely others whose relationship with North Korea simply has not been discovered yet. In fact, given the large number of countries with which North Korea has had military relationships (for profit) in recent years, it is almost a question not of which countries they proliferate to on the African continent, but which countries they do not proliferate to. In fact, Burkina Faso and Madagascar are two more countries rumored to have military ties to North Korea, yet the evidence chain is not as complete or detailed as it is with the other African nations I have described. The examples that I have provided make it clear that North Korea has built a large-scale network on the African continent that grew out of the Cold War and continues into our own times because many of these countries found themselves still in need of help after the Soviet Union collapsed. It would probably be shocking to most people that North Korea has built arms factories in Namibia,

Madagascar, Ethiopia, Uganda, and the Democratic Republic of the Congo. And of course North Korea continues to need the hard cash (or the barter deals) that helps Pyongyang fund its own military needs as well as the luxury goods that keep the elite in the DPRK happy and in line. It is my assessment that, if one is to look at the many deals Pyongyang has on the African continent, it is likely making hundreds of millions of dollars annually. According to former UNSC sanctions expert Enrico Carisch, a specialist who tracked North Korea's illicit activities, Pyongyang's trade in small arms on the African continent is worth around $100 million a year. Carisch did not mention things such as missiles, aircraft, and military training, so the figure could be significantly higher.[89]

In closing, it is, I believe, important to note some of the trends that we have seen in North Korea's military deals in Africa. Several nations that were formerly supplied (often for free) by the Soviet Union still need to acquire and/or maintain Soviet-era weapons cheaply. Some nations are, much like North Korea, either considered pariah states or under sanctions. Some states that actually have received foreign aid from the United States nevertheless also purchased arms and training from North Korea. Perhaps as troubling as anything, there is a lack of transparency when it comes to compliance with UN sanctions, and this has shown no signs of changing to date. And, of course, it is important to note that a key reason many of these states continue to buy from North Korea is because Pyongyang offers the cheapest deals. Policy makers in both Washington and Seoul need to continue to focus on these many military deals (as Seoul has done in the past)[90] because these deals in Africa have the potential to be a legitimate pressure point for Pyongyang.

7

Conclusions and Policy Implications

This book has taken an unusual look at an unusual international dilemma. Mostly for reasons involving academic background, many of the issues addressed in this work have been either largely ignored or, worse, misrepresented. While this is disappointing, it is probably not the fault of those academics who have avoided doing research on what can only be considered one of the key international security concerns relating to North Korea. As of the writing of this work (2018), most of those in the academic community have never served in the military—or even served in roles in which they addressed salient military issues within the government. Today's academic community is largely composed of individuals who have never worn a military uniform.[1] Thus, issues such as military capabilities and readiness (which must be addressed before one can truly understand the impact of military proliferation on a nation-state or a region), whom these systems go to, how the systems (or training, or maintenance) are used, and how they affect where they go are not only difficult for most in the academic community to grapple with; they remain largely untouched. To date, no other author has written a formal book addressing the military capabilities and support for those capabilities that North Korea possesses and often proliferates to the Middle East and Africa (and elsewhere), how these systems (and support) are proliferated, whom these systems are going to, and the types of proliferation that have occurred to specific state and nonstate actors.

In this concluding chapter, I will conduct a summary and analysis of the evidence presented throughout the book—and the significance that it holds for America's policy and the policy of its allies. I will also consider the diplomatic, informational, military, and economic factors (commonly known as the DIME) for this issue, how they have been involved in recent history, and how they have been leveraged to put real pressure on the DPRK government.

I will also go into detail about how I assess the United States and its allies can put real pressure on the Kim family regime in Pyongyang—pressure that could actually bring the regime down or close to economic and political collapse.

Summary and Analysis of Evidence

A summarization of the evidence provides us an opportunity for important analysis. North Korea's military proliferation efforts in the Middle East and Africa are directly related to Pyongyang's need for funding for its nuclear and ballistic missile programs as well as its conventional military. This need has not gone away—with or without sanctions imposed by the United Nations as well as the United States and its allies. Because of this, North Korea has diversified and nuanced the way that it proliferates WMD, conventional weapons, military training, etc. The variety of military systems that it has recently and rapidly developed are likely to be proliferated nearly as fast as those systems are fielded. This has been the modus operandi since the Cold War and shows no signs of ending.[2] And, perhaps as important as anything else, the scope and focus of activities with these countries (the military-related trade and the money), both in the Middle East and in Africa, are surprising to most analysts.

If one looks at the number of systems in North Korea's arsenal that since 2012 have been either newly tested or newly introduced, one finds the greatest increase in the history of the DPRK.[3] But these tests are not simply a prelude to the fielding of these systems. They are also a prelude to the proliferation of these systems to countries that are in the process themselves of constantly upgrading and maintaining their militaries, countries such as Iran.[4] Thus, it is important to note all the developments addressed in detail in chapter 2. While often not referenced in the public arena, nearly all these systems are truly two-headed threats. They are a threat to the region (and, in the case of ICBM missiles, to the United States), and they are a threat to other regions that they are proliferated to. Thus, it is important to note that every time a system is tested—especially a WMD-related system—there is a good chance that it will be proliferated to one of North Korea's major clients—such as Iran or Syria—and used to disrupt regional security, create instability, and enhance violence and death.[5]

A key source of debate among analysts has been how North Korea conducts its proliferation activities and gets around sanctions and how effective it has been. North Korea has managed to work its illicit financial network magic in a variety of diverse ways (not just through banks and not just through China). As documented in chapter 3, it uses front companies in countries all over Asia and elsewhere. China does tend to be the nation with the largest amount of dirty money being run through its banks—but that is of course because of its proximity and size and the fact that it harbors one of the most corrupt financial systems in the world. But North Korea has also made extensive use of front companies in places like Singapore, Malaysia, and elsewhere, including several nations in Africa.[6]

As the international system adjusts to focus more on North Korea, Pyongyang has adjusted its tactics, techniques, and procedures to continue to get around international laws, international detection, and international law enforcement. A great example of this can be seen when one looks at the 2017 deal conducted with Iran, which was purchasing weapons for Syria. The money went from Iranian banks to front companies in Malaysia that then invested it in casinos in Macao.[7] One wonders how, with clever deals like this going on apparently all the time, analysts can determine exactly how much money North Korea is making from its deals in the Middle East and Africa. The answer is that, on the basis of the available evidence, it appears, according to the former Congressional Research Service senior analyst Larry Niksch, that North Korea "may receive from Iran upwards of $2 to $3 billion annually from Iran [sic] for the various forms of collaboration between them."[8] In an interview with the former State Department official and former member of the UN Panel of Experts William Newcomb, I posed the question: "My research indicates North Korea is making hundreds of millions of dollars a year from proliferation agreements with nations in Africa." Newcomb responded: "I concur and that is a conservative estimate."[9] Thus, owing to its sophisticated delivery, the support of highly nuanced financial networks, and a variety of methods that allow it get it around international sanctions and laws, North Korea's military proliferation network continues to flourish and provide the hard currency that can support WMD programs, conventional forces, and the bribing of the elite. These are all things that maintain the power of the Kim family regime.

The evidence shows that, when it comes to proliferation in the Middle East, Iran is by far North Korea's biggest customer. The Iranians simply have more money than anyone else who is willing to do business with North Korea, and they have a need for ballistic missile systems that has existed since the early 1980s. Perhaps as important, Iran wishes to be the hegemon in the

Middle East. In order to accomplish this, it must support a number of proxy groups, including Hezbollah, Hamas, and the Houthis.[10] A key supplier of this effort appears to be North Korea.[11] Thus, as we have seen, Iran appears to be paying billions of dollars a year to North Korea for WMD and the ballistic missiles that can carry them, for conventional weapons systems, and for supplies and training for proxy groups. When it comes to Syria, the civil war has been a big boost for North Korean proliferation activities. Everything from chemical weapons, Scud missiles, and a large variety of conventional weapons has been included in this seemingly endless supply chain. The Syrians need what North Korea has, and North Korea continues to be a source of supply.[12] Perhaps just as importantly, North Korean military specialists have gained valuable information as to how their chemical weapons and the associated platforms work during actual combat.

There are other nation-states and nonstate actors that North Korea supplies in the Middle East, but Iran and Syria (whose bills are often paid by Iran) continue to be its two main customers. When it comes to Africa, it is often a matter of military training, the maintenance of old, Soviet-era systems on which key states remain dependent, and the proliferation of conventional systems.[13] North Korea fills a niche that no one else can, and its services come at a price that these states consider reasonable. Thus, its activity in Africa is unlikely to end unless Western states are willing to take over its role.

There are those (though they are in the minority) who have assessed that the North Korean arms trade has actually declined since 1999. This of course does not take into account that, as sanctions and counter—proliferation initiatives were stepped up, North Korea changed its tactics, techniques, and procedures. In fact, while complete missiles and parts for other systems and capabilities used to be shipped directly from North Korea to customers in Iran and elsewhere, now the North Koreans have constructed fabrication facilities in a number of states, including Iran, Syria, and several African nations (as we have seen).[14] Thus, these states continue to rely on North Korean weaponry, parts, and advisers. This appears not to have been factored in to estimates that proliferation has slowed since, say, 1999. The shipment of parts and pieces of systems rather than whole systems is easier and also much harder to detect, whether it be by interdiction or attempts to examine records (which the North Koreans often destroy) in order to ascertain true numbers and profits.[15] While this research has created some debate, it must be noted that North Korea simply could not move forward with its

WMD programs if the funding from proliferation was not there to support it. Cutting off this proliferation and the financing that supports it is very important, though efforts to stop it have been unsuccessful since 2007 and through at least 2017, largely because Washington did not enforce sanctions and did not have the level of organization that it had during the George W. Bush administration, when a joint task force coordinated successful efforts overseas.[16] In fact, in 2017 William Newcomb stated: "North Korea is speeding up the pace of its WMD and ballistic missile development programs. It is vital to take steps now to disrupt the North's foreign sources of supply of technology and components."[17]

Combating North Korean Military Proliferation: Diplomacy

There has been a debate among both policy makers and academics when it comes to North Korea. Even after the first North Korea nuclear crisis was supposedly resolved in 1994 with the visit of former US president Jimmy Carter to the DPRK, the debate has continued.[18] Should the United States (and its key allies in East Asia) use the carrot or the stick in order to bring denuclearization to the Korean Peninsula? Will an effective strategy be coercion or engagement or some mixture of the two? Clearly, in the years during which I worked on this book, neither tactic has worked.[19] In fact, no mix of coercion or engagement has ever worked. North Korea's nuclear programs and the programs for the platforms that will carry nuclear warheads and other forms of WMD continue to advance in both sophistication and numbers.

An examination of the past history of diplomacy involving North Korea shows what can be described only as the failure of engagement to get North Korea to take realistic steps to disband its nuclear weapons program, its ballistic missile development, and its proliferation. Now that we are in the early years of the Trump era, it is my assessment that diplomatic attempts to deal with North Korea can essentially be categorized into three basic time periods: the Agreed Framework (1994–2002), the Six-Party talks (2003–2008), and the period that the Obama administration categorized as strategic patience (2009–2016).[20]

The sad part about the diplomatic efforts that led to these three periods is that the nations involved became so focused on the denuclearization process that conventional weapons, ballistic missiles, and of course proliferation essentially fell by the wayside. To this day, North Korea remains armed to the teeth, with a higher percentage of its male population serving in the military than almost every other country on earth. Its conventional forces continue to threaten the South and advance their capabilities and numbers.[21] As far as proliferation goes, as this work has documented, this has not slowed, and things such as African nations' need to maintain their old, Soviet-era weapons systems, Syria's need for systems and training for its ongoing civil war, and Iran's never-ending thirst for expensive new weapons systems it can use to target Israel continue to provide the cash that supports North Korea's WMD development and underwrite the elite.

It must be said that the Agreed Framework collapsed in 2002 when it became obvious to the United States and the world that North Korea had been violating the terms of the agreement and was developing a second track to nuclear weaponization—highly enriched uranium.[22] The second Bush administration came up with an alternative, the Six-Party talks. Yet this initiative ended when North Korea balked at transparent verification of its obligations.[23] The Obama administration took no diplomatic action with regard to North Korea and never had meaningful talks with the North Korean leadership during its entire eight-year tenure in the White House. Thus, the name for this policy (or lack thereof) was *strategic patience.*[24] Despite these mostly failed policies, Washington and UN member nations did impose a number of sanctions on North Korea. These sanctions truly began in 2006 and continue today.[25] Unfortunately, enforcement has been an issue. Thus, while appearing to be a reasonable and practical solution to the problem of North Korea's rogue state activities, diplomacy has been largely unsuccessful in the post–Cold War era.

Combating North Korean Proliferation: Information

Information operations, cyber warfare, and information in general have all become a growing, often-confusing aspect of society in this modern age. While the technology and, to be sure, many of the paradigms associated with information have changed, one thing is for sure. It is information that helps nation-states, nonstate actors, and other entities wield power. North Korea is no exception. In fact, in North Korea, information is controlled more than it is in any other country on earth.[26] It is the disruption of this information control, the ability to get information from democratic states (especially the ROK), and the proliferation of that information that have the potential to challenge the government in North Korea.[27]

So too does alerting institutions around the world (including the United Nations) about the inhuman results of North Korea's proliferation and its routine violations of international law.

Information is a tool that has in the past been used successfully by the United States and its allies to alert populations under the yoke of authoritarian Communist regimes that a better life was available to them. Following the American victory in the Cold War, evidence showed that broadcasts directed toward Communist-occupied Eastern Europe were widely listened to.[28] One would hope that this methodology would also work in North Korea, but, as referenced above, information is more contained there than it was in, say, Hungary and the Soviet Union during the Cold War—at least until recently. North Korea now has a cell phone network (Orascom sponsored) that may make North Koreans vulnerable to infiltration.[29] In addition, hundreds of thousands of flash drives and black-market DVDs (at least) have been smuggled into North Korea.[30] This new, compelling development in how information can get into North Korea opens up the possibility that change can actually be brought about by information. Of course, we must keep in mind that East Asian societies are different than European societies; nevertheless, as information finally begins to reach people who have never before had access to it, one can assess that this will disrupt the status quo in North Korea and create opportunities for real change, including bringing about the collapse of a government that proliferates death and destruction to various regions worldwide.

According to press sources, during 2017 the Trump administration issued a presidential directive inaugurating a cybercampaign against North Korea's top overseas intelligence agency, the Reconnaissance General Bureau. This Internet campaign was part of a multiagency effort to put pressure on the North Korean regime[31] and is a key example of one way information can be used against North Korea's assets that are conducting illegal and illicit activities. These types of activities have been conducted only on a small-scale basis in the past. If they are conducted properly and target North Korean targets that are important to the regime, they can put real pressure on entities involved in a wide variety of dirty tricks.

The military proliferation that North Korea has engaged in should be troubling to American policy makers (as well as South Korean and Japanese), not only because of the role that it plays in maintaining rogue regimes and terrorists, but also because it is such an important part of maintaining the power of an illegitimate regime.[32] North Korea has—going back to the 1970s—used methodologies that can be described only as criminal to maintain a regime that most people agree has terrorized its own people, intimidated a transparent democracy in the South, and even made attempts (which are ongoing) to directly threaten the United States. Thus, it is hugely important to bring knowledge of this military proliferation to the attention of important international organizations and the public in democracies all over the world. This will make it easier for governments to put pressure on a regime that is nothing more than a holdover from the Cold War, not having collapsed as it should have in 1991. Thus, it is interesting that this work is actually the first book to focus entirely on North Korean military proliferation and related issues. Do other scholars somehow consider this subject unimportant? It is important—perhaps even crucial—that the globalized world understand how this proliferation disrupts security both locally and globally and continues to shore up the Kim family regime financially.

Combating North Korean Military Proliferation: Military Action

While there have been over the years a number of violent military provocations on the Korean Peninsula, the armistice has remained in effect and war avoided since 1953.[33] Although North Korea maintains one of the largest militaries in the world, it has not gone to war with South Korea and the United States in more than sixty years.[34] Thus, since an uneasy peace has existed for so long on the Peninsula, the question is sure to arise, What military tools can the United States and the rest of the world use to contain North Korea's military proliferation?

The United States has a variety of options in terms of instruments of national power.[35] We have already addressed diplomacy and information, but, other than deterrence on the Korean Peninsula, how can the United States possibly contain North Korea's rogue state behavior directly related to proliferation with military force? The answer is the Proliferation Security Initiative (PSI), formulated by the United States under the George W. Bush administration. Most analysts assess this initiative was the result of difficulties faced by counterproliferation operations.[36] The PSI now has over one hundred members internationally and occasionally has carried out important interdiction missions, both at sea and in the air.[37] That said, most experts assess that the PSI has encountered a variety of challenges and that its interdiction attempts appear to be affecting only a small portion of North Korean or Iranian proliferation.[38] Does that mean that the PSI should be disbanded and its mission abandoned? Absolutely not. At the least, this is an initiative that holds important symbolic meaning. In other words, it shows North Korea that the world will not stand by and do nothing as it engages in rogue state behavior. At best, it is an initiative that can be improved as the number of member nations increases.

The military aspect of containing or perhaps even ending North Korea's profitable proliferation efforts truly comes down to the PSI. Unless policy changes drastically, Washington is not going to bomb cargo ships carrying weapons or send troops into sovereign territory. But the potential for intercepting vessels on the high seas or even aircraft flying through international zones remains an option that has potential. The question of whether it can put a real dent in the proliferation activities of North Korea and other rogue states such as Iran remains unanswered in my opinion because it appears this initiative has come nowhere close to reaching its potential (and that may never happen because of geopolitical challenges). There does remain another option for policy makers to pursue—the economic instrument of power.

Combating North Korean Military Proliferation: Economic Action

If one examines North Korea's actions since the 1990s, it is clear that, as time has moved on, so have the North Koreans. Pyongyang took what started out as a Cold War proxy operation helping the Soviet Union and turned it into a profitable business network that generates what I estimate to be billions of dollars annually for the DPRK. In fact, as time has passed and the world (especially the United States) has reacted to North Korea's proliferation to volatile regions, the network has evolved, becoming far more sophisticated and complex in order to be harder to detect and a real challenge to shut down. Thus, the North Korean international military proliferation operations and the spiderweb of networks that support them have now become, not only a major source of income for the regime in Pyongyang, but also potentially a key leverage point that the United States and its allies can use to put real pressure on the regime.

It is important to note that the evolution of North Korea's international networks is not a minor occurrence and that it did not happen overnight. During the time that the US Treasury Department took its initiatives (which many analysts have called *sanctions*), the designation of Banco Delta Asia (BDA) in Macao as a *money laundering concern* under the Patriot Act created a snowball effect that had banks all over Asia kicking out the North Koreans and their illicitly gained money. The North Koreans even admitted that this action put real pressure on them, telling a high-ranking American government official: "You finally found a way to hurt us."[39] Alas, when the Bush administration lifted the sanctions on BDA, not only did North Korea go back to laundering its money using banks and front companies worldwide, but it also obviously had learned that it must diversify. Thus we are faced with a financial network that will be much more difficult to shut down or even contain.[40]

As Northeast Asia moves forward, it is now obvious that North Korea has front companies—likely numbering in the hundreds —in such diverse areas as China, Malaysia, Singapore, Southeast Asia, the Middle East, and Africa.[41] Thus, disrupting and perhaps even destroying parts of this network will take a counternetwork able to access the necessary resources, orchestrate cooperation among international allies, and maintain constant pressure as the North Koreans attempt to evolve once again to evade international law enforcement. It will also be important to put realistic sanctions and initiatives in place. The reason I say this is that, while during the Obama administration many sanctions were put in place, most targeted North Korean companies, banks, and individuals.[42] While this was certainly a noble effort (even if actual enforcement might have made it far more effective), it is now obvious to many analysts that what we are calling *secondary sanctions* are what must be initiated in order to hit the North Koreans where it truly hurts— the pocketbook. Thus, the statement, It's not just China, and it's not just the banks, is very relevant here. An international network countering North Korea's current operations must go after banks and front companies in China (of course), but it must also go after banks and front companies in countries that are very friendly (and sometimes allies) with the United States in a large-scale, comprehensive effort.

Changing the Paradigm: How to Put Real Pressure on North Korea's Rogue Regime

Throughout this work I have conducted analysis of North Korea's proliferation activity and the illicit financial networks that support it. It should be obvious to anyone who has read all the chapters in this work that North

Korea has stepped up the development and testing of its military systems—particularly those directly related to WMD. In addition, the flow to both state and nonstate actors in the Middle East and Africa appears to have picked up steam in the Kim Jong-un era. Are the two developments related? In other words, is the robust flow of ballistic missiles, technology, and military assistance to places such as Iran directly related to North Korea's uptick in developing and testing its military systems (especially missiles)? The answer to that is probably. Thus, the question is and always has been, How do we put pressure on North Korea's ability to develop, test, deploy, and proliferate military systems and technology that are a threat to the United States and its allies?

The methodology that I used in this chapter to examine how Washington and its allies have used the resources at their disposal to influence North Korea's ability to threaten its neighbors and proliferate weapons to volatile regions of the world is the US Defense Department's instruments of national power analysis. When one looks at how these instruments have worked since their introduction in the 1990s, one comes up with a surprisingly clear assessment. Almost none of them have worked. While the Clinton administration touted its policies as being successful, it is now clear to even the most cynical of analysts that, even as the Agreed Framework was in effect, Pyongyang was cheating by developing a highly enriched uranium weaponization program separate from the program that was at the time frozen in the eyes of the world.[43] The Bush administration also failed in its policies. Believing that North Korea would actually live up to its obligations when it came to verification (despite evidence to the contrary) was perhaps its biggest mistake (among many).[44] And of course the Obama administration followed the policy of strategic patience as North Korea continued to rapidly develop WMD systems and the platforms that would carry them, thus ultimately making this a policy of strategic failure.[45]

If we go back to the first years of the Bush administration, we find a policy that has worked—once. Squeezing North Korea's illicit financial networks worldwide placed real pressure on North Korea. But Washington backed off, thinking that a return to talks would resolve the North Korean nuclear question (it did not). By once again squeezing, not just one bank but several, not just one front company or a few but all of them that are known, and individuals in countries all over the Middle East, East Asia, and Africa, the United States can once again put real pressure on North Korea. What would this result in? I will address that in the following section.

Conclusions and Recommendations

A review of the evidence I have presented in this work shows that, in the two regions I researched, North Korea continues to have a significant impact on security and stability. One can assume nothing else. The arms shipments to Syria during its horrific civil war have probably been an economic boom for the North Koreans as they have significantly stepped up military proliferation to a country that they already had a robust trading relationship with. Iran, of course, is North Korea's biggest and best customer. Not only do the North Koreans sell Iran a wide variety of technology, assistance, components, and training when it comes to ballistic missiles, but they also continue to proliferate a variety of conventional weapons to it as well. In addition, Iran often foots the bill for Syrian acquisition and more often than not that of nonstate actors such as Hezbollah. Africa of course is the place where North Korea's proliferation has been ongoing for many years but largely ignored. More attention needs to be paid to all this proliferation (and to other regions as well not covered here). As this shift in focus occurs, it will become easier to contain or perhaps even shut down the proliferation.

The proliferation that has occurred for many years and appears to have picked up steam in the Kim Jong-un era. This has not only contributed to even more horrific violence on two continents where horrific violence has long been the norm but also been a key factor in generating the funds that allow the DPRK to develop its conventional and WMD-related systems, systems that, once operational, can then be proliferated to state and nonstate actors with an apparently unending thirst for weapons.

What to do about all this? As I have hopefully shown in this book, the road to a denuclearized North Korea is littered with many failed policies. But one policy, initiated for a relatively short time during the George W. Bush administration, did work—going after North Korea's illicit financial networks. It was successful once, and it can be successful again. In fact, as the sanctions expert William Newcomb has stated: "The United States is uniquely capable of sharply increasing the global rate, pace and rigorous enforcement of United Nations sanctions measures on the DPRK through diplomatic encouragement, assistance to capacity-challenged nations, pressure to overcome vested interest and foot-dragging, and the demonstration effect of imposing stiff penalties in cases of willful complicity in evasion or violation. I suggest that even more could be accomplished through coordinated action with like-minded countries."[46] Action can be taken, but it must be comprehensive and widely enforced—something that has not happened since the BDA initiatives. That leads us to the ultimate question: What do we do once our action has brought North Korea to the brink?

On June 12, 2018, President Trump and Kim Jong-un met in Singapore. The occasion was the first time that serving heads of state for the two nations have met. While it is good that the summit took place, the joint statement the two leaders issued afterward is decidedly vague.[47] The United States must keep in mind that North Korea has again and again gone back on its agreements. One hopes that if, once again, North Korea reneges on the details or spirit of the June 12 summit statement and other agreements, Washington will once again step up the economic pressure. One also hopes that North Korea will be subject to economic pressure applied by the United States and other nations unless or until Pyongyang finally ceases its rogue state activities for good—and there are many.

The Bush administration backed off its sanctions and went back to the negotiating table, a move that obviously ended badly. I would submit that, once sanctions that are actually enforced and initiatives that actually have teeth and are backed by adequate resources have brought North Korea to the brink, the United States and its allies should simply continue the pressure. This will likely bring about one of two things: either a cessation of rogue state behavior in the interest of survival or regime collapse. Unless and until this occurs, the United States and the international community will continue to find themselves in an international security quagmire.

Notes

1. Setting the Context

1. For examples of works that address aspects of North Korea's illicit activities or proliferation or its financial networks or the results of these activities, see Robert Daniel Wallace, *Sustaining the Regime: North Korea's Quest for Financial Support* (Lanham, MD: University Press of America, 2006), 21–118; David Kang, "Securitizing Transnational Organized Crime and North Korea's Non-Traditional Society," in *Non-Traditional Security Issues in North Korea,* ed. Kyung-ae Park (Honolulu: University of Hawaii Press, 2013), 75–99; Nicholas Blanford, *Warriors of God: Inside Hezbollah's 30 Year Struggle against Israel* (New York: Random House, 2011), 20–219; and Larry Niksch, "North Korea's Terrorism List Removal," Congressional Research Service, RL30613, January 6, 2010, http://www.dtic.mil/dtic/tr/fulltext/u2/a513061.pdf.

2. "How N. Korea Goes about Exporting Arms," *Chosun Ilbo,* March 10, 2010, http://english.chosun.com/site/data/html_dir/2010/03/10/2010031000953.html.

3. For details on instances of North Korean merchant ships that have been caught reflagging, see Matthew Gianni, "Real and Present Danger: Flag State Failure and Maritime Security and Safety," World Wide Fund for Nature/International Transport Workers' Federation, June 2008, http://assets.panda.org/downloads/flag_state_performance.pdf.

4. "With KPA Assets in Syria and Rumors of Moscow Trip, Gen. Kim Kyok Sik Remains PY Man of the Hour," North Korean Leadership Watch, June 4, 2013, https://nkleadershipwatch.wordpress.com/2013/06/04/with-kpa-assets-in-syria-and-rumors-of-moscow-trip-gen-kimkyok-sik-remains-py-man-of-the-hour/?iframe=true&preview=true/feed.

5. See "N. Korean Army Chief Fingered in Syria Connection," *Chosun Ilbo,* June 11, 2013, http://english.chosun.com/site/data/html_dir/2013/06/11/2013061101459.html.

6. For examples of North Korea's widespread proliferation of conventional weapons on the African continent, see Hugh Griffiths and Lawrence Dermody, "17 July 2013: Shadow Trade: How North Korea's Barter Trade Violates United Nations Sanctions," Stockholm International Peace Research Institute, July 18, 2013, http://www.sipri.org/media/expert-comments/shadow-trade-how-north-koreas-barter-trade-violates-united-nations-sanctions.

2. Understanding the Product

1. For analysis of the weaponization of North Korea's plutonium and highly enriched uranium programs, see Mary Beth Nikitin, "North Korea's Nuclear Weap-

ons: Technical Issues," Congressional Research Service, RL34256, April 3, 2013, https://www.fas.org/sgp/crs/nuke/RL34256.pdf.

2. See Joseph S. Nye, "Understanding the North Korean Threat," Project Syndicate, December 6, 2017, https://www.project-syndicate.org/commentary/understanding-north-korea-threat-by-joseph-s--nye-2017-12.

3. Robert L. Gallucci, "North Korea, Iran, and the Proliferation of Nuclear Weapons: The Threat, U.S. Policy, and the Prescription . . . and the India Deal," in *How to Make America Safe: New Policies for National Security,* ed. Stephan Van Evera (Cambridge, MA: Tobin Project, 2006), http://www.tobinproject.org/sites/tobinproject.org/files/assets/Make_America_Safe_North_Korea_Iran_Nuclear_Proliferation.pdf.

4. For more information about North Korea's first two nuclear tests, see Mark Fitzpatrick, "North Korean Proliferation Challenges: The Role of the European Union," EU Non-Proliferation Consortium, Non-Proliferation Papers, no. 18, June 2012, http://www.sipri.org/research/disarmament/eu-consortium/publications/nonproliferation-paper-18.

5. "N. Korea Resumes Tests for Smaller Missile Warheads," *Chosun Ilbo,* February 26, 2015, http://english.chosun.com/site/data/html_dir/2015/02/26/2015022601825.html.

6. See Victor Cha and Ellen Kim, "North Korea's Third Nuclear Test," Center for Strategic and International Studies, February 12, 2013, http://csis.org/publication/north-koreas-third-nuclear-test; and Kelsey Davenport, "North Korea Conducts Nuclear Test," *Arms Control Today* (Arms Control Association), February 28, 2013, https://www.armscontrol.org/act/2013_03/North-Korea-Conducts-Nuclear-Test.

7. "Iranian Nuke Chief Was in N. Korea for Atomic Test," *The Times of Israel,* February 17, 2013, http://www.timesofisrael.com/iranian-nuke-chief-was-in-n-korea-for-atomic-test.

8. See Jim Wolf, "N. Korea Closer to Nuclear Tipped Missile: U.S. Expert," Reuters, December 28, 2011, http://www.reuters.com/article/2011/12/28/us-korea-north-nuclear-idUSTRE7BR00520111228; Jeffrey Lewis, "North Korea's Nuclear Weapons: The Great Miniaturization Debate," 38 North, February 5, 2015, http://38north.org/2015/02/jlewis020515; and Bill Gertz, "Report: N. Korea Has Nuclear Warheads for Missiles," *Washington Free Beacon,* May 5, 2014, http://freebeacon.com/national-security/report-n-korea-has-nuclear-warheads-for-missiles.

9. Blaine Harden, "Japan Prepares to Shoot Down North Korean Missile in Case of Accident," *Washington Post,* March 28, 2009, http://www.washingtonpost.com/wp-dyn/content/article/2009/03/27/AR2009032700501.html.

10. See "North Korea's Yongbyon Nuclear Facility: New Activity at the Plutonium Production Complex," 38 North, September 8, 2015, http://38north.org/2015/09/yongbyon090815; "N. Korea Digging New Tunnel at Its Nuke Test Site: Official," *Yonhap,* October 30, 2015, http://english.yonhapnews.co.kr/news/2015/10/30/0200000000AEN20151030002800315.html; Andrea Shalal, David Brunnstrom, and Jonathan Landay, "North Korea Nuclear Test Did Not Increase Technical

Capability: U.S.," Reuters, January 19, 2016, http://www.reuters.com/article/us-northkorea-nuclear-usa-idUSKCN0UY042; "North Korea Nuclear Blast Shows 'Uncanny Resemblance' to Last Test—Analyst," Reuters, January 8, 2016, http://in.reuters.com/article/northkorea-nuclear-seismic-idINKBN0UM0KY20160108; Nick Hansen, Robert Kelley, and Allison Puccioni, "North Korean Nuclear Programme Advances," *Jane's Intelligence Review,* March 30, 2016, http://www.janes.com/article/59118/north-korean-nuclear-programme-advances; and "North Korea's Nuclear Programme: How Advanced Is It?" BBC, January 6, 2016, http://www.bbc.com/news/world-asia-pacific-11813699.

11. See Foster Klug and Kim Tong-Hyung, "Rhetoric or Real? N. Korea Nuclear Test May Be a Bit of Both," Associated Press, September 11, 2016, http://bigstory.ap.org/article/f9234cbd0efa4d3caafcbecb88e16576/rhetoric-or-real-n-korea-nuclear-test-may-be-bit-both; and Kang Jin-kyu and Kang Chan-su, "North Korea's Fifth Nuclear Test Strongest Yet," *Joongang Ilbo,* September 10, 2016, http://mengnews.joins.com/view.aspx?aId=3023659.

12. For detailed analysis that supports the assessments of North Korea's sixth nuclear test, see Vladimir Khrustalev, "Thermonuclear Shock: A Detailed Analysis of the Explosion of the DPRK's Hydrogen Bomb and Its Consequences," Defcon Warning System, September 8, 2017, https://defconwarningsystem.com/2017/09/08/thermonuclear-shock-detailed-analysis-explosion-dprks-hydrogen-bomb-consequences; Choe Sang-hun and David E. Sanger, "North Korean Nuclear Test Draws U.S. Warning of 'Massive Military Response,'" *New York Times,* September 2, 2017, https://www.nytimes.com/2017/09/03/world/asia/north-korea-tremor-possible-6th-nuclear-test.html?mcubz=3; James Griffiths and Angela Dewan, "What Is a Hydrogen Bomb and Can North Korea Deliver One?" CNN, September 3, 2017, http://www.cnn.com/2017/09/03/asia/hydrogen-bomb-north-korea-explainer/index.html; and "The Nuclear Explosion in North Korea on 3 September 2017: A Revised Magnitude Assessment," NORSAR, September 12, 2017, https://www.norsar.no/press/latest-press-release/archive/the-nuclear-explosion-in-north-korea-on-3-september-2017-a-revised-magnitude-assessment-article1548-984.html; and Eleanor Albert, "North Korea's Military Capabilities," Council on Foreign Relations, Backgrounder, November 30, 2017, https://www.cfr.org/backgrounder/north-koreas-military-capabilities.

13. See "Aftershocks Likely from September Test Detected from North Korea Nuclear Test Site: USGS," Reuters, December 9, 2017, https://www.reuters.com/article/us-northkorea-missiles-tremors/aftershocks-likely-from-september-test-detected-from-north-korea-nuclear-site-usgs-idUSKBN1E30LD.

14. Jeremy Bender, "Top Norad General: North Korea Has a Nuclear-Capable Missile That Can Hit the US," *Business Insider,* April 10, 2015, http://www.businessinsider.com/us-general-north-korea-has-nuclear-capable-missile-that-can-hit-us-2015-4.

15. See Luis Martinez, "North Korea Can Put a Nuke on a Missile, U.S. Intelligence Agency Believes," ABC News, April 13, 2013, http://abcnews.go.com/Politics/north-korea-put-nuke-missile-us-intelligence-agency/story?id=18935588.

16. Anthony Capaccio, "North Korea Can Miniaturize a Nuclear Weapon: U.S. Says," Bloomberg, April 7, 2015, http://www.bloomberg.com/news/articles/2015-04-07/n-korea-can-mount-miniature-nuclear-weapon-u-s-admiral-says.

17. Richard Sisk, "US General Tells Senate North Korea Can Hit US with Nuclear ICBM," Military.com, April 16, 2015, http://www.military.com/daily-news/2015/04/16/us-general-tells-senate-north-korea-can-hit-us-with-nuclear-icbm.html.

18. For more on the differing assessments of North Korea's ability to put a nuclear warhead on an ICBM capable of hitting the United States, see Baik Sung-won, "US Dismisses Disagreement with Seoul on N Korea Nuclear Threat," Voice of America, April 14, 2015, http://www.voanews.com/content/united-states-dismisses-disagreement-north-korea-nuclear-threat/2719548.html.

19. "N. Korea Claims It Has Miniaturized Nuke Weapons," Yonhap, May 20, 2015, http://english.yonhapnews.co.kr/northkorea/2015/05/20/84/0401000000AEN20150520006853315F.html.

20. For more on the credibility of the North Korean statement made in May 2015 as well as discussion of past exaggerated claims and the debate that has been created as a result of the DPRK announcement, see Choe Sang-hun, "North Korea Claims It Has Built Small Nuclear Warheads," New York Times, May 20, 2015, http://www.nytimes.com/2015/05/21/world/asia/north-korea-claims-it-has-built-small-nuclear-warheads.html?_r=0; and Anna Fifield, "North Korea Claims It Has the Technology to Make Mini–Nuclear Weapons," Washington Post, May 20, 2015, http://www.washingtonpost.com/world/pyongyang-says-it-has-technology-to-make-small-submarined-mounted-nuclear-warheads/2015/05/20/0e96d0bc-fec0-11e4-833c-a2de05b6b2a4_story.html.

21. See "N. Korea Seen Successful in Design of ICBM Vehicle, Nuclear Warhead," Yonhap, March 31, 2016, http://english.yonhapnews.co.kr/northkorea/2016/03/31/0401000000AEN20160331010900315.html; and Adam Taylor, "North Korea's Possible Nuclear Warhead Looks Silly—but It's Still Concerning," Washington Post, March 9, 2016, https://www.washingtonpost.com/news/worldviews/wp/2016/03/09/north-koreas-possible-nuclear-warhead-looks-silly-but-its-still-concerning/?utm_term=.384165afb5f8.

22. For more on the proliferation to Iran of the Scud B missiles, see Alon Levkowitz, "Iran and North-Korea Cooperation: A Partnership within the Axis of Evil," Iran Pulse (Alliance Center for Iranian Studies), no. 10, February 26, 2007, http://humanities1.tau.ac.il/iranian/en/previous-reviews/10-iran-pulse-en/117-10.

23. For an excellent example of an account that shows nothing but contempt for North Korea's ballistic missile capabilities (including testing and not taking into account tests conducted in Iran, Pakistan, Syria, etc.) and claims that North Korea has not produced any reliable missiles, see Markus Schiller, "Characterizing the North Korean Nuclear Missile Threat," Rand Technical Report, 2012, http://www.rand.org/content/dam/rand/pubs/technical_reports/2012/RAND_TR1268.pdf.

24. For more on the training that North Korean specialists received in

China on the Beidou satellite navigation system, see "NK Delegates Received Intensive Training in GPS Technology in China," *Donga Ilbo,* August 2, 2014, http://english.donga.com/srv/service.php3?biid=2014080276698; and "North Koreans Learn about China's Beidou Satellite Navigation System," North Korea Tech, July 31, 2014, https://www.northkoreatech.org/2014/07/31/north-koreans-learn-about-chinas-beidou-satellite-navigation-system.

25. Leo Byrne, "Parts from U.S., UK and SK in North Korean Rocket," *NK News,* March 26, 2014, http://www.nknews.org/2014/03/parts-from-u-s-uk-and-sk-in-north-korean-rocket.

26. See Choe Sang-hun, "North Korea May Soon Have More Powerful Rocket," *New York Times,* August 22, 2014, http://www.nytimes.com/2014/08/23/world/asia/north-korea-may-soon-have-more-powerful-rocket.html?_r=0; Tim Brown, "North Korea: New Construction at the Sohae Satellite Launching Station," 38 North, May 28, 2015, http://38north.org/2015/05/sohae052815; Patrick Cronin, "North Korea's Balance of Terror," Real Clear Defense, May 27, 2015, http://www.realcleardefense.com/articles/2015/05/27/north_koreas_balance_of_terror_107977.html; Koo Jun-hoe, "Construction at Sohae Launch Site to Finish by 2015," *Daily NK,* July 30, 2014, http://www.dailynk.com/english/read.php?num=12151&cataId=nk00100; and Nick Hansen, "North Korea's Sohae Facility: Preparations for Future Large Rocket Launches Progresses [*sic*]; New Unidentified Buildings," 38 North, July 29, 2014, http://38north.org/2014/07/sohae073014.

27. For details and analysis of the events leading up to the launch and the results of the launch as well as the impact of the launch on military planning, see Elizabeth Shim, "North Korea Freight Train en Route to Launch Pad," UPI, October 1, 2015, http://www.upi.com/Top_News/World-News/2015/10/01/North-Korea-freight-train-en-route-to-launch-pad/9091443749385; "Suspicious Activity at North Korea's Sohae Satellite Launching Station," 38 North, January 28, 2016, http://38north.org/2016/01/sohae012816; "US Ship Capable of Tracking NK Rocket Arrives in Japan," *Yonhap,* February 6, 2016, http://english.yonhapnews.co.kr/news/2016/02/06/0200000000AEN20160206001900315.html; David Brunnstrom, "U.S. Officials Say North Korea May Be Nearing Launch," Reuters, February 5, 2016, http://www.reuters.com/article/us-northkorea-satellite-fueling-idUSKCN0VE2C4; Kim Tong-Hyung, "Seoul: N. Korea Moves Up Rocket Launch Window to Feb. 7–14," Associated Press, February 6, 2016, https://www.bostonglobe.com/news/world/2016/02/06/seoul-korea-moves-rocket-launch-window-feb/IXdJEgvR0G5TuP2QpJ0ZPJ/story.html; Jeong Yong-soo, "North Has Prepared a Backup Missile: Sources," *Joongang Ilbo,* February 6, 2016, http://koreajoongangdaily.joins.com/news/article/Article.aspx?aid=3014867; "US to Use Missile Defense System to Monitor North Korea's Upcoming Missile Launch—Carter," TASS, February 6, 2016, http://tass.com/world/854696; Elaine Yu, "North Korea's Planned Rocket Launch: Airlines Re-Route Flights," CNN, February 5, 2016, http://www.cnn.com/2016/02/05/travel/japan-airlines-reroute-flights-north-korea-launch; Jack Kim and Tim Kelly, "US, Allies Aim to Track North Korean Rocket; Launch 'Win-

dow' from Monday," Reuters, February 5, 2016, http://uk.reuters.com/article/
uk-northkorea-satellite-idUKKCN0VE084; "Kim Jong-un 'to Watch Rocket
Launch on Site,'" *Chosun Ilbo,* February 5, 2016, http://english.chosun.com/site/data/
html_dir/2016/02/05/2016020501206.html; Martyn Williams, "Launch Notification Reveals Rocket Drop Zones," North Korea Tech, February 3, 2016, http://
www.northkoreatech.org/2016/02/03/launch-notification-reveals-rocket-drop-
zones; Jack Kim, "North Korea Leader Flies Private Jet to Oversee Rocket Launch,"
Reuters, February 11, 2016, http://www.reuters.com/article/us-northkorea-satellite-
launch-idUSKCN0VK0N2; "North Korea Rocket Launch Deemed Successful and
Deplorable," *Chosun Ilbo,* February 7, 2017, https://article.wn.com/view/2016/02/
07/NKorea_Rocket_Launch_Deemed_Successful_and_Deplorable;
Ju-min Park, "South Korea Says Retrieves Suspected Fairing from North Korean
Rocket," Reuters, February 7, 2016, http://www.reuters.com/article/us-north-
korea-satellite-southkorea-idUSKCN0VG0CF; Sarah Kim and Jeong Yong-soo,
"Navy Finds Missile Launch Debris," *Joongang Ilbo,* February 12, 2016, http://
koreajoongangdaily.joins.com/news/article/article.aspx?aid=3014980; "How North
Korea Surprised the World with Rocket Launch," *Chosun Ilbo,* February 12, 2016,
http://english.chosun.com/site/data/html_dir/2016/02/12/2016021201503.html; Yi
Whan-woo, "North Korea Closer to Developing ICBM," *Korea Times,* February
10, 2016, http://www.koreatimes.co.kr/www/news/nation/2016/02/116_197658.
html; and Michael Elleman, "North Korea Launches Another Large Rocket: Consequences and Options," 38 North, February 10, 2016, http://38north.org/2016/02/
melleman021016.

28. See "N. Korea Fires 25 Short-Range Missiles toward East Sea," *Yonhap,*
March 16, 2014, http://english.yonhapnews.co.kr/national/2014/03/16/90/0301
000000AEN20140316003053315F.html; and "North Korea Fires More Short-
Range Rockets," Aljazeera, March 23, 2014, http://www.aljazeera.com/news/asia-
pacific/2014/03/north-korea-fires-more-short-range-rockets-201432341048349836.
html.

29. See "N. Korea Fires 2 Short-Range Missiles," *Chosun Ilbo,* June 30, 2014,
http://english.chosun.com/site/data/html_dir/2014/06/30/2014063001240.html;
Jung-yoon Choi, "Seoul: North Korea Again Test-Fires Projectiles," Associated
Press, July 12, 2014, http://news.yahoo.com/seoul-north-korea-again-test-fires-
projectiles-012259610.html; "Why Does N. Korea Keep Firing Missiles?" *Chosun Ilbo,*
July 11, 2014, http://english.chosun.com/site/data/html_dir/2014/07/11/2014071
101081.html; Hyung-jin Kim, "North Korea Fires Short-Range Missile into the
Sea," Associated Press, July 26, 2014, http://theadvocate.com/home/9824485-
125/north-korea-fires-short-range-missile (link inactive); Kim Hee-jin and Jeong
Yong-soo, "About 100 Missiles Fired by North into East Sea," *Joongang Ilbo,* July 15, 2014,
http://koreajoongangdaily.joins.com/news/article/article.aspx?aid=2992027; and
Franz-Stefan Gady, "North Korea Fires 2 Ballistic Missiles into Sea," *The Diplomat,*
March 3, 2015. http://thediplomat.com/2015/03/north-korea-fires-2-ballistic-
missiles-into-sea.

30. See Francisco Galamas, "2014: A Year in North Korean Security," *The Diplomat,* December 16, 2014, http://thediplomat.com/2014/12/2014-a-year-in-north-korean-security; "N. Korea Fires Two Ballistic Missiles," *Korea Herald,* March 26, 2014, http://www.koreaherald.com/view.php?ud=20140326001485&mod=skb; and "N. Korea Ready to Fire Medium-Range Nodong Missiles: Military Source," *Yonhap,* March 3, 2015, http://english.yonhapnews.co.kr/national/2015/03/03/24/0 301000000AEN20150303004800315F.html.

31. See Kim Eun-jung, "N. Korea Has 100 KN-02 Missiles with Extended Range," *Yonhap,* March 4, 2014, http://english.yonhapnews.co.kr/news/2014/03/ 05/99/0200000000AEN20140305002300315F.html; and John Grisafi, "Recent Launches Revealed as Surface-to-Surface Missile," *NK News,* August 16, 2014, http:// www.nknews.org/2014/08/recent-launches-revealed-as-surface-to-surface-missile.

32. "North Korea Fires Two Short-Range Missiles into the Sea—South Korea," Reuters, March 10, 2016, http://www.reuters.com/article/northkorea-missiles-idUSL4N16H58W.

33. Lolita C. Baldor, "Seoul: North Korea Fires Ballistic Missile into Sea," Associated Press, March 17, 2016, http://www.militarytimes.com/story/military/2016/03/ 17/seoul-north-korea-fires-ballistic-missile-into-sea/81950254.

34. Jun Ji-hye, "N. Korea Fires Two Mid-Range Missiles," *Korea Times,* March 18, 2016, http://www.koreatimes.co.kr/www/news/nation/2016/09/116_200692. html.

35. "N. Korea Fired 31 Ballistic Missiles in Past 5 Years," *Yonhap,* July 27, 2016, http://english.yonhapnews.co.kr/northkorea/2016/07/27/0401000000AEN201607 27003400315.html.

36. See Lee Yong-soo, "N. Korea Fires Missiles over East Sea," *Chosun Ilbo,* July 20, 2016, http://english.chosun.com/site/data/html_dir/2016/07/20/2016072000730. html; and Kang Jin-kyu, "North Claimed to Have Simulated THAAD Strikes," *Joongang Ilbo,* July 21, 2016, http://koreajoongangdaily.joins.com/news/article/Article .aspx?aid=3021571.

37. Yu Yong-weon, "N. Korea Fires Missile into Japanese-Controlled Waters," *Chosun Ilbo,* August 4, 2016, http://english.chosun.com/site/data/html_dir/2016/08/ 04/2016080400911.html.

38. See Jack Kim and Ju-min Park, "North Korea Missiles Were Medium-Range, Flew 1,000 Km into Japan's Air Defense Zone," Reuters, September 5, 2017, http:// www.reuters.com/article/us-northkorea-missiles-range-idUSKCN11B0FR; and "N. Korea Plays Hide-and-Seek with Spy Satellites," *Chosun Ilbo,* September 9, 2016, http://english.chosun.com/site/data/html_dir/2016/09/09/2016090901365.html.

39. See Tyler Rogoway, "North Korea Says KN-06 SAM System Ready for Production After Successful Test," The Drive, May 28, 2017, http://www.thedrive.com/ the-war-zone/10761/north-korea-says-kn-06-sam-system-ready-for-production-after-successful-test; and "N.K. Leader Inspects Test-Fire of New Anti-Aircraft Weapon," *Yonhap,* May 28, 2017, http://english.yonhapnews.co.kr/northkorea/2017 /05/28/0401000000AEN20170528000300315.html.

40. C. P. Vick, "KN-08: Hwasong-13: The Semi-Mobile Limited Range ICBM, No-Dong-C," Global Security.org, 2015, http://www.globalsecurity.org/wmd/world/dprk/kn-08.htm.

41. "North Korea: Missile," Nuclear Threat Initiative, December 2014, http://www.nti.org/country-profiles/north-korea/delivery-systems.

42. Jack Kim and Phil Stewart, "US to Send Missile Defenses to Guam over North Korea Threat," Reuters, April 4, 2013, http://www.reuters.com/article/2013/04/05/us-korea-north-idUSBRE93002620130405.

43. See Richard Spencer, "N Korea 'Tests New Missile in Iran,'" *The Telegraph*, May 17, 2007, http://www.telegraph.co.uk/news/worldnews/1551868/N-Korea-tests-new-missile-in-Iran.html; and Anthony H. Cordesman and Ashley Hess, *The Evolving Military Balance in the Korean Peninsula and Northeast Asia*, vol. 3, *Missile, DPRK and ROK Nuclear Forces, and External Nuclear Forces*, Report: Center for Strategic and International Studies, July 10, 2013, https://csis-prod.s3.amazonaws.com/s3fs-public/legacy_files/files/publication/130513_KMB_volume3.pdf.

44. For analysis of the North Korean Musudan launches that occurred in April 2016, see Jeong Yong-soo, "Seoul Studies Pyongyang's Missile Move," *Joongang Ilbo*, April 15, 2016, http://koreajoongangdaily.joins.com/news/article/Article.aspx?aid=3017573; Foster Klug and Hyung-jin Kim, "US: North Korean Missile Launch a 'Catastrophic' Failure," Associated Press, April 15, 2016, http://bigstory.ap.org/article/67c278f79593454e868ff3f707606ef3/seoul-says-north-korean-missile-launch-apparently-fails; and Bill Gertz, "North Korean Missile Exploded, Damaged Launcher in Failed Test," *Washington Free Beacon*, April 20, 2016, http://freebeacon.com/national-security/north-korean-missile-exploded-failed.

45. For more analysis of details of what eventually proved to be a successful Musudan launch, see "N. Korea in a Hurry to Prove Mid-Range Ballistic Missile," *Chosun Ilbo*, June 23, 2016, http://english.chosun.com/site/data/html_dir/2016/06/23/2016062301274.html; Kang Jin-Kyu and Jeong Yong-soo, "Two Musudan Missiles Reveal Technical Advance," *Joongang Ilbo*, June 23, 2016, http://koreajoongangdaily.joins.com/news/article/Article.aspx?aid=3020380; "N Korea Conducts Mid-Range Missile Tests," BBC News, June 22, 2016, http://www.bbc.com/news/world-asia-36593321; Park Boram, "N. Korea Fires Off 2 Musudan IRBM Missiles," *Yonhap*, June 22, 2016, http://www.koreatimes.co.kr/www/news/nation/2016/06/485_207574.html; Tal Inbar, "Hwasong-10 Shows the Value [of] North Korea's Perseverance," *NK News*, June 24, 2016, https://www.nknews.org/2016/06/hwasong-10-shows-the-value-north-koreas-perseverance; and Park Boram, "Latest Test Reveals N. Korean Missile Capable of Flying 3,500 Km: Military," *Yonhap*, June 24, 2016, http://english.yonhapnews.co.kr/national/2016/06/24/88/0301000000AEN20160624007651315F.html.

46. Some parts of this chapter were previously published in Bruce E. Bechtol Jr., "The North Korean Military Threat in 2015: The Threat to the ROK-U.S. Alliance and Peninsula Unification," *International Journal of Korean Studies* 19, no. 1 (Spring 2015): 1–35. I would like to thank the editors and staff of the *Interna-*

tional Journal of Korean Studies for their cooperation, collaboration, and support of this research.

47. Bill Gertz, "Inside the Ring: North Korean Missiles Deemed a Serious Threat to the U.S.," *Washington Times,* November 6, 2013, http://www.washingtontimes.com/news/2013/nov/6/inside-the-ring-north-korean-missiles-deemed-a-ser/?page=all.

48. James R. Clapper, "Statement for the Record, Worldwide Threat Assessment of the US Intelligence Community, Senate Select Committee on Intelligence," January 29, 2014, http://www.dni.gov/files/documents/Intelligence%20Reports/2014%20WWTA%20%20SFR_SSCI_29_Jan.pdf.

49. C. D. Haney, "Statement of Admiral C. D. Haney, Commander, United States Strategic Command, before the Senate Committee on Armed Services, 19 March 2015," http://www.defenseinnovationmarketplace.mil/resources/2015_Posture_Statement.pdf.

50. See Andrea Shalal, "U.S. Eyes Iran, North Korea Missile Threats, Boosts Testing Tempo," Reuters, May 18, 2015, http://www.reuters.com/article/2015/03/18/us-usa-military-missiledefense-threat-idUSKBN0ME2ZB20150318; and "U.S. Trying to 'Stay Ahead' of N. Korea's KN-08 Missile Threat: Official," *Korea Herald,* February 4, 2015, http://english.yonhapnews.co.kr/news/2015/02/04/0200000000AEN20150204000200315.html?input=rss.

51. Jon Harper, "NORAD Commander: North Korean KN-08 Missile Operational," *Stars and Stripes,* April 7, 2015, http://www.stripes.com/news/norad-commander-north-korean-kn-08-missile-operational-1.338909.

52. Sisk, "US General Tells Senate North Korea Can Hit US With Nuclear ICBM."

53. John Schilling, "Where's That North Korean ICBM Everyone Was Talking About?" 38 North, March 12, 2015, http://38north.org/2015/03/jschilling031215.

54. See Joseph Bermudez and Henry Kan, "Location of KN-08 Reentry Vehicle Nosecone Identified," 38 North, March 23, 2016, http://38north.org/2016/03/chamjin032316.

55. See Jack Kim and David Brunnstrom, "Declassified: Secretive North Korea Lifts Veil on Arms Program," Reuters, April 12, 2016, http://www.reuters.com/article/us-northkorea-nuclear-idUSKCN0X91LD; and Anna Fifield, "North Korea Unveils Homemade Engine for Missile Capable of Striking U.S.," *Washington Post,* April 8, 2016, https://www.washingtonpost.com/world/north-korea-unveils-home-made-engine-for-missile-capable-of-striking-us/2016/04/08/bd5e3b6e-d3a7-4c81-8d17-98ee5bee03d7_story.html?utm_term=.7469852e9e8e.

56. See "N. Korea Launches New ICBM Unit: Sources," *Yonhap,* February 14, 2016, http://english.yonhapnews.co.kr/northkorea/2016/02/14/43/0401000000AEN20160214001100315F.html.

57. See Richard D. Fisher Jr., "North Korea Unveils New Version of KN-08 ICBM," *Jane's Defense Weekly,* October 12, 2015, http://www.janes.com/article/55190/north-korea-unveils-new-version-of-kn-08-icbm; Scott LaFoy, "Analysis: Redesigned KN-08 Missile Unveiled in Military Parade," *NK News,* October 16, 2015,

https://www.nknews.org/2015/10/analysis-redesigned-kn-08-missile-unveiled-in-military-parade; Tal Inbar, "N. Korea Missiles: No Room for Doubt," *Defense News,* April 4, 2016, 22; and John Schilling, "North Korea's Large Rocket Engine Test: A Significant Step Forward for Pyongyang's ICBM Program," 38 North, April 11, 2016, http://38north.org/2016/04/schilling041116.

58. See Lee Sung-eun, "North Korea Parades What Appears to Be New ICBM," *Joongang Ilbo,* April 15, 2017, http://mengnews.joins.com/view.aspx?aId=3032264; "North Korea Displays New ICBM, Other Missiles," Voice of America, April 15, 2017, http://www.voanews.com/a/north-korea-missiles-icbm/3811277.html; and Ian Williams, "North Korea's New Missiles on Parade," Center for Strategic and International Studies, April 18, 2017, https://www.csis.org/analysis/north-koreas-new-missiles-parade.

59. For details and analysis of the test launch of the extended range, Musudan-based KN-17 (also called the Hwasong-12) missile in the North Korean inventory (as of May 2017), assessments of its capabilities and specifications, and predictions regarding the damage that it could cause to the United States, see Ralph Savelsberg, "A Quick Technical Analysis of the Hwasong-12," 38 North, May 19, 2017, http://www.38north.org/2017/05/hwasong051917; "Hwasong-12," Missile Threat, Center for Strategic and International Studies, May 16, 2017, https://missilethreat.csis.org/missile/hwasong-12; Jonathan Pollack, "Danger Zone: Why North Korea's Latest Missile Is More Worrying Than Any to Date," Brookings Institution, May 17, 2017, https://www.brookings.edu/blog/order-from-chaos/2017/05/17/danger-zone-why-north-koreas-latest-missile-test-is-more-worrying-than-any-to-date; John Schilling, "North Korea's Latest Missile Test: Advancing toward an Intercontinental Ballistic Missile (ICBM) While Avoiding US Military Action," 38 North, May 14, 2017, http://www.38north.org/2017/05/jschilling051417; Lee Chi-dong, "N. Korea Seen Closer to ICBM, Boosted by New Missile Engine," *Yonhap,* May 15, 2017, http://english.yonhapnews.co.kr/northkorea/2017/05/15/0401000000AEN20170515007100315.html; Lee Chul-hae, "North May Have Re-Entry Technology," *Joongang Ilbo,* May 18, 2017, http://koreajoongangdaily.joins.com/news/article/article.aspx?aid=3033474; and Lee Chul-hae, "North May Be Running Low on Mobile Launchers," *Joongang Ilbo,* May 19, 2017, http://koreajoongangdaily.joins.com/news/article/article.aspx?aid=3033539&cloc=joongangdaily%7Chome%7Cnewslist1.

60. For examples of more launches of the Hwasong-12, see Chris Graham, Danny Boyle, and Neil Connor, "North Korea Fires Second Missile over Japan as US Tells China and Russia to Take 'Direct Action,'" *The Telegraph,* September 15, 2017, http://www.telegraph.co.uk/news/2017/09/14/north-korea-files-another-ballistic-missile-japan-residents.

61. See "Hwasong-14 (KN-20)," Center for Strategic and International Studies, Missile Defense Project, 2017, https://missilethreat.csis.org/missile/hwasong-14.

62. For in-depth analysis and details regarding the launch of North Korea's first proven mobile ICBM missile, the location of the missile launch, and the mobile

launcher that transported the missile, see Lee Chi-dong, "N. Korea Claims 'Game Changer' Missile Development," *Yonhap,* July 4, 2017, http://english.yonhapnews .co.kr/focus/2017/07/04/27/1700000000AEN20170704017900315F.html; Uzi Rubin, "Pyongyang Intercontinental Inc.," Real Clear Defense, July 5, 2017, http:// www.realcleardefense.com/articles/2017/07/05/pyongyang_intercontinental_ inc_111730.html; Jack Kim, "North Korea Appeared to Use China Truck in Its First Claimed ICBM Test," Reuters, July 4, 2017, http://www.reuters.com/article/ us-northkorea-missiles-china-truck-idUSKBN19P1J3; Ankit Panda and Vipin Narang, "North Korea's ICBM: A New Missile and a New Era," *The Diplomat,* July 7, 2017, http://thediplomat.com/2017/07/north-koreas-icbm-a-new-missile-and-a-new-era; John Schilling, "North Korea Finally Tests an ICBM," 38 North, July 5, 2017, http://www.38north.org/2017/07/jschilling070517; Joseph Bermudez, "North Korea's Hwasong-14 Missile Launch Site Identified: The Panghyon Aircraft Factory," 38 North, July 6, 2017, http://www.38north.org/2017/07/panghyon070617; Mark Tokola, "The North Korean ICBM Test: A Significant Step but Still Just a Step," The Peninsula, Korea Economic Institute, July 5, 2017, http://blog.keia .org/2017/07/the-north-korean-icbm-test-a-significant-step-but-still-just-a-step; Benjamin Katzeff Silberstein, "North Korea's ICBM Test, Byungjin, and the Economic Logic," *The Diplomat,* July 5, 2017, http://thediplomat.com/2017/07/north-koreas-icbm-test-byungjin-and-the-economic-logic; and Jun Ji-hye, "N. Korea Claims Successful Launch of ICBM," *Korea Times,* July 4, 2017, http://www.koreatimes .co.kr/www/nation/2017/07/103_232404.html.

63. For detailed analysis of the North Korean mobile ICBM launch of July 28, 2017, see Michael Elleman "Early Observations of North Korea's Latest Missile Tests," 38 North, July 28, 2017, http://www.38north.org/2017/07/ melleman072817; "Kim Jong Un Attends Second Hwasong-14 Missile Test," North Korean Leadership Watch, July 29, 2017, http://www.nkleadershipwatch. org/2017/07/29/kim-jong-un-attends-second-hwasong-14-missile-test; David Sanger, Choe Sang-hun, and William J. Broad, "North Korea Tests a Ballistic Missile That Experts Say Could Hit California," *New York Times,* July 28, 2017, https://www.nytimes.com/2017/07/28/world/asia/north-korea-ballistic-missile. html; Colin Dwyer, "North Korea Says Successful ICBM Test Shows U.S. Is in Striking Distance," NPR, July 28, 2017, http://www.npr.org/sections/thetwo-way/ 2017/07/28/540008218/north-korea-h-ballistic-missile-seoul-and-the-pentagon-say; and Leah Crane, "North Korea Launches ICBM with Potential to Reach New York," *New Scientist,* July 28, 2017, https://www.newscientist.com/article/2142224-north-korea-launches-icbm-with-potential-to-reach-new-york.

64. For sources that claim the reentry vehicle may have broken up prior to splashing down in the Pacific Ocean, see Jesse Johnson, "NHK Video Casts Doubt on North Korean ICBM Re-Entry Capabilities and Effectiveness," *Japan Times,* August 1, 2017, http://www.japantimes.co.jp/news/2017/08/01/asia-pacific/nhk-video-casts-doubt-north-korean-icbms-re-entry-capabilities/#.WYQ87jGWyM8. For analysis that assesses there is not enough evidence to support the claim that the reentry vehicle broke

up prior to splashing into the Pacific, see Tal Inbar and Uzi Rubin, "Did the Hwa-song-14 Really Breakup upon Re-entry?" *NK News,* August 7, 2017, https://www.nknews.org/pro/did-the-hwasong-14-really-breakup-upon-re-entry.

65. For assessments that the Hwasong-14 can probably hit Alaska and maybe Hawaii but that weight restrictions may keep it from targets farther away, see Raphael Ofek, "The Puzzle of the North Korean ICBM," Begin-Sadat Center for Strategic Studies, Perspective Paper no. 634, November 5, 2017, https://besacenter.org/perspectives-papers/north-korea-icbm; Theodore A. Postol, Markus Schiller, and Robert Schmucker, "North Korea's 'Not Quite' ICBM Can't Hit the Lower 48 States," *Bulletin of the Atomic Scientists,* August 11, 2017, http://thebulletin.org/north-korea%E2%80%99s-%E2%80%9Cnot-quite%E2%80%9D-icbm-can%E2%80%99t-hit-lower-48-states11012. For assessments that North Korea acquired engines from former Soviet manufacturers in Ukraine that were used for both the Hwasong-12 and the Hwasong-14 missiles, see Michael Elleman, "The Secret to North Korea's ICBM Success," International Institute for Strategic Stud-ies, August 14, 2017, http://www.iiss.org/en/iiss%20voices/blogsections/iiss-voices-2017-adeb/august-2b48/north-korea-icbm-success-3abb. For sources stating that Elleman's assessment has many flaws and cannot be proved and that also reference US government sources disputing it, see Joshua H. Pollack, "How North Korea Makes Its Missiles: Two Reports This Week Made Crucial Mistakes about the DPRK's Rocket Development," *NK News,* August 18, 2017, https://www.nknews.org/2017/08/how-north-korea-makes-its-missiles; and Jonathan Landay, "North Korea Likely Can Make Missile Engines without Imports: U.S.," Reuters, August 15, 2017, https://www.reuters.com/article/us-northkorea-missiles-intelligence-idUSKCN1AV2CK.

66. For discussion of the assessment by US intelligence officials that North Korea now has a nuclear warhead capable of being launched on a long-range mis-sile following its second successful ICBM test launch, see Joby Warrick, "North Korea Defies Predictions—Again—with Early Grasp of Weapons Milestone," *Washington Post,* September 3, 2017, https://www.washingtonpost.com/world/national-security/north-korea-defies-predictions—again—with-early-grasp-of-weapons-milestone/2017/09/03/068ac20c-90db-11e7–89fa-bb822a46da5b_story.html?utm_term=.b41d18abc0cb.

67. For assessments and analysis of the capabilities of the Hwasong-15 (KN-22), motivations behind the building of the missile, and likely implications for tar-geting the United States, see David Brunnstrom and Josh Smith, "North Korea Images Suggest Missile Capable of Hitting All America: U.S. Experts," Reuters, November 30, 2017, https://www.reuters.com/article/us-northkorea-missiles-photos/north-korea-images-suggest-missile-capable-of-hitting-all-america-u-s-experts-idUSKBN1DU0Q5; Jun Ji-hye, "Has North Korea Mastered Re-Entry Technology?" *Korea Times,* November 29, 2017, http://www.koreatimes.co.kr/www/nation/2017/11/103_240133.html, and "North Korea Shows New Features of ICBM," *Korea Times,* November 30, 2017, http://www.koreatimes.co.kr/www/nation/2017/12/103_240183.html; "Military: N. Korea's Hwasong-15 Seems Newly

Developed," *Yonhap*, November 29, 2017, http://english.yonhapnews.co.kr/nationa l/2017/11/30/0301000000AEN20171130001353315.html; "N. Korea Reveals Photos of Hwasong-15 ICBM," *Yonhap*, November 30, 2017, http://english.yonhapnews .co.kr/national/2017/11/30/69/0301000000AEN20171130001300315F.html; Choe Sang-hun, "North Korea's New Missile Is Bigger and More Powerful, Photos Suggest," *New York Times*, November 30, 2017, https://www.nytimes.com/2017/11/30/ world/asia/north-korea-missile-test.html; Zachary Cohen and Ryan Browne, "US Military Says North Korea Launched New ICBM," CNN, November 30, 2017, http://www.cnn.com/2017/11/30/politics/tillerson-china-north-korea-oil/index. html; David Wright, "Reentry of North Korea's Hwasong-15 Missile," Union of Concerned Scientists, December 7, 2017, https://allthingsnuclear.org/dwright/ reentry-of-hwasong-15; Jeff Seldin, "North Korea's New Missile: What We Know," Voice of America, December 1, 2017, https://www.voanews.com/a/north-korea-new-missile-what-we-know/4145056.html; Michael Elleman, "The New Hwasong-15 ICBM: A Significant Improvement That May Be Ready as Early as 2018," 38 North, November 30, 2017, http://www.38north.org/2017/11/melleman113017.

68. Joost Oliemans and Stijn Mitzer, "KPA Flag Ship Undergoing Radical Modernization," *NK News*, December 14, 2015, http://www.nknews.org/2014/12/ kpa-navy-flag-ship-undergoing-radical-modernization.

69. See Zachary Keck, "Who Sold North Korea a New Anti-Ship Missile?" *The Diplomat*, June 13, 2014, http://thediplomat.com/2014/06/who-sold-north-korea-a-new-anti-ship-missile; and "N Korea 'Develops Russian Cruise Missile,'" BBC News, June 17, 2014, http://www.bbc.com/news/world-asia-27881483.

70. Joseph Bermudez Jr., "The Korean People's Navy Tests New Anti-Ship Cruise Missile," 38 North, February 8, 2015, http://38north.org/2015/02/ jbermudez020815.

71. Kang Tae-jun, "North Korea Extends Range of KN01 Anti-Ship Missile—Media," *NK News*, November 25, 2013, http://www.nknews.org/2013/11/ north-korea-extends-range-of-kn01-anti-ship-missile-media.

72. See "N. Korea Builds New High-Speed Infiltration Boat," *Korea Times*, March 23, 2014, http://www.koreatimes.co.kr/www/news/nation/2015/05/205_153862 .html; and Jeong Yong-soo and Ser Myo-ja, "North Has New and Fast Submersible," *Joongang Ilbo*, May 28, 2015, http://koreajoongangdaily.joins.com/news/ article/Article.aspx?aid=3004696.

73. Daniel Dolan, "The North Korean Connection," *U.S. Naval Institute News*, February 14, 2013, https://news.usni.org/2012/06/17/north-korean-connection.

74. See "North Korea's Submarine Capabilities," *Vantage Point* 38, no. 3 (March 2015): 27–28; and "Investigation Result on the Sinking of ROKS 'Cheonan,'" *The Joint Civilian-Military Investigation Group*, May 20, 2010, https://www.globalsecurity .org/jhtml/jframe.html#https://www.globalsecurity.org/military/library/ report/2010/100520_jcmig-roks-cheonan/100520_jcmig-roks-cheonan.pdf.

75. See Ravi Shekhar Narain Singh, *Asian Strategic and Military Perspective* (New Delhi: Lancer, 2008), 231–32.

76. For more very useful information on the new North Korean submarine, see Bill Gertz, "North Korea Building Missile Submarine," *Washington Free Beacon,* August 26, 2014, http://freebeacon.com/national-security/north-korea-building-missile-submarine.

77. See Debalina Ghoshal, "Opinion: North Korea's Sea-Based Deterrent," US Naval Institute, December 1, 2014, http://news.usni.org/2014/12/01/opinion-north-koreas-sea-based-deterrent; and "North Korea Test Fires Submarine Launched Ballistic Missile," AFP, May 9, 2015, http://timesofindia.indiatimes.com/world/rest-of-world/North-Korea-test-fires-submarine-launched-ballistic-missile/articleshow/47214446.cms (link inactive).

78. See "N. Korea Launches Ballistic Missile Submarine: Gov't Sources," *Yonhap,* November 2, 2014, http://english.yonhapnews.co.kr/national/2014/10/31/35/0301000000AEN20141031009551315F.html; and Joseph Bermudez Jr., "North Korea's SINPO-Class Sub: New Evidence of Possible Vertical Launch Tubes; Sinpo Shipyard Prepares for Significant Naval Construction Program," 38 North, January 8, 2015, http://38north.org/2015/01/jbermudez010815.

79. See "S. Korea Spots Signs of N. Korea's Submarine Rocket Development," *Yonhap,* September 14, 2014, http://english.yonhapnews.co.kr/national/2014/09/14/65/0301000000AEN20140914000500315F.html; "N. Korea Conducts Ejection Launcher Test for Submarine Missile: Report," *Yonhap,* November 22, 2014, http://english.yonhapnews.co.kr/national/2014/11/22/39/0301000000AEN20141122000300315F.html; Bill Gertz, "U.S. Confirms North Korean Sub Missiles," *Washington Free Beacon,* March 19, 2015, http://freebeacon.com/national-security/u-s-confirms-north-korean-sub-missiles; Choe Sang-hun, "North Korea Says It Test-Fired Missile from Submarine," *New York Times,* May 8, 2015, http://www.nytimes.com/2015/05/09/world/asia/north-korea-says-it-test-fired-missile-from-submarine.html?_r=0; Bill Gertz, "U.S. Spy Agencies Closely Watched N. Korea Underwater Missile Test," *Washington Free Beacon,* May 11, 2015, http://freebeacon.com/national-security/u-s-spy-agencies-closely-watched-n-korea-underwater-missile-test; Ju-min Park and James Pearson, "North Korea Seen Years from Sub-Launched Missile to Threaten the U.S.," Reuters, May 11, 2015, http://www.reuters.com/article/2015/05/11/us-northkorea-submarine-south-idUSKBN0NW05W20150511; Chang Jae-soon, "Top U.S. Official Strongly Suggests N. Korea's Manipulation of Imagery of SLBM Test," *Yonhap,* May 19, 2015, http://english.yonhapnews.co.kr/full/2015/05/20/26/1200000000AEN20150520000200315F.html; and James Pearson, "North Korea Modified Submarine Missile Launch Photos, Says U.S. Official," Reuters, May 20, 2015, https://uk.reuters.com/article/uk-northkorea-submarine/north-korea-modified-submarine-missile-launch-photos-says-us-official-idUKKBN0O508I20150520.

80. For more details on the ejector device and predicted operational capabilities for the new DPRK SLBM, see Choi Ik-jae and Kang Jin-kyu, "North's Launcher Based on Soviet Device," *Joongang Ilbo,* May 18, 2015, http://koreajoongangdaily.joins.com/news/article/Article.aspx?aid=3004286; and Bruce Klingner, "The Grow-

ing North Korean Missile Threat," *The Daily Signal,* May 17, 2015, http://dailysignal
.com/2015/05/17/the-growing-north-korean-missile-threat.

81. James Dwyer, "North Korea's Submarine Missile Firing Raises the
Nuclear Stakes," *The Conversation,* May 18, 2015, http://theconversation.com/
north-koreas-submarine-missile-firing-raises-the-nuclear-stakes-41667.

82. For analysis of and background on the many North Korean SLBM tests of
2015 and 2016, context on the assessed capabilities of the missile and of the submarine, and in-depth assessments of the threat that the submarine and missile pose to
the United States and its allies in East Asia, see Kang Jin-kyu and Jeong Yong-soo,
"North Korea's SLBM Succeeds, Can Fly 2,000 KM," *Joongang Ilbo,* August 25,
2016, http://mengnews.joins.com/view.aspx?aId=3023037; Ju-min Park and Jack
Kim, "North Korea Fires Submarine-Launched Ballistic Missile towards Japan,"
Reuters, August 24, 2016, http://www.reuters.com/article/us-northkorea-missiles-
idUSKCN10Y2B0; "A New Level of Threat," *Joongang Ilbo,* August 25, 2016, http://
koreajoongangdaily.joins.com/news/article/Article.aspx?aid=3023017; "N. Korea's
Latest Submarine-Launched Ballistic Missile Test Unsuccessful: S. Korea," *Yon-
hap,* July 9, 2016, http://english.yonhapnews.co.kr/news/2016/07/09/0200000000
AEN20160709002253315.html; "N. Korea Apparently Botches Submarine Missile
Test: S. Korean Military," *Yonhap,* April 23, 2016, http://english.yonhapnews.co.kr/
northkorea/2016/04/23/0401000000AEN20160423002554315.html; J. H. Ahn,
"N. Korean Submarine Attempts to Test-Fire Ballistic Missile: MBN," *NK News,*
April 7, 2016, https://www.nknews.org/2016/04/n-korean-submarine-attempts-to-
test-fire-ballistic-missile-mbn; Brian Padden, "UN Security Council Condemns
North Korean Missile Test," Voice of America, April 24, 2016, http://www.voanews.
com/a/un-security-council-north-korea-attempted-missile-launch/3555703.html;
Kim So-hee, "North Claims 'Eye-Opening' Test of an SLBM," *Joongang Ilbo,*
April 25, 2016, http://mengnews.joins.com/view.aspx?aId=3017935; Anna Fifield,
"North Korea Launches Missile from Submarine, Seoul Says," *Washington Post,*
April 23, 2016, https://www.washingtonpost.com/world/north-korea-launches-
missile-from-submarine-seoul-says/2016/04/23/f6ec241b-2773-4aa0-938b-
484bd422c00a_story.html?utm_term=.ca997d03d181; Sarah Kim, "North's Tech
May Be Advancing," *Joongang Ilbo,* January 11, 2016, http://koreajoongangdaily
.joins.com/news/article/article.aspx?aid=3013748; Chang jae-son and Park Boram,
"N. Korea Test-Fired SLBM Last Month: S. Korean Military," *Yonhap,* January 6, 2016, http://english.yonhapnews.co.kr/news/2016/01/06/0200000000
AEN20160106002700315.html; Chang Jae-soon, "N. Korea Successfully Conducts
SLBM Test Last Month: U.S. Report," *Yonhap,* January 6, 2016, http://english
.yonhapnews.co.kr/news/2016/01/06/0200000000AEN20160106000200315.
html; Matthew Pennington, "Institute: N Korea Develops Sub Missile Despite
Setback," *Washington Post,* January 5, 2016, http://www.thejakartapost.com/
news/2016/01/06/us-institute-nkorea-develops-sub-missile-despite-setback.html;
Bill Gertz, "North Korea Conducts Successful Submarine Missile Test," *Washington Free Beacon,* January 5, 2016, http://freebeacon.com/national-security/north-

korea-conducts-successful-submarine-missile-test; Ankit Panda, "North Korea Tests Solid-Fuel Submarine-Launched Ballistic Missile," *The Diplomat,* April 25, 2016, http://thediplomat.com/2016/04/north-korea-tests-solid-fuel-submarine-launched-ballistic-missile; and Bill Gertz, "North Korean Submarine Damaged in Missile Test," *Washington Free Beacon,* December 8, 2015, http://freebeacon.com/national-security/north-korean-submarine-damaged-in-missile-test.

83. See Brian Padden, "Analysts: North Korea to Build New Ballistic Missile Submarine," Voice of America, August 30, 2016, http://www.voanews.com/a/analysts-north-korea-to-build-new-ballistic-missile-submarine/3486125.html; and "N. Korea Developing Larger-Class Submarine for Missile Launch: Expert," *Yonhap,* August 25, 2016, http://www.koreatimes.co.kr/www/news/nation/2016/08/485_212684.html.

84. For background on China's testing of the JL-1 from a Golf-class submarine, see "JL-1 [CSS-N-3]," Federation of American Scientists, June 10, 1998, https://fas.org/nuke/guide/china/slbm/jl-1.htm.

85. See Lee Sang-min, "Security Implications of North Korea's Test-Firing of Solid-Fuel IRBM and South Korea's Countermeasures," *ROK Angle* (Korea Institute for Defense Analyses), no. 152 (March 28, 2017), www.kida.re.kr/cmm/viewBoardImageFile.do?idx=21900; Steve Almasy and Joshua Berlinger, "North Korea Calls Ballistic Missile Test-Fire a Success," CNN, February 13, 2017, http://www.cnn.com/2017/02/11/asia/north-korea-missile; and "N. Korea Employs SLBM Tech in New Intermediate-Range Missile: Military," *Yonhap,* February 13, 2017, http://english.yonhapnews.co.kr/national/2017/02/13/0301000000 AEN20170213008551315.html.

86. For details of the second successful launch of what has been designated the KN-15 by US government officials and the Pukguksong-2 by the North Koreans, see John Schilling, "The Pokguksong-2 Approaches Initial Operational Capability," 38 North, May 24, 2017, http://www.38north.org/2017/05/jschilling052417; and Ju-min Park and Jack Kim, "North Korean Missile Reached Altitude of about 560 Km: Official," Reuters, May 21, 2017, http://www.reuters.com/article/us-northkorea-missiles-height-idUSKBN18H0GR.

87. "Corruption Rampant in N. Korean Army," *Chosun Ilbo,* November 1, 2013, http://english.chosun.com/site/data/html_dir/2013/11/01/2013110100525.html.

88. See Kim Yoo-sung, "Trying Not to Starve in the N. Korean Army," *NK News,* September 9, 2015, https://www.nknews.org/2015/09/trying-not-to-starve-in-the-n-korean-army; and "N. Korean Soldiers Suffering from Malnutrition," *Yonhap,* August 10, 2016, http://english.yonhapnews.co.kr/northkorea/2016/08/10/040 1000000AEN20160810010100315.html.

89. See Lee Yong-soo, "N. Korea Fritters Away 23% of GDP on Defense," *Chosun Ilbo,* December 26, 2016, http://english.chosun.com/site/data/html_dir/2016/12/26/2016122601145.html.

90. See "North Korea's Drones: Made in China?" North Korea Tech, April 20, 2014, http://www.northkoreatech.org/2014/04/20/north-koreas-drones-made-

in-china; Jun Ji-hye, "ROK Surveillance Caught NK Drones," *Korea Times,* June 10, 2014, http://www.koreatimes.co.kr/www/news/nation/2014/06/116_158854. html; and Adam Taylor, "Take a Closer Look at North Korea's Alleged Drones," *Washington Post,* April 2, 2014, http://www.washingtonpost.com/blogs/worldviews/ wp/2014/04/02/take-a-closer-look-at-north-koreas-alleged-drones.

91. Bill Gertz, "Pentagon: North Korea Develops Unmanned Strike Aircraft from Stolen US Drone," *Fox News,* March 6, 2014, http://www.foxnews.com/politics/ 2014/03/06/pentagon-north-korea-develops-unmanned-strike-aircraft-from-stolen-us-drone.

92. See Kyle Mizokami, "Experts: North Korea May Be Developing a Dirty Bomb Drone," *Popular Mechanics,* December 28, 2016, http://www.popularme chanics.com/military/weapons/a24525/north-korea-dirty-bomb-drone; and "N. Korea in Process of Developing Long-Endurance Aerial Drone: Govt," *Yonhap,* December 18, 2016, http://english.yonhapnews.co.kr/news/2016/12/18/02000000 00AEN20161218002851315.html.

93. For a glimpse of the difficult conditions under which North Korean fighter and attack pilots train and fly, see Vasudevan Sridharan, "North Korea's MiG-19 Fighter Jet Crashes during Training Manoeuvres," *International Business Times,* July 30, 2014, http://www.ibtimes.co.uk/north-koreas-mig-19-fighter-jet-crashes-during-training-manoeuvres-1458927.

94. For more on the capabilities of the AN-2, see John Grisafi, "The AN-2: N. Korea's Surprisingly Capable Soviet-Era Biplane," *NK News,* September 16, 2014, http://www.nknews.org/2014/09/the-an-2-n-koreas-surprisingly-capable-aircraft.

95. "North Korea Changes Camouflage of Infiltration Planes," *Chosun Ilbo,* April 6, 2015, http://english.chosun.com/site/data/html_dir/2015/04/06/2015040600863. html.

96. "N. Korea Has about 2,500 Armored Vehicles: Report," *Yonhap,* January 12, 2015, http://english.yonhapnews.co.kr/northkorea/2015/01/12/68/0401000000 AEN20150112003600315F.html.

97. See "North Korean 6×6 APC," *Military Today,* 2017, http://www.military-today.com/apc/north_korean_6×6_apc.htm; and "North Korean 8×8 APC," *Military Today,* 2017, http://www.military-today.com/apc/north_korean_8×8_apc.htm.

98. "N. Korea Builds New High-Speed Infiltration Boat," *Yonhap,* May 23, 2014, http://english.yonhapnews.co.kr/full/2014/03/20/40/1200000000AEN2014 0320008000315F.html.

99. For details and supporting data on the North Korean three-hundred-milli-meter MRL system and the testing that was conducted with it during 2014, see Choe Sang-hun, "North Korea Tests Rocket Launcher with Range beyond Seoul, South Says," *New York Times,* March 4, 2014, http://www.nytimes.com/2014/03/05/ world/asia/north-korea-tests-rocket-launcher-with-longer-range-south-says. html?_r=0; John Grisafi, "The Threat of North Korea's New Rocket Artillery," *NK News,* March 13, 2014, http://www.nknews.org/2014/03/the-threat-of-north-koreas-new-rocket-artillery; "N. Korea Tests New 300-Mm Multiple Rocket

Launchers," *Chosun Ilbo,* March 3, 2014, http://english.chosun.com/site/data/html_
dir/2014/03/03/2014030301647.html; and "N. Korea Fires 5 Short-Range Rockets
into East Sea," *Yonhap,* August 14, 2014, http://english.yonhapnews.co.kr/northkor
ea/2014/08/14/80/0401000000AEN20140814006051315F.html.

100. See John Grisafi, "N. Korea Reveals Details of 300mm Multiple Rocket
Launcher," *NK News,* March 4, 2016, https://www.nknews.org/2016/03/n-korea-
reveals-details-of-300mm-multiple-rocket-launcher; Choe Sang-hun, "North
Korea May Roll Out Rocket System with Greater Reach, South Says," *New York
Times,* April 6, 2016, http://www.nytimes.com/2016/04/07/world/asia/north-
korea-multiple-rocket-launchers.html?_r=0; Jeffrey Lewis, "More Rockets in Kim
Jong Un's Pockets: North Korea Tests a New Artillery System," 38 North, March
7, 2016, http://38north.org/2016/03/jlewis030716; and "N. Korea Fires Missiles
Again," *Chosun Ilbo,* March 22, 2016, http://english.chosun.com/site/data/html_
dir/2016/03/22/2016032200910.html.

101. See "Ex-CIA Director Warns of 'EMP' Weapons Threats from N. Korea,"
Yonhap, July 26, 2014, http://english.yonhapnews.co.kr/full/2014/07/26/65/120
0000000AEN20140726000500315F.html; and "N. Korea Yet to Develop 'EMP'
Bombs: S. Korea," *Yonhap,* July 28, 2014, http://english.yonhapnews.co.kr/northko
rea/2014/07/28/59/0401000000AEN20140728004300315F.html.

102. Rob Nikolewski, "North Korea Amps Up Worries about Potential Threat to
the U.S. Power Grid," *San Diego Union Tribune,* March 13, 2017, http://www.sand
iegouniontribune.com/business/energy-green.   http://www.sandiegouniontribune.
com/business/energy-green/sd-fi-emp-threat-20170309-story.html.

103. For more analysis of the EMP technology and capabilities that the North
Koreans may have, see William R. Graham, "North Korea Nuclear EMP Attack:
An Existential Threat," 38 North, June 2, 2017, http://www.38north.org/2017/06/
wgraham060217.

104. See Henry F. Cooper, "North Korea Dreams of Turning Out the Lights,"
Wall Street Journal, June 8, 2017, https://www.wsj.com/articles/north-korea-dreams-
of-turning-out-the-lights-1496960987?

105. For in-depth analysis of North Korea's claims regarding their recently
assessed thermonuclear test and the range of destruction that an EMP weapon
could produce, see Jamie Seidel, "North Korea Threat: EMP Attack Can Destroy
a Nation's Entire Infrastructure in a Flash," News.com, September 5, 2017, http://
www.news.com.au/technology/science/space/north-korea-threat-emp-attack-can-
destroy-a-nations-entire-infrastructure-in-a-flash/news-story/61b9c40ecef93315fcc
89fa6af4f6fb8.

106. Nicola Smith, "US Report Lays Out Apocalyptic Consequences of
North Korean Electromagnetic Pulse Attack on America," *The Telegraph,* October 24,
2017, http://www.telegraph.co.uk/news/2017/10/24/us-report-lays-apocalyptic-
consequences-north-korean-electromagnetic.

107. For more on the chemical weapons drills and other exercises, see Julian Ryall,
"North Korea Stages Chemical Warfare Drills," *The Telegraph,* February 6, 2015,

http://www.telegraph.co.uk/news/worldnews/asia/northkorea/11394447/North-Korea-stages-chemical-warfare-drills.html.

108. See Bart Marcois, "North Korean WMD Is Not Just Nuclear—OpsLens," *OpsLens,* December 11, 2017, https://www.opslens.com/2017/12/11/north-korean-wmd-is-not-just-nuclear; and Joby Warrick, "Microbes by the Ton: Officials See Weapons Threat as North Korea Gains Biotech Expertise," *Washington Post,* December 10, 2017, https://www.washingtonpost.com/world/national-security/microbes-by-the-ton-officials-see-weapons-threat-as-north-korea-gains-biotech-expertise/2017/12/10/9b9d5f9e-d5f0-11e7-95bf-df7c19270879_story.html?utm_term=.b3ec6a0122e2.

109. See "Kim Jong-nam: Who in North Korea Could Organise a VX Murder?" BBC, February 24, 2017, http://www.bbc.com/news/world-asia-39073839; "Inside the Shadowy North Korean Espionage Agencies Accused of Killing Kim Jong-nam," Reuters, February 24, 2017, http://www.scmp.com/news/asia/east-asia/article/2073675/inside-shadowy-north-korean-espionage-agencies-accused-killing?utm_content=buffer07729&utm_medium=social&utm_source=twitter.com&utm_campaign=buffer; and Ben Farmer, "What Is North Korea's Military Might?" *The Telegraph,* April 19, 2017, http://www.telegraph.co.uk/news/2017/04/03/north-koreas-military-arsenal.

110. See "North Korea Sends Experts in Chemical Weapons to Syria," *Zaman Alwasi,* June 22, 2013, https://en.zamanalwsl.net/news/414.html; Morse Tan, "Syria and North Korea: The Underground Connection," *Jurist,* March 31, 2015, http://www.jurist.org/forum/2015/03/morse-tan-nuclear-programs.php; and Joseph Bermudez, "North Korea's Chemical Warfare Capabilities," 38 North, October 10, 2013, http://38north.org/2013/10/jbermudez101013.

111. See Mari Yamaguchi, "Japan PM: N Korea May Be Capable of Sarin-Loaded Missiles," Associated Press, April 13, 2017, http://www.cnbc.com/2017/04/13/japan-pm-nkorea-may-be-capable-of-sarin-loaded-missiles.html.

112. For more on North Korea's assessed sarin chemical weapons capabilities, see Reid Kirby, "Sea of Sarin: North Korea's Chemical Deterrent," *Bulletin of the Atomic Scientists,* June 21, 2017, http://thebulletin.org/sea-sarin-north-korea%E2%80%99s-chemical-deterrent10856.

113. John Grisafi, "Military Drills and Leadership Changes Top Agenda in January," *NK News,* February 6, 2015, http://www.nknews.org/2015/02/military-drills-and-leadership-changes-top-agenda-in-january.

114. Lee Young-jong and Yoo Sung-woon, "North Practiced a Raid on Incheon Airport: Source," *Joongang Ilbo,* January 24, 2015, http://koreajoongangdaily.joins.com/news/article/article.aspx?aid=2984031.

115. See "N.K. Leader Test-Firing of Multiple Rocket Launcher," *Yonhap,* March 4, 2016, http://www.koreatimes.co.kr/www/news/nation/2016/03/485_199609.html; J. H. Ahn, "North Korea Holds Its Largest Ever Artillery Exercise," *NK News,* March 25, 2016, https://www.nknews.org/2016/03/north-korea-holds-largest-ever-artillery-exercise; and "Kim Jong-un Observes and

Commands Large Live Fire Artillery Exercise," North Korea Leadership Watch, December 2, 2016, https://nkleadershipwatch.wordpress.com/2016/12/02/kim-jong-un-observes-and-commands-large-live-fire-artillery-exercise.

116. See Ju-min Park and Yun Hwan-chae, "North Korea's Kim Guides Special Operations Drill Targeting South," Reuters, December 11, 2016, http://www.reuters.com/article/us-northkorea-southkorea-idUSKBN14004J; and "North Korea's Ability to Wage Special Operations Warfare Has Improved: Think Tank," *Yonhap*, December 18, 2016, http://english.yonhapnews.co.kr/national/2016/12/18/8/0301000000AEN20161218001600315F.html.

117. For an example of the types of training that SOF conduct with state and non-state actors (in a very real way the proliferation of capabilities), see Carl Anthony Wege, "The Hizballah–North Korea Nexus," *Small Wars Journal*, January 23, 2011, http://smallwarsjournal.com/blog/journal/docs-temp/654-wege.pdf.

118. See Jeong Yong-soo and Ser Myo-ja, "Kim Jong-un Ordered a Plan for a 7-Day Asymmetric War: Officials," *Joongang Ilbo*, January 8, 2015, http://korea joongangdaily.joins.com/news/article/article.aspx?aid=2999392.

119. See Hyung-jin Kim and Jung-yoon Choi, "North and South Korea Trade Fire as Residents Evacuate," Associated Press, March 31, 2014, http://pidie27.blogspot.com/2014/03/north-and-south-korea-trade-fire-as.html; Kim Eun-jong, "Koreas Exchange Live Fire Near Western Sea Border," *Yonhap*, March 31, 2014, http://english.yonhapnews.co.kr/national/2014/03/31/2 5/0301000000AEN20140331002554315F.html; "N. Korea Building Military Camps on Border Island: Seoul," *Yonhap*, May 26, 2015, http://english.yon-hapnews.co.kr/national/2015/05/26/95/0301000000AEN201505260015003 15F.html; and "North Korea Fires Artillery Near South Korean Warship," *The Guardian*, May 22, 2014, http://www.theguardian.com/world/2014/may/22/north-korea-fires-artillery-near-south-warship.

120. For more details on the coastal artillery drills the North Koreans conducted in 2016, see "N. Korea Conducts Coastal Artillery Drill," *Chosun Ilbo*, February 22, 2016, http://english.chosun.com/site/data/html_dir/2016/02/22/2016022201034.html.

121. See "The Interview: A Guide to the Cyber-Attack on Hollywood," BBC News, December 29, 2014, http://www.bbc.com/news/entertainment-arts-30512032.

122. See "Statement of General Curtis M. Scaparrotti, Commander, United Nations Command; Commander, United States–Republic of Korea Combined Forces Command; and Commander, United States Forces Korea Before the Senate Armed Services Committee," March 25, 2014, http://www.armed-services.senate.gov/imo/media/doc/Scaparrotti_03-25-14.pdf.

123. Lee Yong-jong and Sarah Kim, "Cyberwarfare Is North's New Priority, Experts Say," *Joongang Ilbo*, November 14, 2013, http://cached.newslookup.com/cached.php?ref_id=342&siteid=2280&id=3700543&t=1384386956.

124. Song Sang-ho, "Korea Vulnerable to Cyberwarfare," *Korea Herald*, July 6, 2014, http://www.koreaherald.com/view.php?ud=20140706000175.

125. "N. Korea Doubles Number of Cyber Warriors over Two Years: Sources," *Yonhap,* July 6, 2014, http://english.yonhapnews.co.kr/national/2014/07/04/2/0301 000000AEN20140704005400315F.html.

126. See Song Sang-ho, "North Korea Bolsters Cyberwarfare Capabilities," *Korea Herald,* July 27, 2014, http://www.koreaherald.com/view.php?ud=20140727000135.

127. David Sanger, Nicole Perlroth, and Eric Schmitt, "U.S. Asks China to Help Rein in Korean Hackers," *New York Times,* December 20, 2014, http://www. nytimes.com/2014/12/21/world/asia/us-asks-china-to-help-rein-in-korean-hackers. html?_r=0.

128. For background and context on the National Defense Commission, see "National Defense Commission," North Korea Leadership Watch, 2016, https:// nkleadershipwatch.wordpress.com/dprk-security-apparatus/national-defense-commission. For analysis of the SAC, see Maria Rosaria Coduti, "Kim Jong Un's North Korea: Leadership Changes under the New Leader," CETRI, December 19, 2016, http://www.cetri.be/Kim-Jong-Un-s-North-Korea?lang=fr.

129. For excellent details regarding the training of cyber-warfare specialists and their background, capabilities, resources, and organization, see Oh Seok-min, "N. Korea Boosts Cyber Operations Capabilities," *Yonhap,* May 10, 2015, http://english .yonhapnews.co.kr/national/2015/05/08/97/0301000000AEN2015050800690 0315F.html; Heesun Lee, "Inside North Korea's Elite Cyberware Unit," CNBC, December 1, 2014, http://www.cnbc.com/id/102226045; Lucy Draper, "North Korea Training Elite Secretive Hacker Unit, Says Defector," *Newsweek,* December 5, 2014, http://europe.newsweek.com/north-korea-training-cyber-warriors-289414; Jenny Jun, Scott LaFoy, and Ethan Sohn, "The Organization of Cyber Operations in North Korea," Center for Strategic and International Studies, December 18, 2014, http://csis.org/publication/organization-cyber-operations-north-korea; Eugene Kim, "We Spoke to a North Korean Defector Who Trained with Its Hackers—What He Said Is Pretty Scary," *Business Insider,* December 24, 2014, http:// www.businessinsider.com/north-korean-defector-jang-se-yul-trained-with-hack ers-2014-12; "Profiling an Enigma: The Mystery of North Korea's Cyber Threat Landscape," HP Security Briefing, Episode 16, August 2014, https://www.slide share.net/crash1980/profiling-an-enigma-the-mystery-of-north-koreas-cyber-threat-landscape; and Alexandre Mansourov, "North Korea's Cyber Warfare and Challenges for the US-ROK Alliance," Korea Economic Institute, Academic Paper Series, December 2, 2014, http://www.keia.org/sites/default/files/publications/kei_ aps_mansourov_final.pdf.

130. For details on North Korean cyberattacks against South Korea and the United States that occurred through 2015 and on units located in China, see Anna Mulrine, "How North Korea Built Up a Cadre of Code Warriors Prepared for Cyberwar," *Christian Science Monitor,* February 6, 2015, http://www.csmonitor .com/World/Passcode/2015/0206/How-North-Korea-built-up-a-cadre-of-code-warriors-prepared-for-cyberwar; Kang Jin-kyu and Shin Yong-ho, "Malware Files Emailed to Nuclear Plant Workers," *Joongang Ilbo,* December 27, 2014, http://korea

joongangdaily.joins.com/news/article/Article.aspx?aid=2998963; "N. Korea Fingered in Email to Sony," *Chosun Ilbo,* January 2, 2015, http://english.chosun.com/site/data/html_dir/2015/01/02/2015010201385.html; Will Ripley, "North Korean Defector: 'Bureau 121' Hackers Operating in China," CNN, January 7, 2015, http://www.cnn.com/2015/01/06/asia/north-korea-hackers-shenyang; and David Sanger and Martin Facklerjan, "N.S.A. Breached North Korean Networks Before Sony Attack, Officials Say," *New York Times,* January 18, 2015, http://www.nytimes.com/2015/01/19/world/asia/nsa-tapped-into-north-korean-networks-before-sony-attack-officials-say.html?_r=0.

131. See Ju-min Park and James Pearson, "Exclusive: North Korea's Unit 180, the Cyber Warfare Cell That Worries the West," Reuters, May 22, 2017, http://www.reuters.com/article/us-cyber-northkorea-exclusive-idUSKCN18H020.

132. See Chae In-taek, "Seoul Still Vulnerable to North Korea's Famed Cyberwarriors," *Joongang Ilbo,* November 18, 2015, http://mengnews.joins.com/view.aspx?aId=3011692; "Latest Cyber Attack Traced to North Korea," *Chosun Ilbo,* January 19, 2016, http://english.chosun.com/site/data/html_dir/2016/01/19/2016011901540.html; and Choe Sang-hun and David E. Sanger, "South Korea Accuses North of Hacking Senior Officials' Phones," *New York Times,* March 6, 2016, http://www.nytimes.com/2016/03/09/world/asia/north-korea-phone-hacking.html?_r=0.

133. Michael S. Rogers, "Statement of Admiral Michael S. Rogers, Commander United States Cyber Command, Before the House Armed Services Committee, Subcommittee on Emerging Threats and Capabilities," March 16, 2016, http://docs.house.gov/meetings/AS/AS26/20160316/104553/HHRG-114-AS26-Wstate-RogersM-20160316.pdf.

134. See Jack Kim, "North Korea Mounts Long-Running Hack of South Korea Computers, Says Seoul," Reuters, June 13, 2016, http://www.reuters.com/article/us-northkorea-southkorea-cyber-idUSKCN0YZ0BE; and Sarah Kim, "North Korean Hackers Strike Again," *Joongang Ilbo,* June 14, 2016, http://koreajoongangdaily.joins.com/news/article/Article.aspx?aid=3019961.

135. Choe Sang-hun, "North Korea Stole Data of Millions of Online Customers, South Says," *New York Times,* July 28, 2016, http://www.nytimes.com/2016/07/29/world/asia/north-korea-hacking-interpark.html.

136. See "S. Korean Military Says Hacking Threats Growing," *Yonhap,* March 21, 2017, http://english.yonhapnews.co.kr/northkorea/2017/03/21/0401000000AEN20170321006451315.html; and "Number of N. Korean Hackers Rises to 7,700: Report," *Yonhap,* March 24, 2017, http://english.yonhapnews.co.kr/news/2017/03/24/0200000000AEN20170324004000315.html.

137. Kevin Dugan, "Kim Jong Un May Be Behind Biggest Bank Heist in History," *New York Post,* March 22, 2017, http://nypost.com/2017/03/22/kim-jong-un-may-be-behind-biggest-bank-heist-in-history.

138. For detailed analysis of North Korea's alleged foray into attacks on financial institutions, see Timothy W. Martin, "North Korea's Army of Hackers Has a New

Target: Bank Accounts," *Wall Street Journal,* July 27, 2017, https://www.wsj.com/articles/north-korean-hackers-hunt-for-cash-1501128326?reflink=article_email_share&shareToken=stfb3637b5f054466a8cb1a9ab81b010fe&mg=prod/accounts-wsj.

139. See Kim Hyo-jin, "Cyberattack: N. Korea's New Cash Source?" *Korea Times,* May 17, 2017, http://www.koreatimes.co.kr/www/nation/2017/05/103_229558.html; Olivia Solon, "WannaCry Ransomware Has Links to North Korea, Cyber-Security Experts Say," *The Guardian,* May 15, 2017, https://www.theguardian.com/technology/2017/may/15/wannacry-ransomware-north-korea-lazarus-group; Scott Campbell, "North Korea Hacking Group Is Thought to Be Behind Cyber Attack Which Wreaked Havoc across the Globe," *The Daily Mail,* May 16, 2017, http://www.dailymail.co.uk/news/article-4508736/North-Korea-global-cyber-hac.html; Jim Kerstetter, "Daily Report: Evidence Points to North Korea in Ransomware Attack," *New York Times,* May 17, 2018, https://www.nytimes.com/2017/05/17/technology/daily-report-evidence-points-to-north-korea-in-ransomware-attack.html?_r=0; "North Korea, Cyber Attacks and 'Lazarus': What We Really Know," Associated Press, June 2, 2017, https://www.apnews.com/1866d617303642488615b118959bc2d8; and Elizabeth Shim, "Report: North Korea behind WannaCry Virus Cyberattack," UPI, June 15, 2017, http://www.upi.com/Top_News/World-News/2017/06/15/Report-North-Korea-behind-WannaCry-virus-cyberattack/1551497539289.

140. Eli Watkins, "White House Officially Blames North Korea for Massive 'WannaCry' Cyberattack," CNN, December 19, 2017, http://www.cnn.com/2017/12/18/politics/white-house-tom-bossert-north-korea-wannacry/index.html.

141. See Christine Kim, "North Korea Hackers Stole South Korea–U.S. Military Plans to Wipe Out North Korea Leadership: Lawmaker," Reuters, October 10, 2017, https://www.reuters.com/article/us-northkorea-cybercrime-southkorea/north-korea-hackers-stole-south-korea-u-s-military-plans-to-wipe-out-north-korea-leadership-lawmaker-idUSKBN1CF1WT; and Kanga Kong, "North Korea Hacks South Korean Warship Blueprints, Report Says," Bloomberg, October 30, 2017, https://www.bloomberg.com/news/articles/2017-10-31/north-korea-hacks-south-korean-warship-blueprints-report-says.

142. Bruce E. Bechtol Jr., *North Korea and Regional Security in the Kim Jong-un Era: A New International Security Dilemma* (London: Palgrave Macmillan, 2014), 40.

143. See Sam Kim, "South Korea Says North Will Pay Severely for Alleged Mine Attack," Bloomberg.com, August 10, 2015, http://www.bloomberg.com/news/articles/2015-08-10/south-korea-says-north-will-pay-severely-for-alleged-mine-attack; and Choe Sang-Hun, "North Korea Placed Mines That Maimed Soldiers at DMZ, South Says," *New York Times,* August 10, 2015, http://www.santafenewmexican.com/news/north-korea-placed-mines-that-maimed-soldiers-at-dmz-south/article_adfe0800-b4c9-5f96-a8ad-77c6f471cb42.html.

144. See Ashley Rowland and Yoo Kyong Chang, "Land Mine Blast Highlights Difficulty of Monitoring Korea's Long DMZ," *Stars and Stripes,* August 16, 2015,

http://www.stripes.com/news/land-mine-blast-highlights-difficulty-of-monitoring-korea-s-long-dmz-1.363176.

145. For more on the activities that occurred after the original North Korean land-mine provocation, see James Rothwell, "North Korea 'Agrees on Truce' with South Korea After Three Days of Crisis Talks: As It Happened August 24," *The Telegraph,* August 24, 2015, http://www.telegraph.co.uk/news/worldnews/asia/northkorea/11815637/North-Korean-troops-ordered-onto-war-footing-by-Kim-Jong-un-live.html;   Choe Sang-hun, "North and South Korea on Alert over Loudspeakers Blaring Propaganda," *New York Times,* August 21, 2015, http://www.nytimes.com/2015/08/22/world/asia/north-korea-attack-on-south-triggered-by-propaganda-loudspeakers.html?_r=0; and John G. Grisafi, "Inter-Korean Tensions Top N. Korean Leadership Agenda in August," *NK News,* September 10, 2015, http://www.nknews.org/2015/09/inter-korean-tensions-top-n-korean-leadership-agenda-in-august.

146. "Army to Toughen Response to N. Korean Incursions," *Chosun Ilbo,* August 12, 2015,   http://english.chosun.com/site/data/html_dir/2015/08/12/2015081201028.html.

147. See David L. Asher, "North Korea's Criminal Activities: Financing the Regime," Hearing before the Committee on Foreign Affairs, House of Representatives, 113th Cong., 1st sess., March 5, 2013, http://docs.house.gov/meetings/FA/FA00/20130305/100436/HHRG-113-FA00-20130305-SD003.pdf; Statement of Sung-yoon Lee, "North Korea's Criminal Activities: Financing the Regime: Hearing before the Committee on Foreign Affairs, House of Representatives," 113th Congress, 1st sess., March 5, 2013, http://docs.house.gov/meetings/FA/FA00/20130305/100436/HHRG-113-FA00-20130305-SD003.pdf.

3. How Do They Do It?

1. See "N. Korea Combines 2 Units Managing Leader's Coffers into One: Seoul," *Yonhap,* September 29, 2016, http://www.koreatimes.co.kr/www/news/nation/2016/09/485_215017.html.

2. For some important background information on Office 39, see Tom Burgis, "North Korea: The Secrets of Office 39," *The Financial Times,* June 24, 2015, https://www.ft.com/content/4164dfe6-09d5-11e5-b6bd-00144feabdc0.

3. For details regarding many of the spiderweb-like activities of the North Korean illicit financial network headed by Office 39, see Alastair Gale, "Defectors Detail How North Korea's Office 39 Feeds Leader's Slush Fund," *Wall Street Journal,* September 15, 2014, http://www.wsj.com/articles/defectors-detail-how-north-koreas-office-39-filters-money-to-kims-private-slush-fund-1410823969.

4. See Andrei Lankov, "How Private Finance Took Hold in North Korea," *NK News,* June 30, 2015, https://www.nknews.org/2015/06/how-private-finance-took-hold-in-north-korea.

5. Alastair Gale, "Q&A: High Level Defector on North Korean Trade," *Wall Street Journal,* September 16, 2014, http://blogs.wsj.com/korearealtime/2014/09/16/qa-high-level-defector-on-north-korean-trade.

6. Bradley O. Babson, "The Demise of Jang Song-taek and the Future of North Korea's Financial System," 38 North, February 24, 2014, http://38north.org/2014/02/bbabson022414.

7. Kim Kwang-jin, "The Defector's Tale: Inside North Korea's Secret Economy," *World Affairs*, September/October 2011, http://www.worldaffairsjournal.org/article/defector%E2%80%99s-tale-inside-north-korea%E2%80%99s-secret-economy. This account gives further, compelling details.

8. See Oliver Hotham, "N. Korea Is among the Most Corrupt Nations on Earth, Says NGO," *NK News,* December 4, 2013, https://www.nknews.org/2013/12/north-korea-is-among-most-corrupt-nations-on-earth-says-ngo.

9. See "N. Korea's Informal Economy Thrives," *Chosun Ilbo,* November 16, 2013, http://english.chosun.com/site/data/html_dir/2013/11/16/2013111600456.html.

10. "Breaking: Regime's Slush Fund Manager Defects in Vladivostok," *New Focus International,* August 26, 2016, http://newfocusintl.com/vladivostokdefection.

11. See Elias Groll, "Gold Smuggling North Korean Diplomat Provides Glimpse at Criminal Empire," *Foreign Policy,* March 6, 2015, http://foreignpolicy.com/2015/03/06/gold-smuggling-north-korean-diplomat-provides-glimpse-at-criminal-empire.

12. Leo Byrne, "North Korea Uses 'Multiple and Tiered' Techniques to Evade Sanctions," *NK News,* March 11, 2014, https://www.nknews.org/2014/03/north-korea-uses-multiple-and-tiered-techniques-to-evade-sanctions.

13. See Lisa Schlein, "N. Korea Defectors Urge Switzerland to Freeze Leaders' Funds," Voice of America, November 17, 2014, http://www.voanews.com/a/north-korea-defectors-urge-switzerland-to-freeze-leadership-money/2523035.html.

14. Elizabeth Shim, "North Korea Requiring Diplomats to Raise Millions in U.S. Currency," UPI, September 29, 2015, http://www.upi.com/Top_News/World-News/2015/09/29/North-Korea-requiring-diplomats-to-raise-millions-in-US-currency/2841443540260.

15. See Yi Whan-woo, "N. Korea Leader's Secret Funds Coming to Light," *Korea Times,* August 21, 2016, http://www.koreatimes.co.kr/www/news/nation/2016/08/485_212381.html.

16. See Staff of US Rep. Ed Royce, "Gangster Regime: How North Korea Counterfeits United States Currency," US House of Representatives, Washington, DC, March 12, 2007, http://royce.house.gov/uploadedfiles/report.3.12.07.final.ganster regime.pdf.

17. See Ahn Sung-kyoo, "North Money Laundering Done in Guangdong," *Joongang Ilbo,* June 5, 2013, http://koreajoongangdaily.joins.com/news/article/article.aspx?aid=2972627.

18. See "How N. Korean Diplomats Launder Counterfeit Money," *Chosun Ilbo,* May 14, 2013, http://english.chosun.com/site/data/html_dir/2013/03/14/2013031401253.html.

19. See "Seoul Sounds Positive Note on Beijing's Closure of N. Korea Account,"

Yonhap, May 9, 2013, http://english.yonhapnews.co.kr/national/2013/05/09/53/03
01000000AEN20130509008100315F.HTML; "How Serious Is China in Cracking Down on N. Korea?" *Chosun Ilbo,* May 9, 2013, http://english.chosun.com/site/
data/html_dir/2013/05/09/2013050901277.html?related_all; and "China Probes
N. Korea's Bank Accounts," *Chosun Ilbo,* May 9, 2013, http://english.chosun.com/
site/data/html_dir/2013/05/09/2013050901215.html.

20. See Nate Thayer, "The Front Companies Facilitating North Korean
Arms Exports," *NK News,* May 30, 2013, https://www.nknews.org/2013/05/
the-front-companies-facilitating-north-korean-arms-exports.

21. "Suspected N. Korean Money Laundering Account Found in Japan,"
KBS News, August 8, 2014, http://world.kbs.co.kr/english/news/news_In_detail.
htm?No=104522&id=In.

22. See "Singapore Charges Company over North Korea Weapons Role," Associated Press, June 10, 2014, http://www.ndtv.com/world-news/singapore-charges-company-over-north-korea-weapons-role-576951; and Hans Sherrer, "Chinpo
Shipping Company, Ltd," Wrongfully Convicted Database Record, May 2017,
http://forejustice.org/db/Shipping-Company-Ltd—Chinpo-.html.

23. According to a former high-ranking North Korean defector, at least one of
the banks in Singapore that the North Koreans have used in the past is the United
Overseas Bank. See Kim Kwang-jin, interview with author, July 19, 2015, Seoul.

24. Anonymous former senior ROK government official, interview with author,
July 27, 2015, Seoul.

25. See James Pearson, "Front Companies, Embassies Mask North Korean
Weapons Trade—U.N.," Reuters, March 11, 2014, http://www.reuters.com/article/
us-korea-korea-un-idUSBREA2A08020140311.

26. See James Pearson and Marius Zaharia, "Singapore 'Closely Studying' U.N.
Report on North Korea Arms Trade," Reuters, March 9, 2017, http://www.reuters.
com/article/us-northkorea-singapore-arms-idUSKBN16G13S.

27. See Scott A. Snyder, "Malaysia's Front Office Role in Enabling North Korean WMD
Procurement," Asia Unbound, March 6, 2017, http://blogs.cfr.org/asia/2017/03/06/
malaysias-front-office-role-enabling-north-korean-wmd-procurement.

28. See Hugh Griffiths and Lawrence Dermody, "Loopholes in UN Sanctions against North Korea," 38 North, May 6, 2014, http://38north.org/2014/05/
griffithdermod050614.

29. See Hugh Griffiths and Lawrence Dermody, "Feb 13: Sanctions beyond Borders: How to Make North Korea Sanctions Work," Stockholm International Peace
Research Institute, February 28, 2013, https://www.sipri.org/node/329.

30. See Juan Zarate, Testimony before the Senate Banking, Housing, and Urban
Affairs Subcommittee on National Security and International Trade and Finance,
May 10, 2017, https://www.banking.senate.gov/public/_cache/files/32fc800c-312f-
4e68-ad3f-3be5a6eae989/F5431B8F84661542DF1C9C3E23CC102A.zarate-
testimony-5-10-17.pdf.

31. "N. Korea Uses Civilian Airliners to Haul Hard Currency," *Chosun Ilbo,* July

3, 2015, http://english.chosun.com/site/data/html_dir/2015/07/03/2015070301475.html.

32. Hamish Macdonald, "U.S. Sanctions KPA Unit, Shipping Companies, N. Koreans Overseas," *NK News,* December 9, 2015, https://www.nknews.org/2015/12/u-s-sanctions-kpa-unit-shipping-companies-n-koreans-overseas.

33. See Brian Padden, "UN Security Council Approves New Sanctions on North Korea," Voice of America, March 2, 2016, http://www.voanews.com/a/un-counts-the-ways-north-korea-evaded-sanctions/3215914.html.

34. See "Iran, North Korea, and Syria Nonproliferation Act Sanctions," US Department of State, Office of the Spokesperson, March 24, 2017, https://www.state.gov/r/pa/prs/ps/2017/03/269084.htm; "Imposition of Nonproliferation Measures against Foreign Persons, Including a Ban on U.S. Government Procurement," US Department of State, Public Notice 9939, March 30, 2017, https://www.federalregister.gov/documents/2017/03/30/2017-06225/imposition-of-nonproliferation-measures-against-foreign-persons-including-a-ban-on-us-government; Vivian Salama, "US Imposes Sanctions on China, North Korea Entities, People," Associated Press, March 24, 2017, https://apnews.com/840c799486a6438391cc651d33a93b44; and "Victor Cha: US Sends 'Secondary Sanctions' Warning to China through Blacklisting of NK Firm," *Yonhap,* April 3, 2017, http://english.yonhapnews.co.kr/northkorea/2017/04/03/0401000000AEN20170403000400315.html.

35. For more details on activities that involved a complicated web of banks and front companies in China, Singapore, and Panama (to name the major players), see Sangwan Yoon, Sam Kim, and Andrea Tan, "How North Korea Funnels Cash into the Country," Bloomberg, February 21, 2016, https://www.bloomberg.com/news/articles/2016-02-21/china-at-the-heart-of-north-korea-s-illicit-cash-flow-funnel; Jack Hands, "The Panama Papers Underscore the Futility of North Korean Sanctions," *The Diplomat,* April 6, 2016, http://thediplomat.com/2016/04/the-panama-papers-underscore-the-futility-of-north-korea-sanctions; and Mirren Gidda, "Panama Papers: British Banker Helped North Korea Sell Arms, Expand Nuclear Program," *Newsweek,* April 6, 2016, http://www.newsweek.com/panama-papers-mossack-fonseca-north-korea-444452.

36. See "Treasury Sanctions Agents Linked to North Korea's Weapons of Mass Destruction Proliferation and Financial Networks," US Department of the Treasury, March 31, 2017, https://www.treasury.gov/press-center/press-releases/Pages/sm0039.aspx.

37. See Chang Jae-soon and Roh Hyo-dong, "U.S. Blacklisting of N.K. Unlikely to Be as Powerful as BDA Sanctions: Expert," *Yonhap,* June 12, 2016, http://english.yonhapnews.co.kr/news/2016/06/13/0200000000AEN20160613000300315.html.

38. John Park, "To Curb North Korea's Nuclear Program, Follow the Money," *The Conversation,* September 20, 2016, http://theconversation.com/to-curb-north-koreas-nuclear-program-follow-the-money-65462.

39. "Proliferation Security Initiative," US Department of State, 2016, https://www.state.gov/t/isn/c10390.htm.

40. Daniel Drezner, "An Analytically Eclectic Approach to Sanctions and Non-proliferation," in *Sanctions, Statecraft, and Nuclear Proliferation,* ed. Etel Solingen (Cambridge: Cambridge University Press, 2012), 161.

41. Leo Byrne, "Murky Waters: North Korea's Ships in South Korean Seas," *NK News,* November 6, 2014, https://www.nknews.org/2014/11/murky-waters-north-koreas-ships-in-south-korean-seas.

42. For more details on North Korean reflagging of merchant ships, the front companies used to support this effort, and the ongoing proliferation that occurs as a result of all this, see Elizabeth Shim, "Report: North Korea Ships under Sierra Leone Flag Issued Warning," UPI, March 25, 2016, http://www.upi.com/Top_News/World-News/2016/03/25/Report-North-Korea-ships-under-Sierra-Leone-flag-issued-warning/7471458960074; Andrea Berger, "North Korea's Friends in Singapore Running Flags of Convenience," 38 North, June 22, 2015, http://38north.org/2015/06/aberger062215; and "N. Korea Runs 9 Merchant Ships under Foreign Flags: Report," *Yonhap,* October 28, 2016, http://english.yonhapnews.co.kr/news/2016/10/28/33/0200000000AEN20161028004100315F.html.

43. See Seana K. Magee, "N. Korea Tactically Evading Sanctions on a Large Scale: UN Report," *Kyodo News,* February 8, 2017, http://abc140.blog.fc2.com/blog-entry-17001.html.

44. See Michelle Nichols, "U.N. Bans Four Ships over North Korea Coal, U.S. Delays Four More," Reuters, October 10, 2017, https://www.reuters.com/article/us-northkorea-missiles-un/u-n-bans-four-ships-over-north-korea-coal-u-s-delays-four-more-idUSKBN1CF2MV; and Paul Sonne and Felicia Schwartz, "U.S. Pressure on North Korea's Global Ties Bears Fruit," *Wall Street Journal,* October 8, 2017, https://www.wsj.com/articles/state-department-pressure-on-north-koreas-global-ties-bears-fruit-1507492004.

45. See "How N. Korea Goes about Exporting Arms." See also Bruce E. Bechtol Jr., *The Last Days of Kim Jong-il: The North Korean Threat in a Changing Era* (Washington, DC: Potomac, 2013), 111–28.

46. Anthony Ruggiero, "UN Report Reveals North Korea's Sanctions Evasion," Foundation for Defense of Democracies, FDD Policy Brief, March 7, 2017, http://www.defenddemocracy.org/media-hit/anthony-ruggiero-un-report-reveals-north-koreas-sanctions-evasion.

47. See Richard Nephew, "Paper Tigers: DPRK PoE Report Shows Deep Problems with Enforcement," 38 North, March 16, 2017, http://38north.org/2017/03/rnephew031617.

48. For analysis of how much money—projected to be billions of dollars—the North Korean illicit activities bring in annually, see "North Korea's Informal Economy Thrives."

49. For an example of an estimate that proliferation to Iran alone is worth $2–$3 billion a year, see Larry Niksch, "The Iran–North Korea Strategic Relationship," Testimony to the House Committee on Foreign Affairs, July 28, 2015, http://docs.house.gov/meetings/FA/FA18/20150728/103824/HHRG-114-FA18-Wstate-NikschL-20150728.pdf.

50. For detailed analysis of North Korean proliferation to a wide variety of African nations, see Samuel Ramani, "North Korea's Africa Strategy," *The Diplomat*, July 15, 2015, http://thediplomat.com/2015/07/north-koreas-african-strategy.

51. See "The DPRK Is Capitalist When It Wants to Be: The Story of Drugs Incorporated (Parts 1 & 2)," New Focus International, August 18, 2012, http://newfocusintl.com/the-dprk-is-capitalist-when-it-wants-to-be-the-story-of-drugs-incorporated-parts-12.

52. "N. Korean Opium Floods Northeast China," *Chosun Ilbo*, August 15, 2014, http://english.chosun.com/site/data/html_dir/2014/08/15/2014081500517.html.

53. See "N. Korean Diplomats 'Sell Millions of Dollars' Worth of Drugs,'" *Chosun Ilbo*, March 20, 2013, http://www.neogaf.com/forum/showthread.php?t=527601.

54. For important details of North Korea's government-sponsored drug operations, particularly ice, and how these activities are conducted, see Isaac Stone Fish, "Inside North Korea's Crystal Meth Trade," *Foreign Policy*, November 21, 2013, http://foreignpolicy.com/2013/11/21/inside-north-koreas-crystal-meth-trade; and Pierre Thomas, Jack Date, Josh Margolin, and Aaron Katersky, "North Korea May Be Pushing Meth into the United States," ABC News, November 20, 2013, http://abcnews.go.com/International/north-korea-pushing-meth-united-states/story?id=20955416.

55. See Geoffrey Ingersoll, "The Quality of the Meth Coming out of North Korea Would Make Even Walter White's Eyes Pop," Business Insider, November 22, 2013, http://www.businessinsider.com/north-koreas-got-breaking-bad-meth-2013-11; and "North Korea Could Be Making 'Breaking Bad' Amounts of Meth," Associated Press, November 24, 2013, http://nypost.com/2013/11/24/north-korea-could-be-making-breaking-bad-amounts-of-meth.

56. See "N. Korean Stimulant Smuggling Networks Extend to Japan, South Korea," *Japan Times*, August 19, 2014, http://www.intellasia.net/n-korean-stimulant-smuggling-networks-extend-to-japan-korea-2-382493.WIiTSjEzWM8.

57. See Oh Hyun Oo, "Drug Trade Continues to Prove Lucrative," *Daily NK*, January 3, 2014, http://www.dailynk.com/english/read.php?num=11339&cataId=nk01500.

58. See Joshua McMorrow-Hernandez, "Paper Money—Whatever Happened to North Korean Counterfeit U.S. $100 Bills?" Coin Week, March 29, 2016, http://www.coinweek.com/people-in-the-news/crime-and-fraud/paper-money-whatever-happened-north-korean-counterfeit-u-s-100-bills.

59. See Julian Ryall, "North Korea May Have Resumed Counterfeiting Operation," *The Telegraph*, June 28, 2016, http://www.telegraph.co.uk/news/2016/06/28/north-korea-may-have-resumed-counterfeiting-operation.

60. See Yi Whan-woo, "N. Korea Selling Counterfeit Money to Terrorists," *Korea Times*, June 27, 2016, http://www.koreatimes.co.kr/www/news/nation/2016/06/485_207990.html.

61. For more on the reasons behind North Korea's apparent renewal of large-scale counterfeiting operations, see Brian R. Moore and Riza De Los Reyes, "What's

behind North Korea's Recent Counterfeiting?" *The Diplomat,* July 6, 2016, http://thediplomat.com/2016/07/whats-behind-north-koreas-recent-counterfeiting.

62. See Christina Gathman, "Inside North Korea's State-Sanctioned Criminal Empire," *International Affairs Review* 23, no. 1 (Fall 2014), http://iar-gwu.org/sites/default/files/articlepdfs/4-Inside%20North%20Koreas%20Criminal%20Empire-Gathman.pdf.

63. See Bruce E. Bechtol Jr., "Military Proliferation in the Kim Jong-un Era: The Impact on Human Rights in North Korea," *International Journal of Korean Studies* 18, no. 1 (Spring 2014), http://www.icks.org/data/ijks/1482467285_add_file_5.pdf.

64. See Paige Gance, "Obama Administration Sanctions Myanmar General for Dealings with North Korea," Reuters, July 2, 2013, http://www.reuters.com/article/us-usa-sanctions-idUSBRE9610QF20130702.

65. See "Ed Royce: New North Korean Sanctions Will Sting," *Yonhap,* July 30, 2014, http://www.koreatimes.co.kr/www/news/nation/2014/07/485_161957.html.

66. See Yonho Kim, "US Treasury Issues Advisory on Financial Transactions with N. Korea," Voice of America, August 7, 2014, http://www.voanews.com/a/us-treasury-issues-advisory-on-financial-transactions-with-north-korea/2406604.html.

67. For more details on the US sanctions against North Korean entities issued in January 2015, see Carol Morello and Greg Miller, "U.S. Imposes Sanctions on N. Korea Following Attack on Sony," *Washington Post,* January 2, 2015, https://www.washingtonpost.com/world/national-security/us-imposes-sanctions-on-n-korea-following-attack-on-sony/2015/01/02/3e5423ae-92af-11e4-a900-9960214d4cd7_story.html?utm_term=.1f4f4287ddc7; "[Editorial] Coordinated Position: Pyongyang's Outmoded Tactics Will Not Pay Off," *Korea Herald,* January 16, 2015, http://www.koreaherald.com/view.php?ud=20150116000387; and "Treasury Imposes Sanctions against the Government of the Democratic People's Republic of Korea," US Department of the Treasury, January 2, 2015, https://www.treasury.gov/press-center/press-releases/Pages/jl9733.aspx.

68. "U.S. Issues New Advisory on Financial Deals with N. Korea," *Korea Herald,* March 18, 2015, http://www.koreaherald.com/view.php?ud=20150318000713.

69. See "U.S. Leaves Out N. Korea from Terrorism Sponsors List," *Yonhap,* June 2, 2015, http://english.yonhapnews.co.kr/national/2016/06/03/26/0301000000AEN20160603000200315F.html.

70. See Jim Geramone, "Gates Gives Frank Assessments of World Trouble Spots," *Defense News,* August 13, 2010, http://archive.defense.gov/news/newsarticle.aspx?id=60425.

71. See "US Expands North Korea Sanctions over Arms Trade," BBC, December 9, 2015, http://www.bbc.com/news/world-asia-35048138; and "US Sanctions North Korea over Arms Trade," AFP, December 9, 2015, http://www.dailymail.co.uk/wires/afp/article-3351645/US-sanctions-N-Korea-arms-trade.html.

72. See "Vietnam—Banking Systems," Export.gov, November 2, 2016, https://www.export.gov/article?id=Vietnam-Banking-Systems.

73. See "Executive Order—Blocking Property of the Government of North Korea and the Workers' Party of Korea, and Prohibiting Certain Transactions with Respect to North Korea," White House, Office of the Press Secretary, March 16, 2016, https://obamawhitehouse.archives.gov/the-press-office/2016/03/16/executive-order-blocking-property-government-north-korea-and-workers.

74. See "Impact of Int'l Sanctions on N. Koreans Remain [sic] Minimal: RFA," *Yonhap,* May 29, 2016, http://english.yonhapnews.co.kr/northkorea/2016/05/29/33/0401000000AEN20160529004100315F.html.

75. See "Treasury Takes Actions to Further Restrict North Korea's Access to the U.S. Financial System," US Department of the Treasury, June 1, 2016, https://www.treasury.gov/press-center/press-releases/Pages/j10471.aspx; Matthew Pennington, "US Designates North Korea 'Primary Money Laundering Concern,'" Associated Press, June 2, 2016, https://apnews.com/5cbca899f29c4be298466f08b9219768; Patricia Zengerle, "U.S. Takes Further Steps to Block North Korea's Access to Financial System," Reuters, June 2, 2016, http://www.reuters.com/article/us-northkorea-usa-treasury-idUSKCN0YN4TM.

76. For more on how effective a shutdown of North Korean access to the SWIFT system could be, see Sarah Kim, "U.S. to Shutter North's Overseas Banking," *Joongang Ilbo,* September 29, 2016, http://koreajoongangdaily.joins.com/news/article/Article.aspx?aid=3024297.

77. Scott A. Snyder, "Four Ways to Unilaterally Sanction North Korea," Asia Unbound, September 28, 2016, http://blogs.cfr.org/asia/2016/09/28/four-ways-to-unilaterally-sanction-north-korea.

78. "Treasury Finalizes Action to Further Restrict North Korea's Access to the U.S. Financial System," US Department of the Treasury, November 4, 2016, https://www.treasury.gov/press-center/press-releases/Pages/j10603.aspx.

79. "U.S. Sanctions North Korean Companies, Officials After Nuclear Test," Reuters, December 2, 2016, http://www.reuters.com/article/us-usa-northkorea-treasury-idUSKBN13R1YD.

80. See "Treasury Targets Chinese and Russian Entities and Individuals Supporting the North Korean Regime," US Treasury Department, August 22, 2017, https://www.treasury.gov/press-center/press-releases/Pages/sm0148.aspx.

81. See Elizabeth Shim, "North Korea Banks under U.S. Sanctions Have Partners in China, Singapore," UPI, September 27, 2017, https://www.upi.com/Top_News/World-News/2017/09/27/North-Korea-banks-under-US-sanctions-have-partners-in-China-Singapore/6171506530537.

82. Ryan Pickrell, "Trump's Exec Order on North Korea Is a Big Step That Should Have Been Taken Years Ago," *Daily Caller,* September 23, 2017, http://dailycaller.com/2017/09/23/trumps-exec-order-on-north-korea-is-a-big-step-that-should-have-been-taken-years-ago.

83. Sarah Kim, "As UN Names Firms Aiding North, U.S. Seeks More Sanctions," *Joongang Ilbo,* October 9, 2017, http://mengnews.joins.com/view.aspx?aId=3039187.

84. Paul Sonne and Felicia Schwartz, "U.S. Pressure on North Korea's Global

Ties Bears Fruit," *Wall Street Journal,* October 8, 2017, https://www.wsj.com/articles/
state-department-pressure-on-north-koreas-global-ties-bears-fruit-1507492004.

85. See Ian Talley, "Treasury Blocks Chinese Bank from U.S. Financial System
over North Korea Ties," *Wall Street Journal,* November 2, 2017, https://www.wsj.
com/articles/treasury-blocks-chinese-bank-from-u-s-financial-system-over-north-
korea-ties-1509667328; and "The Forex Effect: US Dollars, Overseas Networks,
and Illicit North Korean Finance," Center for Advanced Defense Studies, December 12, 2017, https://static1.squarespace.com/static/566ef8b4d8af107232d5358a/
t/5a3292079140b73f73f92efd/1513263687907/The+Forex+Effect.pdf.

86. See Lee Haye-ah, "U.S. Designates N. Korea as State Sponsor of Terrorism,"
Yonhap, November 21, 2017, http://english.yonhapnews.co.kr/national/2017/11/21/
0301000000AEN20171121000355315.html.

87. See Bruce Klingner, "Debunking Six Myths about North Korean Sanctions," *The Daily Signal,* December 22, 2014, http://dailysignal.com/2014/12/22/
debunking-six-myths-north-korean-sanctions.

88. Parts of this chapter were previously published in Bruce E. Bechtol Jr.,
"North Korean Illicit Activities and Sanctions: A National Security Dilemma," *Cornell International Law Journal* 51, no. 1 (2018). I would like to thank the editors and
staff of the *Cornell International Law Journal* for their cooperation, collaboration,
and support of this research.

89. For more about the first North Korean nuclear crisis that culminated in the
Agreed Framework, see Curtis H. Martin, "Lessons of the Agreed Framework for
Using Engagement as a Nonproliferation Tool," *The Nonproliferation Review,* Fall
1999, https://www.nonproliferation.org/wp-content/uploads/npr/martin64.pdf.

90. The JCPOA was the agreement signed with Iran in 2015 freezing its nuclear
weaponization program. It has often been compared to the North Korean series of
talks. For an example of this, see Thomas Ricks, "To Start Talks with North Korea,
Look to the Iran Deal—but Don't Hold Your Breath," *Foreign Policy,* September 12, 2016, http://foreignpolicy.com/2016/09/12/to-start-talks-with-north-korea-
look-to-the-iran-deal-but-dont-hold-your-breath.

91. See Parameswaran Ponnudurai, "Global Bid to Cripple North Korea's Illicit
Trade," Radio Free Asia, March 5, 2013, http://www.rfa.org/english/news/korea/
illicit-03052013150916.html.

92. See Yang Jung A, "Banks Put a Big Fly in NK Ointment," *Daily NK,* May 9,
2013, http://www.dailynk.com/english/read.php?cataId=nk00400&num=10560;
Antoni Slodkowski and Warren Strobel, "Japan, Australia to Sanction North
Korean Bank as Part of U.S.-Led Crackdown," Reuters, March 26, 2013, http://
www.reuters.com/article/us-korea-north-bank-idUSBRE92P04T20130326; and
Margaret Brennan, "U.S. Urges Nations to Cut North Korea's Financial Link,"
CBS News, April 5, 2013, http://www.cbsnews.com/news/us-urges-nations-to-cut-
north-koreas-financial-link.

93. See Yonho Kim and Jee Abbey Lee, "Money Laundering Watchdog Calls
on North Korea to Fulfill Pledge," Voice of America, March 2, 2015, http://www.

voanews.com/a/money-laundering-watchdog-calls-on-north-korea-to-fulfill-pledge/2665115.html; "Advisory: Advisory on the FATF-Identified Jurisdictions with AML/CFT Deficiencies," US Department of the Treasury, Financial Crimes Enforcement Network, March 16, 2015, https://www.fincen.gov/news/news-releases/advisory-fatf-identified-jurisdictions-amlcft-deficiencies; and Yonho Kim and Jee Abbey Lee, "Watchdog Warns of N. Korea Money Laundering," Voice of America, June 29, 2015, http://www.voanews.com/a/watchdog-warns-of-north-korea-money-laundering/2842448.html.

94. See Mark Hosenball, "Anti–Money Laundering Body Urges More Scrutiny of Iran, North Korea," Reuters, February 19, 2016, http://www.reuters.com/article/us-iran-economy-moneylaundering-idUSKCN0VS2LM.

95. For a list of UN sanctions resolutions on North Korea, see "Security Council Committee Established Pursuant To Resolution 1718 (2006)," UN Security Council, November 2016, https://www.un.org/sc/suborg/en/sanctions/1718/resolutions.

96. See Louis Charbonneau and Michelle Norris, "U.N. Imposes Harsh New Sanctions on North Korea Drafted by US, China," Reuters, March 2, 2016, http://www.hurriyetdailynews.com/un-imposes-harsh-new-sanctions-on-north-korea-drafted-by-us-china.aspx?pageID=238&nid=95970&NewsCatID=359; "Security Council Imposes Fresh Sanctions on Democratic People's Republic of Korea, Unanimously Adopting Resolution 2270 (2016)," UN Security Council, March 2, 2016, http://www.un.org/press/en/2016/sc12267.doc.htm; and Bradley O. Babson, "UNSCR 2270: The Good, the Bad, and the Perhaps Surprising Opportunity for the North Korean Economy," 38 North, March 21, 2016, http://38north.org/2016/03/bbabson032116.

97. See "Anti–Money Laundering Body Calls for Cutting Ties with N. Korean Banks," Yonhap, October 24, 2016, http://english.yonhapnews.co.kr/northkorea/2016/10/24/0401000000AEN20161024008800320.html.

98. See Benjamin Katzeff Silberstein, "The November 2016 North Korea Sanctions: Some Perspective," North Korean Economy Watch, December 2, 2016, http://www.nkeconwatch.com/2016/12/01/the-november-2016-sanctions-some-perspective; and Kang Mi Jin, "How Sanctions Affected North Korea's Economy in 2016," Daily NK, December 26, 2016, http://www.dailynk.com/english/read.php?num=14270&cataId=nk02900.

99. See Don Weinland, "North Korean Banks Banned from Swift Transaction System," Financial Times, March 8, 2017, https://www.ft.com/content/69dd9512-03d9-11e7-ace0-1ce02ef0def9; and Jeremy Wagstaff and Tom Bergin, "SWIFT Messaging System Bans North Korean Banks Blacklisted by U.N.," Reuters, March 8, 2017, http://www.reuters.com/article/us-northkorea-banks-swift-idUSKBN16F0NI.

100. For details of the UN sanctions imposed on North Korea during August 2017, see "U.N. Security Council Unanimously Adopts New Sanctions on N. Korea," Yonhap, August 6, 2017, http://english.yonhapnews.co.kr/northkorea/2017/08/06/0401000000AEN20170806000453315.html.

101. For more on the unique aspects of what the Kim family regime entails, see David S.

Maxwell, "Is the Kim Family Regime Rational and Why Don't the North Korean People Rebel?" Foreign Policy Research Institute, January 27, 2012, http://www.fpri.org/ article/2012/01/is-the-kim-family-regime-rational-and-why-dont-the-north-korean-people-rebel.

102. See "Midterm Report of the Panel of Experts Established Pursuant to Resolution 1874 (2009)," UN Security Council, North Korea, Panel of Experts, September 5, 2017, http://www.un.org/ga/search/view_doc.asp?symbol=S/2017/742.

103. See "Resolutions," United Nations Security Council, December 2017, https://www.un.org/sc/suborg/en/sanctions/1718/resolutions.

104. For an example of Russia and China insisting on watering down UN sanctions against North Korea, see Demetri Sevastopulo and Katrina Manson, "UN Agrees Stronger Sanctions against North Korea," Financial Times, September 11, 2017. https://www.ft.com/content/f07c6800-9736-11e7-b83c-9588e51488a0.

105. See Baik Sungwon, Ham Ji-ha, and Jenny Lee, "Will New Sanctions Restrain Kim Jong Un? Maybe Not," Voice of America, August 9, 2017, https://www.voanews.com/a/will-new-sanctions-restrain-kim-jong-un-maybe-not/3978217.html.

106. For an example of analysis regarding how China will or will not put pressure on North Korea that dates to 2006 but is still relevant today, see Christopher P. Twomey, "China Policy towards North Korea and Its Implications for the United States: Balancing Competing Concerns," Strategic Insights 5, no. 7 (September 2006), https://www.hsdl.org/?view&did=466572.

107. "N. Korea 'Deliberately Breached' Chinese Contract over Missile Vehicles: U.N. Report," Yonhap, June 26, 2013, http://english.yonhapnews.co.kr/news/2013/ 06/26/50/0200000000AEN20130626005000315F.HTML.

108. See "China Mulls Impact of N. Korea Regime Collapse on Border Area," Kyodo News International, May 4, 2014, https://fortunascorner.wordpress.com/ 2014/05/05/china-mulls-impact-of-north-korean-regime-collapse-on-border/ comment-page-1; Jin Dong Hyeok, "Report: China's Military Prepared for Collapse Scenario," Daily NK, May 5, 2014, https://www.dailynk.com/english/ read.php?num=11836&catald=nk00100; Yun Sun, "The North Korean Contingency: Why China Will Not Cooperate," 38 North, July 25, 2014, http://38north .org/2014/07/ysun072514; and Parris Chang, "China Manipulating Both Koreas," Taipei Times, June 21, 2014, http://www.taipeitimes.com/News/editorials/ archives/2014/06/21/2003593271.

109. Kim Ga Young, "A North Korea without Chinese Oil Supplies," Daily NK, January 15, 2016, http://www.dailynk.com/enlish/read.php?catald=nk00400&num= 13698.

110. See Jeong Yong-soo, "China Suddenly Gives North Fuel for Planes," Joongang Ilbo, January 31, 2015, http://koreajoongangdaily.joins.com/news/article/Article .aspx?aid=3000349.

111. For an analysis of North Korea's aviation and rocket fuel situation as of March 2016, see Peter Hayes, David von Hippel, and Roger Cavazos, "Sanctioning Kerosene and Jet Fuel in North Korea," Nautilus Institute, NAPSNet Pol-

icy Forum, March 10, 2016, http://nautilus.org/napsnet/napsnet-policy-forum/sanctioning-kerosene-and-jet-fuel-in-north-korea.

112. "N. Korea's Exports to Russia Jump 32 Pct in 2014: Report," *Yonhap,* March 18, 2015, http://english.yonhapnews.co.kr/full/2015/03/18/99/1200000000AEN20150318002300315F.html.

113. Curtis Melvin, "North Korea Building New Transport Corridor and Border Crossing," 38 North, May 4, 2015, http://38north.org/2015/05/cmelvin050415.

114. See Anna Fifield and Michael Birnbaum, "North Korea Might Be Courting Russia, but China Still Looms Larger," *Washington Post,* May 5, 2015, https://www.washingtonpost.com/world/north-korea-might-be-courting-russia-but-its-still-no-match-for-china/2015/05/04/6ca7bd46-c90d-4c99-8fce-de58d93608a7_story.html?utm_term=.71f19f6239c5.

115. For more about the modus operandi for moving cash across the China–North Korea border in 2016, see Seol Song Ah, "Traders Send Piles of Cash by Train to Evade Remittance Block," *Daily NK,* March 31, 2016, http://www.dailynk.com/english/read.php?num=13837&cataId=nk01500.

116. See Choi Song Min, "Military Items Smuggled through Chinese Customs Despite Sanctions," *Daily NK,* April 4, 2016, http://www.dailynk.com/english/read.php?num=13839&cataId=nk01500; and John Bacon, "China Joins Global Effort to Squeeze North Korea," *USA Today,* April 5, 2016, http://www.usatoday.com/story/news/world/2016/04/05/china-joins-global-effort-squeeze-north-korea/82653582.

117. See Kim Oi-hyun, "China Issues Official List of North Korea Embargo Products," *Hankyoreh Ilbo,* April 6, 2016, http://english.hani.co.kr/arti/english_edition/e_northkorea/738498.html; Yeh Young-june, "Beijing Implements UN Sanctions," *Joongang Ilbo,* April 7, 2016, http://koreajoongangdaily.joins.com/news/article/Article.aspx?aid=3017197; and "China Imposes Trade Sanctions on N. Korea," *Chosun Ilbo,* April 8, 2016, http://english.chosun.com/site/data/html_dir/2016/04/06/2016040601266.html.

118. See Elizabeth Shim, "China Trade with North Korea Up 20 Percent—Before Sanctions," UPI, April 13, 2016, http://www.upi.com/Top_News/World-News/2016/04/13/China-trade-with-North-Korea-up-20-percent-before-sanctions/1431460560493.

119. See Shin Jin-ho, "Despite Official Claims, Crude Still Flows from China," *Joongang Ilbo,* May 16, 2016, http://koreajoongangdaily.joins.com/news/article/article.aspx?aid=3018740.

120. See Sarah Kim, "China–North Korea Ties Get Some Momentum," *Joongang Ilbo,* June 3, 2016, http://koreajoongangdaily.joins.com/news/article/Article.aspx?aid=3019552.

121. See Gordon Chang, "China Likely Cheating, Again, on North Korean Sanctions," *World Affairs Journal,* June 15, 2016, http://www.worldaffairsjournal.org/blog/gordon-g-chang/china-likely-cheating-again-north-korea-sanctions.

122. See "China-N.K. Trade Surges in August," *Yonhap,* September 22, 2016, http://english.yonhapnews.co.kr/news/2016/09/22/0200000000AEN20160922006100315.html.

123. See Jane Perlez, Yufan Huang, and Paul Mozurmay, "How North Korea Managed to Defy Years of Sanctions," *New York Times,* May 12, 2017, https://www.nytimes.com/2017/05/12/world/asia/north-korea-sanctions-loopholes-china-united-states-garment-industry.html?_r=0.

124. See Hamish Macdonald, "China Accused of Inaction on N. Korea Sanctions in Senate Hearing," *NK News,* September 28, 2016, https://www.nknews.org/2016/09/china-accused-of-inaction-on-n-korea-sanctions-in-senate-hearing.

125. See Kim Myong-song, "N. Korea, China in Clandestine Trade in Coastal Waters," *Chosun Ilbo,* October 21, 2016, http://english.chosun.com/site/data/html_dir/2016/10/21/2016102101270.html; and "China Exports of Jet Fuel to N. Korea Up Nearly 400 Pct in September: Data," *Yonhap,* October 26, 2016, http://english.yonhapnews.co.kr/news/2016/10/26/0200000000AEN20161026006300320.html.

126. Chang Jae-soon, "US Actively Investigating More Chinese Firms for Dealings with N. Korea," *Yonhap,* September 29, 2016, http://english.yonhapnews.co.kr/national/2016/09/29/26/0301000000AEN20160929000251315F.html.

127. For the complete Justice Department report, see "Four Chinese Nationals and China-Based Company Charged with Using Front Companies to Evade U.S. Sanctions Targeting North Korea's Nuclear Weapons and Ballistic Missile Programs," US Department of Justice, Office of Public Affairs, September 26, 2016, https://www.justice.gov/opa/pr/four-chinese-nationals-and-china-based-company-charged-using-front-companies-evade-us.

128. See "China Keeps Importing U.N.-Sanctioned Minerals from N.K.," *Yonhap,* March 29, 2017, http://english.yonhapnews.co.kr/northkorea/2017/03/29/0401000000AEN20170329005400315.html.

129. "China Exports US$4.25 Mln Banned Items to N. Korea Last Year: VOA," *Yonhap,* March 9, 2017, http://english.yonhapnews.co.kr/northkorea/2017/03/09/53/0401000000AEN20170309008100315F.html.

130. For more information and analysis regarding Chinese action taken against North Korean parties using banks in China, see "Beijing Orders Banks to Close Accounts for North Koreans," *Daily NK,* September 9, 2017, http://www.dailynk.com/english/read.php?num=14709&cataId=nk01500.

131. For an example of anecdotal evidence suggesting that China has been violating UN sanctions in order to keep North Korea supplied with petroleum products, see "North Korea: South Seizes Ship amid Row over Illegal Oil Transfer," BBC, December 29, 2017, http://www.bbc.com/news/world-asia-42510783.

132. See Keegan Hamilton, "North Korean Meth, Motorcycle Gangs, Army Snipers, and a Guy Named Rambo," Vice News, March 18, 2014, https://news.vice.com/article/north-korean-meth-motorcycle-gangs-army-snipers-and-a-guy-named-rambo.

133. See Josh Meyer, "Squeeze on North Korea's Money Supply Yields Results," *Los Angeles Times,* November 2, 2006, http://www.latimes.com/world/la-fg-macao2nov02-story.html.

134. For examples of the diversification of North Korea's illegal and illicit financial networks since the end of the BDA sanctions and the failed Six-Party

talks, see Yoon, Kim, and Tan, "How North Korea Funnels Cash into the Country"; and Daniel Wertz and Ali Vaez, "Sanctions and Nonproliferation in North Korea and Iran," Federation of American Scientists, https://fas.org/issue-brief/sanctions-nonproliferation-north-korea-iran.

135. "U.S. to Further Tighten Sanctions on N. Korea, Go After Third Country Entities," *Yonhap,* May 16, 2016, http://english.yonhapnews.co.kr/northkorea/2017/05/17/0401000000AEN20170517000451315.html.

136. "Treasury Sanctions Suppliers of North Korea's Nuclear and Weapons Proliferation Programs," US Department of the Treasury, June 1, 2017, https://www.treasury.gov/press-center/press-releases/Pages/sm0099.aspx.

137. See Aaron Arnold, "Watch Out for the Blowback of Secondary Sanctions on North Korea," *The Diplomat,* April 28, 2017, http://thediplomat.com/2017/04/watch-out-for-the-blowback-of-secondary-sanctions-on-north-korea.

138. For more details on the blacklisting of the Bank of Dandong, see "Treasury Sanctions 4 Chinese Entities, Targeting North Korea," *The Whim,* July 4, 2017, http://www.thewhim.com/treasury-sanctions-4-chinese-entities-targeting-north-korea; Ken Bredemeier, "US Blacklists Chinese Bank It Says Has Been Funding N. Korean Weapons Development," Voice of America, June 29, 2017, https://www.voanews.com/a/us-blacklists-chinese-bank-it-says-has-been-funding-north-korean-weapons-developement/3921814.html; Elizabeth Shim, "China Condemns U.S. Sanctions against Entities with Suspected North Korea Ties," UPI, June 30, 2017, https://www.upi.com/China-condemns-US-sanctions-against-entities-with-suspected-North-Korea-ties/3361498829713; Tony Munroe and Shu Zhang, "Blacklisted China Bank Cited as a North Korea Conduit to Global Finance," Reuters, June 30, 2017, http://www.reuters.com/article/us-usa-northkorea-china-sanctions-dandon-idUSKBN19L1MD; and "Treasury Acts to Increase Economic Pressure on North Korea and Protect the U.S. Financial System," US Department of the Treasury, June 29, 2017, https://www.treasury.gov/press-center/press-releases/Pages/sm0118.aspx.

139. For two key examples of moves that the US government has taken against financial entities following the blacklisting of the Bank of Dandong, see Matt Spetalnick and David Brunnstrom, "Exclusive: U.S. Prepares New Sanctions on Chinese Firms over North Korea Ties—Officials," Reuters, July 13, 2017, http://www.reuters.com/article/us-northkorea-usa-sanctions-exclusive-idUSKBN19Y28A; and Julian Berlinger, "Guns and Money: Why US' Top North Korea Diplomat Is in Southeast Asia," CNN, July 17, 2017, http://www.cnn.com/2017/07/16/asia/north-korea-myanmar-singapore/index.html.

140. For details on the entities and individuals targeted by the Treasury Department in August 2017, see "Treasury Targets Chinese and Russian Entities and Individuals Supporting the North Korean Regime," US Department of the Treasury, August 22, 2017, https://www.treasury.gov/press-center/press-releases/Pages/sm0148.aspx; and "North Korean Designations; Non-Proliferation Designations; Counter Narcotics Designations Removals and Update; Transnational Criminal Organizations, Designations Removals and Update; Counter Terrorism Designa-

tion Removal; Cuba Designation Removal," US Department of the Treasury, August 22, 2017, https://www.treasury.gov/resource-center/sanctions/OFAC-Enforcement/Pages/20170822.aspx.

141. Stefan D. Cassella and Michael Zeldin, "On Russia and North Korea, Shell Companies Conceal the Truth," CNN, September 8, 2017, http://www.cnn.com/2017/09/08/opinions/shell-companies-russia-probe-north-korea-opinion-zeldin-cassella.

142. For more details on one of the complaints filed by the Department of Justice (specifically by the US Attorney's Office in Washington, DC), see "United States Files Complaint to Forfeit More Than $1.9 Million from China-Based Company Accused of Acting as a Front for Sanctioned North Korea Bank," US Department of Justice, US Attorney's Office, District of Columbia, June 15, 2017, https://www.justice.gov/usao-dc/pr/united-states-files-complaint-forfeit-more-19-million-china-based-company-accused-acting.

143. For detailed analysis of the executive order issued by President Trump and the potential for real pressure on North Korea, see "Turning the Screws on North Korea," *Wall Street Journal,* September 22, 2017, https://www.wsj.com/articles/turning-the-screws-on-north-korea-1506118397; and Donald J. Trump, "Presidential Executive Order on Imposing Additional Sanctions with Respect to North Korea," Executive Order, The White House, September 21, 2017, https://www.whitehouse.gov/the-press-office/2017/09/21/presidential-executive-order-imposing-additional-sanctions-respect-north.

144. For analysis of UN sanctions created with the hope of changing North Korea's behavior, see Dwayne Melendez, "Financial Sanctions on North Korea: Prospects and Challenges in the Age of the Tax Havens," *North Korean Review,* August 7, 2016, https://www.northkoreanreview.net/single-post/2016/08/08/Financial-Sanctions-on-North-Korea-Prospects-and-Challenges-in-the-Age-of-the-Tax-Havens.

145. See Patrick McClanahan, "North Korea: China's Liability?" *Harvard Political Review,* November 13, 2016, http://harvardpolitics.com/world/north-korea-chinas-liability.

4. North Korea and Military Proliferation to Iran

1. For details on the congressional minority in both houses of Congress that was large enough for the Obama Iran nuclear deal to go forward, see Jennifer Steinhauer, "Democrats Hand Victory to Obama on Iran Nuclear Deal," *New York Times,* September 10, 2015, http://www.nytimes.com/2015/09/11/us/politics/iran-nuclear-deal-senate.html?_r=0.

2. See "Joint Comprehensive Plan of Action," US Department of State, Diplomacy in Action, 2017, https://www.state.gov/e/eb/tfs/spi/iran/jcpoa.

3. For more on A. Q. Khan's nuclear bazaar, see Ishaan Tharoor, "A. Q. Khan's Revelations: Did Pakistan's Army Sell Nukes to North Korea?" *Time,* July 7, 2011, http://world.time.com/2011/07/07/a-q-khans-revelations-did-pakistans-army-sell-nukes-to-north-korea.

4. North Korea has a long history of proliferating a variety of conventional weapons systems to many countries, including Iran. See Bertil Lintner, "The Long Reach of North Korea's Missiles," *Asia Times,* June 21, 2006, http://www.atimes.com/atimes/Korea/HF21Dg02.html.

5. See R. Jeffrey Smith and Joby Warrick, "Pakistani Scientist Khan Describes Iranian Efforts to Buy Nuclear Bombs," *Washington Post,* March 14, 2010, http://www.washingtonpost.com/wp-dyn/content/article/2010/03/13/AR20100 31302258.html.

6. See Matthew Kroenig, *Exporting the Bomb: Technology Transfer and the Spread of Nuclear Weapons* (Ithaca, NY: Cornell University Press, 2010), 144.

7. See David E. Sanger, "The Khan Network" (paper presented at the Conference on South Asia and the Nuclear Future, June 4–5, 2004, Stanford University, sponsored by the Center for International Security and Cooperation and the US Army War College), http://fsi.stanford.edu/sites/default/files/evnts/media//Khan_network-paper.pdf.

8. Iran has yet to test a nuclear weapon, while North Korea has tested several times and has (probably) been working on its nuclear weaponization program for several years longer than Iran. See Moshe Arens, "As North Korea Blunders, the Iranian Clock Ticks Away," *Haaretz,* April 21, 2013, http://www.haaretz.com/opinion/as-north-korea-blusters-the-iranian-nuclear-clock-ticks-away.premium-1.516715.

9. Douglas Frantz, "Iran Closes in on Ability to Build a Nuclear Bomb," *Los Angeles Times,* August 4, 2003, http://articles.latimes.com/2003/aug/04/world/fg-nuke4.

10. See "Douglas Frantz: Assistant Secretary, Bureau of Public Affairs," US Department of State, 2016, http://www.state.gov/r/pa/ei/biog/213904.htm.

11. Pakistan and North Korea were actively involved in the deployment and testing of the No Dong during the late 1990s. See "Pakistan's Nuclear Capable Missiles," Wisconsin Project on Nuclear Arms Control, January 1, 1999, http://www.wisconsinproject.org/pakistans-nuclear-capable-missiles.

12. The warhead design for a 500 kilogram warhead is likely at least one of the designs that North Korean scientists, engineers, and technicians have been working on for several years with the Iranians, and the original designs came from China, but were then reportedly proliferated by Pakistan to Libya, Iran, and North Korea, see Seongwhun Cheon, "Assessing the Threat of North Korea's Nuclear Capability," *Korean Journal of Defense Analysis* 18, no. 3 (Fall 2006): 35–69.

13. Iran and Pakistan both reportedly attended the first No Dong test in North Korea during 1993. They also both purchased large orders of No Dong missiles from North Korea in the mid- to late 1990s. See "Shahab 3," Missile Threat.com, April 17, 2013, http://missilethreat.com/missiles/shahab-3; and Adrian Levy and Catherine Scott-Clark, *Deception: Pakistan, the United States, and the Secret Trade in Nuclear Weapons* (London: Walker, 2007), 245.

14. "N Korea May Already Have Nuclear Warheads: Ex-CIA Official," AFP, September 26, 2008, http://www.spacewar.com/reports/NKorea_may_already_have_nuclear_warheads_ex-CIA_official_999.html.

15. The No Dong has a range of as far as fifteen hundred kilometers. See "Pakistan Missile Chronology," Nuclear Threat Initiative, May 2011, http://www.nti.org/media/pdfs/pakistan_missile.pdf?_=1316466791.

16. See Robin Hughes, "Tehran Takes Steps to Protect Nuclear Facilities," *Jane's Defence Weekly,* January 25, 2006, 4–5.

17. Michael V. Hayden, "Director's Remarks at the Los Angeles World Affairs Council," Central Intelligence Agency, September 16, 2008, https://www.cia.gov/news-information/speeches-testimony/speeches-testimony-archive-2008/directors-remarks-at-lawac.html.

18. See James Woolsey, "Breaking the Iran, North Korea, Syria Nexus," Testimony before the US Congress, House Committee on Foreign Affairs, Washington, DC, April 11, 2013, http://docs.house.gov/meetings/FA/FA13/20130411/100636/HHRG-113-FA13-Wstate-WoolseyJ-20130411.pdf.

19. See "Ex-Iranian Official Revealed Syrian Nuke Plan: Report," Associated Press, March 21, 2009, http://www.taipeitimes.com/News/world/archives/2009/03/21/2003438992.

20. Leonard S. Spector, "Can Iran's Accelerating Nuclear Program Be Stopped?" Yale Global, March 11, 2010, http://www.english.globalarabnetwork.com/201003105141/World-Politics/can-irans-accelerating-nuclear-program-be-stopped.html.

21. For more details regarding the software the DPRK allegedly provided Iran to support its nuclear weapons program, see "North Korea Supplied Nuclear Software to Iran: German Report," Reuters, August 4, 2011, http://www.reuters.com/article/2011/08/24/us-nuclear-northkorea-iran-idUSTRE77N2FZ20110824.

22. "Hundreds of N. Koreans Working at Iran Nuke Facilities," *Chosun Ilbo,* November 14, 2011, http://english.chosun.com/site/data/html_dir/2011/11/14/2011111400526.html.

23. Joby Warrick, "IAEA Says Foreign Expertise Has Brought Iran to Threshold of Nuclear Capability," *Washington Post,* November 6, 2011, https://www.washingtonpost.com/world/national-security/iaea-says-foreign-expertise-has-brought-iran-to-threshold-of-nuclear-capability/2011/11/05/gIQAc6hjtM_story.html.

24. For more on North Korean assistance to Iran's plutonium reactor construction, see Jay Solomon, "Iran Seen Trying New Path to a Bomb," *Wall Street Journal,* August 5, 2013, https://www.wsj.com/articles/SB10001424127887323997004578644140963633244; Ephraim Asculai, "The Plutonium Track: Implications for the Completion of Iran's Heavy Water Reactor at Arak," Discussion Meeting, International Institute for Strategic Studies, Arundel House, London, September 11, 2013, http://www.iiss.org/en/events/events/archive/2013--5126/september-03c7/the-plutonium-track-766d; "N. Korea's Nuclear Facilities Located Mostly at Yongbyon: Gov't," *Yonhap,* October 14, 2013, http://english.yonhapnews.co.kr/news/2013/10/14/0200000000AEN20131014008600315.html; and Jang Yong-seung and Ahn Jeong-hoon, "Meir Dagan: N. Korea Is Already Nuclear Power," *Maeil Business Newspaper,* October 15, 2013, http://news.mk.co.kr/english/newsRead.php?rss=Y&sc=30800011&year=2013&no=986632.

25. For analysis of and evidence about the Iranians who observed the nuclear test, the money paid to North Korea so that high-ranking Iranian officials could attend the test, and analysis suggesting that the test was of a miniaturized warhead, see "Report: Iranians at N. Korea Nuclear Test," UPI, February 15, 2013, http://www.upi.com/Top_News/World-News/2013/02/15/Report-Iranians-at-N-Korea-nuclear-test/UPI-22931360904909; "Fears Rise about Iran–North Korea Nuclear Connection," *NK News,* February 18, 2013, http://www.nknews.org/2013/02/fears-rise-about-iran-north-korea-nuclear-connection; "Iran 'Paid Millions for Ringside Seat at N. Korean Nuke Test,'" *Chosun Ilbo,* February 18, 2013, http://english.chosun.com/site/data/html_dir/2013/02/18/2013021801176.html; "Iranian Nuclear Chief Observed Korean Nuke Test," *Jerusalem Post,* February 17, 2013, http://www.jpost.com/IranianThreat/News/Article.aspx?id=303499; Lee Sang-yong, "Evidence of Iranian Test Involvement Mounts," *Daily NK,* February 19, 2013, http://www.dailynk.com/english/read.php?cataId=nk00100&num=10327; "NK Nuke Was Bought and Paid for by a Key End-User: Iran," *Korea Times,* February 20, 2013, http://www.koreatimes.co.kr/www/news/nation/2013/02/511_130797.html; Vincent Pry, "Understanding North Korea and Iran," Family Security Matters, February 26, 2013, http://www.familysecuritymatters.org/publications/detail/understanding-north-korea-and-iran; Nikitin, "North Korea's Nuclear Weapons: Technical Issues"; and David E. Sanger and Choe Sang-hun, "Defying UN, North Korea Confirms Third Nuclear Test," AsianTown.net, February 12, 2013, http://news.asiantown.net/r/28361/defying-un—north-korea-confirms-third-nuclear-test-prompting-emergency-un-meeting.

26. "Iran, North Korea Discuss Expansion of Ties," FARS News Agency, February 24, 2014, http://english.farsnews.com/newstext.aspx?nn=13921205001438.

27. For more information about allegations that Iran may be housing nuclear materials in North Korea, an allegation for which there is no supporting evidence to date, see Adam Kredo, "Experts: Iran Housing Nuke Materials in North Korea, Syria," *Washington Free Beacon,* March 31, 2015, http://freebeacon.com/national-security/experts-iran-housing-nuke-materials-in-north-korea-syria.

28. See John Irish, "North Korean Nuclear, Missile Experts Visit Iran—Dissidents," Reuters, May 28, 2015, https://af.reuters.com/article/worldNews/idAFKBN0OD08020150528; Alireza Jafarzadeh, "Iran's Cooperation with North Korea Includes Nuclear Warhead Technology," *The Hill,* June 3, 2015, http://thehill.com/blogs/congress-blog/foreign-policy/243787-irans-cooperation-with-north-korea-includes-nuclear; Kellan Howell, "Iran Working with North Korea to Thwart U.N. Nuclear Inspections: Report," *Washington Times,* September 4, 2015, http://www.washingtontimes.com/news/2015/sep/4/iran-working-north-korea-thwart-un-nuclear-inspect/?page=all; and "Iran: Nuclear Cooperation between Iran Regime & North Korea, NCRI Reveals," National Council of Resistance of Iran, August 2015, http://www.ncr-iran.org/en/media-gallery/187-iran-nuclear-cooperation-between-iran-regime-north-korea-ncri-reveals.

29. For more details and context about the exchange of North Korean nuclear

technology with Iran and the concerns it has caused US officials, see Adam Kredo, "North Korea Nuclear Progress Puts Iran on Renewed Pathway to Bomb," *Washington Free Beacon,* September 4, 2017, http://freebeacon.com/national-security/north-korea-nuclear-progress-puts-iran-renewed-pathway-bomb.

30. Larry Niksch, "Responding to North Korea's Nuclear and Missile Test: Ending the U.N. Security Council Pretense," Institute for Corean American Studies, February 26, 2016, http://www.icasinc.org/2016/2016l/2016llan.html.

31. Chung-min Lee, "North Korean Missiles: Strategic Implications and Policy Responses," *Pacific Review* 14, no. 1 (2001), http://unpan1.un.org/intradoc/groups/public/documents/apcity/unpan012791.pdf.

32. Min-ha Lee, "North Korea's Missiles," Radio Free Asia, February 25, 2009, http://www.rfa.org/english/multimedia/InteractiveNorthKoreaMissile-02252009171048.html.

33. "Chronology of North Korea's Missile Trade and Developments: 1980–1989," James Martin Center for Nonproliferation Studies, 2003, http://cns.miis.edu/research/korea/chr8089.htm.

34. "Hwasong 6/Scud C," Federation of American Scientists, February 17, 2015, http://fas.org/nuke/guide/dprk/missile/hwasong-6.htm.

35. For more on the key evidence that Iran is reliant on foreign parts and assistance (largely North Korean) in order to assemble its ballistic missiles, see Michael Elleman, "Iran's Ballistic Missile Program," Iran Primer, United States Institute of Peace, August 2015. http://iranprimer.usip.org/resource/irans-ballistic-missile-program.

36. See "N Korea Develops New Scud Missile for Export," *World Tribune,* February 22, 2005, http://rense.com/general63/page.htm; Michael Arthur, "Scud ER," Missile Advocacy Alliance, 2015, http://missiledefenseadvocacy.org/threats/north-korea/scud-er; and Alex Kogan, "The Secretive Syrian–N. Korean Alliance," *Jerusalem Post,* September 18, 2007, http://www.jpost.com/International/The-secretive-Syrian-N-Korean-alliance.

37. See David C. Wright and Timur Kadyshev, "An Analysis of the North Korean Nodong Missile," *Science and Global Security* 4 (1994), http://scienceandglobalsecurity.org/archive/sgs04wright.pdf; Anthony Cordesman, *Iran's Military Forces in Transition* (Westport, CT: Praeger, 1999), 302–3; and Stephen J. Cimbala, *Nuclear Strategy in the Twenty-First Century* (Santa Barbara, CA: Praeger, 2000), 82.

38. See Choe Sang-hun, "Iran–North Korea Talks May Harden U.S. Stance," *New York Times,* November 27, 2005, http://www.nytimes.com/2005/11/27/world/asia/irannorth-korea-talks-may-harden-us-stance.html; "Tehran to Pyongyang: Trade Oil for Nuke Help," WorldNet Daily, November 27, 2005, http://www.wnd.com/2005/11/33600; and "Iran's Long-Range Missile Program: Nato's Next Challenge," Defense Update News Commentary, January 19, 2005, http://www.defense-update.com/2005/01/irans-long-range-missile-program-natos.html.

39. See Jonathan Karl, "Iranian Missile Hits Diplomatic Nerve," ABC News, July 9, 2008, http://abcnews.go.com/GMA/story?id=5338337&page=1; Edwin Black, "The Iranians Are Almost There: This Is How They Did It," *The Times of*

Israel, September 4, 2012, http://www.timesofisrael.com/the-iranians-are-almost-there-this-is-how-they-did-it; and David Albright, "North Korea Miniaturization," 38 North, February 13, 2013, http://38north.org/2013/02/albright021313.

40. Tim Hume, "Iran Test-Fires New Generation Long-Range Ballistic Missiles, State Media Report," CNN, October 11, 2015, http://www.cnn.com/2015/10/11/middleeast/iran-ballistic-missile-test.

41. See Joseph S. Bermudez Jr., "North Korea Deploys New Missiles," *Jane's Defence Weekly*, August 2, 2004, 4; and Sonni Efron, "N. Korea Working on Missile Accuracy," *Los Angeles Times*, September 12, 2003, http://articles.latimes.com/2003/sep/12/world/fg-norkor12.

42. There were a variety of press and academic reports alleging that North Korea proliferated the eighteen Musudan MRBM systems to Iran. But, in 2010, US government documents leaked on WikiLeaks confirmed the sale. See Alon Ben-David, "Iran Acquires Ballistic Missiles from DPRK," Pakistan Defence, 29 December 2005, https://defence.pk/pdf/threads/iran-acquires-ballistic-missiles-from-dprk.593; "Iran 'Bought' 18 North Korean Missiles," *Taipei Times*, December 17 2005, http://www.taipeitimes.com/News/world/archives/2005/12/17/2003284803; and "Missile Technology Control Regime (Mtcr): North Korea's Missile Program," US State Department, October 6, 2009, https://wikileaks.org/plusd/cables/09STATE103755_a.html (document disclosed on WikiLeaks).

43. "Iran Develops Missile with 4,000-Km Range," Middle East Newsline, March 2, 2006, http://regimechangeiran.blogspot.com/2006/03/iran-develops-missile-with-4000-km.html; Bharath Gopalaswamy, "Is an Iranian Missile Threat Imminent?" International Network of Engineers and Scientists against Proliferation, April 2008, http://www.inesap.org/bulletin-28/iranian-missile-threat-imminent.

44. See Charles P. Vick, "The Operational Shahab-4/No-Dong-B Flight Tested in Iran for Iran & North Korea Confirmed," Global Security.Org, 2006, http://www.globalsecurity.org/wmd/library/report/2006/cpvick-no-dong-b_2006.htm; and Al J. Venter, *Allah's Bomb: The Islamic Quest for Nuclear Weapons* (Lanham, MD: Lyons, 2007), 128.

45. "Iran Missile Test May Have Been Variant of NK Musudan," Center for Strategic and International Studies, Missile Defense Project, February 2, 2017, https://missilethreat.csis.org/iran-missile-test-may-variant-nk-musudan.

46. See Bill Chappell, "Iran Shows Off New Ballistic Missile at Military Parade," National Public Radio, September 22, 2017, https://www.npr.org/sections/thetwo-way/2017/09/22/552942917/iran-shows-off-new-ballistic-missile-at-military-parade; and South Front, "North Korea and Its Missile Program—All What [*sic*] You Need to Know," Global Research, November 18, 2017, https://www.globalresearch.ca/north-korea-and-its-missile-program-all-what-you-need-to-know/5618993.

47. For more analysis of the North Korea–Iran missile proliferation issue and the source of the map shown in this chapter, see "Recognizing Iran as a Strategic Threat: An Intelligence Challenge for the United States," Staff Report of the US House of Representatives Permanent Select Committee on Intelligence, Subcom-

mittee on Intelligence Policy, August 23, 2006, http://permanent.access.gpo.gov/lps73446/IranReport082206v2.pdf.

48. Brian Harvey, Henk H. F. Smid, and Theo Pirard, *Emerging Space Powers: The New Space Programs of Asia, the Middle East and South-America* (Berlin: Springer Praxis, 2010), 459.

49. See "Iran Military Engineers on Hand for N. Korea Missile Launch," *World Tribune,* July 12, 2006, http://www.worldtribune.com/worldtribune/06/front2453929.001388889.html; and Barbara Demick, "N. Korea–Iran Ties Seem to Be Growing Stronger," *Los Angeles Times,* July 27, 2006, http://articles.latimes.com/2006/jul/27/world/fg-missile27.

50. See "North Korean Engineers Visited Iran" (in Japanese), *Sankei Shimbun,* May 26, 2009, http://www.sankei.co.jp.

51. "Iran to Observe North Korea Missile Test," Missile Threat, December 7, 2012, http://missilethreat.com/iran-to-observe-north-korea-missile-test.

52. Henry Taylor, "Graphic: North Korea Successfully Launches Three Stage Rocket," *The Telegraph,* December 12, 2012, http://www.telegraph.co.uk/news/worldnews/asia/northkorea/9739822/Graphic-North-Korea-successfully-launches-three-stage-rocket.html.

53. See "Israeli TV Shows 'Iranian Missile' That 'Can Reach Far beyond Europe,'" *The Times of Israel,* January 21, 2015, http://www.timesofisrael.com/israeli-tv-shows-iranian-missile-that-can-reach-far-beyond-europe. The article also shows a striking photo of the new Iranian missile, which looks remarkably like a Taepo Dong.

54. The State Department cables exposed on WikiLeaks leave no doubt that the Iranian Safir missile system (sometimes called an SLV) is derived from technology acquired from North Korea. See "Update concerning Conversion of Space Launch Vehicles to Ballistic Missiles," US Department of State, September 30, 2009, https://wikileaks.org/plusd/cables/09STATE101892_a.html (document disclosed on WikiLeaks); and "U.S.-Russia Joint Threat Assessment Talks—December 2009," US State Department, February 24, 2010, https://wikileaks.org/plusd/cables/10STATE17263_a.html (document disclosed on WikiLeaks).

55. Stephanie Nebehay, "U.S. Calls for Shutting Down Iran, North Korea Arms Networks," Reuters, May 3, 2013, http://www.reuters.com/article/2013/05/03/us-nuclear-usa-iran-northkorea-idUSBRE9420I520130503.

56. Bill Gertz, "Iran, North Korea Secretly Developing New Long-Range Rocket Booster for ICBMs," *Washington Free Beacon,* November 26, 2013, http://freebeacon.com/national-security/iran-north-korea-secretly-developing-new-long-range-rocket-booster-for-icbms.

57. "U.S. Intel: Iran Financing North Korean ICBMs in Exchange for Technology, Components," *World Tribune,* December 4, 2013, http://www.worldtribune.com/archives/u-s-intel-iran-financing-north-korean-icbms-in-exchange-for-technology-components.

58. Bill Gertz, "North Korea Transfers Missile Goods to Iran during

Nuclear Talks," *Washington Free Beacon,* April 15, 2015, http://freebeacon.com/national-security/north-korea-transfers-missile-goods-to-iran-during-nuclear-talks.

59. John G. Grisafi, "DPRK, Iran Strong Partners in Missile Tech—Middle East Experts," *NK News,* January 19, 2015, http://www.nknews.org/2015/01/dprk-iran-strong-partners-in-missile-tech-middle-east-experts.

60. For explicit details on the sanctions imposed on Iran for collaborating with North Korea on an eighty-ton rocket booster for an ICBM, see "Treasury Department Sanctions Those Involved in Ballistic Missile Procurement for Iran," US Department of the Treasury, January 17, 2016, https://www.treasury.gov/press-center/press-releases/Pages/jl0322.aspx.

61. See Elizabeth Shim, "Sanctioned North Korean Firm Active in Iran, Source Says," UPI, March 28 2016, http://www.upi.com/Top_News/World-News/2016/03/28/Sanctioned-North-Korea-firm-active-in-Iran-source-says/2301459177912.

62. Yi, "North Korea Closer to Developing ICBM."

63. See Steve Herman, Brian Padden, and Carla Babb, "North Korea Tests Powerful New Rocket Engine," Voice of America, March 19, 2017, http://www.voanews.com/a/north-korea-tillerson-rocket-engine-test/3772372.html; and Eric Talmadge, "North Korea Tests Newly Developed High-Thrust Rocket Engine," Associated Press, March 19, 2017, http://bigstory.ap.org/article/e3076f09ddd14beb8f5c1a39ee4e904f/north-korea-tests-newly-developed-high-thrust-rocket-engine.

64. Parts of this chapter were previously published in Bruce E. Bechtol Jr., "North Korea and Military Proliferation to Iran: An International Security Dilemma," *ChiMoKoJa—Histories of China, Mongolia, Korea and Japan* 2 (2016): 71–95. I would like to thank the editors and staff of *ChiMoKoJa* for their cooperation, collaboration, and support of this research.

65. See "On Khamenei's Orders, Tehran Accelerates Missile Activities and Tests After the Iran Nuclear Deal," Iran Watch, June 20, 2017, http://www.iranwatch.org/library/private-viewpoints/khameneis-orders-tehran-accelerates-missile-activities-tests-after-iran-nuclear-deal.

66. See "Iran Abandons Its Human Spaceflight Ambitions," Spacewatch Middle East, June 2017, https://spacewatchme.com/2017/06/iran-abandons-human-spaceflight-ambitions.

67. For more analysis of the Iranian missile launch during July 2017 and of the missile that was launched, see "Will Iran's Simorgh Space Launcher Appear in North Korea?" Nuclear Threat Initiative, July 8, 2016, http://www.nti.org/analysis/articles/will-irans-simorgh-space-launcher-appear-north-korea; and Lucas Tomlinson, "Iran Launched Rocket Carrying Satellite, Official Says," FOX News, July 27, 2017, http://www.foxnews.com/world/2017/07/27/iran-launched-rocket-carrying-satellite-official-says.html.

68. For more on the new missile system shown in Iran in September 2017 and its direct correlation to assistance from the North Koreans, see Joseph Trevithick, "Iran's New Ballistic Missile Looks a Lot Like a Modified North Korean One," The Drive, September 23, 2017, http://www.thedrive.com/the-war-zone/14572/

irans-new-ballistic-missile-looks-a-lot-like-a-modified-north-korean-one; and "Iran 'Successfully Launches Ballistic Missile,'" Euro News, September 23, 2017, https:// www.youtube.com/watch?v=K1TMyPcovrQ.

69. "Iran Launches Missile Strike into Syria in Response to Tehran Attacks," *The Times of Israel,* June 18, 2017, https://www.timesofisrael.com/iran-launches-missile-strike-into-syria-for-tehran-attacks.

70. See Kevin M. Woods, Williamson Murray, and Thomas Holaday, "Saddam's War: An Iraqi Military Perspective of the Iran-Iraq War," McNair Paper no. 70, National Defense University, March 2009, 54–55, http://ndupress.ndu.edu/Portals/ 68/Documents/Books/saddams-war.pdf; John J. Metzler, *Divided Dynamism: The Diplomacy of Separated Nations: Germany, Korea, China* (Lanham, MD: University Press of America, 2014), 101; David Hambling, "Decisive Weapons of the Next Korean War," *Popular Mechanics,* November 4, 2010, http://www.popularmechanics .com/military/weapons/a6211/north-korea-conflict-weapons-available; and Chad O'Carroll and John G. Grisafi, "North Korea's Million Man Army: Potential Mercenary Force?" *NK News,* May 15, 2015, http://www.nknews.org/2015/05/ north-koreas-million-man-army-potential-mercenary-force.

71. For an interesting example of this, see Senator Pat Roberts, Opening State-ment Before the Senate Select Committee on Intelligence, US Senate, at the Hear-ing entitled "Current and Projected National Security Threats to the United States," Washington, DC, February 2, 2006, https://books.google.com/books?id=yEKq 90a70foC&pg=PA3&lpg=PA3&dq=iran+continues+to+buy+conventional+weap ons+from+north+korea&source=bl&ots=ZREa1Ea8dm&sig=ADh1kxOdYaE4V 9SxgkMe5EgtGs4&hl=en&sa=X&ved=0CFUQ6AEwCWoVChMIyZGAi9LcyA IVSD0-Ch1ehwIR#v=onepage&q=iran%20continues%20to%20buy%20conven tional%20weapons%20from%20north%20korea&f=false (link inactive).

72. The information on the 2017 arms shipment from North Korea to Syria paid for by Iran came from a source that has proved to repeatedly be very reliable in the past. See Anonymous former senior ROK government official, interview with author, June 29, 2017, Seoul.

73. See Daniel Martin, Ulla Fernandez-Arcaya, Paula Tirado, E'ric Dutrieux, and Jordi Corbera, "Relationships between Shallow-Water Cumacean Assemblages and Sediment Characteristics Facing the Iranian Coast of the Persian Gulf," *Journal of the Marine Biological Association of the United Kingdom,* 90, no. 1 (2010), https://www .researchgate.net/publication/233414586_Relationships_between_shallow-water_ cumacean_assemblages_and_sediment_characteristics_facing_the_Iranian_ coast_of_the_Persian_Gulf.

74. Dolan, "The North Korean Connection."

75. See Ahmad Majidyar, "U.S. Officials: Iran's Latest Missile Launch Hints Teh-ran-Pyongyang Cooperation," Middle East Institute, May 5, 2017, http://www.mei. edu/content/io/us-officials-iran-s-latest-missile-launch-hints-tehran-pyongyang-cooperation; Alex Hollings, "Could China Be Funneling Missile Technology to North Korea through Iran?" SOFREP: Special Forces News, May 6, 2017, https://sofrep.

com/80694/china-funneling-missile-technology-north-korea-iran; "Yono Class/ Ghadir Class Midget Submarine," Global Security.org, 2017, http://www.glo balsecurity.org/military/world/iran/ghadir.htm; "Yono Class (Ghadir)," Military Edge, The Foundation for Defense of Democracies, 2017, http://militaryedge. org/armaments/ghadir; Lucas Tomlinson, "Iran Attempted Missile Launch from Submarine, US Officials Say," FOX News, May 3, 2017, http://www.foxnews .com/world/2017/05/03/iran-attempted-misile-launch-from-submarine-us-officials-say.html; Ariel Zilber, "Iran Conducts 'Failed Missile Test from Same Submarine Used by North Korea' Just Days After Near Incident with US Warship in the Strait of Hormuz," *Daily Mail,* May 3, 2017, http://www.dailymail.co.uk/news/article-4471140/Iran-conducts-failed-missile-test-submarine.html; Kenneth Katzman, "Iran's Long-Range Missile Capabilities," Iran Watch, Wisconsin Project on Nuclear Arms Control, July 15, 1998, http://www.iranwatch.org/library/government/ united-states/congress/legislation-reports/irans-long-range-missile-capabilities; and "North Korea Modernises Submarine Fleet," *Jane's Intelligence Review,* May 10, 2016, http://www.janes360.com/images/assets/463/57463/North_Korea_modernises_ submarine_fleet1.pdf.

76. See Taimur Khan, "Weapons Seizures Show Iran's 'Arms Pipeline' to Yemen's Houthi Rebels," *The National,* November 30, 2016, http://www.thenational.ae/ world/middle-east/weapons-seizures-show-iran-arms-pipeline-to-yemens-houthi-rebels; and Joost Oliemans and Stijn Mitzer, "N. Korean Arms Found in Vessel Intercepted Off Coast of Oman," *NK News,* March 16th, 2016, https://www.nknews .org/2016/03/n-korean-arms-found-in-vessel-intercepted-off-coast-of-oman.

77. For information on the proliferation of North Korean Scud missiles to Yemen, the proliferation of Scuds to Iran, and the assistance with Iran's Scud missile program Pyongyang has provided and context on the assistance Iran has provided to the Houthis (which points to an assessment that it may also be assisting them with the operation of missiles they captured from the previous government), see Anthony Cordesman and Bryan Gold, *The Gulf Military Balance: The Missile and Nuclear Connections* (Washington, DC: Center for Strategic and International Studies, 2014), 60–61; Abdullah al-Shihri, "Houthi Rebels Fire Scud Missile from Yemen into Saudi Arabia," *Washington Post,* June 6, 2015, https://www.wash ingtonpost.com/world/houthi-rebels-fire-scud-missile-from-yemen-into-saudi-ara bia/2015/06/06/00e39c44-0c89-11e5-a7ad-b430fc1d3f5c_story.html?utm_term=. a820f06ac085; "North Korea Likely Supplied Scud Missiles Fired at Saudi Arabia by Yemen's Houthi Rebels," Vice News, July 29, 2015, https://news.vice.com/article/ north-korea-likely-supplied-scud-missiles-fired-at-saudi-arabia-by-yemens-houthi-rebels; and Yara Bayoumy and Phil Stewart, "Exclusive: Iran Steps Up Weapons Supply to Yemen's Houthis via Oman—Officials," Reuters, October 20, 2016, http://www.reuters.com/article/us-yemen-security-iran-idUSKCN12K0CX.

78. "Iran, North Korea, and Syria Nonproliferation Act Sanctions."

79. See Shuaib Almosawa and Anne Barnard, "Saudis Intercept Missile Fired from Yemen That Came Close to Riyadh," *New York Times,* November 4, 2017,

https://www.nytimes.com/2017/11/04/world/middleeast/missile-saudi-arabia-riyadh.html; Lewis Tallon, "Rockets and Round-Ups: Dangerous Times in the Kingdom," *Encyclopedia Geopolitica,* November 5, 2017, https://encyclopedia geopolitica.com/2017/11/05/rockets-and-round-ups-dangerous-times-in-the-kingdom; Jon Gambrell, "US Air Force Official: Missile Targeting Saudis Was Iranian," Associated Press, November 10, 2017, https://apnews.com/f132794ad 69b42f78ca3e39727432d2f; Dion Nissenbaum and Felicia Schwartz, "U.S. Seeks to Bolster Saudi Arabia in Face of Expanding Iranian Threat," *Wall Street Journal,* November 17, 2017, https://www.wsj.com/articles/u-s-seeks-to-bolster-saudi-arabia-in-face-of-expanding-iranian-threat-1510962715; and Rebeccah Heinrichs, "Did the Saudis Shoot Down a Houthi Missile on Nov. 4? It Doesn't Much Matter," Defense One, December 11, 2017, http://www.defenseone.com/ideas/2017/12/did-saudis-shoot-down-houthi-missile/144451.

80. See Keck, "Who Sold North Korea a New Anti-Ship Missile?"; and "N Korea 'Develops Russian Cruise Missile.'"

81. Joseph Bermudez Jr., "The Korean People's Navy Tests New Anti-Ship Cruise Missile," 38 North, February 8, 2015, http://38north.org/2015/02/jbermudez020815.

82. "Combat Fleets 16th Edition: Iranian Frigates and Patrol Craft," US Naval Institute, August 2013, http://www.usni.org/combat-fleets-2012-iranian-frigates-and-patrol-craft-0.

83. Geramone, "Gates Gives Frank Assessments of World Trouble Spots."

84. "Hezbollah a North Korea–Type Guerilla Force," *Intelligence Online,* no. 529, August 25–September 7, 2006, http://www.oss.net/dynamaster/file_archive/060902/26241feaf4766b4d441a3a78917cd55c/Intelligence%20Online%20on%20Hezbolllah.pdf.

85. Moon Chung-in, "[Outlook] The Syrian Nuke Connection," *Joongang Ilbo,* November 26, 2007, http://joongangdaily.joins.com/article/view.asp?aid=2883146.

86. "Hezbollah a North Korea–Type Guerilla Force."

87. Lenny Ben-David, "Mining for Trouble in Lebanon," *Jerusalem Post,* October 29, 2007, http://www.jpost.com/Opinion/Op-Ed-Contributors/Mining-for-trouble-in-Lebanon.

88. Ali Nouri Zadeh, "Iranian Officer: Hezbollah Has a Commando Naval Unit," Asharq Alawsat, July 29, 2006, http://english.aawsat.com/2006/07/article55265861/iranian-officer-hezbollah-has-a-commando-naval-unit.

89. "Hezbollah Training in North Korea," The Intelligence Summit, April 25, 2007, http://intelligence-summit.blogspot.com/2007/04/hezbollah-training-in-north-korea.html.

90. For an example of continued North Korean weapons sales to Hezbollah (and Hamas) in this particular instance sales that were foiled by Thai authorities, see Yoko Kubota, "Israel Says North Korean Arms Were for Hamas, Hezbollah," Reuters, May 12, 2010, http://www.reuters.com/article/2010/05/12/us-israel-korea-north-idUSTRE64B18520100512.

91. For an example of an arms shipment bound for Hamas fighters (as well as nonstate actors), see Joby Warrick, "Arms Smuggling Heightens Fears Iran May Be Building Arsenal," *Washington Post,* December 3, 2009, http://www.washington post.com/wp-dyn/content/article/2009/12/02/AR2009120203923.html.

92. For examples of reports providing evidence of the Iran-brokered North Korea–Hamas deal that was uncovered in 2014, see Curt Coughlin, "Hamas and North Korea in Secret Arms Deal," *The Telegraph,* July 26, 2014, http://www.telegraph.co.uk/news/worldnews/middleeast/palestinianauthority/10992921/Hamas-and-North-Korea-in-secret-arms-deal.html; Kim Hee-jin, "Pyongyang, Hamas Talk Arms Deal," *Joongang Ilbo,* July 28, 2014, http://koreajoongangdaily.joins.com/news/article/Article.aspx?aid=2992623; and Emanuele Ottolenghi, "Time for a Strong U.S. Effort to Cripple the IRGC," The National Interest, July 18, 2014, http://nationalinterest.org/blog/the-buzz/time-strong-us-effort-cripple-the-irgc-10912.

93. See Larry Niksch, "North Korea's Nuclear Weapons Development and Diplomacy," Congressional Research Service, RL33590, January 5, 2010, http://fas.org/sgp/crs/nuke/RL33590.pdf; and Matt M. Matthews, "We Were Caught Unprepared: The 2006 Hezbollah-Israeli War," The Long War Series, Occasional Paper no. 26, US Army Combined Arms Center, Combat Studies Institute Press, 2008, http://carl.army.mil/download/csipubs/matthewsOP26.pdf.

94. See Shane Harris, "Extensive Hamas Tunnel Network Points to Israeli Intelligence Failure," The Cable, July 31, 2014, http://thecable.foreignpolicy.com/posts/2014/07/31/extensive_hamas_tunnel_network_points_to_israeli_intelligence_failure_harris; and Jared Sichel, "Why Would North Korea Help Hamas Build Tunnels?" *Jewish Journal,* July 28, 2014, http://jewishjournal.com/news/los_angeles/131430.

95. Victor D. Cha and Gabriel Scheinmann, "North Korea's Hamas Connection: Below the Surface?" *The National Interest,* September 4, 2014, http://nationalinterest.org/feature/north-koreas-hamas-connection-below-the-surface-11195.

96. See "Everything You Need to Know about Hamas' Underground City of Terror," Israel Defense Forces, July 31, 2014, https://www.idfblog.com/blog/2014/07/31/everything-need-know-hamas-underground-city-terror.

97. For analysis of and evidence regarding North Korean sales of shoulder-fired antiaircraft missiles and antitank weapons to Hamas (and the capabilities of these weapons), see Moath al-Amoudi, "Is North Korea Supplying Arms to Palestinian Factions?" *Al-Monitor,* August 22, 2016, http://www.al-monitor.com/pulse/originals/2016/08/palestinian-resistance-factions-weapons-deals-black-market.html; "Hamas Acquires North Korean Laser-Guided Missiles," Virtual Jerusalem, January 24, 2017, http://virtualjerusalem.com/news.php?Itemid=25124; and Kyle Mizokami, "North Korea Says Its New Missile Can Turn Tanks into 'Boiled Pumpkins,'" *Popular Mechanics,* February 29, 2016, http://www.popularmechanics.com/military/weapons/a19663/north-korea-anti-tank-missile.

98. Niksch, "The Iran–North Korea Strategic Relationship."

5. North Korea and Syria

1. See Peter Lee and Jang Ji-Hyang, "Middle East Q/A: Intervening in Syria and Lessons for North Korea," Issue Brief, Asan Institute for Policy Studies, September 5, 2013, http://en.asaninst.org/contents/issue-brief-no-69-middle-east-qa-intervening-in-syria-and-lessons-for-north-korea.

2. See Marisa Sullivan, "Hezbollah in Syria," Middle East Security Report no. 19, Institute for the Study of War, April 2014, http://www.understandingwar.org/sites/default/files/Hezbollah_Sullivan_FINAL.pdf.

3. Yonhap News Agency, *North Korea Handbook* (London: Routledge, 2014), 992.

4. David McCarthy, *The Sword of David: The Israeli Air Force at War* (New York: Skyhorse, 2014), 9.

5. Alexandre Mansourov, "North Korea: Entering Syria's Civil War," 38 North, November 25, 2013, http://38north.org/2013/11/amansourov112513.

6. Ibid.

7. Nate Thayer, "The Violent Consequences of the North Korea–Syria Arms Trade," *NK News,* June 20, 2013, http://www.nknews.org/2013/06/the-violent-consequences-of-the-north-korea-syria-arms-trade.

8. J. Berkshire Miller, "North Korea's Chemical Weapons Shop of Horrors," *The National Interest,* October 6, 2014, http://nationalinterest.org/commentary/north-koreas-chemical-shop-horrors-9056.

9. See "Scientific Studies and Research Center," Nuclear Threat Initiative, August 1, 2010, http://www.nti.org/facilities/481.

10. "With KPA Assets in Syria and Rumors of Moscow Trip, Gen. Kim Kyok Sik Remains PY Man of the Hour."

11. See Choe Sang-hun, "Kim Kyok-sik, North Korean General Tied to Attacks, Dies at 77," *New York Times,* May 11, 2015, http://www.nytimes.com/2015/05/12/world/asia/kim-kyok-sik-hard-line-north-korean-general-dies-at-77.html?_r=0.

12. Anshel Pfeffer, "Russian, North Korean Arms Ships to Dock in Syria as Bloody Crackdown Continues," *Haaretz,* May 26, 2012, http://www.haaretz.com/news/middle-east/russian-north-korean-arms-ships-to-dock-in-syria-as-bloody-crackdown-continues-1.432709.

13. "Syria: Missile," Nuclear Threat Initiative, August 2014, http://www.nti.org/country-profiles/syria/delivery-systems.

14. See "U.S. and West Can Never Overpower Might of Syria and DPRK: Syrian President," KCNA, March 10, 2015, http://www.kcna.co.jp/item/2015/201503/news10/20150310-14ee.html.

15. See Jerrold M. Post, "Kim Jong-il of North Korea: In the Shadow of His Father," *International Journal of Applied Psychoanalytic Studies* 5, no. 3 (2008): 191–210.

16. See Geoffrey Cain, "Syria's Other Key Ally: North Korea," *Global Post,* September 8, 2013, http://www.globalpost.com/dispatch/news/regions/asia-pacific/north-korea/130906/syria-north-korea-alliance-chemical-weapons.

17. "Syrian Delegation Visits North Korean Leader Kim Jong-un," *Syria News*, July 26, 2013, http://www.syrianews.cc/syrian-delegation-north-korea.

18. See "Prime Minister to DPRK Foreign Minister: Syria Is on Its Way to Achieve Stability," *Syria News*, June 18, 2014, http://www.sana.sy/en/?p=3403; and "DPRK Foreign Minister Meets with Bashar al-Assad," North Korea Leadership Watch, June 18, 2014, https://nkleadershipwatch.wordpress.com/2014/06/19/dprk-foreign-minister-meets-with-bashar-al-assad.

19. See "Ninety-Six Percent of Syria's Declared Chemical Weapons Destroyed— UN-OPCW Mission Chief," UN News Centre, September 4, 2014, http://www.un.org/apps/news/story.asp?NewsID=48642#.VSOEHpUtGM8.

20. Hayden, "The CIA's Counterproliferation Efforts."

21. "Background Briefing with Senior Intelligence Officials on Syria's Covert Nuclear Reactor and North Korea's Involvement," Office of the Director of National Intelligence, April 24, 2008, https://fas.org/irp/news/2008/04/odni042408.pdf.

22. Ibid.

23. See Mark Mazzetti and Helene Cooper, "Israeli Nuclear Suspicions Linked to Raid in Syria," *New York Times*, September 17, 2007, http://www.nytimes.com/2007/09/18/world/asia/18korea.html; Michael Sheridan, "Kim Jong-il Builds 'Thunderbirds' Runway for War in North Korea," *Sunday Times*, April 27, 2008, http://www.timesonline.co.uk/tol/news/world/asia/article3822538.ece; "North Korea Provide [*sic*] Raw Uranium to Syria in 2007: Sources," *Kyodo News*, February 28, 2010, http://www.istockanalyst.com/article/viewiStockNews/articleid/3903101 (link inactive); and Kim So-hyun, "Worries Surface over N.K.-Iranian Nuclear Deals," *Korea Herald*, March 18, 2010, http://www.koreaherald.co.kr/national/Detail.jsp?newsMLId=20100318000038 (link inactive).

24. Caroline Glick, "Column One: Israel and the Axis of Evil," *Jerusalem Post*, May 27, 2009, http://www.jpost.com/servlet/Satellite?cid=1243346492707&pagename=JPost%2FJPArticle%2FShowFull.

25. See "Syrians with Secret CBW Material on Train That Exploded?" IMRA.com, May 15, 2004, http://www.imra.org.il/story.php3?id=20828; and "Source Notes Syrian Technicians Killed in Yongch'on Train Explosion," *Tokyo Sankei Shimbum*, May 7, 2004, A07.

26. James Hider, "Blast at Secret Syrian Missile Site Kills Dozens," *The Times*, September 20, 2007, http://www.timesonline.co.uk/tol/news/world/middle_east/article2489930.ece.

27. See "Test-Firing of New Scud Missiles in Syria by N. Korea, Syria, Iran in May Failed Killing over 20," Independent Media Review Analysis, August 15, 2009, http://imra.org.il/story.php3?id=45208.

28. For more information on North Korea's assistance in Syria's chemical weapons programs and its ties to artillery and ballistic missiles, which North Korea also produces and proliferates to Syria, see Vasidevam Sridharan, "North Korea 'Assisting' Regime with Chemical Weapons," *IB Times*, June 17, 2015, http://www.ibtimes.co.uk/north-korea-syria-chemical-weapons-assad-pyongyang-479554; "N.

Korea 'Exporting Chemical Weapons Parts to Syria,'" *Chosun Ilbo,* June 17, 2013, http://english.chosun.com/site/data/html_dir/2013/06/17/2013061700887.html; and John McCreary, NightWatch, October 7, 2013, http://www.kforcegov.com/NightWatch/NightWatch_13000212.aspx.

29. David Sanger, Eric Schmitt, and Jodi Rudoren, "Israeli Strike into Syria Said to Damage Research Site," *New York Times,* February 3, 2013, http://www.nytimes.com/2013/02/04/world/middleeast/syrian-weapons-center-said-to-be-damaged.html?_r=0 I.

30. "Reports: Cash-Strapped N. Korea 'Stepped Up' Chemical Weapons Shipments to Syria," *World Tribune,* August 26, 2013, http://www.worldtribune.com/archives/reports-cash-strapped-n-korea-stepped-up-chemical-weapons-shipments-to-syria.

31. Gordon Chang, "Punishing Assad's WMD Supplier," *World Affairs,* August 28, 2013, http://www.worldaffairsjournal.org/blog/gordon-g-chang/punishing-assads-wmd-supplier.

32. Joseph S. Bermudez Jr., "North Korea's Chemical Warfare Capabilities," 38 North, October 10, 2013, http://38north.org/2013/10/jbermudez101013.

33. See Nate Thayer, "North Korea and Syrian Chemical and Missile Programs," *NK News,* June 19, 2013, http://www.nknews.org/2013/06/north-korea-and-syrian-chemical-and-missile-programs.

34. Ibid.

35. Parts of this chapter were previously published in Bruce E. Bechtol Jr., "North Korea and Syria: Partners in Destruction and Violence," *Korean Journal of Defense Analysis* 27, no. 3 (September 2015): 277–92. I would like to thank the editors and staff for their cooperation, collaboration, and support of this research.

36. "Syria Capabilities: Scud C," Nuclear Threat Initiative, August 2004, http://www.nti.org/e_research/profiles/Syria/Missile/4126_4337.html (link inactive).

37. "Syria Capabilities: Scud D," Nuclear Threat Initiative, August 2004, http://www.nti.org/e_research/profiles/Syria/Missile/4126_4338.html (link inactive).

38. "Syria Improves Its SCUD D Missile with Help from North Korea," Geostrategy-Direct, February 22, 2006, http://www.geostrategy-direct.com/geostrategy%2Ddirect.

39. See Aaron Klein, "N. Korea Rebuilding Damaged Syrian Missiles," World Net Daily, June 18, 2013, http://www.wnd.com/2013/06/n-korea-rebuilding-damaged-syrian-missiles; and Oliver Hotham, "N. Korea Assisting Syria in Improving Missile Capabilities: Report," *NK News,* January 30, 2014, http://www.nknews.org/2014/01/n-korea-assisting-syria-in-improving-missile-capabilities-report.

40. Avi Issacharoff, "Bypassing Sanctions and with Help from Iran, Syria Steps Up Missile Production," *The Times of Israel,* January 28, 2014, http://www.timesofisrael.com/syria-accelerates-missile-production-despite-sanctions.

41. "SSRC: Spectre at the Table," *Jane's Defence Weekly,* November 29, 2012, http://www.janes360.com/images/assets/839/32839/syrian_chem_weapons.pdf.

42. Louis Charbonneau and Michelle Nichols, "U.N. Confirms Sarin Used in Syria Attack; U.S., UK, France Blame Assad," Reuters, September 16, 2013, http://www.reuters.com/article/2013/09/16/us-syria-crisis-un-idUSBRE98F0ED20130916.

43. Mansourov, "North Korea: Entering Syria's Civil War."

44. Joost Oliemans and Stijn Mitzer, "N Korean Upgraded Tanks Still in Use in Syrian Civil War," *NK News,* December 1, 2014, http://www.nknews. org/2014/12/n-korean-upgraded-tanks-still-in-use-in-syrian-civil-war.

45. "North Korean MANPADS Showing Up in the Hands of Fighters of the Islamic State?" Oryx Blog, August 27, 2014, http://spioenkop.blogspot. com/2014/08/north-korean-manpads-showing-up-in.html.

46. "With KPA Assets in Syria and Rumors of Moscow Trip, Gen. Kim Kyok Sik Remains PY Man of the Hour."

47. See "N. Korea Tried to Export Gas Masks to Syria: Media," Breitbart, August 27, 2013, http://www.breitbart.comnational-security/2013/08/27/n-korea-tried-to-export-gas-masks-to-syria-media.

48. For background on this issue, see "Arms Control and Proliferation Profile: North Korea," Arms Control Association, February 2015, https://www.armscontrol .org/factsheets/northkoreaprofile.

49. Mansourov, "North Korea: Entering Syria's Civil War."

50. For more details, see "N. Korean Officers 'Helping Syrian Gov't Forces,'" *Chosun Ilbo,* June 5, 2013, http://english.chosun.com/site/data/html_ dir/2013/06/05/2013060501134.html.

51. Olivia Alabaster, "North Korea Boosting Ground Support to Regime," *Daily Star,* June 8, 2013, http://www.dailystar.com.lb/News/Middle-East/2013/Jun-08/ 219763-north-korea-boosting-ground-support-to-regime.ashx#axzz2ySminqFx.

52. Aaron Klein, "Iran, N. Korea Run Operations Room in Syria," World Net Daily, August 27, 2013, http://www.wnd.com/2013/08/iran-n-korea-run-operations-room-in-syria.

53. For more analysis of North Korean advisers supporting Syrian air force, artillery, and missile units, see Oliver Hotham, "Activist: Assad Has Hired N. Korean Pilots for Air Strikes," *NK News,* October 29, 2013, http://www.nknews .org/2013/10/activist-assad-has-hired-n-korean-pilots-for-air-strikes; Jonathan Spyer, "Behind the Lines: Assad's North Korean Connection," *Jerusalem Post,* November 2, 2013, http://www.jpost.com/Features/Front-Lines/Behind-The-Lines-Assads-North-Korean-connection-330303; and "North Korean Pilots 'Helping Syrian Gov't in Raids on Rebels,'" *Chosun Ilbo,* November 11, 2013, http://english.chosun. com/site/data/html_dir/2013/11/11/2013111101689.html.

54. Spyer, "Behind the Lines."

55. For more analysis of North Korea's support to Syria's missile programs during the ongoing civil war, see Thayer, "North Korea and Syrian Chemical and Missile Programs"; Klein, "N. Korea Rebuilding Damaged Syrian Missiles"; and Hotham, "N. Korea Assisting Syria in Improving Missile Capabilities."

56. Elizabeth Shim, "North Korea Troops Fighting in Syrian Civil War, Delegate Says," UPI, March 22, 2016, http://www.upi.com/Top_News/World-News/ 2016/03/22/North-Korea-troops-fighting-in-Syrian-civil-war-delegate-says/ 1021458696828.

57. Ali Richter, "North Korean Type 73 GPMGs in Iraq, Syria, & Yemen," Armament Research Service, March 16, 2016, http://armamentresearch.com/north-korean-type-73-gpmgs-in-iraq-syria-yemen.

58. See Anonymous former senior ROK government official, interview with author, June 29, 2017, Seoul.

59. For analysis and details on the two reported shipments of weapons to Syria as seen in a UN report leaked early to Reuters, see Michelle Nichols, "North Korea Shipments to Syria Chemical Arms Agency Intercepted: UN Report," Reuters, August 21, 2017, https://www.reuters.com/article/us-northkorea-syria-un-idUSKCN1B12G2.

60. See Martin Chulov, "Two North Korean Shipments to Syria Intercepted in Six Months, UN Told," *The Guardian*, August 22, 2017, https://www.theguardian.com/world/2017/aug/22/two-north-korean-shipments-to-syria-intercepted-in-six-months-un-told.

61. For specific details regarding recent Syrian–North Korean arms deals, see "Midterm Report of the Panel of Experts Established Pursuant to Resolution 1874 (2009)."

62. The UN Panel of Experts report from early 2018 was leaked to several major press outlets during the first week of February. The author obtained an early draft of the leaked report on February 8, 2018. Valuable details from the leaked report were discussed in several important press reports. See Michelle Nichols, "Exclusive: North Korea Earned $200 Million from Banned Exports, Sends Arms to Syria, Myanmar-U.N. Report," Reuters, February 2, 2018, https://af.reuters.com/article/world-News/idAFKBN1FM2NH; "North Korea Arming Syria, Myanmar: UN Report," Al Jazeera, February 3, 2018, http://www.aljazeera.com/news/2018/02/north-korea-arming-syria-myanmar-report-180203064444145.html; Taryn Tarrant-Cornish, "North Korea Selling Chemical Weapons to Syria and Ballistic Missiles to Myanmar, UN Claim," *The Express*, February 4, 2018, https://www.express.co.uk/news/world/914184/North-Korea-chemical-weapons-Syria-Myanmar-ballistic-missiles-sanctions-trade-selling. For complete details, see: "Final Report of the Panel of Experts Submitted Pursuant to Resolution 2345 (2017)." UN Security Council, Panel of Experts, March 5, 2018. http://www.un.org/ga/search/view_doc .asp?symbol=S/2018/171.

63. "Hezbollah a North Korea–Type Guerilla Force."

64. See Wege, "The Hizballah–North Korean Nexus."

65. Anshel Pfeffer, "IDF Reveals Intel on Huge Hezbollah Arms Stockpile in Southern Lebanon," *Haaretz*, July 8, 2010, http://www.haaretz.com/print-edition/news/idf-reveals-intel-on-huge-hezbollah-arms-stockpile-in-southern-lebanon-1.300656.

66. See "N. Korea to Mass-Produce Syria-Provided Missile," Associated Press, June 2, 2009, https://www.thefreelibrary.com/N.+Korea+to+mass-produce+Syria-provided+missile.-a0202321247.

67. "VOA: N. Korea Supplied WMD to Hezbollah," KBS News, December 3, 2011, http://world.kbs.co.kr/english/news/news_In_detail.htm?No=86476.

68. "North Korea 'Helped Syria Build Missile Factory,'" *Chosun Ilbo*, November 28, 2011, http://english.chosun.com/site/data/html_dir/2011/11/28/2011112800692.html.

69. Richard Beeston, Nicholas Blanford, and Sheera Frenkel, "Embattled Syrian Regime Still Sending Missiles to Lebanese Militants," *The Times,* July 15, 2011, https://www.thetimes.co.uk/article/embattled-syrian-regime-still-sending-missiles-to-lebanese-militants-jw3hsrqblhw.

70. See "North Korea Slams Reports of Arms Deals with Hamas, Hezbollah," Yahoo News, July 29, 2014, http://news.yahoo.com/n-korea-slams-reports-arms-deals-hamas-hezbollah-012140239.html.

71. For more information regarding the transfer of chemical weapons to Hezbollah, see Yori Yanover, "Defecting Syrian Officer: Chemical Weapons Already Transferred to Hezbollah," Jewish Press, December 9, 2012, http://www.jewishpress.com/news/defecting-syrian-officer-chemical-weapons-have-already-been-transferred-to-hezbollah/2012/12/09.

72. See Alon Levkowitz, "North Korea and the Middle East," Mideast Security and Policy Studies no. 127. Begin-Sadat Center for Strategic Studies, January 2017. https://besacenter.org/wp-content/uploads/2017/01/MSPS-Levkowitz-Web-.pdf.

73. See Jay Solomon, "North Korea's Alliance with Syria Reveals a Wider Proliferation Threat," The Washington Institute, Policywatch 2885, November 2, 2017, http://www.washingtoninstitute.org/policy-analysis/view/north-koreas-alliance-with-syria-reveals-a-wider-proliferation-threat.

6. North Korean Proliferation on the African Continent

1. For examples of North Korean proliferation to Africa in the 1970s, see "North Korea, Foreign Policy Goals: Chapter 3A," Federation of American Scientists, DIA Excerpt, October 1991, https://fas.org/irp/dia/product/knfms/knfms_chp3a.html.

2. For an excellent example of some of the violent regimes in Africa that North Korea has supported with military arms or training in recent years, see Samuel Ramani, "North Korea's African Allies," *The Diplomat,* June 4, 2016, http://thediplomat.com/2016/06/north-koreas-african-allies.

3. See Chan Kyong-park, "Sanctions-Busting N. Korea Runs Barter Trade: Analysts," AFP, July 18, 2013, http://www.koreaherald.com/view.php?ud=20130718000738.

4. See Peter Nadin, "Sanctions and Why They Don't Work (Very Well)," Our World, United Nations University, September 5, 2014, https://ourworld.unu.edu/en/sanctions-and-why-they-dont-work-very-well.

5. See Annie DuPre, Nicolas Kasprzyk, and Noël Stott, "Cooperation between African States and the Democratic People's Republic of Korea," Institute for Security Studies, ISS Research Report, 2016, https://issafrica.s3.amazonaws.com/site/uploads/research-report-dprk.pdf.

6. For a very good example of an African nation that was being supported by the Soviet Union and is now being supported by North Korea, see Jeremy Bervoets, "The Soviet Union in Angola: Soviet and African Perspectives on the Failed Socialist Transformation," *Vestnik: The Journal of Russian and Asian Studies,* November 5, 2011, http://www.sras.org/the_soviet_union_in_angola.

7. For some examples of African nations that have ignored UN sanc-

tions on North Korea in the past, see Mark Fitzpatrick, "Squeezing North Korea's Foreign Earnings," International Institute for Strategic Studies, June 3, 2016, http://www.iiss.org/en/shangri-la%20voices/blogsections/2016-588c/ squeezing-north-koreas-foreign-earnings-4678.

8. See "Egypt, Events of 2016," Human Rights Watch, 2017, https://www.hrw. org/world-report/2017/country-chapters/egypt.

9. For more on the US-Egypt relationship and foreign assistance, see Emily Tamkin, "Time to Rethink the US-Egypt Relationship, Experts Tell Senate," *Foreign Policy,* April 25, 2017, http://foreignpolicy.com/2017/04/25/time-to-rethink-the-u-s-egypt-relationship-experts-tell-senate.

10. See "Final Report of the Panel of Experts Submitted Pursuant to Resolution 2276 (2016)," UN Security Council, Panel of Experts, February 27, 2017, http://www. un.org/ga/search/view_doc.asp?symbol=S/2017/150; Edith M. Lederer, "North Korea Uses New Ways to Flout Sanctions," *Jakarta Post,* March 2, 2017, https:// www.pressreader.com/indonesia/the-jakarta-post/20170302/281883003123659; Leo Byrne, "UN PoE Finds N. Korea Continues to Sell Military, Sanctioned Items," *NK News,* March 2, 2017, https://www.nknews.org/2017/03/un-poe-finds-n-korea-continues-to-sell-military-sanctioned-items; "Egypt's Missile Efforts Succeed with Help from North Korea," Wisconsin Project on Nuclear Arms Control, September 1, 1996, http://www.wisconsinproject.org/egypts-missile-efforts-succeed-with-help-from-north-korea; "US Confirms Egypt Has Tested N. Korean Missiles," *World Tribune,* September 18, 2002, http://www.rense.com/general29/asnr.htm; and Oliver Hotham, "Amid Missile Deal Rumor, N. Korea & Egypt Sign Cultural Cooperation Plan," *NK News,* November 19, 2013, https://www.nknews.org/2013/11/ amid-missile-deal-rumor-n-korea-egypt-sign-cultural-cooperation-plan.

11. For detailed coverage of the August 2017 act, see Gardiner Harris and Declan Walshaug, "U.S. Slaps Egypt on Human Rights Record and Ties to North Korea," *New York Times,* August 22, 2017, https://www.nytimes.com/2017/08/22/us/politics/ us-aid-egypt-human-rights-north-korea.html?mcubz=3.

12. For further details of Egypt's situation in 2017 because of its importation of North Korean ballistic missiles and missile parts, see Megha Rajagopalan and Maged Atef, "Trump Wants Other Countries to Stop Trading with North Korea; That's Easier Said Than Done," Buzzfeed, September 6, 2017, https://www.buzzfeed. com/meghara/trump-wants-other-countries-to-stop-trading-with-north?utm_ term=.clLMEJwjx#.tk0EGk413.

13. For details and analysis of the rocket-propelled grenade shipment from North Korea, see Joby Warrick, "A North Korean Ship Was Seized Off Egypt with a Huge Cache of Weapons Destined for a Surprising Buyer," *Washington Post,* October 1, 2017, https://www.washingtonpost.com/world/national-security/a-north-korean-ship-was-seized-off-egypt-with-a-huge-cache-of-weapons-destined-for-a-surprising-buyer/2017/10/01/d9a4e06e-a46d-11e7-b14f-f41773cd5a14_story.html.

14. "Final Report of the Panel of Experts Submitted Pursuant to Resolution 2276 (2016)."

15. See Oscar Nkala, "Namibia Confirms North Korean–Built Arms and Ammunition Factory," *Defense News,* March 17, 2016, http://www.defense-news.com/story/defense/international/2016/03/17/namibia-north-korean-arms-ammunition-factory/81902650.

16. For more details and analysis of the assistance that the North Koreans gave to the Namibian military, see Andrea Berger, "The 2016 UN Panel of Experts Report: An Eye-Opening Account of Persistent Blindness," 38 North, April 19, 2016, http://38north.org/2016/04/aberger041916; John Grobler, "Report Namibia Caught Violating North Korea Sanctions," *NK News,* April 15, 2016, https://www.nknews.org/2016/04/report-namibia-caught-violating-north-korea-sanctions; and Samuel Oakford, "UN Report Details North Korea's Exploits in Africa, Including Training Cops in Martial Arts," Vice News, February 29, 2016, https://news.vice.com/article/un-report-details-north-koreas-exploits-in-africa-including-training-cops-in-martial-arts.

17. For an excellent example articulating how North Korea is involved in supporting rogue states and terrorists through KOMID, see Joseph Klein, "New UN Security Council Resolution Strengthens Sanctions against North Korea," *Canada Free Press,* December 1, 2016, http://canadafreepress.com/article/new-un-security-council-resolution-strengthens-sanctions-against-north-kore.

18. See Max Weylandt, "Is It All over between Namibia and North Korea?" African Arguments, July 13, 2016, http://africanarguments.org/2016/07/13/is-it-all-over-between-namibia-and-north-korea.

19. "North Koreans Still Operating in Namibia," *The Namibian,* January 13, 2017, http://www.namibian.com.na/160087/archive-read/North-Koreans-still-operating-in-Namibia.

20. "Namibia Dismisses U.N. Expert's Claims on North Korea Ties," Reuters, October 24, 2017, https://www.reuters.com/article/us-namibia-north-korea/namibia-dismisses-u-n-experts-claims-on-north-korea-ties-idUSKBN1CT257.

21. See "Sudan Human Rights," Amnesty International, 2017, http://www.amnestyusa.org/our-work/countries/africa/sudan.

22. See Eric Reeves, "Sudan: Aerial Military Attacks on Civilians and Humanitarians 'They Bombed Everything That Moved,' 1999–2012," African Arguments, January 18, 2012, http://africanarguments.org/2012/01/18/they-bombed-everything-that-moved-aerial-military-attacks-on-civilians-and-humanitarians-in-sudan-1999-2012-by-eric-reeves.

23. "Final Report of the Panel of Experts Submitted Pursuant to Resolution 2276 (2016)."

24. Salem Solomon, "Sanctioned and Shunned, North Korea Finds Arms Deals in Africa," Voice of America, March 22, 2017, http://www.voanews.com/a/sanctioned-and-shunned-north-korea-finds-arms-deals-in-africa/3777262.html.

25. For an excellent example of analysis conducted on the Sudan's violations of sanctions and the sanctions placed on the Sudan, see John Prendergast and Brad Brooks-Rubin, "Modernized Sanctions for Sudan: Unfinished Business for the Obama Administration," The Enough Project, April 2016, http://www.enoughproject.org/files/Modernized_Sanctions_for_Sudan_042016.pdf.

26. "Sudan Completely Severs Military Ties with N. Korea: Foreign Minister," *Yonhap,* November 2, 2016, http://english.yonhapnews.co.kr/news/2016/11/02/020 0000000AEN20161102003100315.html.

27. The Sudan remained under close scrutiny during 2017 because of its dealings with North Korea. See "The Administration Extends Sanctions Review Period," press release, US Department of State, July 11, 2017, https://www.state .gov/r/pa/prs/ps/2017/07/272539.htm; and Andrea Berger, "Trump Puts Sudan (and the World) 'on Notice' over DPRK," Arms Control Wonk, July 12, 2017, http://www.armscontrolwonk.com/archive/1203587/trump-puts-sudan-and-the-world-on-notice-over-dprk.

28. See "Sudan Cut Diplomatic Relations with North Korea to Get Sanctions Lifted: Report," *Sudan Tribune,* October 5, 2017, http://www.sudan tribune.com/spip.php?article63676; and Lily Kuo, "North Korea Is Losing Its Friends in Africa," Quartz Africa, October 5, 2017, https://qz.com/1095163/ north-korea-sudan-cuts-ties-as-north-korea-loses-more-friends-in-africa.

29. See Matt Spetalnick, "U.S. Lifts Sudan Sanctions, Wins Commitment against Arms Deals with North Korea," Reuters, October 6, 2017, https://www.reuters .com/article/us-sudan-usa-sanctions/u-s-lifts-sudan-sanctions-wins-commitment-against-arms-deals-with-north-korea-idUSKBN1CB26Q.

30. For some interesting and relevant analysis and history of the North Korea–Uganda relationship, see Shannon Ebrahim, "Africa Oiling North Korea," *Pretoria News,* February 19, 2016, https://www.pressreader.com/south-africa/ pretoria-news/20160219/281827167828468.

31. See "Uganda-US Relations," Global Security.org, 2017, http://www.globalse curity.org/military/world/uganda/forrel-us.htm.

32. See "Uganda–North Korea Ties Skirt Limits of Sanctions," *World Politics Review,* January 12, 2015, http://www.worldpoliticsreview.com/trend-lines/14832/ uganda-north-korea-ties-skirt-limits-of-sanctions; "North Korea Visit Not Linked to Arms Supply: Uganda," AFP, June 15, 2013, http://www.breitbart.com/news/ cng-d16019e8b0214aceaabf05b24a156bc5-741; Chad O'Carroll, "Exclusive: North Korean Minister Inspects Ugandan Police Force," *NK News,* June 14, 2013, https:// www.nknews.org/2013/06/exclusive-north-korean-minister-inspects-ugandan-police-force; and Andrew Bagala, "Uganda to Learn from North Korea—Kayi-hura," *Daily Monitor,* June 13, 2013http://www.monitor.co.ug/News/National/ Uganda-to-learn-from-North-Korea—-Kayihura/688334-1881202-16ocpv/index. html.

33. For more on the interesting events of 2014 and the context of what occurred between North Korea and Uganda before that time, see Andrea Berger, "A Legal Precipice? The DPRK-Uganda Security Relationship," 38 North, November 13, 2014, http://38north.org/2014/11/aberger111314.

34. For more on Uganda's lack of transparency when it comes to revealing ties with North Korea, evidence of ongoing ties to North Korea's military, past contracts and military assistance, see Risdel Kasasira, "Africa: No Buying Weap-

ons from North Korea, Says Minister," *The Monitor,* December 11, 2016, http://allafrica.com/stories/201612120064.html; "Uganda Angered at Claim It Has Cut Military Ties with North Korea," *Japan Times,* May 30, 2016, http://www.japantimes.co.jp/news/2016/05/30/asia-pacific/uganda-angered-at-claim-it-has-cut-military-ties-with-north-korea/#.WR_8aDGGOM8; "South Korean President Visits Uganda to Talk Business," Associated Press, May 28, 2016, https://apnews.com/a24fbcc7c844494eb6a04f556e829206/south-korean-president-visits-uganda-talk-business-trade; "Uganda to Suspend Security, Military Cooperation with N. Korea," *Korea Times,* May 30, 2016, http://www.koreatimes.co.kr/www/news/nation/2016/05/485_205805.html; Hamish Macdonald, "Uganda Reveals Another Military Contract with North Korea," *NK News,* July 20, 2016, https://www.nknews.org/pro/uganda-reveals-another-military-contract-with-north-korea; and "Final Report of the Panel of Experts Submitted Pursuant to Resolution 2276 (2016)."

35. See Daryl Plunk, "North Korea: Exporting Terrorism?" Heritage Foundation, February 25, 1988, http://www.heritage.org/terrorism/report/north-korea-exporting-terrorism.

36. See W. Martin James III, *A Political History of the Civil War in Angola: 1974– 1990* (London: Routledge, 2011), 218.

37. For more on how North Korea assisted African nations during the Cold War, see André Vltchek, "North Korea Punished for Helping to Liberate Africa," Voltaire Network, March 26, 2016, http://www.voltairenet.org/article190923.html.

38. For more on how the end of the Cold War represented a paradigm shift and how it affected African states, see Jeffrey James Byrne, "Africa's Cold War," in *The Cold War in the Third World,* ed. Robert J. McMahon (Oxford: Oxford University Press, 2013), https://cisac.fsi.stanford.edu/sites/default/files/2013_byrne_africas_cold_war_oxford_cold_war_third_world_mcmahon_us_letter.pdf.

39. See "Angola: Arms Trade and Violations of the Laws of War since the 1992 Elections," Human Rights Watch, November 1994, https://www.hrw.org/sites/default/files/reports/ANGOLA94N.PDF.

40. See Bill Gertz, "N. Korea Violating UN Sanctions with Angolan Military Aid," *Washington Free Beacon,* June 12, 2015, http://freebeacon.com/national-security/n-korea-violating-un-sanctions-with-angolan-military-aid.

41. See Tatenda Gwaambuka, "North Korea's African Allies—Equatorial Guinea, Angola and DRC," The African Exponent, June 19, 2016, https://www.africanexponent.com/post/7344-north-koreas-african-allies-equatorial-guinea-angola-drc; and Hamish Macdonald, "Angola Discusses Public Security Cooperation with North Korea," *NK News,* April 8, 2016, https://www.nknews.org/2016/04/angola-discusses-public-security-cooperation-with-north-korea.

42. "N. Korean Workers Die of Yellow Fever in Angola: RFA," *Yonhap,* April 8, 2016, http://english.yonhapnews.co.kr/northkorea/2016/04/08/15/0401000000AEN20160408005500315F.html.

43. See "Angola Submits Implementation Report of Sanctions on N. Korea," *Yonhap,* August 6, 2016. http://english.yonhapnews.co.kr/national/2016/08/06/21/

0301000000AEN20160806001700315F.html; and Ju-min Park and Tony Munroe, "Squeezing North Korea: Old Friends Take Steps to Isolate Regime," Reuters, September 26, 2016, http://www.reuters.com/article/us-northkorea-nuclear-squeeze-idUSKCN11V0WE.

44. See "Final Report of the Panel of Experts Submitted Pursuant to Resolution 2276 (2016)."

45. See James Jeffrey, "Tension High between Ethiopia and Eritrea Despite Harmony in Region," *Irish Times,* August 3, 2016, http://www.irishtimes.com/news/world/africa/tension-high-between-ethiopia-and-eritrea-despite-harmony-in-region-1.2742951.

46. Connor Gaffey, "Eritrea Slams US for 'Inexplicable' Sanctions Following North Korea Report," *Newsweek,* April 17, 2017, http://www.newsweek.com/eritrea-north-korea-sanctions-579347.

47. See Salem Solomon, "US Imposes New Sanctions on Eritrea's Navy over North Korea Links," Voice of America, April 8, 2017, http://www.voanews.com/a/us-sanctions-eritrea-navy-over-north-korea-links/3802651.html; and "Final Report of the Panel of Experts Submitted Pursuant to Resolution 2276 (2016)."

48. See Hamish Macdonald, "North Korean Machine Guns Were Found on Boat Bound for Somalia in 2016," *NK News,* November 14, 2017, https://www.nknews.org/2017/11/north-korean-machine-guns-were-found-on-boat-bound-for-somalia-in-2016-report.

49. "NATO Intercepts Military Cargo Ship Bound for Eritrea—UN," *Sudan Tribune,* May 11, 2011, http://www.sudantribune.com/spip.php?article38864.

50. See Small Arms Survey Group, *Small Arms Survey 2012: Moving Targets* (Cambridge: Cambridge University Press, 2012), 346, 347.

51. Anonymous former senior ROK government official, interview with author, July 27, 2015, Seoul.

52. See "Al-Shabaab Biggest Threat to Peace in Somalia, Committee Chair Tells Security Council, as Delegates Air Differences over Sanctions," United Nations, Meeting Coverage and Press Releases, Security Council, 7925th Meeting, April 13, 2017, https://www.un.org/press/en/2017/sc12795.doc.htm.

53. For more analysis of the Soviet Union's expansion and support to nations around the world and in Africa and the fact that it brought these nations into its satellite sphere, see Geoffrey Kemp and Robert Harkavy, *Strategic Geography and the Changing Middle East* (Washington, DC: Brookings Institution Press, 1997).

54. "Ethiopia: US Assistance to Ethiopia," *Ethiopian Herald,* July 28, 2015, http://allafrica.com/stories/201507280885.html.

55. For more on the Ethiopia-Eritrea War, see "Ethiopia-Eritrea Civil War (1974–1991)," Political Economy Research Institute, University of Massachusetts, Amherst, 2017, http://www.peri.umass.edu/fileadmin/pdf/Ethiopia1.pdf.

56. See *Ethiopia: A Country Study,* ed. Thomas P. Ofcansky and LaVerle Berry (Washington, DC: Library of Congress, Federal Research Division, 1993).

57. See Fantahun Ayele, *The Ethiopian Army: From Victory to Collapse, 1977–1991* (Chicago: Northwestern University Press, 2014), 50–51.

58. See Jason McLure, "The Troubled Horn of Africa," *CQ Researcher* 3, no. 6 (June 2009), http://library.cqpress.com/cqresearcher/document.php?id=cqrglobal 2009060000.

59. See Michael R. Gordon and Mark Mazzetti, "Ethiopia Bought Arms from North Korea with U.S. Assent," *New York Times,* April 8, 2007, http://www.nytimes.com/2007/04/08/world/americas/08iht-arms.4.5191534.html?pagewanted=all.

60. "North Korea Sells Arms to Ethiopia with U.S. OK: NYT," Reuters, April 7, 2007, http://www.reuters.com/article/us-korea-ethiopia-arms-idUSN072828 8520070407.

61. For more details on the North Korea–Ethiopia military collaboration, which appears to have been ongoing as of 2014, see "Report of the Panel of Experts Established Pursuant to Resolution 1874 (2009)," UN Security Council, North Korea, Panel of Experts, March 6, 2014, http://www.un.org/ga/search/view_doc.asp?symbol=S/2014/147; Andrea Berger, "Is Ethiopia Violating UN Sanctions against North Korea?" 38 North, December 23, 2014, http://38north.org/2014/12/aberger122314; and Armin Rosen, "Here's Why North Korea May Still Be Selling Weapons to a US Ally," *Business Insider,* January 6, 2015, http://www.business insider.com/heres-why-north-korea-may-still-be-selling-weapons-to-a-us-ally-2015-1.

62. See Mark Fitzpatrick and Hannah Schwartz, "North Korea's Illicit Trade: Every Little Bit Hurts," *IISS Voices* (International Institute for Strategic Studies), May 24, 2017, http://www.iiss.org/en/iiss%20voices/blogsections/iiss-voices-2017-adeb/may-8636/north-korea-illicit-trade-e676.

63. For an excellent example of what the rule of Mugabe has been like for nearly forty years, see Ashish Kumar Sen, "Zimbabwe's Robert Mugabe, After 33 Years of Brutal Misrule, Seeks Another Term," *Washington Times,* July 29, 2013, http://www.washingtontimes.com/news/2013/jul/29/zimbabwes-robert-mugabe-after-33-years-brutal-misr.

64. See Laura Mowat, "Zimbabwe Latest: Robert Mugabe Misses Mnangagwa Sworn in as He and Grace Disappear," *Daily Express,* November 24, 2017, https://www.express.co.uk/news/world/883769/Zimbabwe-coup-latest-news-Robert-Mugabe-safe-Emerson-Mnangagwa-president.

65. See Alan Cowell, "Mugabe's Fifth Brigade: Grounded in Loyalty," *New York Times,* March 6, 1983, http://www.nytimes.com/1983/03/06/world/mugabes-fifth-brigade-grounded-in-loyalty.html; "Zimbabwe: The ZANU-ZAPU Rivalry," Central Intelligence Agency, April 1983, https://www.cia.gov/library/reading-room/docs/CIA-RDP84S00552R000200030002-4.pdf (sanitized copy approved for release 2011/07/05); and "Fifth Brigade—Zimbabwe," Terrorism Research and Analysis Consortium, 2017, https://www.trackingterrorism.org/group/fifth-brigade-zimbabwe.

66. See Byoung-Lo Kim, *Two Koreas in Development: A Comparative Study of Principles and Strategies of Capitalist and Communist Third World Development* (London: Routledge, 1991), 166–67.

67. See Katherine Shrader, "North Korea Arms Trade Seen as Threat," Associ-

ated Press, October 12, 2006, http://www.washingtonpost.com/wp-dyn/content/article/2006/10/12/AR2006101200953_pf.html.

68. Julian Ryall, "North Korea Losing African, South American Allies," *Deutsche Welle,* June 21, 2016, http://www.dw.com/en/north-korea-losing-african-south-american-allies/a-19344851; and Itai Mushekwe, "Zimbabwe in 'Arms for Uranium' Pact with North Korea," Nehanda Radio, September 19, 2013, http://nehandaradio.com/2013/09/19/zimbabwe-in-arms-for-uranium-pact-with-north-korea.

69. Samuel Ramani, "The Iran–North Korea Connection," *The Diplomat,* August 20, 2016, http://thediplomat.com/2016/04/the-iran-north-korea-connection.

70. "Zimbabwe: Mugabe Speaks on Loss of Contact with North Korea, Says Willing to Re-Establish Ties," *New Zimbabwe,* March 30, 2016, http://allafrica.com/stories/201603310075.html.

71. See Karl Maier, *Conspicuous Destruction: War, Famine and the Reform Process in Mozambique* (New Haven, CT: Yale University Press; New York: Human Rights Watch, 1993), 180.

72. See "Final Report of the Panel of Experts Submitted Pursuant to Resolution 2276 (2016)."

73. See "North Korea, Foreign Policy Goals: Chapter 3A."

74. Oliver Hotham, "Tanzania Won't Deny N. Korea Is Providing Military Assistance," *NK News,* August 15, 2013, https://www.nknews.org/2013/08/tanzania-wont-deny-n-korea-is-providing-military-assistance.

75. Megan Slack, "President Obama Visits Tanzania," The White House, July 1, 2013, https://obamawhitehouse.archives.gov/blog/2013/07/01/president-obama-visits-tanzania.

76. For an example of US-Tanzania relations, mutual interests, and foreign aid over the years, see Tony Waters, "Markets and Morality: American Relations with Tanzania," *African Studies Quarterly* 8, no. 3 (Spring 2006), https://asq.africa.ufl.edu/waters_spring06.

77. Barbara Among, "Uganda, Tanzania on UN Radar over North Korea Links," *Africa Review,* April 13, 2014, http://www.africareview.com/news/Uganda-Tanzania-on-UN-radar-over-North-Korea-links-/979180-2278036-4kf380/index.html.

78. See Ian Whytock, "North Korea's African Safari," NATO Association of Canada, February 6, 2014, http://natoassociation.ca/north-koreas-african-safari.

79. See "Report of the Panel of Experts Established Pursuant to Resolution 1874 (2009)."

80. See Shannon Ebrahim, "Africa's Empowerment of N Korea," *The Star,* February 19, 2016, http://www.iol.co.za/the-star/africas-empowerment-of-n-korea-1987162.

81. For specific details regarding Tanzanian–North Korean recent arms deals, see "Midterm Report of the Panel of Experts Established Pursuant to Resolution 1874 (2009)."

82. For an excellent example of the DRC's violent history, see Herbert Weiss, "A History of Resistance in the Congo," African Futures, December 12, 2012, http://forums.ssrc.org/african-futures/2012/12/08/african-futures-history-of-resistance-in-congo.

83. See "North Korea Helps Fine-Tune DRC Army," *Africa News,* April 27, 2000, http://www.iol.co.za/news/africa/north-korea-helps-fine-tune-drc-army-35829.

84. See "N. Korean Arms 'Sold to Congolese Insurgents,'" *Chosun Ilbo,* December 24, 2009, http://english.chosun.com/site/data/html_dir/2009/12/24/2009122400291.html.

85. See George F. Ward, "Africa and North Korea: Monuments and Munitions," *Africa Watch* (Institute for Defense Analysis) 15 (May 4, 2017), https://www.ida.org/idamedia/Corporate/Files/Publications/AfricaWatch/africawatch-May-04-2017-v0115.ashx.

86. See Michelle Nichols, "Exclusive—Rwanda Aids Burundi Rebels, North Korea Arms Congo: U.N. Experts," Reuters, May 13, 2016, http://uk.reuters.com/article/uk-burundi-rwanda-congodemocratic-un-idUKKCN0Y4014; and Cara Anna, "North Korea Used Africa to Get around Sanctions, UN Report Shows," Associated Press, March 4, 2017, https://www.thestar.com/news/world/2017/03/04/north-korea-used-africa-to-get-around-sanctions-un-report-says.html.

87. See "DR Congo Denies Getting Pistols from North Korea," AFP, May 16, 2016, http://www.qatar-tribune.com/news-details/id/1320/d/20160516. ·

88. See "Final Report of the Panel of Experts Submitted Pursuant to Resolution 2276 (2016)."

89. See Kambiz Foroohar, "The UN's Problem with North Korea Is Africa," Bloomberg, November 29, 2017, https://www.bloomberg.com/news/articles/2017-11-30/north-korean-arms-trade-among-loopholes-un-struggling-to-close; Lily Kuo, "North Korea Is Losing Its Friends in Africa," Bloomberg, October 5, 2017, https://www.bloomberg.com/news/articles/2017-11-30/north-korean-arms-trade-among-loopholes-un-struggling-to-close; Kim Young-nam, Salem Solomon, and Eric Manirakiza, "Burkina Faso Pledges to End North Korea Trade," Voice of America, December 21, 2017, https://www.voanews.com/a/burkina-faso-pledges-end-to-north-korea-trade/4173544.html; and Philippe Alfroy, "N. Korea's African Friends Face Test of Loyalty," *The Straits Times,* December 10, 2017, http://www.straitstimes.com/asia/east-asia/north-koreas-african-friends-face-test-of-loyalty.

90. For an excellent example of how South Korea attempted to use its economic instrument of power to influence African nations and perhaps wean them away from their military deals with North Korea, see Jared Ward, "Two Koreas Battle for Hearts and Minds in Africa," *NK News,* July 28, 2016, https://www.nknews.org/2016/07/two-koreas-battle-for-hearts-and-minds-in-africa.

7. Conclusions and Policy Implications

1. For an excellent example of a university that is lacking in faculty who have a background of military service, see Stuart Wolpert, "Army Veteran, a UCLA Student, Teaches Class on Combat and Military Life," *UCLA News,* April 5, 2013, http://newsroom.ucla.edu/releases/ucla-army-veteran-a-student-to-244663.

2. For an excellent analysis of how the end of the Cold War actually changed the proliferation paradigms of countries like North Korea, see Harald Müller,

"Viewpoint: Neither Hype nor Complacency: WMD Proliferation After the Cold War," *The Nonproliferation Review,* Winter 1997, https://www.nonproliferation.org/wp-content/uploads/npr/muller42.pdf.

3. For an excellent example of the many weapons tests that the North Koreans have conducted in the Kim Jong-un era, see Scott W. Bray, "North Korea's Nuclear Weapons and Missile Capability" (speech presented to the Institute for Corean-American Studies, June 26, 2017), https://www.dni.gov/files/ODNI/documents/20170726-NIM-East-Asia-Speech-to-ICAS-on-North-Koreas-Nulcear-and-Ballistic-Missile-Programs.pdf.

4. See Donald Kirk, "Iran's Partnership with North Korea on Nukes and Missiles May Scuttle Any Deal," *Forbes,* February 20, 2015, https://www.forbes.com/sites/donaldkirk/2015/02/20/irans-irans-long-time-partnership-with-north-korea-on-nukes-and-missiles-may-scuttle-a-real-deal/#253ece28b61b.

5. For a very good discussion of the military trade between North Korea and Iran, see "Complexities of the Iranian and North Korean Threats," The Soufan Group, February 21, 2017, http://www.soufangroup.com/tsg-intelbrief-complexities-of-the-iranian-and-north-korean-threats.

6. For an excellent example of the front company networks that North Korea uses, see Scott Snyder, "How North Korea Evades UN Sanctions through International 'Front' Companies," *Forbes,* March 3, 2017, https://www.forbes.com/sites/scottasnyder/2017/03/03/how-north-korea-evades-un-sanctions-through-international-front-companies/#7595fb36788b.

7. Anonymous former senior ROK government official, interview with author, June 29, 2017, Seoul.

8. See Niksch, "The Iran–North Korea Strategic Relationship."

9. William Newcomb, interview with author, June 30, 2017, Seoul.

10. See Joost Hilterman and April Longley Alley, "The Houthis Are Not Hezbollah," *Foreign Policy,* February 27, 2017, http://foreignpolicy.com/2017/02/27/the-houthis-are-not-hezbollah; Jack Moore, "Iran to 'Renew Funding' for Hamas, Despite Trump's Riyadh Speech," *Newsweek,* May 31, 2017, http://www.newsweek.com/iran-renew-funding-hamas-despite-trumps-riyadh-speech-617996; and David Daoud, "Meet the Proxies: How Iran Spreads Its Empire through Terrorist Militias," *The Tower,* March 2015, http://www.thetower.org/article/meet-the-proxies-how-iran-spreads-its-empire-through-terrorist-militias.

11. See Michael Freund, "Comment: The North Korean Threat to Israel," *Jerusalem Post,* August 25, 2015, http://www.jpost.com/Opinion/Fundamentally-Freund-The-North-Korean-threat-to-Israel-413133.

12. For an example of how North Korea has been supplying the Assad regime during the Syrian civil war, see Alex Diaz, "North Korea, Syria and Decades of Chemical Weapons," Fox News, April 10, 2017, http://www.foxnews.com/world/2017/04/10/north-korea-syria-and-decades-chemical-weapons.html.

13. For analysis of and context regarding post–Cold War African states, see Marina Ottaway, Jeffrey Herbst, and Greg Mills, "Africa's Big States: Toward a New

Realism," Carnegie Endowment, Policy Outlook, February 2004, http://carnegie endowment.org/files/PolicyOutlookOttaway.pdf.

14. See Dinshaw Mistry, *Containing Missile Proliferation: Strategic Technology, Security Regimes, and International Cooperation in Arms Control* (Seattle: University of Washington Press, 2005), 105–7; Patrick Goodenough, "Report: Iran Collaborating with N. Korea on Extensive Ballistic Missile Development," CNS News, June 21, 2017, https://www.cnsnews.com/news/article/patrick-goodenough/report-iran-collaborating-n-korea-extensive-ballistic-missile; Solomon, "Sanctioned and Shunned, North Korea Finds Arms Deals in Africa"; and Rosen, "Here's Why North Korea May Still Be Selling Weapons to a US Ally."

15. For an excellent example of published research assessing that North Korea's profits from military proliferation have declined since 1999, which seems unlikely given its high volume of sales of missiles, conventional arms, and reported nuclear technology to Iran and Syria as well as the many arms deals with African nations, the paradigm shift from transporting whole missiles to transporting components, spare parts, engineers, and technicians to on-site fabrication facilities in several countries built and operated with North Korean assistance, and support (direct or indirect) to groups such as Hezbollah and Hamas, see Stephan Haggard and Marcus Noland, *Hard Target: Sanctions, Inducements, and the Case of North Korea* (Stanford, CA: Stanford University Press, 2017), 59–104.

16. See David L. Asher, "The Impact of U.S. Policy on North Korean Illicit Activities," Heritage Lectures, April 18, 2017, http://s3.amazonaws.com/thf_media/2007/pdf/h11024.pdf.

17. See David Thompson, "Risky Business: System-Level Analysis of the North Korean Proliferation Financing System,"C4ADS,2017, https://static1.squarespace.com/static/566ef8b4d8af107232d5358a/t/59413c8bebbd1ac3194eafb1/1497447588968/Risky+Business-C4ADS.pdf.

18. For commentary that looks back to Jimmy Carter's negotiations and what the former president has said about the incident more recently, see R. B. A. Di Muccio, "How Jimmy Carter and I Were Wrong on North Korea—and How Carter Is Still Wrong," Center for Visions and Values, Grove City College, December 13, 2010, http://www.visionandvalues.org/2010/12/how-jimmy-carter-and-i-were-wrong-on-north-korea%E2%80%94and-how-carter-is-still-wrong.

19. For examples of how the carrot-or-stick debate has played out to date and is likely to play out in the future, see Rose Blanchard, Meghan McCall, and Geoff Wilson, eds., "Diplomacy-Minded President Moon Complicates Trump's North Korea Strategy," Ploughshares Fund, May 17, 2017, http://www.ploughshares.org/issues-analysis/early-warning/diplomacy-minded-president-moon-complicates-trump%E2%80%99s-north-korea; and "No Time for Friction with South Korea," *New York Times,* May 11, 2017, https://www.nytimes.com/2017/05/11/opinion/south-korea-president.html?partner=rssnyt&emc=rss.

20. See Paul Kerr and Daryl Kimball, "The Agreed Framework at a Glance," Arms Control Association, September 2004, https://www.armscontrol.org/system/

files/agreedframework.pdf; Matthew Martin, "The Six-Party Talks and New Opportunities to Strengthen Regional Nonproliferation and Disarmament Efforts" (conference organized by the Stanley Foundation, the National Committee on North Korea, the China Arms Control and Disarmament Association, and the Institute for Foreign Policy Analysis and coordinated by the Stanley Foundation, Beijing, October 23–24, 2008), https://www.stanley foundation.org/publications/report/6partytalksrpt309.pdf; and William Tobey, "Obama's 'Strategic Patience' on North Korea Is Turning into Strategic Neglect," *Foreign Policy,* February 14, 2013, http://foreignpolicy.com/2013/02/14/ obamas-strategic-patience-on-north-korea-is-turning-into-strategic-neglect.

21. See Raymond Farrell, "Thunder Run to Seoul: Assessing North Korea's War Plan," Real Clear Defense, April 25, 2017, http://www.realcleardefense. com/articles/2017/04/25/thunder_run_to_seoul_assessing_north_koreas_war_ plan_111241.html.

22. See Olly Terry, "What Can the U.S. Learn from the Agreed Framework?" *International Policy Digest,* January 15, 2015, https://intpolicydigest.org/2015/01/15/ can-u-s-learn-agreed-framework.

23. See "The Six-Party Talks and President Obama's North Korea Policy," Nuclear Threat Initiative, February 1, 2009, http://www.nti.org/analysis/articles/ obamas-north-korea-policy.

24. For deeper analysis of Obama's policy on North Korea, which most analysts (on both the Left and the Right) agree was a failure, see Walter Russell Mead, "No More 'Strategic Patience' on North Korea," Hudson Institute, March 17, 2017, https:// www.hudson.org/research/13457-no-more-strategic-patience-on-north-korea.

25. See "Resolutions," UN Security Council, Security Council Committee Established Pursuant to Resolution 1718 (2006), 2017, https://www.un.org/sc/ suborg/en/sanctions/1718/resolutions.

26. For examples of how tightly information is controlled in North Korea, see Jenny Jun, Scott LaFoy, and Ethan Sohn, "North Korea's Cyber Operations: Strategy and Responses," Report of the Korea Chair, Center for Strategic and International Studies, December 2015, https://csis-prod.s3.amazonaws.com/s3fs-public/legacy_ files/files/publication/151216_Cha_NorthKoreasCyberOperations_Web.pdf.

27. For more analysis on how information can influence North Korea, see Kenny Sokan, "Fighting North Korea's Dictatorship through Flash Drives," Public Radio International, March 28, 2016, https://www.pri.org/stories/2016-03-28/ fighting-north-koreas-dictatorship-through-flashdrives.

28. See Cissie Dore Hill, "Voices of Hope: The Story of Radio Free Europe and Radio Liberty," *Hoover Digest,* 2001, no. 4 (October 30), http://www.hoover.org/ research/voices-hope-story-radio-free-europe-and-radio-liberty.

29. For more on the Orascom–North Korea connection and how the influx of cell phones has changed North Korean society, see "The North Korean Connection," Finance Uncovered, February 3, 2016, http://www.financeuncovered.org/ investigations/the-north-korean-connection.

30. See Benjamin Ismaïl, "North Korea: Frontiers of Censorship," Reporters without Borders, October 2011, https://rsf.org/sites/default/files/rsf_north-korea_2011.pdf.

31. For more analysis of the cybercampaign and other initiatives, see Karen De Young, Ellen Nakashima, and Emily Rauhala, "Trump Signed Presidential Directive Ordering Actions to Pressure North Korea," *Washington Post,* September 30, 2017, https://www.washingtonpost.com/world/national-security/trump-signed-presidential-directive-ordering-actions-to-pressure-north-korea/2017/09/30/97c672 2a-a620-11e7-b14f-f41773cd5a14_story.html?utm_term=.322599812255.

32. For examples of how the Kim regime has kept itself in power in the past, see Daniel L. Byman and Jennifer Lind, "Keeping Kim: How North Korea's Regime Stays in Power," Belfer Center for Science and International Affairs, Policy Brief, July 2010, http://www.belfercenter.org/sites/default/files/files/publication/byman-lind-policybrief-final.pdf.

33. For an excellent example of a North Korean violent provocation, see David Eunpyoung Jee, "North Korea's Addiction to Provocation," *The Diplomat,* August 11, 2015, http://thediplomat.com/2015/08/north-koreas-addiction-to-provocation.

34. For more on North Korea's military, see Sung-chool Lee, "The ROK-US Joint Political and Military Response to North Korean Armed Provocations," Report of the Korea Chair, Center for Strategic and International Studies, October 2011, https://csis-prod.s3.amazonaws.com/s3fs-public/legacy_files/files/publication/111006_Lee_ROKUSJointResponse_web.pdf.

35. For a definition of *instruments of national power,* examples of how those instruments are used, and doctrine regarding how they relate to policy, see "Doctrine for the Armed Forces of the United States," Joint Publication 1, US Department of Defense, March 25, 2013, http://www.dtic.mil/doctrine/new_pubs/jp1.pdf.

36. For analysis of why the PSI was established and how its mission was formed, see Emma Belcher, "The Proliferation Security Initiative: Lessons for Using Nonbinding Agreements," Council on Foreign Relations, Working Paper, July 2011, https://www.cfr.org/content/publications/attachments/IIGG_WorkingPaper6_PSI.pdf.

37. For the latest list of PSI member states, see "Proliferation Security Initiative," Nuclear Threat Initiative, February 20, 2017, http://www.nti.org/learn/treaties-and-regimes/proliferation-security-initiative-psi.

38. For an analysis of the challenges that the PSI has encountered, see Jacek Durkalec, "The Proliferation Security Initiative: Evolution and Future Prospects," EU Non-Proliferation Consortium, Non-Proliferation Papers, no. 16, June 2012, http://www.nonproliferation.eu/web/documents/nonproliferationpapers/jacek-durkalec4fcc7fd95cfff.pdf.

39. For more on how the action taken against Banco Delta Asia really hurt the North Koreans, see Jeff Daniels, "Ex-CIA Agent Says US Sanctions against Chinese Bank Aiding Pyongyang 'Extremely Long Overdue,'" CNBC, June 29, 2017, http://www.cnbc.com/2017/06/29/ex-cia-agent-says-us-sanctions-against-chinese-bank-

long-overdue.html; and Meyer, "Squeeze on North Korea's Money Supply Yields Results."

40. For an excellent example that explains how North Korea has adjusted and diversified following the BDA initiative, see "The U.S. Wants to Choke Off North Korea's Access to Global Banks," *Reuters*, June 2, 2016, http://fortune.com/2016/06/02/us-north-korea-banks.

41. For examples of front companies and banks in countries outside North Korea and China, see Berlinger, "Guns and Money"; and Jonathan Cheng, "The Global Web That Keeps North Korea Running," *Fox Business*, July 6, 2017, http://www.foxbusiness.com/features/2017/07/06/global-web-that-keeps-north-korea-running.html.

42. For an example of the types of sanctions initiated against North Korea during the Obama administration, see Julie Hirshfield Davis, "Obama Places Sanctions on Kim Jong-un and Other Top North Koreans for Rights Abuses," *New York Times,* July 6, 2016, https://www.nytimes.com/2016/07/07/world/asia/obama-puts-sanctions-on-north-korean-leaders-for-human-rights-abuse.html.

43. For in-depth context and analysis of the Agreed Framework and the fact that North Korea was cheating on it, see William J. Perry, "Proliferation on the Peninsula: Five North Korea Nuclear Crises" (speech delivered by the former secretary of defense at the Carnegie Endowment for International Peace, November 2005), https://cisac.fsi.stanford.edu/sites/default/files/Perry_Proliferation_on_the_Peninsula.pdf.

44. For background on and the context of the final versions of the Six-Party talks during the Bush administration and how the talks ultimately failed because of disputes over verification, see Shin-yon Kim, "The Tortuous Dilemma: The 2008 Six-Party Talks and U.S. DPRK Relations," *SAIS U.S.-Korea Yearbook 2008,* John Hopkins University, 2010, http://uskoreainstitute.org/wp-content/uploads/2010/02/KimSY.pdf.

45. For an example of scholarship that is critical of the policy of strategic patience, see James E. Goodby and Donald Gross, "Strategic Patience Has Become Strategic Passivity," Brookings Institution, December 22, 2010, https://www.brookings.edu/articles/strategic-patience-has-become-strategic-passivity.

46. See William Newcomb, "Testimony before the House Committee on Financial Services at the Hearing 'Restricting North Korea's Access to Finance,'" July 19, 2017, https://financialservices.house.gov/uploadedfiles/hhrg-115-ba19-wstate-wnewcomb-20170719.pdf.

47. "Joint Statement of President Donald J. Trump of the United States of America and Chairman Kim Jong Un of the Democratic People's Republic of Korea at the Singapore Summit." The White House, June 12, 2018. https://www.whitehouse.gov/briefings-statements/joint-statement-president-donald-j-trump-united-states-america-chairman-kim-jong-un-democratic-peoples-republic-korea-singapore-summit/.

Selected Bibliography

"The Administration Extends Sanctions Review Period." Press release, US Department of State, July 11, 2017. https://www.state.gov/r/pa/prs/ps/2017/07/272539. htm.

"Advisory: Advisory on the FATF-Identified Jurisdictions with AML/CFT Deficiencies." United States Department of the Treasury, Financial Crimes Enforcement Network, March 16, 2015. https://www.fincen.gov/news/news-releases/advisory-fatf-identified-jurisdictions-amlcft-deficiencies.

Ahn, J. H. "North Korea Holds Its Largest Ever Artillery Exercise." *NK News,* March 25, 2016. https://www.nknews.org/2016/03/north-korea-holds-largest-ever-artillery-exercise.

———. "N. Korean Submarine Attempts to Test-Fire Ballistic Missile: MBN." *NK News,* April 7, 2016. https://www.nknews.org/2016/04/n-korean-submarine-attempts-to-test-fire-ballistic-missile-mbn.

Albert, Eleanor. "North Korea's Military Capabilities." Council on Foreign Relations, CFR Backgrounder, November 30, 2017. https://www.cfr.org/backgrounder/north-koreas-military-capabilities.

Albright, David. "North Korea Miniaturization." 38 North, February 13, 2013. http://38north.org/2013/02/albright021313.

"Al-Shabaab Biggest Threat to Peace in Somalia, Committee Chair Tells Security Council, as Delegates Air Differences over Sanctions." United Nations, Meeting Coverage and Press Releases, Security Council, 7925th Meeting, April 13, 2017. https://www.un.org/press/en/2017/sc12795.doc.htm.

"Angola: Arms Trade and Violations of the Laws of War since the 1992 Elections." Human Rights Watch, November 1994. https://www.hrw.org/sites/default/files/reports/ANGOLA94N.PDF.

Anonymous former senior ROK government official. Interview with author, June 29, 2017, Seoul.

Anonymous former senior ROK government official. Interview with author, July 27, 2015, Seoul.

"Arms Control and Proliferation Profile: North Korea." Arms Control Association, February 2015. https://www.armscontrol.org/factsheets/northkoreaprofile.

Arnold, Aaron. "Watch Out for the Blowback of Secondary Sanctions on North Korea." *The Diplomat,* April 28, 2017. http://thediplomat.com/2017/04/watch-out-for-the-blowback-of-secondary-sanctions-on-north-korea.

Arthur, Michael. "Scud ER." Missile Defense Advocacy Alliance, 2015. http://missile defenseadvocacy.org/threats/north-korea/scud-er.

Asculai, Ephraim. "The Plutonium Track: Implications for the Completion of Iran's Heavy Water Reactor at Arak." Discussion Meeting, International Institute for Strategic Studies, Arundel House, London, September 11, 2013. http://www.iiss.org/en/events/events/archive/2013--5126/september-03c7/the-plutonium-track-766d.

Asher, David L. "North Korea's Criminal Activities: Financing the Regime." Hearing before the Committee on Foreign Affairs, House of Representatives, 113th Cong., 1st sess., March 5, 2013. http://docs.house.gov/meetings/FA/FA00/20130305/100436/HHRG-113-FA00-20130305-SD003.pdf.

———. "The Impact of U.S. Policy on North Korean Illicit Activities." Heritage Foundation, April 18, 2007. https://www.heritage.org/asia/report/the-impact-us-policy-north-korean-illicit-activities.

Ayele, Fantahun. *The Ethiopian Army: From Victory to Collapse, 1977–1991.* Chicago: Northwestern University Press, 2014.

Babson, Bradley O. "The Demise of Jang Song Thaek and the Future of North Korea's Financial System." 38 North, February 24, 2014. http://38north.org/2014/02/bbabson022414.

———. "UNSCR 2270: The Good, the Bad, and the Perhaps Surprising Opportunity for the North Korean Economy." 38 North, March 21, 2016. http://38north.org/2016/03/bbabson032116.

"Background Briefing with Senior Intelligence Officials on Syria's Covert Nuclear Reactor and North Korea's Involvement." Office of the Director of National Intelligence, April 24, 2008. https://fas.org/irp/news/2008/04/odni042408.pdf.

Baik, Sungwon. "US Dismisses Disagreement with Seoul on N Korea Nuclear Threat." Voice of America, April 14, 2015. http://www.voanews.com/content/united-states-dismisses-disagreement-north-korea-nuclear-threat/2719548.html.

Bechtol, Bruce E., Jr. *The Last Days of Kim Jong-il: The North Korean Threat in a Changing Era.* Washington DC: Potomac, 2013.

———. "Military Proliferation in the Kim Jong-un Era: The Impact on Human Rights in North Korea." *International Journal of Korean Studies* 18, no. 1 (Spring 2014). http://www.icks.org/data/ijks/1482467285_add_file_5.pdf.

———. *North Korea and Regional Security in the Kim Jong-un Era: A New International Security Dilemma.* London: Palgrave Macmillan, 2014.

———. "North Korea and Syria: Partners in Destruction and Violence." *Korean Journal of Defense Analysis* vol. 27, no. 3 (September 2015): 277–92.

———. "The North Korean Military Threat in 2015: The Threat to the ROK-U.S. Alliance and Peninsula Unification." *International Journal of Korean Studies* 19, no. 1 (Spring 2015). http://www.icks.org/data/ijks/1482467975_add_file_1.pdf.

———. "North Korea and Military Proliferation to Iran: An International Security Dilemma." *ChiMoKoJa—Histories of China, Mongolia, Korea and Japan,* vol. 2 (2016). http://maxoki161.blogspot.com/2016/09/north-korea-and-military-proliferation.html.

"Beijing Orders Banks to Close Accounts for North Koreans." *Daily NK,* September 9, 2017. http://www.dailynk.com/english/read.php?num=14709&catald=nk01500.

Belcher, Emma. "The Proliferation Security Initiative: Lessons for Using Nonbinding Agreements." Council on Foreign Relations, Working Paper, July 2011. https://www.cfr.org/content/publications/attachments/IIGG_WorkingPaper6_PSI.pdf.

Ben-David, Alon. "Iran Acquires Ballistic Missiles from DPRK." Pakistan Defence, December 29, 2005. https://defence.pk/pdf/threads/iran-acquires-ballistic-missiles-from-dprk.593.

Berger, Andrea. "Is Ethiopia Violating UN Sanctions against North Korea?" 38 North, December 23, 2014. http://38north.org/2014/12/aberger122314.

———. "A Legal Precipice? The DPRK-Uganda Security Relationship." 38 North, November 13, 2014. http://38north.org/2014/11/aberger111314.

———. "North Korea's Friends in Singapore Running Flags of Convenience." 38 North, June 22, 2015. http://38north.org/2015/06/aberger062215.

———. "The 2016 UN Panel of Experts Report: An Eye-Opening Account of Persistent Blindness." 38 North, April 19, 2016. http://38north.org/2016/04/aberger041916.

———. "Trump Puts Sudan (and the World) 'on Notice' over DPRK." *Arms Control Wonk,* July 12, 2017. http://www.armscontrolwonk.com/archive/1203587/trump-puts-sudan-and-the-world-on-notice-over-dprk.

Bermudez, Joseph S., Jr. "North Korea Deploys New Missiles." *Jane's Defence Weekly,* August 2, 2004, 4.

———. "North Korea's Chemical Warfare Capabilities." 38 North, October 10, 2013. http://38north.org/2013/10/jbermudez101013.

———. "The Korean People's Navy Tests New Anti-Ship Cruise Missile." 38 North, February 8, 2015. http://38north.org/2015/02/jbermudez020815.

———. "North Korea's SINPO-Class Sub: New Evidence of Possible Vertical Launch Tubes; Sinpo Shipyard prepares for Significant Naval Construction Program." 38 North, January 8, 2015. http://38north.org/2015/01/jbermudez010815.

Bermudez, Joseph S., Jr. and Henry Kan. "Location of KN-08 Reentry Vehicle Nosecone Identified." 38 North, March 23, 2016. http://38north.org/2016/03/chamjin032316.

Bermudez, Joseph S., Jr. and Frank Pabian. "North Korea's Hwasong-14 Missile Launch Site Identified: The Panghyon Aircraft Factory." 38 North, July 6, 2017. http://www.38north.org/2017/07/panghyon070617.

Bervoets, Jeremy. "The Soviet Union in Angola: Soviet and African Perspectives on the Failed Socialist Transformation." *Vestnik: The Journal of Russian and Asian Studies,* November 5, 2011. http://www.sras.org/the_soviet_union_in_angola.

Blanchard, Rose, Meghan McCall, and Geoff Wilson, eds. "Diplomacy-Minded President Moon Complicates Trump's North Korea Strategy." Ploughshares Fund, May 17, 2017. http://www.ploughshares.org/issues-analysis/early-warning/diplomacy-minded-president-moon-complicates-trump%E2%80%99s-north-korea.

Bray, Scott W. "North Korea's Nuclear Weapons and Missile Capability." Speech Presented to the Institute for Corean-American Studies, June 26, 2017. https://www.dni.gov/files/ODNI/documents/20170726-NIM-East-Asia-Speech-to-ICAS-on-North-Koreas-Nulcear-and-Ballistic-Missile-Programs.pdf.

"Breaking: Regime's Slush Fund Manager Defects in Vladivostok." *New Focus International,* August 26, 2016. http://newfocusintl.com/vladivostokdefection.

Bredemeier, Ken. "US Blacklists Chinese Bank It Says Has Been Funding N. Korean Weapons Development." Voice of America, June 29, 2017. https://www.voanews.com/a/us-blacklists-chinese-bank-it-says-has-been-funding-north-korean-weapons-developement/3921814.html.

Brown, Tim. "North Korea: New Construction at the Sohae Satellite Launching Station." 38 North, May 28, 2015. http://38north.org/2015/05/sohae052815.

Byman, Daniel L., and Jennifer Lind. "Keeping Kim: How North Korea's Regime Stays in Power." Belfer Center for Science and International Affairs, Policy Brief, July 2010. http://www.belfercenter.org/sites/default/files/files/publication/byman-lind-policybrief-final.pdf.

Byrne, Leo. "Murky Waters: North Korea's Ships in South Korean Seas." *NK News,* November 6, 2014. https://www.nknews.org/2014/11/murky-waters-north-koreas-ships-in-south-korean-seas.

———. "North Korea Uses 'Multiple and Tiered' Techniques to Evade Sanctions." *NK News,* March 11, 2014. https://www.nknews.org/2014/03/north-korea-uses-multiple-and-tiered-techniques-to-evade-sanctions.

———. "Parts from U.S., UK and SK in North Korean Rocket." *NK News,* March 26, 2014. http://www.nknews.org/2014/03/parts-from-u-s-uk-and-sk-in-north-korean-rocket.

———. "UN PoE Finds N. Korea Continues to Sell Military, Sanctioned Items." *NK News,* March 2, 2017. https://www.nknews.org/2017/03/un-poe-finds-n-korea-continues-to-sell-military-sanctioned-items.

Cha, Victor, and Ellen Kim. "North Korea's Third Nuclear Test." Center for Strategic and International Studies, February 12, 2013. http://csis.org/publication/north-koreas-third-nuclear-test.

Cha, Victor D., and Gabriel Scheinmann. "North Korea's Hamas Connection: 'Below' the Surface?" *The National Interest,* September 4, 2014. http://nationalinterest.org/feature/north-koreas-hamas-connection-below-the-surface-11195.

Chang, Gordon G. "Punishing Assad's WMD Supplier." *World Affairs,* August 28, 2013. http://www.worldaffairsjournal.org/blog/gordon-g-chang/punishing-assads-wmd-supplier.

———. "China Likely Cheating, Again, on North Korean Sanctions." *World Affairs,* June 15, 2016. http://www.worldaffairsjournal.org/blog/gordon-g-chang/china-likely-cheating-again-north-korea-sanctions.

Chappell, Bill. "Iran Shows Off New Ballistic Missile at Military Parade." National

Public Radio, September 22, 2017. https://www.npr.org/sections/thetwo-way/2017/09/22/552942917/iran-shows-off-new-ballistic-missile-at-military-parade.

Cheon, Seongwhun. "Assessing the Threat of North Korea's Nuclear Capability." *Korean Journal of Defense Analysis* 18, no. 3 (Fall 2006): 35–69.

Choi, Song Min. "Military Items Smuggled through Chinese Customs Despite Sanctions." *Daily NK,* April 4, 2016. http://www.dailynk.com/english/read.php?num=13839&cataId=nk01500.

"Chronology of North Korea's Missile Trade and Developments: 1980–1989." James Martin Center for Nonproliferation Studies, 2003. http://www.nonproliferation.org/chronology-of-north-koreas-missile-trade-and-developments-1980-1989.

Cimbala, Stephen J. *Nuclear Strategy in the Twenty-First Century.* Santa Barbara, CA: Praeger, 2000.

Clapper, James R. "Statement for the Record, Worldwide Threat Assessment of the US Intelligence Community, Senate Select Committee on Intelligence." January 29, 2014. http://www.dni.gov/files/documents/Intelligence%20Reports/2014%20WWTA%20%20SFR_SSCI_29_Jan.pdf.

Coduti, Maria Rosaria, "Kim Jong Un's North Korea: Leadership Changes under the New Leader." CETRI, December 19, 2016. http://www.cetri.be/Kim-Jong-Uns-North-Korea?lang=fr.

The Cold War in the Third World. Edited by Robert J. McMahon. Oxford: Oxford University Press, 2013.

"Combat Fleets 16th Edition: Iranian Frigates and Patrol Craft." United States Naval Institute, August 2013. http://www.usni.org/combat-fleets-2012-iranian-frigates-and-patrol-craft-0.

"Complexities of the Iranian and North Korean Threats." The Soufan Group, February 21, 2017. http://www.soufangroup.com/tsg-intelbrief-complexities-of-the-iranian-and-north-korean-threats.

Cordesman, Anthony. *Iran's Military Forces in Transition.* Westport, CT: Praeger, 1999.

Cordesman, Anthony, and Bryan Gold. *The Gulf Military Balance: The Missile and Nuclear Connections.* Washington, DC: Center for Strategic and International Studies, 2014.

Cordesman, Anthony H., and Ashley Hess. *The Evolving Military Balance in the Korean Peninsula and Northeast Asia.* Vol. 3, *Missile, DPRK and ROK Nuclear Forces, and External Nuclear Forces.* Center for Strategic and International Studies Report, June 2013. https://csis-prod.s3.amazonaws.com/s3fs-public/legacy_files/files/publication/130513_KMB_volume3.pdf.

Crane, Leah. "North Korea Launches ICBM with Potential to Reach New York." *New Scientist,* July 28, 2017. https://www.newscientist.com/article/2142224-north-korea-launches-icbm-with-potential-to-reach-new-york.

Cronin, Patrick. "North Korea's Balance of Terror." *Real Clear Defense,* May 27, 2015. http://www.realcleardefense.com/articles/2015/05/27/north_koreas_balance_of_terror_107977.html.

Daoud, David. "Meet the Proxies: How Iran Spreads Its Empire through Terrorist Militias." *The Tower,* March 2015. http://www.thetower.org/article/meet-the-proxies-how-iran-spreads-its-empire-through-terrorist-militias.

Davenport, Kelsey. "North Korea Conducts Nuclear Test." *Arms Control Today,* February 28, 2013. https://www.armscontrol.org/act/2013_03/North-Korea-Conducts-Nuclear-Test.

Di Muccio, R. B. A. "How Jimmy Carter and I Were Wrong on North Korea—and How Carter Is Still Wrong." Center for Visions and Values, December 13, 2010. http://www.visionandvalues.org/2010/12/how-jimmy-carter-and-i-were-wrong-on-north-korea%E2%80%94and-how-carter-is-still-wrong.

"Doctrine for the Armed Forces of the United States." Joint Publication 1, US Department of Defense, March 25, 2013. http://www.dtic.mil/doctrine/new_pubs/jp1.pdf.

Dolan, Daniel. "The North Korean Connection." *US Naval Institute News,* February 14, 2013. https://news.usni.org/2012/06/17/north-korean-connection.

"Douglas Frantz: Assistant Secretary, Bureau of Public Affairs." US Department of State, 2016. http://www.state.gov/r/pa/ei/biog/213904.htm.

"DPRK Foreign Minister Meets with Bashar al-Assad." North Korea Leadership Watch, June 18, 2014. https://nkleadershipwatch.wordpress.com/2014/06/19/dprk-foreign-minister-meets-with-bashar-al-assad.

"The DPRK Is Capitalist When It Wants to Be: The Story of Drugs Incorporated (Parts 1 & 2)." *New Focus International,* August 18, 2012. http://newfocusintl.com/the-dprk-is-capitalist-when-it-wants-to-be-the-story-of-drugs-incorporated-parts-12.

Draper, Lucy. "North Korea Training Secretive Elite Hacker Unit, Says Defector." *Newsweek,* December 5, 2014. http://europe.newsweek.com/north-korea-training-cyber-warriors-289414.

DuPre, Annie, Nicolas Kasprzyk, and Noël Stott. "Cooperation between African States and the Democratic People's Republic of Korea." Institute for Security Studies Research Report, 2016. https://issafrica.s3.amazonaws.com/site/uploads/research-report-dprk.pdf.

Durkalec, Jacek. "The Proliferation Security Initiative: Evolution and Future Prospects." EU Non-Proliferation Consortium, Non-Proliferation Papers, no. 16, June 2012. http://www.nonproliferation.eu/web/documents/nonproliferation papers/jacekdurkalec4fcc7fd95cfff.pdf.

Dwyer, Colin. "North Korea Says Successful ICBM Test Shows U.S. Is in Striking Distance." NPR, July 28, 2017. http://www.npr.org/sections/thetwo-way/2017/07/28/540008218/north-korea-h-ballistic-missile-seoul-and-the-pentagon-say.

Dwyer, James. "North Korea's Submarine Missile Firing Raises the Nuclear Stakes." *The Conversation,* May 18, 2015. http://theconversation.com/north-koreas-submarine-missile-firing-raises-the-nuclear-stakes-41667.

"Egypt, Events of 2016." Human Rights Watch, 2017. https://www.hrw.org/world-report/2017/country-chapters/egypt.

"Egypt's Missile Efforts Succeed with Help from North Korea." Wisconsin Project on Nuclear Arms Control, September 1, 1996. http://www.wisconsinproject.org/egypts-missile-efforts-succeed-with-help-from-north-korea.

Elleman, Michael. "Iran's Ballistic Missile Program." Iran Primer, US Institute of Peace, August 2015. http://iranprimer.usip.org/resource/irans-ballistic-missile-program.

———. "North Korea Launches Another Large Rocket: Consequences and Options." 38 North, February 10, 2016. http://38north.org/2016/02/melleman021016.

———. "Early Observations of North Korea's Latest Missile Tests." 38 North, July 28, 2017. http://www.38north.org/2017/07/melleman072817.

———. "The New Hwasong-15 ICBM: A Significant Improvement That May Be Ready as Early as 2018." 38 North, November 30, 2017. http://www.38north.org/2017/11/melleman113017.

———. "The Secret to North Korea's ICBM Success." *IISS Voices* (International Institute for Strategic Studies), August 14, 2017. http://www.iiss.org/en/iiss%20voices/blogsections/iiss-voices-2017-adeb/august-2b48/north-korea-icbm-success-3abb.

Ethiopia: A Country Study. Edited by Thomas P. Ofcansky and LaVerle Berry. Washington, DC: Library of Congress, Federal Research Division, 1993.

"Ethiopia-Eritrea Civil War (1974–1991)." Political Economy Research Institute, University of Massachusetts, Amherst, 2017. http://www.peri.umass.edu/fileadmin/pdf/Ethiopia1.pdf.

"Everything You Need to Know about Hamas' Underground City of Terror." Israel Defense Forces, July 31, 2014. https://www.idfblog.com/blog/2014/07/31/everything-need-know-hamas-underground-city-terror.

"Executive Order—Blocking Property of the Government of North Korea and the Workers' Party of Korea, and Prohibiting Certain Transactions with Respect to North Korea." White House, Office of the Press Secretary, March 16, 2016. https://obamawhitehouse.archives.gov/the-press-office/2016/03/16/executive-order-blocking-property-government-north-korea-and-workers.

Farrell, Raymond. "Thunder Run to Seoul: Assessing North Korea's War Plan." *Real Clear Defense,* April 25, 2017. http://www.realcleardefense.com/articles/2017/04/25/thunder_run_to_seoul_asessing_north_koreas_war_plan_111241.html.

"Fears Rise about Iran–North Korea Nuclear Connection." *NKNews,* February 18, 2013. http://www.nknews.org/2013/02/fears-rise-about-iran-north-korea-nuclear-connection.

"Fifth Brigade—Zimbabwe." Terrorism Research and Analysis Consortium, 2017. https://www.trackingterrorism.org/group/fifth-brigade-zimbabwe.

"Final Report of the Panel of Experts Submitted Pursuant to Resolution 2276 (2016)." UN Security Council, Panel of Experts, February 27, 2017. http://www.un.org/ga/search/view_doc.asp?symbol=S/2017/150.

"Final Report of the Panel of Experts Submitted Pursuant to Resolution 2345

(2017)." UN Security Council, Panel of Experts, March 5, 2018. http://www
.un.org/ga/search/view_doc.asp?symbol=S/2018/171.

Fish, Isaac Stone. "Inside North Korea's Crystal Meth Trade." *Foreign Policy,* November 21, 2013. http://foreignpolicy.com/2013/11/21/inside-north-koreas-crystal-meth-trade.

Fisher, Richard D., Jr. "North Korea Unveils New Version of KN-08 ICBM." *Jane's Defense Weekly,* October 12, 2015. http://www.janes.com/article/55190/north-korea-unveils-new-version-of-kn-08-icbm.

Fitzpatrick, Mark. "North Korean Proliferation Challenges: The Role of the European Union." EU Non-Proliferation Consortium, Non-Proliferation Papers, no. 18, June 2012. http://www.sipri.org/research/disarmament/eu-consortium/publications/nonproliferation-paper-18.

———. "Squeezing North Korea's Foreign Earnings." International Institute for Strategic Studies, June 3, 2016. http://www.iiss.org/en/shangri-la%20voices/blogsections/2016-588c/squeezing-north-koreas-foreign-earnings-4678.

Fitzpatrick, Mark, and Hannah Schwartz. "North Korea's Illicit Trade: Every Little Bit Hurts." *IISS Voices* (International Institute for Strategic Studies), May 24, 2017. http://www.iiss.org/en/iiss%20voices/blogsections/iiss-voices-2017-adeb/may-8636/north-korea-illicit-trade-e676.

"Four Chinese Nationals and China-Based Company Charged with Using Front Companies to Evade U.S. Sanctions Targeting North Korea's Nuclear Weapons and Ballistic Missile Programs." United States Department of Justice, Office of Public Affairs, September 26, 2016. https://www.justice.gov/opa/pr/four-chinese-nationals-and-china-based-company-charged-using-front-companies-evade-us.

Gady, Franz-Stefan. "North Korea Fires 2 Ballistic Missiles into Sea." *The Diplomat,* March 3, 2015. http://thediplomat.com/2015/03/north-korea-fires-2-ballistic-missiles-into-sea.

Gaffey, Connor. "Eritrea Slams US for 'Inexplicable' Sanctions Following North Korea Report." *Newsweek,* April 17, 2017. http://www.newsweek.com/eritrea-north-korea-sanctions-579347.

Galamas, Francisco. "2014: A Year in North Korean Security." *The Diplomat,* December 16, 2014. http://thediplomat.com/2014/12/2014-a-year-in-north-korean-security.

Gathman, Christina. "Inside North Korea's State-Sanctioned Criminal Empire." *International Affairs Review* 23, no. 1 (Fall 2014). http://iar-gwu.org/sites/default/files/articlepdfs/4-Inside%20North%20Koreas%20Criminal%20Empire-Gathman.pdf.

Ghoshal, Debalina. "Opinion: North Korea's Sea-Based Deterrent." *US Naval Institute News,* December 1, 2014. http://news.usni.org/2014/12/01/opinion-north-koreas-sea-based-deterrent.

Gidda, Mirren. "Panama Papers: British Banker Helped North Korea Sell Arms, Expand Nuclear Program." *Newsweek,* April 6, 2016. http://www.newsweek.com/panama-papers-mossack-fonseca-north-korea-444452.

Goodby, James E., and Donald Gross. "Strategic Patience Has Become Strategic Passivity." Brookings Institution, December 22, 2010. https://www.brookings.edu/articles/strategic-patience-has-become-strategic-passivity.

Gopalaswamy, Bharath. "Is an Iranian Missile Threat Imminent?" International Network of Engineers and Scientists against Proliferation, April 2008. http://www.inesap.org/bulletin-28/iranian-missile-threat-imminent.

Graham, William R. "North Korea Nuclear EMP Attack: An Existential Threat." 38 North, June 2, 2017. http://www.38north.org/2017/06/wgraham060217.

Griffiths, Hugh, and Lawrence Dermody. "Feb 13: Sanctions beyond Borders: How to Make North Korea Sanctions Work." Stockholm International Peace Research Institute, February 28, 2013. https://www.sipri.org/node/329.

———. "Loopholes in UN Sanctions against North Korea." 38 North, May 6, 2014. http://38north.org/2014/05/griffithdermod050614.

Grisafi, John G. "The AN-2: N. Korea's Surprisingly Capable Soviet-Era Biplane." NK News, September 16, 2014. http://www.nknews.org/2014/09/the-an-2-n-koreas-surprisingly-capable-aircraft.

———. "Recent Launches Revealed as Surface-to-Surface Missile." NK News, August 16, 2014. http://www.nknews.org/2014/08/recent-launches-revealed-as-surface-to-surface-missile.

———. "The Threat of North Korea's New Rocket Artillery." NK News, March 13, 2014. http://www.nknews.org/2014/03/the-threat-of-north-koreas-new-rocket-artillery.

———. "DPRK, Iran Strong Partners in Missile Tech—Middle East Experts." NK News, January 19, 2015. http://www.nknews.org/2015/01/dprk-iran-strong-partners-in-missile-tech-middle-east-experts.

———. "Inter-Korean Tensions Top N. Korean Leadership Agenda in August." NK News, September 10, 2015. http://www.nknews.org/2015/09/inter-korean-tensions-top-n-korean-leadership-agenda-in-august.

———. "Military Drills and Leadership Changes Top Agenda in January." NK News, February 6, 2015. http://www.nknews.org/2015/02/military-drills-and-leadership-changes-top-agenda-in-january.

———. "N. Korea Reveals Details of 300mm Multiple Rocket Launcher." NK News, March 4, 2016. https://www.nknews.org/2016/03/n-korea-reveals-details-of-300mm-multiple-rocket-launcher.

Grobler, John. "Report Namibia Caught Violating North Korea Sanctions." NK News, April 15, 2016. https://www.nknews.org/2016/04/report-namibia-caught-violating-north-korea-sanctions.

Groll, Elias. "Gold Smuggling North Korean Diplomat Provides Glimpse at Criminal Empire." Foreign Policy, March 6, 2015. http://foreignpolicy.com/2015/03/06/gold-smuggling-north-korean-diplomat-provides-glimpse-at-criminal-empire.

Gwaambuka, Tatenda. "North Korea's African Allies—Equatorial Guinea, Angola and DRC." African Exponent, June 19, 2016. https://www.africanexponent.com/post/7344-north-koreas-african-allies-equatorial-guinea-angola-drc.

Hambling, David. "Decisive Weapons of the Next Korean War." *Popular Mechanics,* November 4, 2010. http://www.popularmechanics.com/military/weapons/a6211/north-korea-conflict-weapons-available.

Hands, Jack. "The Panama Papers Underscore the Futility of North Korean Sanctions." *The Diplomat,* April 6, 2016. http://thediplomat.com/2016/04/the-panama-papers-underscore-the-futility-of-north-korea-sanctions.

Haney, C. D. "Statement of Admiral C. D. Haney, Commander, United States Strategic Command, before the Senate Committee on Armed Services, 19 March 2015." http://www.defenseinnovationmarketplace.mil/resources/2015_Posture_Statement.pdf.

Hansen, Nick. "North Korea's Sohae Facility: Preparations for Future Large Rocket Launches Progresses [*sic*]; New Unidentified Buildings." 38 North, July 29, 2014. http://38north.org/2014/07/sohae073014.

Hansen, Nick, Robert Kelley, and Allison Puccioni. "North Korean Nuclear Programme Advances." *Jane's Intelligence Review,* March 30, 2016. http://www.janes.com/article/59118/north-korean-nuclear-programme-advances.

Harris, Shane, "Extensive Hamas Tunnel Network Points to Israeli Intelligence Failure." The Cable, July 31, 2014. http://thecable.foreignpolicy.com/posts/2014/07/31/extensive_hamas_tunnel_network_points_to_israeli_intelligence_failure_harris.

Harvey, Brian Henk, H. F. Smid, and Theo Pirard. *Emerging Space Powers: The New Space Programs of Asia, the Middle East and South-America.* Berlin: Springer Praxis, 2010.

Hayden, Michael V. "Director's Remarks at the Los Angeles World Affairs Council." Central Intelligence Agency, September 16, 2008. https://www.cia.gov/news-information/speeches-testimony/speeches-testimony-archive-2008/directors-remarks-at-lawac.html.

Hayes, Peter, David von Hippel, and Roger Cavazos. "Sanctioning Kerosene and Jet Fuel in North Korea." Nautilus Institute, NAPSNet Policy Forum, March 10, 2016. http://nautilus.org/napsnet/napsnet-policy-forum/sanctioning-kerosene-and-jet-fuel-in-north-korea.

Heinrichs, Rebeccah. "Did the Saudis Shoot Down a Houthi Missile on Nov. 4? It Doesn't Much Matter." Defense One, December 11, 2017, http://www.defenseone.com/ideas/2017/12/did-saudis-shoot-down-houthi-missile/144451.

Herman, Steve, Brian Padden, and Carla Babb. "North Korea Tests Powerful New Rocket Engine." Voice of America, March 19, 2017. http://www.voanews.com/a/north-korea-tillerson-rocket-engine-test/3772372.html.

"Hezbollah a North Korea–Type Guerilla Force." *Intelligence Online,* no. 529, August 25–September 7, 2006. http://www.oss.net/dynamaster/file_archive/060902/26241feaf4766b4d441a3a78917cd55c/Intelligence%20Online%20on%20Hezbolllah.pdf.

"Hezbollah Training in North Korea." The Intelligence Summit, April 25, 2007. http://intelligence-summit.blogspot.com/2007/04/hezbollah-training-in-north-korea.html.

Hill, Cissie Dore. "Voices of Hope: The Story of Radio Free Europe and Radio Liberty." *Hoover Digest,* 2001 no. 4 (October 30, 2001). http://www.hoover.org/research/voices-hope-story-radio-free-europe-and-radio-liberty.

Hilterman, Joost, and April Longley Alley. "The Houthis Are Not Hezbollah." *Foreign Policy,* February 27, 2017. http://foreignpolicy.com/2017/02/27/the-houthis-are-not-hezbollah.

Hotham, Oliver. "Activist: Assad Has Hired N. Korean Pilots for Air Strikes." *NK News,* October 29, 2013. http://www.nknews.org/2013/10/activist-assad-has-hired-n-korean-pilots-for-air-strikes.

———. "Amid Missile Deal Rumor, N. Korea & Egypt Sign Cultural Cooperation Plan." *NK News,* November 19, 2013. https://www.nknews.org/2013/11/amid-missile-deal-rumor-n-korea-egypt-sign-cultural-cooperation-plan.

———. "N. Korea Is among the Most Corrupt Nations on Earth, Says NGO." *NK News,* December 4, 2013. https://www.nknews.org/2013/12/north-korea-is-among-most-corrupt-nations-on-earth-says-ngo.

———. "Tanzania Won't Deny N. Korea Is Providing Military Assistance." *NK News,* August 15, 2013. https://www.nknews.org/2013/08/tanzania-wont-deny-n-korea-is-providing-military-assistance.

———. "N. Korea Assisting Syria in Improving Missile Capabilities: Report." *NK News,* January 30, 2014. http://www.nknews.org/2014/01/n-korea-assisting-syria-in-improving-missile-capabilities-report.

How to Make America Safe: New Policies for National Security. Edited by Stephan Van Evera. Cambridge, MA: Tobin Project, 2006.

Hughes, Robin. "Tehran Takes Steps to Protect Nuclear Facilities." *Jane's Defence Weekly,* January 25, 2006, 4–5.

"Hwasong 6/Scud C." Federation of American Scientists, February 17, 2015. http://fas.org/nuke/guide/dprk/missile/hwasong-6.htm.

"Hwasong-12." Missile Threat, Center for Strategic and International Studies, May 16, 2017. https://missilethreat.csis.org/missile/hwasong-12.

"Imposition of Nonproliferation Measures against Foreign Persons, Including a Ban on U.S. Government Procurement." US Department of State, Public Notice 9939, March 30, 2017. https://www.federalregister.gov/documents/2017/03/30/2017-06225/imposition-of-nonproliferation-measures-against-foreign-persons-including-a-ban-on-us-government.

Inbar, Tal. "Hwasong-10 Shows the Value [of] North Korea's Perseverance." *NK News,* June 24, 2016. https://www.nknews.org/2016/06/hwasong-10-shows-the-value-north-koreas-perseverance.

———. "N. Korea Missiles: No Room for Doubt." *Defense News,* April 4, 2016, 22.

"Investigation Result on the Sinking of ROKS 'Cheonan.'" The Joint Civilian-Military Investigation Group, May 20, 2010. https://www.globalsecurity.org/jhtml/jframe.html#https://www.globalsecurity.org/military/library/report/2010/100520_jcmig-roks-cheonan/100520_jcmig-roks-cheonan.pdf.

"Iran: Nuclear Cooperation between Iran Regime & North Korea, NCRI Reveals." National Council of Resistance of Iran, August 2015. http://www.ncr-iran.org/

en/media-gallery/187-iran-nuclear-cooperation-between-iran-regime-north-korea-ncri-reveals.

"Iran Missile Test May Have Been Variant of NK Musudan." Center for Strategic and International Studies, Missile Defense Project, February 2, 2017. https://missilethreat.csis.org/iran-missile-test-may-variant-nk-musudan.

"Iran, North Korea, and Syria Nonproliferation Act Sanctions." US Department of State, Office of the Spokesperson, March 24, 2017. https://www.state.gov/r/pa/prs/ps/2017/03/269084.htm.

"Iran to Observe North Korea Missile Test." Missile Threat, December 7, 2012. http://missilethreat.com/iran-to-observe-north-korea-missile-test.

Ismaïl, Benjamin. "North Korea: Frontiers of Censorship." Reporters without Borders, October 2011. https://rsf.org/sites/default/files/rsf_north-korea_2011.pdf.

Jafarzadeh, Alireza. "Iran's Cooperation with North Korea Includes Nuclear Warhead Technology." The Hill, June 3, 2015. http://thehill.com/blogs/congress-blog/foreign-policy/243787-irans-cooperation-with-north-korea-includes-nuclear.

James, Martin W., III. A Political History of the Civil War in Angola: 1974–1990. London: Routledge, 2011.

Jee, David Eunpyoung. "North Korea's Addiction to Provocation." The Diplomat, August 11, 2015. http://thediplomat.com/2015/08/north-koreas-addiction-to-provocation.

Jin, Dong Hyeok. "Report: China's Military Prepared for Collapse Scenario." Daily NK, May 5, 2014. https://www.dailynk.com/english/read.php?num=11836&catald=nk00100.

"JL-1 [CSS-N-3]." Federation of American Scientists, June 10, 1998. https://fas.org/nuke/guide/china/slbm/jl-1.htm.

"Joint Comprehensive Plan of Action." US Department of State, Diplomacy in Action, 2017. https://www.state.gov/e/eb/tfs/spi/iran/jcpoa.

Jun, Jenny, Scott LaFoy, and Ethan Sohn. "The Organization of Cyber Operations in North Korea." Center for Strategic and International Studies, December 18, 2014. http://csis.org/publication/organization-cyber-operations-north-korea.

———. "North Korea's Cyber Operations: Strategy and Responses." Report of the Korea Chair. Center for Strategic and International Studies, December 2015. https://csis-prod.s3.amazonaws.com/s3fs-public/legacy_files/files/publication/151216_Cha_NorthKoreasCyberOperations_Web.pdf.

Kang, Mi Jin. "How Sanctions Affected North Korea's Economy in 2016." Daily NK, December 26, 2016. http://www.dailynk.com/english/read.php?num=14270&catald=nk02900.

Kang, Tae-jun. "North Korea Extends Range of KN01 Anti-Ship Missile—Media." NK News, November 25, 2013. http://www.nknews.org/2013/11/north-korea-extends-range-of-kn01-anti-ship-missile-media.

Katzman, Kenneth. "Iran's Long-Range Missile Capabilities." Iran Watch, Wisconsin Project on Nuclear Arms Control, July 15, 1998. http://www.iranwatch.org/library/government/united-states/congress/legislation-reports/irans-long-range-missile-capabilities.

Keck, Zachary. "Who Sold North Korea a New Anti-Ship Missile?" *The Diplomat,* June 13, 2014. http://thediplomat.com/2014/06/who-sold-north-korea-a-new-anti-ship-missile.

Kemp, Geoffrey, and Robert Harkavy. *Strategic Geography and the Changing Middle East.* Washington, DC: Brookings Institution Press, 1997.

Kerr, Paul, and Daryl Kimball. "The Agreed Framework at a Glance." Arms Control Association, September 2004. https://www.armscontrol.org/system/files/agreed-framework.pdf.

Khan, Taimur. "Weapons Seizures Show Iran 'Arms Pipeline' to Yemen's Houthi Rebels." *The National,* November 30, 2016. http://www.thenational.ae/world/middle-east/weapons-seizures-show-iran-arms-pipeline-to-yemens-houthi-rebels.

Khrustalev, Vladiamr. "Thermonuclear Shock: A Detailed Analysis of the Explosion of the DPRK's Hydrogen Bomb and Its Consequences." Defcon Warning System, September 8, 2017. https://defconwarningsystem.com/2017/09/08/thermonuclear-shock-detailed-analysis-explosion-dprks-hydrogen-bomb-consequences.

Kim, Byoung-Lo. *Two Koreas in Development: A Comparative Study of Principles and Strategies of Capitalist and Communist Third World Development.* London: Routledge, 1991.

Kim, Ga Young. "A North Korea without Chinese Oil Supplies." *Daily NK,* January 15, 2016. http://www.dailynk.com/english/read.php?cataId=nk00400&num=13698.

"Kim Jong Un Attends Second Hwasong-14 Missile Test." North Korean Leadership Watch, July 29, 2017. http://www.nkleadershipwatch.org/2017/07/29/kim-jong-un-attends-second-hwasong-14-missile-test.

"Kim Jong-un Observes and Commands Large Live Fire Artillery Exercise." North Korea Leadership Watch, December 2, 2016. https://nkleadershipwatch.wordpress.com/2016/12/02/kim-jong-un-observes-and-commands-large-live-fire-artillery-exercise.

Kim, Kwang-jin. "The Defector's Tale: Inside North Korea's Secret Economy." *World Affairs,* September/October 2011. http://www.worldaffairsjournal.org/article/defector%E2%80%99s-tale-inside-north-korea%E2%80%99s-secret-economy.

———. Interview with author, July 19, 2015, Seoul.

Kim, Shin-yon. "The Tortuous Dilemma: The 2008 Six-Party Talks and U.S. DPRK Relations." *SAIS U.S.-Korea Yearbook 2008,* John Hopkins University, 2010. http://uskoreainstitute.org/wp-content/uploads/2010/02/KimSY.pdf.

Kim, Yonho. "US Treasury Issues Advisory on Financial Transactions with N. Korea." Voice of America, August 7, 2014. http://www.voanews.com/a/us-treasury-issues-advisory-on-financial-transactions-with-north-korea/2406604.html.

Kim, Yonho, and Jee Abbey Lee. "Money Laundering Watchdog Calls on North Korea to Fulfill Pledge." Voice of America, March 2, 2015. http://www.voanews.com/a/money-laundering-watchdog-calls-on-north-korea-to-fulfill-pledge/2665115.html.

———. "Watchdog Warns of N. Korea Money Laundering." Voice of America, June 29, 2015. http://www.voanews.com/a/watchdog-warns-of-north-korea-money-laundering/2842448.html.

Kim, Yoo-sung. "Trying Not to Starve in the N. Korean Army." *NK News,* September 9, 2015. https://www.nknews.org/2015/09/trying-not-to-starve-in-the-n-korean-army.

Kirby, Reid. "Sea of Sarin: North Korea's Chemical Deterrent." *Bulletin of the Atomic Scientists,* June 21, 2017. http://thebulletin.org/sea-sarin-north-korea%E2%80%99s-chemical-deterrent10856.

Kirk, Donald. "Iran's Partnership with North Korea on Nukes and Missiles May Scuttle Any Deal." *Forbes,* February 20, 2015. https://www.forbes.com/sites/donaldkirk/2015/02/20/irans-irans-long-time-partnership-with-north-korea-on-nukes-and-missiles-may-scuttle-a-real-deal/#253ece28b61b.

Klein, Aaron. "N. Korea Rebuilding Damaged Syrian Missiles." *World Net Daily,* June 18, 2013. http://www.wnd.com/2013/06/n-korea-rebuilding-damaged-syrian-missiles.

Klingner, Bruce. "Debunking Six Myths about North Korean Sanctions." *The Daily Signal,* December 22, 2014. http://dailysignal.com/2014/12/22/debunking-six-myths-north-korean-sanctions.

———. "The Growing North Korean Missile Threat." *The Daily Signal,* May 17, 2015. http://dailysignal.com/2015/05/17/the-growing-north-korean-missile-threat.

Koo, Jun-hoe. "Construction at Sohae Launch Site to Finish by 2015." *Daily NK,* July 30, 2014. http://www.dailynk.com/english/read.php?num=12151&cataId=nk00100.

Kroenig, Matthew. *Exporting the Bomb: Technology Transfer and the Spread of Nuclear Weapons.* Ithaca NY: Cornell University Press, 2010.

LaFoy, Scott. "Analysis: Redesigned KN-08 Missile Unveiled in Military Parade." *NK News,* October 16, 2015. https://www.nknews.org/2015/10/analysis-redesigned-kn-08-missile-unveiled-in-military-parade.

Lankov, Andrei. "How Private Finance Took Hold in North Korea." *NK News,* June 30, 2015. https://www.nknews.org/2015/06/how-private-finance-took-hold-in-north-korea.

Lee, Chung-min. "North Korean Missiles: Strategic Implications and Policy Responses." *The Pacific Review* 14, no. 1 (2001). http://unpan1.un.org/intradoc/groups/public/documents/apcity/unpan012791.pdf.

Lee, Min-ha. "North Korea's Missiles." Radio Free Asia, February 25, 2009. http://www.rfa.org/english/multimedia/InteractiveNorthKoreaMissile-02252009171048.html.

Lee, Peter, and Jang Ji-Hyang. "Middle East Q/A: Intervening in Syria and Lessons for North Korea." Issue Brief, Asan Institute for Policy Studies, September 5, 2013. http://en.asaninst.org/contents/issue-brief-no-69-middle-east-qa-intervening-in-syria-and-lessons-for-north-korea.

Lee, Sang-min. "Security Implications of North Korea's Test-Firing of Solid-Fuel

IRBM and South Korea's Countermeasures." *ROK Angle* (Korea Institute for Defense Analyses), no. 152 (March 28, 2017). www.kida.re.kr/cmm/viewBoardImageFile.do?idx=21900.

Lee, Sang-yong. "Evidence of Iranian Test Involvement Mounts." *Daily NK,* February 19, 2013. http://www.dailynk.com/english/read.php?cataId=nk00100&num=10327.

Lee, Sung-chool. "The ROK-US Joint Political and Military Response to North Korean Armed Provocations." Report of the Korea Chair. Center for Strategic and International Studies, October 2011. https://csis-prod.s3.amazonaws.com/s3fs-public/legacy_files/files/publication/111006_Lee_ROKUSJointResponse_web.pdf.

Lee, Sung-yoon. "North Korea's Criminal Activities: Financing the Regime." Hearing before the Committee on Foreign Affairs, House of Representatives, 113th Cong., 1st sess., March 5, 2013. http://docs.house.gov/meetings/FA/FA00/20130305/100436/HHRG-113-FA00-20130305-SD003.pdf.

Levkowitz, Alon. "Iran and North-Korea Cooperation: A Partnership within the Axis of Evil." *Iran Pulse* (Alliance Center for Iranian Studies), no. 10, February 26, 2007. http://humanities1.tau.ac.il/iranian/en/previous-reviews/10-iran-pulse-en/117-10.

————. "North Korea and the Middle East." Mideast Security and Policy Studies no. 127. Begin-Sadat Center for Strategic Studies, January 2017. https://besacenter.org/wp-content/uploads/2017/01/MSPS-Levkowitz-Web-.pdf.

Levy, Adrian, and Catherine Scott-Clark. *Deception: Pakistan, the United States, and the Secret Trade in Nuclear Weapons.* London: Walker, 2007.

Lewis, Jeffrey. "North Korea's Nuclear Weapons: The Great Miniaturization Debate." 38 North, February 5, 2015. http://38north.org/2015/02/jlewis020515.

————. "More Rockets in Kim Jong-un's Pockets: North Korea Tests a New Artillery System." 38 North, March 7, 2016. http://38north.org/2016/03/jlewis030716.

Lintner, Bertil. "The Long Reach of North Korea's Missiles." *Asia Times,* June 21, 2006. http://www.atimes.com/atimes/Korea/HF21Dg02.html.

Macdonald, Hamish. "U.S. Sanctions KPA Unit, Shipping Companies, N. Koreans Overseas." *NK News,* December 9, 2015. https://www.nknews.org/2015/12/u-s-sanctions-kpa-unit-shipping-companies-n-koreans-overseas.

————. "Angola Discusses Public Security Cooperation with North Korea." *NK News,* April 8, 2016. https://www.nknews.org/2016/04/angola-discusses-public-security-cooperation-with-north-korea.

————. "China Accused of Inaction on N. Korea Sanctions in Senate Hearing." *NK News,* September 28, 2016. https://www.nknews.org/2016/09/china-accused-of-inaction-on-n-korea-sanctions-in-senate-hearing.

————. "Uganda Reveals Another Military Contract with North Korea." *NK News,* July 20, 2016. https://www.nknews.org/pro/uganda-reveals-another-military-contract-with-north-korea.

Maier, Karl. *Conspicuous Destruction: War, Famine and the Reform Process in Mozam-*

bique. New Haven, CT: Yale University Press; New York: Human Rights Watch, 1993.

Majidyar, Ahmad. "U.S. Officials: Iran's Latest Missile Launch Hints Tehran-Pyongyang Cooperation." Middle East Institute, May 5, 2017. http://www.mei.edu/content/io/us-officials-iran-s-latest-missile-launch-hints-tehran-pyongyang-cooperation.

Mansourov, Alexandre. "North Korea: Entering Syria's Civil War." 38 North, November 25, 2013. http://38north.org/2013/11/amansourov112513.

———. "North Korea's Cyber Warfare and Challenges for the US-ROK Alliance." Academic Paper Series. Korea Economic Institute, December 2, 2014. http://www.keia.org/sites/default/files/publications/kei_aps_mansourov_final.pdf.

Martin, Curtis H. "Lessons of the Agreed Framework for Using Engagement as a Nonproliferation Tool." *The Nonproliferation Review,* Fall 1999. https://www.nonproliferation.org/wp-content/uploads/npr/martin64.pdf.

Martin, Daniel, Ulla Fernandez-Arcaya, Paula Tirado, Éric Dutrieux, and Jordi Corbera. "Relationships between Shallow-Water Cumacean Assemblages and Sediment Characteristics Facing the Iranian Coast of the Persian Gulf." *Journal of the Marine Biological Association of the United Kingdom* 90, no. 1 (2010). https://www.researchgate.net/publication/233414586_Relationships_between_shallow-water_cumacean_assemblages_and_sediment_characteristics_facing_the_Iranian_coast_of_the_Persian_Gulf.

Martin, Matthew. "The Six-Party Talks and New Opportunities to Strengthen Regional Nonproliferation and Disarmament Efforts." Conference organized by the Stanley Foundation, the National Committee on North Korea, the China Arms Control and Disarmament Association, and the Institute for Foreign Policy Analysis and coordinated by the Stanley Foundation, Beijing, October 23–24, 2008. https://www.stanleyfoundation.org/publications/report/6partytalksrpt309.pdf.

Matthews, Matt M. "We Were Caught Unprepared: The 2006 Hezbollah-Israeli War." The Long War Series, Occasional Paper no. 26, US Army Combined Arms Center, Combat Studies Institute Press, 2008. http://carl.army.mil/download/csipubs/matthewsOP26.pdf.

Maxwell, David S. "Is the Kim Family Regime Rational and Why Don't the North Korean People Rebel?" Foreign Policy Research Institute, January 27, 2012. http://www.fpri.org/article/2012/01/is-the-kim-family-regime-rational-and-why-dont-the-north-korean-people-rebel.

McCarthy, David. *The Sword of David: The Israeli Air Force at War.* New York: Skyhorse, 2014.

McClanahan, Patrick. "North Korea: China's Liability?" *Harvard Political Review,* November 13, 2016. http://harvardpolitics.com/world/north-korea-chinas-liability.

McCreary, John. NightWatch, October 7, 2013. http://www.kforcegov.com/NightWatch/NightWatch_13000212.aspx (link inactive).

McLure, Jason. "The Troubled Horn of Africa." *CQ Researcher* 3, no. 6 (June 2009). http://library.cqpress.com/cqresearcher/document.php?id=cqrglobal2009060000.

McMorrow-Hernandez, Joshua. "Paper Money—Whatever Happened to North Korean Counterfeit U.S. $100 Bills?" *Coin Week,* March 29, 2016. http://www.coinweek.com/people-in-the-news/crime-and-fraud/paper-money-whatever-happened-north-korean-counterfeit-u-s-100-bills.

Mead, Walter Russell. "No More 'Strategic Patience' on North Korea." Hudson Institute, March 17, 2017. https://www.hudson.org/research/13457-no-more-strategic-patience-on-north-korea.

Melendez, Dwayne. "Financial Sanctions on North Korea: Prospects and Challenges in the Age of the Tax Havens." *North Korean Review,* August 7, 2016. https://www.northkoreanreview.net/single-post/2016/08/08/Financial-Sanctions-on-North-Korea-Prospects-and-Challenges-in-the-Age-of-the-Tax-Havens.

Melvin, Curtis. "North Korea Building New Transport Corridor and Border Crossing." 38 North, May 4, 2015. http://38north.org/2015/05/cmelvin050415.

Metzler, John J. *Divided Dynamism: The Diplomacy of Separated Nations: Germany, Korea, China.* Lanham, MD: University Press of America, 2014.

"Midterm Report of the Panel of Experts Established Pursuant to Resolution 1874 (2009)." UN Security Council, North Korea, Panel of Experts, September 5, 2017. http://www.un.org/ga/search/view_doc.asp?symbol=S/2017/742.

Miller, J. Berkshire. "North Korea's Chemical Weapons Shop of Horrors." *The National Interest,* October 6, 2014. http://nationalinterest.org/commentary/north-koreas-chemical-shop-horrors-9056.

"Missile Technology Control Regime (Mtcr): North Korea's Missile Program." US State Department Official Document, October 6, 2009. https://wikileaks.org/plusd/cables/09STATE103755_a.html. Document disclosed on WikiLeaks.

Mistry, Dinshaw. *Containing Missile Proliferation: Strategic Technology, Security Regimes, and International Cooperation in Arms Control.* Seattle: University of Washington Press, 2005.

Mizokami, Kyle. "Experts: North Korea May Be Developing a Dirty Bomb Drone." *Popular Mechanics,* December 28, 2016. http://www.popularmechanics.com/military/weapons/a24525/north-korea-dirty-bomb-drone.

———. "North Korea Says Its New Missile Can Turn Tanks into 'Boiled Pumpkins.'" *Popular Mechanics,* February 29, 2016. http://www.popularmechanics.com/military/weapons/a19663/north-korea-anti-tank-missile.

Moore, Brian R., and Riza De Los Reyes. "What's Behind North Korea's Recent Counterfeiting?" *The Diplomat,* July 6, 2016. http://thediplomat.com/2016/07/whats-behind-north-koreas-recent-counterfeiting.

Moore, Jack. "Iran to 'Renew Funding' for Hamas, Despite Trump's Riyadh Speech." *Newsweek,* May 31, 2017. http://www.newsweek.com/iran-renew-funding-hamas-despite-trumps-riyadh-speech-617996.

Müller, Harald. "Viewpoint: Neither Hype nor Complacency: WMD Proliferation after the Cold War." *The Nonproliferation Review,* Winter 1997. https://www.nonproliferation.org/wp-content/uploads/npr/muller42.pdf.

Nadin, Peter. "Sanctions and Why They Don't Work (Very Well)." Our World,

United Nations University, September 5, 2014. https://ourworld.unu.edu/en/sanctions-and-why-they-dont-work-very-well.

"National Defense Commission." North Korea Leadership Watch, 2016. https://nkleadershipwatch.wordpress.com/dprk-security-apparatus/national-defense-commission.

Nephew, Richard. "Paper Tigers: DPRK POE Report Shows Deep Problems with Enforcement." 38 North, March 16, 2017. http://38north.org/2017/03/rnephew031617.

Newcomb, William. Interview with the author, June 30, 2017, Seoul.

———. Testimony before the House Committee on Financial Services at the Hearing "Restricting North Korea's Access to Finance." July 19, 2017. https://financialservices.house.gov/uploadedfiles/hhrg-115-ba19-wstate-wnewcomb-20170719.pdf.

Nikitin, Mary Beth. "North Korea's Nuclear Weapons: Technical Issues." Congressional Research Service, RL34256, April 3, 2013. https://www.fas.org/sgp/crs/nuke/RL34256.pdf.

Niksch, Larry. "North Korea's Nuclear Weapons Development and Diplomacy." Congressional Research Service, RL33590, January 5, 2010. http://fas.org/sgp/crs/nuke/RL33590.pdf.

———. "The Iran–North Korea Strategic Relationship." Testimony to the House Committee on Foreign Affairs, July 28, 2015. http://docs.house.gov/meetings/FA/FA18/20150728/103824/HHRG-114-FA18-Wstate-NikschL-20150728.pdf.

———. "Responding to North Korea's Nuclear and Missile Test: Ending the U.N. Security Council Pretense." Institute for Corean American Studies, February 26, 2016. http://www.icasinc.org/2016/2016l/2016llan.html.

"Ninety-Six Percent of Syria's Declared Chemical Weapons Destroyed—UN-OPCW Mission Chief." UN News Centre, September 4, 2014. http://www.un.org/apps/news/story.asp?NewsID=48642#.VSOEHpUtGM8.

"North Korea: Missile." Nuclear Threat Initiative, December 2014. http://www.nti.org/country-profiles/north-korea/delivery-systems.

"North Korea Displays New ICBM, Other Missiles." Voice of America, April 15, 2017. http://www.voanews.com/a/north-korea-missiles-icbm/3811277.html.

"North Korea, Foreign Policy Goals: Chapter 3A." Federation of American Scientists, DIA Excerpt, October 1991. https://fas.org/irp/dia/product/knfms/knfms_chp3a.html.

"North Korea Modernises Submarine Fleet." Jane's Intelligence Review, May 10, 2016. http://www.janes360.com/images/assets/463/57463/North_Korea_modernises_submarine_fleet1.pdf.

"The North Korean Connection." Finance Uncovered, February 3, 2016. http://www.financeuncovered.org/investigations/the-north-korean-connection.

"North Korean Designations; Non-Proliferation Designations; Counter Narcotics Designations Removals and Update; Transnational Criminal Organizations,

Designations Removals and Update; Counter Terrorism Designation Removal; Cuba Designation Removal." US Treasury Department, August 22, 2017. https://www.treasury.gov/resource-center/sanctions/OFAC-Enforcement/Pages/20170822.aspx.

"North Korean 6×6 APC." *Military Today*, 2017. http://www.military-today.com/apc/north_korean_6x6_apc.htm.

"North Korean 8×8 APC." *Military Today*, 2017. http://www.military-today.com/apc/north_korean_8x8_apc.htm.

"North Korea's Drones: Made in China?" North Korea Tech, April 20, 2014. http://www.northkoreatech.org/2014/04/20/north-koreas-drones-made-in-china.

"North Korea's Submarine Capabilities." *Vantage Point* 38, no. 3 (March 2015): 1–14.

"North Korea's Yongbyon Nuclear Facility: New Activity at the Plutonium Production Complex." 38 North, September 8, 2015. http://38north.org/2015/09/yongbyon090815.

"North Koreans Learn about China's Beidou Satellite Navigation System." North Korea Tech, July 31, 2014. https://www.northkoreatech.org/2014/07/31/north-koreans-learn-about-chinas-beidou-satellite-navigation-system.

"The Nuclear Explosion in North Korea on 3 September 2017: A Revised Magnitude Assessment." NORSAR, September 12, 2017. https://www.norsar.no/press/latest-press-release/archive/the-nuclear-explosion-in-north-korea-on-3-september-2017-a-revised-magnitude-assessment-article1548-984.html.

Nye, Joseph S. "Understanding the North Korea Threat." Project Syndicate, December 7, 2017. https://www.project-syndicate.org/commentary/understanding-north-korea-threat-by-joseph-s—nye-2017-12.

O'Carroll, Chad. "Exclusive: North Korean Minister Inspects Ugandan Police Force." *NK News*, June 14, 2013. https://www.nknews.org/2013/06/exclusive-north-korean-minister-inspects-ugandan-police-force.

O'Carroll, Chad, and John G. Grisafi. "North Korea's Million Man Army: Potential Mercenary Force?" *NK News*, May 15, 2015. http://www.nknews.org/2015/05/north-koreas-million-man-army-potential-mercenary-force.

Ofek, Raphael. "The Puzzle of the North Korean ICBM." Begin-Sadat Center for Strategic Studies, Perspective Paper No. 634, November 5, 2017, https://besacenter.org/perspectives-papers/north-korea-icbm.

Oh, Hyun Oo. "Drug Trade Continues to Prove Lucrative." *Daily NK*, January 3, 2014. http://www.dailynk.com/english/read.php?num=11339&cataId=nk01500.

Oliemans, Joost, and Stijn Mitzer. "N. Korean Upgraded Tanks Still in Use in Syrian Civil War." *NK News*, December 1, 2014. http://www.nknews.org/2014/12/n-korean-upgraded-tanks-still-in-use-in-syrian-civil-war.

———. "KPA Flag Ship Undergoing Radical Modernization." *NK News*, December 14, 2015. http://www.nknews.org/2014/12/kpa-navy-flag-ship-undergoing-radical-modernization.

———. "N. Korean Arms Found in Vessel Intercepted Off Coast of Oman." *NK*

News, March 16, 2016. https://www.nknews.org/2016/03/n-korean-arms-found-in-vessel-intercepted-off-coast-of-oman.

"On Khamenei's Orders, Tehran Accelerates Missile Activities and Tests After the Iran Nuclear Deal." Iran Watch, June 20, 2017. http://www.iranwatch.org/library/private-viewpoints/khameneis-orders-tehran-accelerates-missile-activities-tests-after-iran-nuclear-deal.

Ottaway, Marina, Jeffrey Herbst, and Greg Mills. "Africa's Big States: Toward a New Realism." Carnegie Endowment, Policy Outlook, February 2004. http://carnegie endowment.org/files/PolicyOutlookOttaway.pdf.

Ottolenghi, Emanuele. "Time for a Strong U.S. Effort to Cripple the IRGC." *The National Interest,* July 18, 2014. http://nationalinterest.org/blog/the-buzz/time-strong-us-effort-cripple-the-irgc-10912.

Padden, Brian. "Analysts: North Korea to Build New Ballistic Missile Submarine." Voice of America, August 30, 2016. http://www.voanews.com/a/analysts-north-korea-to-build-new-ballistic-missile-submarine/3486125.html.

———. "UN Security Council Approves New Sanctions on North Korea." Voice of America, March 2, 2016. http://www.voanews.com/a/un-counts-the-ways-north-korea-evaded-sanctions/3215914.html.

———. "UN Security Council Condemns North Korean Missile Test." Voice of America, April 24, 2016. http://www.voanews.com/a/un-security-council-north-korea-attempted-missile-launch/3555703.html.

"Pakistan Missile Chronology." Nuclear Threat Initiative, May 2011. http://www.nti.org/media/pdfs/pakistan_missile.pdf?_=1316466791.

"Pakistan's Nuclear Capable Missiles." Wisconsin Project on Nuclear Arms Control, January 1, 1999. http://www.wisconsinproject.org/pakistans-nuclear-capable-missiles.

Panda, Ankit. "North Korea Tests Solid-Fuel Submarine-Launched Ballistic Missile." *The Diplomat,* April 25, 2016. http://thediplomat.com/2016/04/north-korea-tests-solid-fuel-submarine-launched-ballistic-missile.

Panda, Ankit, and Vipin Narang. "North Korea's ICBM: A New Missile and a New Era." *The Diplomat,* July 7, 2017. http://thediplomat.com/2017/07/north-koreas-icbm-a-new-missile-and-a-new-era.

Park, John. "To Curb North Korea's Nuclear Program, Follow the Money." *The Conversation,* September 20, 2016. http://theconversation.com/to-curb-north-koreas-nuclear-program-follow-the-money-65462.

Perry, William J. "Proliferation on the Peninsula: Five North Korea Nuclear Crises." Speech delivered by the former Secretary of Defense at the Carnegie Endowment for International Peace, November 2005. https://cisac.fsi.stanford.edu/sites/default/files/Perry_Proliferation_on_the_Peninsula.pdf.

Plunk, Daryl. "North Korea: Exporting Terrorism?" The Heritage Foundation, February 25, 1988. http://www.heritage.org/terrorism/report/north-korea-exporting-terrorism.

Pollack, Jonathan. "Danger Zone: Why North Korea's Latest Missile Is More Worrying Than Any to Date." Brookings Institution, May 17, 2017. https://www.

brookings.edu/blog/order-from-chaos/2017/05/17/danger-zone-why-north-koreas-latest-missile-test-is-more-worrying-than-any-to-date.

Pollack, Joshua H. "How North Korea Makes Its Missiles: Two Reports This Week Made Crucial Mistakes about the DPRK's Rocket Development." *NK News,* August 18, 2017. https://www.nknews.org/2017/08/how-north-korea-makes-its-missiles.

Ponnudurai, Parameswaran. "Global Bid to Cripple North Korea's Illicit Trade." Radio Free Asia, March 5, 2013. http://www.rfa.org/english/news/korea/illicit-03052013150916.html.

Post, Jerrold M. "Kim Jong-il of North Korea: In the Shadow of His Father." *International Journal of Applied Psychoanalytic Studies* 5, no. 3 (2008): 191–210.

Postol, Theodore A., Markus Schiller, and Robert Schmucker. "North Korea's 'Not Quite' ICBM Can't Hit the Lower 48 States." *Bulletin of the Atomic Scientists,* August 11, 2017. http://thebulletin.org/north-korea%E2%80%99s-%E2%80%99Cnot-quite%E2%80%9D-icbm-can%E2%80%99t-hit-lower-48-states11012.

Prendergast, John, and Brad Brooks-Rubin. "Modernized Sanctions for Sudan: Unfinished Business for the Obama Administration." The Enough Project, April 2016. http://www.enoughproject.org/files/Modernized_Sanctions_for_Sudan_042016.pdf.

"Proliferation Security Initiative." US Department of State, 2016. https://www.state.gov/t/isn/c10390.htm.

"Proliferation Security Initiative." Nuclear Threat Initiative, February 20, 2017. http://www.nti.org/learn/treaties-and-regimes/proliferation-security-initiative-psi.

"Profiling an Enigma: The Mystery of North Korea's Cyber Threat Landscape." HP Security Briefing, Episode 16, August 2014. https://www.slideshare.net/crash1980/profiling-an-enigma-the-mystery-of-north-koreas-cyber-threat-landscape.

Pry, Vincent. "Understanding North Korea and Iran." Family Security Matters, February 26, 2013. http://www.familysecuritymatters.org/publications/detail/understanding-north-korea-and-iran.

Ramani, Samuel. "North Korea's Africa Strategy." *The Diplomat,* July 15, 2015. http://thediplomat.com/2015/07/north-koreas-african-strategy.

———. "North Korea's African Allies." *The Diplomat,* June 4, 2016. http://thediplomat.com/2016/06/north-koreas-african-allies.

"Recognizing Iran as a Strategic Threat: An Intelligence Challenge for the United States." Staff Report of the US House of Representatives Permanent Select Committee on Intelligence, Subcommittee on Intelligence Policy, August 23, 2006. http://permanent.access.gpo.gov/lps73446/IranReport082206v2.pdf.

Reeves, Eric. "Sudan: Aerial Military Attacks on Civilians and Humanitarians 'They Bombed Everything That Moved,' 1999–2012." African Arguments, January 18, 2012. http://africanarguments.org/2012/01/18/they-bombed-everything-that-moved-aerial-military-attacks-on-civilians-and-humanitarians-in-sudan-1999-2012-by-eric-reeves.

"Report of the Panel of Experts Established Pursuant to Resolution 1874 (2009)." UN Security Council, North Korea, Panel of Experts, March 6, 2014. http://www.un.org/ga/search/view_doc.asp?symbol=S/2014/147.

"Resolutions." UN Security Council, Security Council Committee Established Pursuant to Resolution 1718 (2006), 2017. https://www.un.org/sc/suborg/en/sanctions/1718/resolutions.

Richter, Ali. "North Korean Type 73 GPMG's in Iraq, Syria, and Yemen." Armament Research Service, March 16, 2016. http://armamentresearch.com/north-korean-type-73-gpmgs-in-iraq-syria-yemen.

Ricks, Thomas. "To Start Talks with North Korea, Look to the Iran Deal—But Don't Hold Your Breath." *Foreign Policy,* September 12, 2016. http://foreignpolicy.com/2016/09/12/to-start-talks-with-north-korea-look-to-the-iran-deal-but-dont-hold-your-breath.

Roberts, Pat. Opening Statement Before the Senate Select Committee on Intelligence, US Senate, at the Hearing Entitled "Current and Projected National Security Threats to the United States." Washington, DC, February 2, 2006. https://books.google.com/books?id=yEKq90a70foC&pg=PA3&lpg=PA3&dq=iran+continues+to+buy+conventional+weapons+from+north+korea&source=bl&ots=ZREa1Ea8dm&sig=ADh1kxOdYaE4V9SxgkMe5Egt Gs4&hl=en&sa=X&ved=0CFUQ6AEwCWoVChMIyZGAi9LcyAIVSD0-Ch1ehwIR#v=onepage&q=iran%20continues%20to%20buy%20conventional%20weapons%20from%20north%20korea&f=false.

Rogers, Michael S. "Statement of Admiral Michael S. Rogers, Commander United States Cyber Command, Before the House Armed Services Committee, Subcommittee on Emerging Threats and Capabilities." March 16, 2016. http://docs.house.gov/meetings/AS/AS26/20160316/104553/HHRG-114-AS26-Wstate-RogersM-20160316.pdf.

Rogoway, Tyler. "North Korea Says KN-06 SAM System Ready for Production After Successful Test." *The Drive,* May 28, 2017. http://www.thedrive.com/the-war-zone/10761/north-korea-says-kn-06-sam-system-ready-for-production-after-successful-test.

Rubin, Uzi. "Pyongyang Intercontinental Inc." Real Clear Defense, July 5, 2017. http://www.realcleardefense.com/articles/2017/07/05/pyongyang_intercontinental_inc_111730.html.

Ruggiero, Anthony. "UN Report Reveals North Korea's Sanctions Evasion." Foundation for Defense of Democracies, FDD Policy Brief, March 7, 2017. http://www.defenddemocracy.org/media-hit/anthony-ruggiero-un-report-reveals-north-koreas-sanctions-evasion.

Ryall, Julian. "North Korea Losing African, South American Allies." *Deutsche Welle,* June 21, 2016. http://www.dw.com/en/north-korea-losing-african-south-american-allies/a-19344851.

Sanctions, Statecraft, and Nuclear Proliferation. Edited by Etel Solingen. Cambridge: Cambridge University Press, 2012.

Sanger, David E. "The Khan Network." Paper presented at the Conference on South Asia and the Nuclear Future, June 4–5, 2004, at Stanford University, sponsored by the Center for International Security and Cooperation and the US Army War College. http://fsi.stanford.edu/sites/default/files/evnts/media//Khan_network-paper.pdf.

Savelsberg, Ralph. "A Quick Technical Analysis of the Hwasong-12." 38 North, May 19, 2017. http://www.38north.org/2017/05/hwasong051917.

Schlein, Lisa. "N. Korea Defectors Urge Switzerland to Freeze Leaders' Funds." Voice of America, November 17, 2014. http://www.voanews.com/a/north-korea-defectors-urge-switzerland-to-freeze-leadership-money/2523035.html.

Schiller, Markus. "Characterizing the North Korean Nuclear Missile Threat." Rand Technical Report, 2012. http://www.rand.org/content/dam/rand/pubs/technical_reports/2012/RAND_TR1268.pdf.

Schilling, John. "Where's That North Korean ICBM Everyone Was Talking About?" 38 North, March 12, 2015. http://38north.org/2015/03/jschilling031215.

———. "North Korea's Large Rocket Engine Test: A Significant Step Forward for Pyongyang's ICBM Program." 38 North, April 11, 2016. http://38north.org/2016/04/schilling041116.

———. "North Korea Finally Tests an ICBM." 38 North, July 5, 2017. http://www.38north.org/2017/07/jschilling070517.

———. "North Korea's Latest Missile Test: Advancing toward an Intercontinental Ballistic Missile (ICBM) While Avoiding US Military Action." 38 North, May 14, 2017. http://www.38north.org/2017/05/jschilling051417.

———. "The Pokguksong-2 Approaches Initial Operational Capability." 38 North, May 24, 2017. http://www.38north.org/2017/05/jschilling052417.

"Scientific Studies and Research Center." Nuclear Threat Initiative, August 1, 2010. http://www.nti.org/facilities/481.

"Security Council Committee Established Pursuant to Resolution 1718 (2006)." UN Security Council, November 2016. https://www.un.org/sc/suborg/en/sanctions/1718/resolutions.

"Security Council Imposes Fresh Sanctions on Democratic People's Republic of Korea, Unanimously Adopting Resolution 2270 (2016)." UN Security Council, March 2, 2016. http://www.un.org/press/en/2016/sc12267.doc.htm.

Seldin, Jeff. "North Korea's New Missile: What We Know." Voice of America, December 1, 2017. https://www.voanews.com/a/north-korea-new-missile-what-we-know/4145056.html.

Seol, Song Ah. "Traders Send Piles of Cash by Train to Evade Remittance Block." Daily NK, March 31, 2016. http://www.dailynk.com/english/read.php?num=13837&catald=nk01500.

"Shahab 3." Missile Threat.com, April 17, 2013. http://missilethreat.com/missiles/shahab-3.

Sichel, Jared. "Why Would North Korea Help Hamas Build Tunnels?" Jewish Journal, July 28, 2014. http://jewishjournal.com/news/los_angeles/131430.

Silberstein, Benjamin Katzeff. "North Korea's ICBM Test, Byungjin, and the Economic Logic." *The Diplomat,* July 5, 2017. http://thediplomat.com/2017/07/north-koreas-icbm-test-byungjin-and-the-economic-logic.

Singh, R. S. N. *Asian Strategic and Military Perspective.* New Delhi: Lancer, 2008.

Sisk, Richard. "US General Tells Senate North Korea Can Hit US with Nuclear ICBM." Military.com, April 16, 2015. http://www.military.com/daily-news/2015/04/16/us-general-tells-senate-north-korea-can-hit-us-with-nuclear-icbm.html.

"The Six-Party Talks and President Obama's North Korea Policy." Nuclear Threat Initiative, February 1, 2009. http://www.nti.org/analysis/articles/obamas-north-korea-policy.

Slack, Megan. "President Obama Visits Tanzania." The White House, July 1, 2013. https://obamawhitehouse.archives.gov/blog/2013/07/01/president-obama-visits-tanzania.

Small Arms Survey Group. *Small Arms Survey 2012: Moving Targets.* Cambridge: Cambridge University Press, 2012.

Snyder, Scott A. "Four Ways to Unilaterally Sanction North Korea." *Asia Unbound,* September 28, 2016. https://www.cfr.org/blog/four-ways-unilaterally-sanction-north-korea.

———. "How North Korea Evades UN Sanctions through International 'Front' Companies." *Forbes,* March 3, 2017. https://www.forbes.com/sites/scottasnyder/2017/03/03/how-north-korea-evades-un-sanctions-through-international-front-companies/#7595fb36788b.

———. "Malaysia's Front Office Role in Enabling North Korean WMD Procurement." *Asia Unbound,* March 6, 2017. http://blogs.cfr.org/asia/2017/03/06/malaysias-front-office-role-enabling-north-korean-wmd-procurement.

Sokan, Kenny. "Fighting North Korea's Dictatorship through Flash Drives." Public Radio International, March 28, 2016. https://www.pri.org/stories/2016-03-28/fighting-north-koreas-dictatorship-through-flashdrives.

Solomon, Jay. "North Korea's Alliance with Syria Reveals a Wider Proliferation Threat." The Washington Institute, Policywatch 2885, November 2, 2017, http://www.washingtoninstitute.org/policy-analysis/view/north-koreas-alliance-with-syria-reveals-a-wider-proliferation-threat.

Solomon, Salem. "Sanctioned and Shunned, North Korea Finds Arms Deals in Africa." Voice of America, March 22, 2017. http://www.voanews.com/a/sanctioned-and-shunned-north-korea-finds-arms-deals-in-africa/3777262.html.

———. "US Imposes New Sanctions on Eritrea's Navy over North Korea Links." Voice of America, April 8, 2017. http://www.voanews.com/a/us-sanctions-eritrea-navy-over-north-korea-links/3802651.html.

South Front. "North Korea and Its Missile Program—All What [*sic*] You Need to Know." Global Research, November 18, 2017. https://www.globalresearch.ca/north-korea-and-its-missile-program-all-what-you-need-to-know/5618993.

Spector, Leonard S. "Can Iran's Accelerating Nuclear Program Be Stopped?"

Yale Global, March 11, 2010. http://www.english.globalarabnetwork.com/ 201003105141/World-Politics/can-irans-accelerating-nuclear-program-be-stopped.html.

"SSRC: Spectre at the Table." *Jane's Defence Weekly,* November 29, 2012. http://www. janes360.com/images/assets/839/32839/syrian_chem_weapons.pdf.

Staff of US Rep. Ed Royce. "Gangster Regime: How North Korea Counterfeits U.S. Currency." US House of Representatives, Washington DC, March 12, 2007. http://royce.house.gov/uploadedfiles/report.3.12.07.final.gansterregime.pdf.

"Statement of General Curtis M. Scaparrotti, Commander, United Nations Command; Commander, United States–Republic of Korea Combined Forces Command; and Commander, United States Forces Korea Before the Senate Armed Services Committee." March 25, 2014. http://www.armed-services.senate.gov/ imo/media/doc/Scaparrotti_03-25-14.pdf.

"Sudan Human Rights." Amnesty International, 2017. http://www.amnestyusa.org/ our-work/countries/africa/sudan.

Sullivan, Marisa. "Hezbollah in Syria." Middle East Security Report no. 19, Institute for the Study of War, April 2014. http://www.understandingwar.org/sites/default/ files/Hezbollah_Sullivan_FINAL.pdf.

"Suspicious Activity at North Korea's Sohae Satellite Launching Station." 38 North, January 28, 2016. http://38north.org/2016/01/sohae012816.

"Syria: Missile." Nuclear Threat Initiative, August 2014. http://www.nti.org/country-profiles/syria/delivery-systems.

"Syria Capabilities: Scud C." Nuclear Threat Initiative, August 2004. http://www.nti. org/e_research/profiles/Syria/Missile/4126_4337.html (link inactive).

"Syria Capabilities: Scud D." Nuclear Threat Initiative, August 2004. http://www. nti.org/e_research/profiles/Syria/Missile/4126_4338.html (link inactive).

"Syria Improves Its SCUD D Missile with Help from North Korea." Geostrategy-Direct, February 22, 2006. http://www.geostrategy-direct.com/ geostrategy%2Ddirect.

Tallon, Lewis. "Rockets and Round-Ups: Dangerous Times in the Kingdom." *Encyclopedia Geopolitica,* November 5, 2017. https://encyclopediageopolitica. com/2017/11/05/rockets-and-round-ups-dangerous-times-in-the-kingdom.

Tamkin, Emily. "Time to Rethink the US-Egypt Relationship, Experts Tell Senate." *Foreign Policy,* April 25, 2017. http://foreignpolicy.com/2017/04/25/time-to-rethink-the-u-s-egypt-relationship-experts-tell-senate.

Tan, Morse. "Syria and North Korea: The Underground Connection." *Jurist,* March 31, 2015. http://www.jurist.org/forum/2015/03/morse-tan-nuclear-programs.php.

Terry, Olly. "What Can the U.S. Learn from the Agreed Framework?" *International Policy Digest,* January 15, 2015. https://intpolicydigest.org/2015/01/15/can-u-s-learn-agreed-framework.

Tharoor, Ishaan. "A. Q. Khan's Revelations: Did Pakistan's Army Sell Nukes to North Korea?" *Time,* July 7, 2011. http://world.time.com/2011/07/07/a-q-khans-revelations-did-pakistans-army-sell-nukes-to-north-korea.

Thayer, Nate. "The Front Companies Facilitating North Korean Arms Exports." *NK News,* May 30, 2013. https://www.nknews.org/2013/05/the-front-companies-facilitating-north-korean-arms-exports.

——. "North Korea and Syrian Chemical and Missile Programs." *NK News,* June 19, 2013. http://www.nknews.org/2013/06/north-korea-and-syrian-chemical-and-missile-programs.

——. "The Violent Consequences of the North Korea–Syria Arms Trade." *NK News,* June 20, 2013. http://www.nknews.org/2013/06/the-violent-consequences-of-the-north-korea-syria-arms-trade.

Thompson, David. "Risky Business: A System-Level Analysis of the North Korean Proliferation Financing System." Center for Advanced Defense Studies, 2017. https://static1.squarespace.com/static/566ef8b4d8af107232d5358a/t/59413c8 bebbd1ac3194eafb1/1497447588968/Risky+Business-C4ADS.pdf.

Tobey, William. "Obama's 'Strategic Patience' on North Korea Is Turning into Strategic Neglect." *Foreign Policy,* February 14, 2013. http://foreignpolicy. com/2013/02/14/obamas-strategic-patience-on-north-korea-is-turning-into-strategic-neglect.

Tokola, Mark. "The North Korean ICBM Test: A Significant Step, but Still Just a Step." The Peninsula, Korea Economic Institute, July 5, 2017. http://blog. keia.org/2017/07/the-north-korean-icbm-test-a-significant-step-but-still-just-a-step.

"Treasury Acts to Increase Economic Pressure on North Korea and Protect the U.S. Financial System." US Department of the Treasury, June 29, 2017. https://www. treasury.gov/press-center/press-releases/Pages/sm0118.aspx.

"Treasury Imposes Sanctions against the Government of the Democratic People's Republic of Korea." US Department of the Treasury, January 2, 2015. https:// www.treasury.gov/press-center/press-releases/Pages/jl9733.aspx.

"Treasury Department Sanctions Those Involved in Ballistic Missile Procurement for Iran." US Department of the Treasury, January 17, 2016. https://www.treasury. gov/press-center/press-releases/Pages/jl0322.aspx.

"Treasury Finalizes Action to Further Restrict North Korea's Access to the U.S. Financial System." US Department of the Treasury, November 4, 2016. https:// www.treasury.gov/press-center/press-releases/Pages/jl0603.aspx.

"Treasury Sanctions Agents Linked to North Korea's Weapons of Mass Destruction Proliferation and Financial Networks." US Department of the Treasury, March 31, 2017. https://www.treasury.gov/press-center/press-releases/Pages/sm0039.aspx.

"Treasury Sanctions Suppliers of North Korea's Nuclear and Weapons Proliferation Programs." US Department of the Treasury, June 1, 2017. https://www.treasury. gov/press-center/press-releases/Pages/sm0099.aspx.

"Treasury Takes Actions to Further Restrict North Korea's Access to the U.S. Financial System." US Department of the Treasury, June 1, 2016. https://www. treasury.gov/press-center/press-releases/Pages/jl0471.aspx.

"Treasury Targets Chinese and Russian Entities and Individuals Supporting the

North Korean Regime." US Department of the Treasury, August 22, 2017. https://www.treasury.gov/press-center/press-releases/Pages/sm0148.aspx.

Trevithick, Joseph. "Iran's New Ballistic Missile Looks a Lot Like a Modified North Korean One." The Drive, September 23, 2017. http://www.thedrive.com/the-war-zone/14572/irans-new-ballistic-missile-looks-a-lot-like-a-modified-north-korean-one.

Trump, Donald J. "Presidential Executive Order on Imposing Additional Sanctions with Respect to North Korea." Executive Order, The White House, September 21, 2017. https://www.whitehouse.gov/the-press-office/2017/09/21/presidential-executive-order-imposing-additional-sanctions-respect-north.

Twomey, Christopher P. "China Policy towards North Korea and Its Implications for the United States: Balancing Competing Concerns." *Strategic Insights* 5, no. 7 (September 2006). https://www.hsdl.org/?view&did=466572.

"Uganda–North Korea Ties Skirt Limits of Sanctions." *World Politics Review,* January 12, 2015. http://www.worldpoliticsreview.com/trend-lines/14832/uganda-north-korea-ties-skirt-limits-of-sanctions.

"Uganda-US Relations." Global Security.org, 2017. http://www.globalsecurity.org/military/world/uganda/forrel-us.htm.

"United States Files Complaint to Forfeit More Than $1.9 Million from China-Based Company Accused of Acting as a Front for Sanctioned North Korea Bank." US Department of Justice, US Attorney's Office, District of Columbia, June 15, 2017. https://www.justice.gov/usao-dc/pr/united-states-files-complaint-forfeit-more-19-million-china-based-company-accused-acting.

"Update Concerning Conversion of Space Launch Vehicles to Ballistic Missiles." US Department of State, September 30, 2009. https://wikileaks.org/plusd/cables/09STATE101892_a.html. Document disclosed on WikiLeaks.

"U.S. and West Can Never Overpower Might of Syria and DPRK: Syrian President." KCNA, March 10, 2015. http://www.kcna.co.jp/item/2015/201503/news10/20150310-14ee.html (link inactive).

"U.S.-Russia Joint Threat Assessment Talks—December 2009." US State Department, February 24, 2010. https://wikileaks.org/plusd/cables/10STATE17263_a.html. Document disclosed on WikiLeaks.

Venter, Al J. *Allah's Bomb: The Islamic Quest for Nuclear Weapons.* Lanham, MD: Lyons, 2007.

Vick, Charles P. "The Operational Shahab-4/No-Dong-B Flight Tested in Iran for Iran & North Korea Confirmed." Global Security.Org, May 2, 2006. https://www.globalsecurity.org/wmd/library/report/2006/cpvick-no-dong-b_2006.htm.

———. "KN-08: Hwasong-13: The Semi-Mobile Limited Range ICBM, No-Dong-C." Global Security.org, 2015. http://www.globalsecurity.org/wmd/world/dprk/kn-08.htm.

"Vietnam—Banking Systems." Export.gov, November 2, 2016. https://www.export.gov/article?id=Vietnam-Banking-Systems.

Vltchek, André. "North Korea Punished for Helping to Liberate Africa." Voltaire Network, March 26, 2016. http://www.voltairenet.org/article190923.html.

Ward, George F. "Africa and North Korea: Monuments and Munitions." *Africa Watch* (Institute for Defense Analysis), vol. 15 (May 4, 2017). file:///C:/Users/Joe%20 Brown/Downloads/africawatch-May-04-2017-vol15.pdf.

Ward, Jared. "Two Koreas Battle for Hearts and Minds in Africa." *NK News,* July 28, 2016. https://www.nknews.org/2016/07/two-koreas-battle-for-hearts-and-minds-in-africa.

Waters, Tony. "Markets and Morality: American Relations with Tanzania." *African Studies Quarterly* 8, no. 3 (Spring 2006). https://asq.africa.ufl.edu/waters_ spring06.

Wege, Carl Anthony. "The Hizballah–North Korea Nexus." *Small Wars Journal,* January 23, 2011. http://smallwarsjournal.com/blog/journal/docs-temp/654-wege. pdf.

Weiss, Herbert. "A History of Resistance in the Congo." African Futures, December 12, 2012. http://forums.ssrc.org/african-futures/2012/12/08/african-futures-history-of-resistance-in-congo.

Wertz, Daniel, and Ali Vaez. "Sanctions and Nonproliferation in North Korea and Iran." Federation of American Scientists, FAS Issue Brief, June 2012. https://fas. org/issue-brief/sanctions-nonproliferation-north-korea-iran.

Weylandt, Max. "Is It All over between Namibia and North Korea?" African Arguments, July 13, 2016. http://africanarguments.org/2016/07/13/is-it-all-over-between-namibia-and-north-korea.

Whytock, Ian. "North Korea's African Safari." NATO Association of Canada, February 6, 2014. http://natoassociation.ca/north-koreas-african-safari.

"Will Iran's Simorgh Space Launcher Appear in North Korea?" Nuclear Threat Initiative, July 8, 2016. http://www.nti.org/analysis/articles/will-irans-simorgh-space-launcher-appear-north-korea.

Williams, Ian. "North Korea's New Missiles on Parade." Center for Strategic and International Studies, April 18, 2017. https://www.csis.org/analysis/north-koreas-new-missiles-parade.

Williams, Martyn. "Launch Notification Reveals Rocket Drop Zones." North Korea Tech, February 3, 2016. http://www.northkoreatech.org/2016/02/03/launch-notification-reveals-rocket-drop-zones.

"With KPA Assets in Syria and Rumors of Moscow Trip, Gen. Kim Kyok Sik Remains PY Man of the Hour." North Korea Leadership Watch, June 5, 2013. https://nkleadershipwatch.wordpress.com/2013/06/04/with-kpa-assets-in-syria-and-rumors-of-moscow-trip-gen-kim-kyok-sik-remains-py-man-of-the-hour/?iframe=true&preview=true/feed.

Wolpert, Stuart. "Army Veteran, a UCLA Student, Teaches Class on Combat and Military Life." *UCLA News,* April 5, 2013. http://newsroom.ucla.edu/releases/ucla-army-veteran-a-student-to-244663.

Woods, Kevin M., Williamson Murray, and Thomas Holaday. "Saddam's War: An Iraqi

Military Perspective of the Iran-Iraq War." McNair Paper no. 70, National Defense University, March 2009. http://ndupress.ndu.edu/Portals/68/Documents/Books/saddams-war.pdf.

Woolsey, James. "Breaking the Iran, North Korea, Syria Nexus." Testimony before the US Congress, House Committee on Foreign Affairs, Washington, DC, April 11, 2013. http://docs.house.gov/meetings/FA/FA13/20130411/100636/HHRG-113-FA13-Wstate-WoolseyJ-20130411.pdf.

Wright, David C., and Timur Kadyshev. "An Analysis of the North Korean Nodong Missile." *Science and Global Security* 4 (1994). http://scienceandglobalsecurity.org/archive/sgs04wright.pdf.

Wright, David. "Reentry of North Korea's Hwasong-15 Missile." Union of Concerned Scientists, December 7, 2017, https://allthingsnuclear.org/dwright/reentry-of-hwasong-15.

Yang, Jung A. "Banks Put a Big Fly in NK Ointment." *Daily NK,* May 9, 2013. http://www.dailynk.com/english/read.php?catId=nk00400&num=10560.

Yanover, Yori. "Defecting Syrian Officer: Chemical Weapons Already Transferred to Hezbollah." Jewish Press, December 9, 2012. http://www.jewishpress.com/news/defecting-syrian-officer-chemical-weapons-have-already-been-transferred-to-hezbollah/2012/12/09.

Yonhap News Agency. *North Korea Handbook.* London: Routledge, 2014.

"Yono Class (Ghadir)." Military Edge, Foundation for Defense of Democracies, 2017. http://militaryedge.org/armaments/ghadir.

"Yono Class/Ghadir Class Midget Submarine." Global Security.org, 2017, http://www.globalsecurity.org/military/world/iran/ghadir.htm.

Yun, Sun. "The North Korean Contingency: Why China Will Not Cooperate." 38 North, July 25, 2014. http://38north.org/2014/07/ysun072514.

Zarate, Juan. Testimony Before the Senate Banking, Housing, and Urban Affairs Subcommittee on National Security and International Trade and Finance, May 10, 2017. https://www.banking.senate.gov/public/_cache/files/32fc800c-312f-4e68-ad3f-3be5a6eae989/F5431B8F84661542DF1C9C3E23CC102A.zarate-testimony-5-10-17.pdf.

"Zimbabwe: The ZANU-ZAPU Rivalry." Central Intelligence Agency, April 1983. https://www.cia.gov/library/readingroom/docs/CIA-RDP84S00552R000200030002-4.pdf. Sanitized copy approved for release 2011/07/05.

Index